THE SELF IN JUNGIAN PSYCHOLOGY

Theory and Clinical Practice

Leslie Stein

CHIRON PUBLICATIONS • ASHEVILLE, NORTH CAROLINA

www.ChironPublications.com

Cover design by Celeste Stein
Cover image: Inside the Crystal from 'The Text of Light' series, © Robert Owen 2021
Interior design by Danijela Mijailovic
Printed primarily in the United States of America.

ISBN 978-1-63051-980-3 paperback
ISBN 978-1-63051-981-0 hardcover
ISBN 978-1-63051-982-7 ebook
ISBN 978-1-63051-983-4 limited edition paperback

Library of Congress Cataloging-in-Publication Data

Names: Stein, Leslie M., author.
Title: The self in Jungian psychology : theory and clinical practice / Leslie Stein.
Description: Asheville, North Carolina : Chiron Publications, [2022] | Includes bibliographical references and index. | Summary: "Realizing the Self is the absolute goal of Jungian psychology. Yet as a concept it is impossibly vague as it defines a center of our being that also embraces the mystery of existence. This work synthesizes the thousands of statements Jung made about the Self in order to bring it to ground, to unravel its true purpose, and to understand how it might be able to manifest"— Provided by publisher.
Identifiers: LCCN 2021049604 (print) | LCCN 2021049605 (ebook) | ISBN 9781630519803 (paperback) | ISBN 9781630519810 (hardcover) | ISBN 9781630519827 (ebook)
Subjects: LCSH: Jungian psychology. | Self.
Classification: LCC BF173.J85 S734 2022 (print) | LCC BF173.J85 (ebook) | DDC 150.19/54—dc23/eng/20211202
LC record available at https://lccn.loc.gov/2021049604
LC ebook record available at https://lccn.loc.gov/2021049605

Contents

List of Figures

Introduction

Establishing the existence of a central point located somewhere within our being that also embraces the unending totality is bound to create great confusion as to what it is and what it means. Yet, this is what Jung proposes as the Self, a preexistent center of psyche containing the entirety of all that is known and unknown and, furthermore, that experiencing this Self is the ultimate goal of life.

This is not a concept shared by other psychological traditions. In most therapeutic theory, the "self" is considered to be a cohesive self-representation formed by experience and memory. For Jungian theory and clinical practice, the Self is a personality within our being, perhaps with its own energy and agency, that is the true guiding spirit of every life, and the purpose of psychoanalysis is to reveal that truth. Such a concept could have been assigned to the category of speculative, metaphysical thought, except that Jung declares it to be a psychological fact when the Self is fully known to ego consciousness.

The concept of a preexistent internal center has a natural appeal because it is observable that there exists a centering process to bring us to a still point, or otherwise we would have no orientation to be able to confront the confusion and chaos of our lives, tossed and turned as we are by unconscious forces. A center in our being matches the human need for structure and order, to be able to discover a means to hold onto something solid in a brutal world. The Self as a center therefore makes sense but also does not make sense; its existence can be understood hypothetically and, for some, experientially, but its substance, the manner in which it operates, its origins, its location, and even the fact that it exists, is beyond comprehension. It is a complete mystery that can never be fully understood, yet we can accept that we all cleave to a central point, a place of balance, a location where there is a possible reconciliation of conflicting desires where we can find and derive meaning from the order its realization provides.

Treading very carefully because of the unknowability of the full extent of the concept of the Self, I offered only one view of the nature of the Self as having primarily magnetic properties that draws us closer to a center and that reflects an innate wholeness, during a lecture that I presented at the 2019 Congress of the International Association for Analytical Psychology in Vienna. During question time, one psycho-analyst asserted that my view of the Self was completely different from what Jung proposes and what I offered was highly unorthodox. I was very surprised that I had evoked such a reaction because Jung clearly expounds this idea of magnetism in explaining Gnostic images of the Self, and it is to me a profound explanation of the nature of the Self. Later that day, I spoke with a distinguished analyst who had written his own detailed commentaries on the Self, and he said that he thought "without question" that my view was indeed the correct one and I had made an appropriate interpretation. I was confused and thought perhaps my first interlocutor's strong opinion was an anomaly or maybe he merely misunderstood what I was proposing about the Self. Remarkably, when I submitted the paper for publication, one reviewer commented that I had misunderstood the nature of the Self, and yet another senior analyst who read the paper said that I had clarified what Jung meant. What I thought was understandable became instead a controversial subject, but having spent many years writing an earlier book on the process of realizing the Self— *Becoming Whole: Jung's Equation for Realizing God*—I was surprised that the idea remained so unclear to my colleagues. Or, I thought on reflection, perhaps I had got it wrong and it was more confusing to me than I was prepared to admit.

Before I started this work in the hope of achieving some clarification, I was aware that there are considerable headwinds in even contemplating writing a book about the Self. The first is that the Self is so intimately tied by Jung to Christianity that it is difficult to tear the real essence of it from Christ and to make it primarily a psychological subject matter. In an interview with James Hillman, he stresses this issue:

> (The Self) has been amalgamated with Christology and monotheistic unity because we are a Christian culture. So when Jungians use the term 'self' they can't help but be in

the old monotheistic senex structure of unity and centering. It's a hopeless circle of hoping to get out of the ego and into the self.... [1]

The second headwind I faced is that it is very difficult to say *with precision* what Jung had in mind as he extolled the concept of the Self. He made so many references to the Self with varied meanings in a multitude of contexts that it is difficult to interrelate comments and be conclusive. Looked at from the point of view of extracting from Jung's copious writings an intellectual and logical explanation of the Self, Aldous Huxley's comments come to mind. He calls Jungian literature "a vast quaking bog" with no "firm intellectual ground to rest on, and only rarely, in that endless expanse of jelly, the blessed relief of a hard, concrete, particular fact."[2]

This work, therefore, makes no claim of tying up all of the loose ends of Jung's utterances about the Self, although that is continuously attempted for the narrative to have coherence. Instead, this work has the primary objective to explicate his ideas through examining his revelations as to the Self over time. Looked at in this way, myself, and any writer (or reader), can only understand Jung's realizations about the Self according to *their own* insights, their religious, mystical, philosophical, psychoanalytic orientation, and life experience. In Jungian terms, explaining his realizations reflects the degree of that individual's development in the process of individuation. For each of us, there can only be a sense of certainty about the true nature of the Self as aspects of it become a psychological fact when it has been realized by consciousness. Outside that exceptional situation, Jung's realizations of the Self will always carry the uncertainty of a metaphysical discussion with the ideal of full realization of the Self a distant goal, and we can thus read his ideas as informing us what that realization could be and what that brings.

Realization of the Self, if that occurs, is a bulwark against both headwinds as the Self becomes a polestar, indelibly absorbed into our hearts and minds where it achieves clarity. It does not have to be realized in a particular form or according to any rules. In inspired exchanges with the

---

[1] Hillman 1983, p. 83
[2] Huxley 1956, p. 172

late John Dourley, a Jungian Analyst and Catholic priest, just prior to his death, he expressed to me a deep realization of the Self, primarily from a religious, transcendent position exemplified by Christian mystics. Huxley is absolutely correct that there is no intellectual ground to stand on in explaining the Self, but the Self, as Dourley illustrates, is not calling out to the intellect. Instead, it speaks to our religious and spiritual longing through a primal desire in all of us to experience peace, the wholeness within ourselves, that gives our lives meaning.

The main reason to write this book is that it is my witness statement about the Self. It is my experience, the extent of my realization such as it is, my past, present, and future, in my search for the *Deus absconditus,* the hidden God, undertaken in a Jungian form by this attempt to understand the Self. The Self is the point! And by whatever name it is given and what form it has been sought by me, it is the fundamental question that seeks an answer. It is an irrepressible quest, and I seek to address it here in this context because it is indeed the work of my lifetime.

There is much that has been already written about the Self, as would be expected, but it is not possible to rely for revelation of the true nature of the Self on the knowledge of psychoanalysts or this book. The Self is only truly understood by its realization, even a partial glimpse of that essential wholeness that it represents. Yet, as the center and goal of the process of psychological growth, there is also, at least for me, an intellectual need for it to be put under the microscope for an examination of its deepest core, to give the idea some dimension and scope, to make it real, so that when encountered, it may be recognized.

To convey Jung's realizations and ideas about the Self requires that he be quoted extensively, *most often* in words and expressions that are confusing and mysterious. It is no wonder that Jung's writings have been charged with "creating a neo-gnostic metaphysics, a reestablishment of Neoplatonic hypostases."[3] His psychological, religious, and spiritual assertions drift into each other, as they must with the Self, and appear often as the merging of ever-changing admixtures of concepts. There is no solidity or *even a moment of certainty* in Jung's comments, and it is most accurate to describe the Self as an ever-turning vortex filled with

---

[3] Corbin 2014, p. 109

the ingredients for the difficult induction of the psyche into the revelation of a central function, and the sacred, mystical insight of something beyond consciousness that is as ancient as time. In this vast, swirling mixture, the enquiry must still be made as Louis Zinkin explains:

> It cannot remain something which those 'in the know' understand, but which cannot be explained to others; not, that is, if analytical psychology has any claims to be a theory of psychology which can be explicated, rather than a mystery-cult to which one has to be initiated and whose secrets must never be revealed to others. But if we make such a claim, we have to do our best to untangle the contradictions or paradoxes which confront us when we try to be coherent.[4]

The only approach to the Self is to write about Jung's revelations as generating hypotheses that can be analyzed in intelligible parts. That turns it into an exercise in logic even though the Self is so much more than that. Thus, I follow down every narrow alley that arises from his words, and there are many, some clear and others obscure, where I am forced to hold onto logic as the only way out. This is the only form of writing, I believe, that can unknot the puzzle of the Self, to make it alive as resting on a bedrock that corresponds to our deepest instincts. It is not meant, therefore, to create a rough bunch of ideas of what is the Self or to impose another system overlayed on top, but rather it is an attempt to wrestle with it and say what I believe it is, even when the reasoning only follows some breadcrumbs he lays down, as best as that can be accomplished.

To accomplish a full analysis, my essential proposition is that Jung's writings on the Self are a series of steps he traversed, ever higher, evolving over time, building on past experiences, reinforcing his views by analogies, and consistently calling on the concept to describe the fundamental wholeness we all seek. I therefore start at the beginning with Jung's dream that reveals the Self to him, then try to locate where he believes that Self as a center lies in an individual's psyche, and then how it embraces totality, a concept that he introduced that has been most confusing. The result of explaining the Self as having a form is that its

---

[4] Zinkin 2008a, p. 389

powerful nature inevitably leads to it being presented as an internal substance with its own power, and therefore linked to transcendent notions of God and the soul that elevate the qualities of the Self. This attribution of the Self to wider forces is explored, and, thereafter, attention is paid to where else that attribution occurs, such as discovering a guiding spirit, relying on an internal voice, or by valuing a self-conscious witnessing. I dwell on the veracity of his most convincing comparison of the Hindu *Atman* with the Self because therein lies its closest approximation. To examine this comparison with Eastern religion, I also enter briefly the crosswinds of the Buddhist no-Self and the Hindu *Advaita* Self, which offer their own insights into the transcendent dimensions of the Self. This journey to this transcendent nature of the inner Self prompts examination of the relationship between the personal realization of the Self and the larger community and world issues. Finally, I concentrate on the key clinical questions related to how the Self might operate by use of vignettes in the text and some notes on how it may be best addressed in analysis.

Fundamental to an understanding of the Self is the obvious enquiry of what it indeed is: Is it a brain function, a psychic entity, an archetype? As would be expected, the idea has attracted prodigious commentary and debate. On the one hand, it has been perceived as a separate entity with agency working ceaselessly in our being, responsible for psychological growth from infancy to old age. On the other, it has been seen as a fascinating center that attracts everything to it, but without agency. A specific attempt is made in this book to analyze the convoluted options and to venture the most appropriate theory. As that is no more than speculation about what cannot be known, in submitting to logic, the analysis is inevitably circuitous and frustrating, but it helps explain where theories of the Self have gone adrift.

The development of the concept of the Self, as it is the central theme of the entire Jungian opus, is not a stand-alone idea but embraces all aspects of Jung's insights and writing, so references, quotes, and cross-references to different ideas abound. It touches, as a few examples, on his encounter with Nietzsche's ideas, the influence of German Romanticism that was prominent at that time, visions he had after an illness, his engagement with the Self in alchemy, Gnosticism, Daoism, and Hinduism, and his profound later period when he advanced metaphysical ideas. As a consequence, with such vast material, I have only drawn on that which is useful in explicating his approach to the Self, often avoiding layers of subtlety that may be interesting but that would require an unnecessary sojourn from the topic at hand.

It can be said that the realization of the Self, finding a central organizing place in our being where the conflicts can be held is, for all of us, an endless life process, round and round in a spiral evolving both inwardly and outwardly. In the same way, writing about the Self has been a similar journey. What seemed clear at one point then became complicated, and what was complicated took weeks and often months to give up its secrets. Searching for the scope, dimension and nature of "totality," however, a concept Jung uses in relation to the Self became very dangerous, as I explain, and I was indeed injured during this period, so I know now that it is not our business to make this inquiry of totality too deeply as it contains light and darkness in equal measure.

As many quotes from Jung have, as mentioned, subtle distinctions and explain multiple issues, some will be used more than once to serve different contexts. Again, this is to capture his evolving realizations that create shifts in his language, such as replacing the word "soul" with "Self" in 1921 and moving from God to the God-image, as those concepts were refined. There are also some expressions that initially appear confusing but which Jung clarified many years or decades later.

I have been as thorough as I could tolerate in order to examine the Self from so many vantage points that some of its secrets are revealed and disparate statements can be unified. What never left me in writing this work is a statement made by Jung in a conversation with E.A. Bennet when Jung was contemplating his biography; Bennet reports, "he said it would require a full understanding of his thought, and no one understood it completely."[5] This brought home to me that it is not possible to fully understand his view of the Self because it is constructed from his private realizations, his unsaid numinous experiences, and interpretations of his own dreams and visions. This may be obvious, but it requires enunciation, not as an excuse, but rather as justifying the statement that the Self is understood fully only when it is realized by an individual.

---

[5] Bennet 1985, p. 61

I use the term "Self" with a capital "S." There is a long-standing debate as to whether the Self in Jungian writing should instead have a small "s" as it appears in the English edition of Jung's *Collected Works*, or a capital "S" to indicate it is more than the self as when it is used in the phrase "my self." Murray Stein states, "…let's not capitalize it, lest we confuse the self with Divinity."[6] In 1932, in the *Visions* seminars, Jung was asked by an attendee that when he speaks of a mandala symbol that is a symbol of the Self: "It is her Self—with a capital?" and he answers "Yes."[7] Perls and Stephens, pioneering Gestalt therapists, state that "many psychologists like to write the self with a capital S, as if the self is something precious, something extraordinarily valuable. … The self means nothing but this thing as it is defined by otherness."[8] They were not writing about Jung's concept of the Self, but they are certainly correct that it can be regarded as yet another "other" in our psyche as it appears as a phenomenon outside ego consciousness and deserves no more capitalization that any other inner mystery. In a recorded conversation between analysts about the Self, it is mentioned that "Well, I think Michael Fordham (who wrote about the Self) asked Jung and suggested small 's' would be more suitable for everything and Jung agreed."[9] In this work, with respect to the different views, the Self will be capitalized because it is the centerpiece of the entirety of the Jungian opus, but, more importantly, it is the specific subject matter of this book.

I have actively sought advice from Paul Bishop, Sonu Shamdasani, and Murray Stein, all of whom responded enthusiastically and offered insights that came from that weathered sense of Jung. My wife, Dr. Miriam Stein, also a Jungian Analyst, pointed out many blind alleys where I had become lost and helped bring me back into the light. I thank them all and appreciate that they offered me the chance to more deeply refine my understanding.

Sydney, Australia

June 24, 2021

---

[6] Stein 2008, p. 306
[7] Jung 1997, p. 535
[8] Perls & Stephens 1982, p. 8
[9] Zinkin, et al. 2008b, p. 412

Chapter 1. Approaching the Self

In an unpublished, original typescript held in the Kristine Mann Library in New York, the Indologist Heinrich Zimmer recounts meeting Jung at the Zurich Club in 1932 and asking him about the Self:

> (I) asked him naively what was his opinion about the Hindu idea of the transcendental Self, indwelling man, underlying his conscious personality as well as the vast depth of the unconscious including the archetypes. But he, without as much as disclosing his lips, while from the bottle in his right hand he poured the gin, with the forefinger of his left, persistently pointed to the rising level of the liquid in the glass, until I hastily said 'stop, stop, thank you.' That was the gentle and inspiring way of the Zen-master to make me say 'stop stop' to my own talking. It implied this advice to come down from the lofty level of my question to more earthbound facts and enjoyment, to approach the soaring speculative flight to transcendental spheres which can't be reached by mere words of abstract conceptions.

The Self, no matter what explanation is offered or what nuance of expression is used, is an indescribable concept. What indeed is a center in our being? It cannot be brought to ground as it does not rest on a logical bedrock that there *must* be a center point in psyche. As well, its importance does not present to the world-at-large as a shared, agreed truth, and it does not evoke any direct Western comparisons. It has no relationship to science and has, in fact, been called a "scientific obscenity."[1] The Self stands apart from culture, does not draw meaning from historical or current events, and is not reliably informed yet by neuroscience, but only by Eastern religion and Western esoterica. It

---

[1] Allport 1955, p. 37

cannot, in the end, be perfectly communicated, and any explanation will always fall short of what it might be. Finding the true, clear meaning will, accordingly, fail; it will necessarily always be opaque. The Self, as Jung admits, is "a construct that serves to express an unknowable essence which we cannot grasp as such, since by definition it transcends our powers of comprehension."[2]

Jacques Derrida's comments on Martin Heidegger's avoidance of the term "spirit" are briefly instructive as a parallel. In his essay, *Of Spirit*, Derrida points out that "Rather than a value, spirit seems to designate, beyond a deconstruction, the very resource for any deconstruction and the possibility of any evaluation."[3] Spirit cannot be deconstructed (examined to expose bias, flaws, or inconsistencies) because it is a term without an explicable meaning and which has no binary attributes—spirit or nonspirit—that could, at least, provide a comparison. Heidegger, according to Derrida, therefore indicated that the Spirit is an ontological obscurity that precedes all biology, anthropology, and psychology, so that Heidegger initially only used it in quotation marks and then rejected its use.

The concept of the Self that parallels the issue Heidegger faced with "spirit" is, however, at the very heart of Jungian Analytical Psychology; it is accurate to say that, without it, psychoanalysis is unmoored. The entire basis of psychological growth is postulated on the existence and realization of the Self by a process that seeks it as a goal. The Self must therefore be understood in spite of its obscurity because its realization, all Jungians accept, is the key to psychological development; Jung was absolutely clear about that. To have an interest in Jung and his ideas necessitates holding some explanation of the nature and process of the Self. Yet, like the blind men grasping the elephant, there are many different opinions as to its substance and also its operation in the therapeutic process.

The term "Self" is ancient, as Jung explains: "This nomenclature is no invention of mine. It existed with the same meaning for the same thing thousands of years before I did. ... I was obliged to choose this concept

---

[2] CW 7, § 399
[3] Derrida, et al. 1989, p. 461

or else prove that it meant something different."[4] Its meaning is therefore overlayed with many centuries of metaphysical, philosophical, and psychological commentary. It persists as an idea because it is a reference to the means to crystalize a universal need to find a center to balance the chaos; seeking order, peace, and apparent meaning, define the human experience. It exists, therefore, as a critical idea because of the imperative for redemption from the absurdities of life amplified by conflict, pain, and a lack of unity in our experiences.

There is, in addition to its elaborate history and unknowability, significant confusion in Jungian thought as to its meaning for, at a minimum, four notable factors. The first caused a split between the Zurich Jungians, oriented to adherence to Jung's concepts, and the London-based developmental school led by Michael Fordham. In his classic 1947 paper, Fordham extended the *a priori* existence of the Self to neonates and, more importantly, disputed the scope of the Self as proposed by Jung. As will be explained, his logic and orientation required him to offer a different understanding of the Self. This has had the effect of creating a lasting, alternative view as to its scope and nature. The second factor, as already mentioned, is that in hundreds of statements, Jung invokes the concept of the Self in different ways in very many contexts and most often in language that is vague as mixed in with complex, intertwined psychological ideas. This has caused commentators to rely on some quotes and ignore others, moving the Self in different directions within the corpus of Jungian thought. The third is that because the Self has a numinous, revelatory nature when it is experienced, it slides in and out of other transcendent postulates relating to the soul, spirit, and God, adding a mystical or spiritual quality to his ideas. This leads then to comparisons of the Self with God that go too far, such as, "The self is conceived almost impersonally, as a celestial body, and precisely because it is impersonal it is looked upon as divine."[5] There is, however, for that reason, no expressed view of the Self that has not conveyed a vague transcendent quality. Finally, there appears to be a reticence on the part of Jung, perhaps as a matter of great wisdom as exhibited in his reply to Zimmer, to attempt to be too precise or didactic.

---

[4] *Letters*, Vol. 1, p. 359
[5] Pulver 1960, p. 250

This detected reluctance of Jung to be conclusive as to the nature of the Self is, most likely, because it was always an emerging phenomenon for him where gradual, subtle, new realizations arose over time. It was always a work-in-progress that coincided with different phases of his own psychological development and his theoretical and professional emphases. When the concept of the Self was applicable in the context of different subject matters, he would then insert the view of the Self he held at that time. The view often added to what he had said previously, but not necessarily in similar words. It was not until just the year before his death that he proposed a formal definition of the Self that now appears in Volume 6 of the English *Collected Works* attached to the *Psychological Types* essays. This definition did not appear in the earliest version of that essay, published in German in 1921 in Zurich, where only hints of the purpose of the Self were mentioned under a different definitional heading for the Ego function. The Editorial Note to the *Collected Works* confirms that it was only for the publication of the revised edition of the Swiss Collected Works, the *Gesammelte Werke* in 1960, that Jung decided to insert a formal definition of the Self.

It is unclear if this late-in-life definition, when Jung was 84, was an attempt to clarify what he meant, as it lacks the feeling and content of the revelatory, numinous insights that he explained over time when writing about the Self. There has to be a distinct reason because he was no longer interested, it has been said, in explaining his work in his later years but insisted that the reader "would have to meet him where he was."[6] It is difficult to escape the conclusion that a final definition was necessary because the Self had, until that time, been effectively offered by him as an insoluble puzzle of a thousand pieces to be understood *by way of deduction* from his abstract references to it in the *Collected Works* and other writings.

Unfortunately, as will be explored, the Definition does not gather in all of the nuances Jung uses when bringing the Self into the many dimensions of psychological growth. It does not stand alone as the final description as the more dramatic, mystical aspects of the Self are detached from the Definition. If we are then thrown back on the multitude of ideas of the Self he raises in different ways over more than 60 years, we face another

---

[6] Edinger 1996a, p. 11

significant problem that is crucially important. In at least four instances in the *Collected Works*, as will also be explicated, the inaccuracy of the translation from the German into the English version drastically changes the meaning of the Self and complicates the manner in which it is viewed thereafter. The paramount error is the English translation of a critical description of the scope of the Self in a lecture he presented in German at the Eranos conference in Ascona, Switzerland, in 1935. This lecture was not translated accurately in the English *Collected Works* as a key phrase that he had marked "*n.b.*" in the German edition was left out of the English version. That one phrase, as will be analyzed, changed the entire emphasis and understanding of the Self. There is thus, for all non-German speaking Jungians, a frustrating missing connection as to whether the conventional English R.F.C. Hull translation of the *Collected Works* can be considered reliable in unraveling the nature of the Self. We must, however, rely on Hull's translation for the entirety of the English *Collected Works,* so it has always been assumed that it is accurate, even though it disrupts the manner in which the Self is thereafter understood. We are often reminded by German-speaking colleagues that there are indeed translation issues; Murray Stein, for instance, points to another significant translation error by Hull that relates to the Self and confuses understanding,[7] as will be discussed.

How to Read Jung on the Self

Jung had deep experiences of the Self and, like a poet rather than a scientist, he spent his entire professional life describing these experiences in as many ways as he was moved. When the Self is found it can never be lost, and it then is the centerpiece of one's existence. It is therefore apparent that these experiences altered Jung's consciousness indelibly so that the Self became for him a psychological fact whose many facets were continuously being enlivened in his writing. It is reported that Jung said, "The way I am and the way I write are a unity."[8] Accordingly, the Self as written by him is not derived or explained primarily by reason but by an exposition of his unmediated revelations tailored to the context of the subject matter of his consideration.

---

[7] Stein 2008, p. 309
[8] Bair 2004, p. 777

Unlike the bases of other psychologies, the Self is not derived from external observations of infants, patients, or logic. The Self in Jungian psychology is based on the *revelations of its founder*. The Self appeared to Jung in such a profound way that he oriented his entire doctrine to its revelation, and his writings draw us into the magical qualities of what he proposes so that we can relate to what to him was the essence of human life. His statements about the Self are meant to speak to us, and in reading his ideas, we can almost hear his voice, even if the illusions sometimes are vague and their meaning uncertain. We are left always with a sense that the Self is pointing to some profound organizing principle, however described, that brings us home to ourselves in moments when we are confused or disoriented.

The analyst Wolfgang Giegerich argues that Jung

> was conceptually not really up to his own experience. He did not make it easy for his audience and readers to see what the Self was really about. He made many different, contradictory statements about the Self and individuation speaking one way to theological critics and the opposite to scientific critics.[9]

There are no actual contradictory statements that can be found, but rather there are different emphases as to the nature of the Self that were a product of his emerging realizations that he presented in different contexts. This certainly cannot be considered a failure, but it is the case that his statements do not create a straightforward, sequential, logically positive explanation about the Self. He is, instead, each time it is mentioned, pointing at his experience and offering us to share in that experience so that we can realize the Self for ourselves. As Jung reminds us: "The needful thing is not to the know the truth but to *experience* it. Not to have an intellectual conception of things, but to find our way to the inner, and perhaps wordless, irrational experience...."[10] We can have that experience and that will be our understanding and do not need to approximate Jung's experience of the Self to touch its basic nature.

---

[9] Giegerich 2005, p. 185
[10] CW 18, § 1292

We can observe that if Jung was merely pushing a psychological theory, as perhaps Giegerich is suggesting, rather than elucidating profound revelations of his own, he would have had to make the Self non-falsifiable. This is not his approach and thus any argument about inconsistencies or ones that find lack of logic is missing the point. It is not that Jung is beyond criticism, but rather it is his revelations that are being explained. They are, as anthropologists and social scientists refer to them, *etic* statements, that are entirely personal to the observer. If there is any proselytizing of the Self by its continuous mention in his writings, it is to invite others to an experience that would foster a separation from the mob, an essential element of psychological development. This approach is reminiscent of the *Kuzari Principle*, a biblical argument that personal experience is *equal to* and as good as an uninterrupted historical tradition.[11]

Jung positions the Self at the heart of psychological growth, but it remains only a debatable, mere metaphysical idea *until it is realized by an individual,* as it was for him. It obtains some verification thereafter by the *consensus generum,* the ancient historical agreement of the people. It was thus necessary for Jung, after his own realizations and in the absence of mass realizations of the Self, to offer some verification elsewhere: alchemy, Gnosticism, Eastern religion, and Western mystics. In drawing on other traditions, he steeps us in metaphysical concepts repeatedly to explain the existence of the images that became real for him in his psyche. These comparisons are not the subject matter of his realizations but are intellectual or metaphysical representations of what he experienced. He is not vouching for their authenticity by his vast scholarship and intellectual reasoning but is elucidating and making patent the power of the Self as a primordial archetype that came to him: "Analysis of the unconscious has long since demonstrated the existence of powers in the form of archetypal images, which, be it noted, *are not identical with the corresponding intellectual concepts.*"[12]

Jung also had to face as the founder of a school of psychology that there is not a vast amount of personal testimony that echoes his realizations of the Self so that it can be thereafter conveniently argued that it is capable

---

[11] Explained fully in Halevi 2001.
[12] CW 18, § 1505, emphasis supplied.

of being realized by all. The second rule of the *Kuzari Principle* is that the truth will increase by the number of reliable observers who claim to have the revelation; the greater the observers of the revelation, the less that it can be said that it is an idea of one person. As well, the more credible the observers, the less likely it is that it will be doubted. What permeates then through Jungian thought is an orientation to the Self as the *primary* goal of the entire psychological process that contains an implied promise that every individual has the chance to become that complete person and thereby champion the Self. It is thus expressed by Jung as the key and hope to the full flowering of the individual,[13] a hidden secret that is the Philosopher's Stone, a special spiritual journey. Underlying his comments is always that promise of the goal that is so alluring that it calls us by his use of transcendent, lofty expressions that make it the treasure worth seeking. It is fair to say that the mystery in which it is described is necessary for it to be accepted because it offers a hope that logic cannot provide.

It is unlikely, however, that those who come for analysis would have had or will have an expansive experience of the Self as did Jung. It is not a revelation of a magnitude that is common or that derives its significance because it has been shared at once by a large group of people, such as the revelation on Mount Sinai before an entire nation. It is a unique revelation and because he deems his own realization as the goal of psychological growth and explains it in such high-level terms, it creates a clinical tendency for the rest of us to search for evidence of its existence. This takes the form of equating any aspect of psychological development, such as a momentary sense of peace or a dream of a strong figure, as pointing to the Self. Jung, however, did not seek to make every intimation or symbol work that hard as a form of realization but instead grounds the Self on a single *idea* that there is, indeed, an orientation to a center in psyche that is possible as a personal experience. When read this way as his specific revelation repeated in different contexts and, as well, with the allure of wholeness as the goal, he establishes a promise that it is possible to approximate some degree of the truth of what he is proposing, no matter how far away that seems.

---

[13] CW 7, § 404

His writings on the Self are indeed a continuous invitation to have that experience. "It is a field of personal experience which leads directly to the experience of individuation, the attainment of the self." The promise defines his opus: "this self is the world, if only a consciousness could see it. That is why we must know who we are."[14] Knowing who we are is the process of individuation where the Self is the matrix, the process, and the end state. It appears that in addition to creating the Self as a promise, there is an ongoing attempt to make it attractive, to offer it up for others as a solution to all ills and to make it an exciting enterprise.

As the experience was so powerful for Jung and because he then finds comparisons within Eastern religions and Western esoteric traditions, his explanations most often turn from a practical idea of the Self as the center of psyche to one that is transcendent, partaking of the religious, spiritual, or mystical. Those kinds of statements predominate in his explanation of the Self. The moment that this shift is made from a practical center or centering process to one that has religious, transcendent qualities, the Self becomes equated with the higher divinity, and it is then expressed differently. This is a reflection of his experience but also his confirming background research. He therefore speaks freely of the divine spirit and the soul of the world as if it were a necessary continuation of the Self and the nature of the unconscious. This is, however, a potential source of confusion in reading about the Self because some statements have a different valence than others. If, for instance, he adds that the Self is identical to cosmic forces,[15] this adds a gloss that may seem to be unrelated to it being a center of psyche and moves it from the precise to the abstract. This requires one to move from the psychological to the transcendent and back and is then the only way in which Jung's experience of the Self can be understood that often makes understanding a daunting proposition. He often starts one way, practically and precise, and ends a different way where the Self sometimes seems to exist as a mist. This is how the Self is to be read as paradoxically both the center of psyche but also that which encapsulates the highest form of spiritual understanding.

---

[14] *Ibid,* para. 46
[15] CW 13, § 373n5

It should also be briefly mentioned, as a fuller discussion will be necessary, that fundamental to reading about the Self is the issue of whether it is being accorded its own power and agency that could create our lives for its own purposes (the "agency model"), or whether it is always there, passively, and we are drawn to its recognition (the "magnet model"). This is an underlying backdrop to Jung's thousands of statements about the Self. If it is the former, the agency view, then there is tendency to read into his statements that the Self initiates the display of itself in symbols and signs, and so our realization of it is the Self's doing. Psychologically, that means that it is an independent, autonomous actor that has its hand on our shoulder as the guiding spirit. If it is the latter form, the magnet view, our continued realization of the Self is different, like the metallurgic notion of annealing where layer and layer of insight is laid down because we are continually drawn to it, bringing us out of identification with the collective and closer to our own individuality. Each statement about the Self is open to either interpretation and is an unanswered question that makes reading about the Self a greater mystery.

Early Interest in the Self

Jung's interest in the concept of the Self spans a lifetime. He indicates that when he was 23 in 1898, he had read Nietzsche's *Zarathustra*, and, even that young, he had an inclination toward or intuition about the Self as he later reports: "I was already interested in the concept of the Self, but I was not clear how I should understand it."[16] Nietzsche's comments about the Self that he would have read as to the Self are introduced early in *Thus Spake Zarathustra* in the section on *Despisers of the Body* to indicate that there exists within us a spirit and, as well, senses that are instruments of the body so that "The Self seeks with the eyes of the sense, it listens with the ears of the spirit. ... Behind your thoughts and feelings, my brother, stands a mighty commander, an unknown sage—he is called Self."[17] Sonu Shamdasani, the Jung historian, explains that this last passage was underlined in Jung's copy of *Zarathustra*.[18] In a later seminar

---

[16] *Zarathustra*, Vol I, p. 391
[17] Nietzsche 1961, p. 62
[18] Shamdasani 2009, p. 477n29

Jung presented on *Zarathustra*, he adds, "later in the winter of 1914-15, I studied it very carefully and made a lot of notations. ... I made my marks, when I came across these passages, and they seemed very important to me. Yet I could not make use of it because one misses in Zarathustra, the concept of the unconscious...."[19]

Paul Bishop comprehensively elucidates that although Nietzsche's concept of the Self and Jung's Self are different in many ways, such as Nietzsche's identifying the Self with the ego and Jung locating aspects of the Self in the unconscious, they join together conceptually as they both are concerned with the idea of wholeness obtained from the uniting of the opposites.[20] This appears as an early orientation to wholeness that absorbed Jung even though Nietzsche's ideas were not later directly employed when Jung came to explain the Self.

The concept of the Self therefore confirmed for Jung, to the great extent that he absorbed Nietzsche, that there must be an organizing principle, a unity or wholeness, for an individual lost in the chaos of the opposites. This is evident in all Jung's writings but no more so than in his 1916 work, *Septem Sermones ad Mortuous,*[21] the *Seven Sermons to the Dead*, that he published using the author's name of the Gnostic Basilides. This is Jung's early sounding of how an individual is to orient in random existence through the Self. Although it is written as would an ancient Gnostic text and therefore is often obtuse, its echo resounds thereafter in all his writings on the Self.

In this work, he describes the infinite dimension of the primordial firmament as the *Pleroma* that contains everything as undifferentiated opposites. It is the archaic totality before creation, unrestricted, with no apparent center or possibility of order. This absolute chaos of the *Pleroma* is therefore never in a static state, so a center cannot be possible, and this, he explains, is "to free you from the delusion that somewhere, either without or within, there standeth something fixed, or in some way established, from the beginning."[22] There is no center or wholeness in a chaotic universe before creation.

---

[19] *Zarathustra*, Vol. 1, p. 391
[20] Bishop 1996, pp. 345-356
[21] *Memories*, Appendix V
[22] *Ibid*, p. 379

The *Pleroma*, undifferentiated chaos, is in us, and we are its children, Jung asserts, and what can be brought to ground in an individual and fixed occurs through *Creatura*, the creative capacity of man to be able to apply discrimination to the qualities of the *Pleroma*, which consists of endless pairs of opposites. Some years later, he explains that "Creation ... begins with an act of division of the opposites ..."[23] There is thus no creation, nothing is born or progresses without the opposites being examined and made the subject of discrimination as until then they stay suspended in a state of a mere promise of some reconciliation: "In a state of 'promise' before they become, they are nonexistent, there is neither black nor white, good nor bad."[24]

This is Jung's creation myth where the ground of being is derived from a universe of opposites through seeking their reconciliation. The individual achieves reconciliation by a fixedness arising from the process of holding the opposites together at a point at the deepest level of the unconscious, the place that strives for the continued creation of our own being. This place is where all opposites, such as good and evil, matter and spirit, conscious and unconscious, can be held in balance so that we are not swept away in the primordial confusion. This is, of course, abstract and a series of ideas actually proposed by Basilides, but it becomes in Jung's later writing the underlying basis of the Self: finding fixedness, an orientation to a central position in the play of opposites, and as what is necessary to stand in the face of the chaos of the *Pleroma*. The Self in this early 1916 formulation, is of a fixed point—a center as a goal and also suggesting that center point to hold the opposites. As Jung later explains, "The self is made manifest in the opposites and the conflicts between them; it is a '*coincidentia oppositorum,* '"[25] the coincidence of opposites within us that it mediates.

The Self contains *within it* all of the opposites, but it is also a point that is the place to reconcile those opposites. For this reconciliation to occur, there needs to be that point that is not dragged into either of the opposites and that can hold the great tension between them. In the *Seven Sermons*, Jung exposes this critical process of balancing the opposites not through

---

[23] CW 9.i, § 632
[24] Jung 1984, p. 131
[25] CW 12, § 259

an ideal of beauty as suggested by Plato, but by invoking the ancient Gnostic god *Abraxas*. Although portrayed as a flawed demiurge, *Abraxas* is a representation of the center as he stands as the mid-point between God and the Devil and therefore is capable of balancing the entirety of all of the opposite qualities of the *Pleroma*; the "sum" of Abraxas is therefore 365, meaning it contains all. Here lies the introduction by Jung of the paradox that *Abraxas* is the center, but yet contains all of the opposites. Thus, the Self, when conflated with *Abraxas*, must always be seen as a paradox, able to contain everything but yet also the center.

This process of finding a center in the chaos and thereby being able to hold the conflicting opposites is the manner in which psychological growth occurs. The Self offers the center or balance point, an essential orientation, and, as well, holds the opposites. It thus becomes, as Jung states about *Abraxas*, the pure "creative drive of form and formation."[26] It is creative because it is the process of human development to bring the opposites to a center point so that the well-spring of that creativity, continuous flowing formations, can rise with less impediment.

It is necessary to create this structure of a center that potentially holds the tension of opposites because, as Jung proposes, "If you marry the ordered to the chaos you produce the divine child, the supreme meaning beyond meaning and meaninglessness."[27] The divine child is a representation of a divine potential without any conflict, the unmanifested state of pure innocence. That state results from the uniting of all of the opposites so life is connected with a higher level, the divine, that takes that unity beyond the day-to-day of the opposites of having meaning then feeling meaningless. The divine child holds *all* of the opposites of the *Pleroma* in one central point, establishing the supreme meaning that creates profound, indelible order by establishing a divine structure at the center of a void, revealing the true goal of life.

The structure Jung creates in *Seven Sermons* is the clear foundation of the Self, at that time and thereafter, resulting from the ontological need to ground the chaos of the *Pleroma*, the chaos in each individual, through finding a fixed place to integrate the opposites. The role of each individual

---

[26] *Red Book*, p. 370n164
[27] *Ibid,* p.236

is therefore to realize the center point to more effectively hold these opposites that then offers the possibility of creating collective order in psyche and the world, even as an interregnum. Without that point, there is nothing but undifferentiated chaos, which means an individual is subject to the unconscious whims of the collective and lacks real meaning, a phenomenon not too hard to find.

This underlying theme of the necessity of finding a potential unity for conflicting opposites can also be found in Jung's early and continued orientation to unravelling the nature of what it is to be one's own person: individuality. He raises the question of what creates individuality in his 1898 *Zofingia* lecture to his medical fraternity when he was just 19.[28] The themes in that lecture are more fully developed in a later essay that "individuality" arises by a combination of "psychological elements."[29] The multiplicity of those elements that yields individuality therefore naturally suggests that there must be a way in which they can be unified or integrated, and in 1928 he writes: "Multiplicity and inner division are opposed by an integrative unity whose power is as great as that of the instincts."[30] Individuality, consequently, depends on a balance developing between the tension resulting from opposite pulls, and the capacity to come to a center where that tension is held.

Individuality is just one of many ideas in his opus that repeat Jung's emphasis on the importance of a unity and centering function as a balancing and ordering principle. As another early example, in the same year as the *Seven Sermons*, 1916, Jung wrote *Die transzendente Funcktion*, (*The Transcendent Function*,) which was not published in English until 1958. The Transcendent Function is a concept that is derived from the constant transitioning back and forth between conscious and unconscious material, suggesting a mutual interconnection because in each there "*seems to be the regulating principle of the other.*"[31] This regulating principle exerts an ordering function that strives to bring the two into balance by the creation of a third thing, the Transcendent Function.

---

[28] Jung 1983, p. 86
[29] CW 7, § 514
[30] CW 8, § 96
[31] *Ibid,* § 177, emphasis supplied.

As Jung was giving prime importance to a unity as balancing opposites in the period of 1914-17,[32] which includes the *Seven Sermons* and *The Transcendent Function,* this may explain the crystallization of this theorem in *Scrutinies,* an initially missing part of *The Red Book* manuscript that was written in 1917.[33] In *Scrutinies,* he explains that we must "re-establish the connection with the self, since it is torn apart all too often," and adds, "Through uniting with the self we reach the God."[34] The connection with the Self is indeed repeatedly lost, which we can all attest to, but if, he explains, we can unite with that center, we can reach a state of transcendence. This early revelation, for that is what it must be, is consistent with the *Seven Sermons* as the Self contains all opposites in the *Pleroma* and their uniting would be tantamount to transcendence. He is not being particularly clear in these statements as they were made at the dawning of his revelations, but when viewed, as it must, as his realization that the warring opposites need to be balanced by an ordering function, it is the early enunciation of a foundational requirement of psychological development.

In an Editorial Note to the *Collected Works,*[35] it is explained that the term "Self" first appeared in 1916 in the essay *The Structure of the Unconscious* as "The unconscious personal contents constitute the self, the unconscious and subconscious ego."[36] This early usage, however, is unrelated to how the Self was later formulated and analyzed. It appears as perhaps a first attempt to integrate his revelation at that time into his framework of the ego being contained within a larger, unconscious Self, a theme he develops later.

The Editorial Note further explains that there was no further comment from Jung about the Self until 1921, when its mention appeared in the German version of *Psychologische Typen* but "even as late as the 1950 Swiss edition," the Note suggests, it was used interchangeably with the ego: "(T)his confusion (of using the term ego to be the Self) is made worse confounded because through (the early English Baynes' translation

---

[32] *Memories*, p. 391
[33] *Red Book*, p. xiii
[34] *Ibid*, p. 338
[35] CW 6, § 183n85
[36] CW 7, § 512

published in 1923) this whole passage Ich=ego is more often than not translated as 'self.'"[37]

The various contexts subject to the Bayne translation, where the idea of the Self was adumbrated with the ego, do not harm the development of the concept of the Self as it was clear that the Self, as Jung explains it in this period, is being presented as the unity of the opposites. This lack of harm is also apparent because by having postulated the existence of the unconscious, the ego could not become its center as psyche obviously extends beyond what is conscious. It is noteworthy that the mere explanation of a difference between the ego and the unconscious always was going to lead to the Self as center because the unconscious needed to be separated out from the ego. When the revised English translation of *Psychological Types* was published in 1971, it creates even a clearer distinction between the ego and the Self: "the I is only the centre of my field of consciousness, it is not identical with the totality of my psyche. ... I therefore distinguish between the I and the *self*...."[38]

In commentary on the *Black Books,* Jung's personal diaries, Sonu Shamdasani confirms that the soundings of the Self in 1921 in *Psychologische Typen* were derived from Jung's lectures emphasizing the idea of reconciling the opposites beginning in 1916.[39] At this early stage it can be said, interweaving the various statements, that the Self was conceived as the center of all that Jung was, his individuality, his totality.[40] This is an idea that did not yet explain the nature of the Self and would await further development as a concept some 20 years later.

Wolfgang Giegerich, a critic of many of Jung's ideas, attempts to trace back Jung's interest in the Self to two experiences that Giegerich promotes as formative. The first was Jung's need, expressed in 1912, to find a modern myth that the Church could no longer supply,[41] and the second came out of Jung's realization in 1925 when he was in East Africa where, observing herds of animals, he found his uniqueness in contradistinction to the herd and thus created a personal myth in terms of the power of his own consciousness.[42] How these led to the finding of the Self is unclear, and

---

[37] CW 6, § 183n85
[38] *Ibid,* § 706, emphasis supplied.
[39] *Black Books*, Vol. 1, p. 74
[40] CW 6, § 230
[41] Giegerich 2005, p. 172
[42] *Ibid*, pp. 172-3

Giegerich calls these experiences of Jung's not a vision, but arising from a thought.[43] He states that the East Africa experience "is the ground on which his later psychology of the Self exists."[44]

It is difficult to advance this proposition that Jung created a concept of the Self to establish a new myth based on privileging his consciousness because of what he experienced in Africa. Deidre Bair, one of his biographers, reports Jung saying as to his East Africa experience, "You could say I passed through it as a tourist."[45] It could be that the thought attributed to him by Giegerich was in some general way part of the structure that led him to understanding the Self as it highlighted the self-reflective power of consciousness, but the origin of the Self can be explained better in other ways. These other ways, as already expressed, are concerned with his need, expressed early in his life, to locate a structure that is in psyche that can hold and perhaps balance the opposites. In a lecture given in June 1925, four months *before* sailing for Africa in October of that year, Jung presents a diagram indicating that he was attuned primarily to conceiving a center in the psyche, the totality of all that is conscious and unconscious.

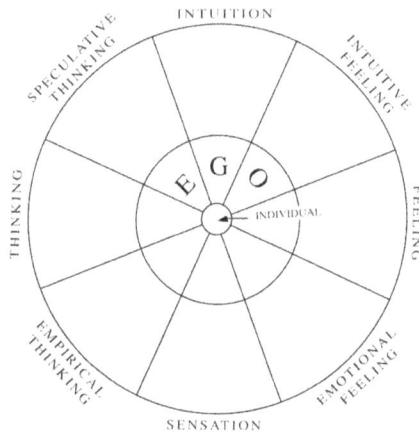

Figure 1: 1925 Use of the Center[46]

---

[43] *Ibid*, p. 176
[44] *Ibid,* p. 178
[45] Bair 2004, p. 427
[46] Jung, 2014a, p. 119. Republished with permission of Taylor and Francis (Books) Limited UK). *Analytical Psychology: Notes of the Seminar given in 1925 by C.G. Jung.* W. McGuire, Ed. p. 119; permission conveyed through Copyright Clearance Center.

"Individual" is at the very center of this diagram and is separated and bounded from the circle of the ego, and Jung describes it in this drawing as the "virtual nucleus I call the Self."[47] This is an early, not yet refined, statement about the Self as a center point of conflicting psychological types. It is tentative and an idea that is not yet complete, as this sentence reveals: "I have assumed (the Self) as existing; it is something that is susceptible of proof. Instead of one center, we may have two …."[48] He also states: "The center of self-regulation, then, is a postulate that is assumed."[49] This is unrelated to a "thought," as Giegerich suggests, that he had in Africa as to the primacy of his consciousness, and indicates that the Self had already been emerging for him as an important construct prior to that journey.

The place of the center as contained within the ego, a small circle of the Self within a larger circle of the ego, is described by him in this diagram as an ordering function, a "central government." He adds, however, "I have represented the self as a point in the middle of the diagram, but it could just as well be thought of as including the whole, or indeed as spreading out all over the world…"[50] In this 1925 lecture, the Self is given a greater role than just a center, as it includes the whole. Jung thereby reiterates the paradox hinted at in the *Seven Sermons*, that the Self is a separate entity in psyche that contains all opposites and, as well, it is also a virtual center that can serve to balance those opposites. As containing all opposites, it then has no boundaries and thus Jung is immediately drawn into a different realm of a mystical or numinous entity within psyche.

The intimation of a Self as spreading out over the world, a totality, is because, like *Abraxas*, it contains the sum of all that exists. This idea could only be a testament to a deep experience that Jung had that can be called mystical and that has never been explicated.[51] This mystical experience in the chronology of the Self would have had to be prior to the *Seven Sermons* in 1916 because it was not an insight previously explained until that time. It also did not follow logically from the mere

---

[47] *Ibid*, p. 120
[48] *Ibid*
[49] *Ibid*
[50] *Ibid*
[51] Stein 2015

idea of the existence of a center in a psychological sense. The experience of totality creates a confluence of the Self with the Godhead and no doubt drew Jung closer to the philosophical and religious history of God as all-encompassing as well as a center point. As Marie-Louise von Franz suggests, "(I)t was only gradually that he came upon the far-reaching historical parallels to his experience."[52] This 1925 lecture was that moment or the expression of a moment in which a realization had occurred that the Self is an entity or force that not only offers us a balance but has a transcendent nature that goes beyond logic and suggests a religious recasting of its purpose that occurs in his later writings.

The idea of the Self having two aspects, a center and totality, in fact connects with the revelations in the 1916 *Seven Sermons* that the *Pleroma* exists within us, unmanifested in our being as the total of opposites, which is anchored by the *Creatura* at a point where these opposites can be balanced. The 1925 lecture, as an early development of the concept of the Self as including more than a center, may also be considered to have arisen because of the context of the topic of that lecture of the multiple functions of consciousness. The different psychological ego types require a regulatory function that accords with the notion of a central government, as Jung puts it, to control diverse and contradictory conscious emphases. This idea follows naturally from the need to mediate and balance disparate opposites or forces that are in conflict: most importantly, consciousness and the unconscious.

The need for this regulatory function for different types also appears in an even earlier form in the first edition of *Psychologische Typen* in 1921. The nature of the Self at that time was, as mentioned, included in the Definition of *Ich* ("I") as being other than the ego, and as the subject of the entire psyche that Jung explains appears symbolically as an ideal or superior personality, such as Faust or Zarathustra.[53] This early formulation in 1921 conveyed the idea of the Self as a superior function beyond a mere center. This formulation of a superior function in 1921, and the 1925 idea of the Self having transcendent aspects, made it the goal that was to be established firmly as the *summum metam*, the highest goal of psychological growth several years later after Jung's dream in 1927,

---

[52] von Franz 1975, p. 143
[53] Jung 1921, S. 630

discussed in Chapter 2. For him, thereafter, this highest form of growth is consistently expressed as the key to the psychological process of self-realization.[54]

The Significance of Opposites

The Self as containing and mediating opposites is the core of Jung's concept; there is no Self without that tension of opposites. A belief over centuries that there is a need for a mediating function for opposites such as the Self, is linked not only to philosophy but also to anthropology as an ancient, universal desire to manage complexities and inconsistencies.[55] In this orientation of seeking a balance, it is even argued that Freud's structural model of the psyche—id, ego, and superego—can be translated as different self-representations over time that arise to carry out this mediating function.[56] Hans Kohut, the originator of what is called "self-psychology," bases his notion of a self on this need:

> Whenever we are observing a person who strives for pleasure or pursues vengeful and destructive purposes or who is in conflict concerning those aims or opposes them, it is possible to discern a self which, while it includes drives (and/or defences) in its organization, has become a supra-ordinate configuration whose significance transcends that of the sum of its parts.[57]

Mario Jacoby explains that this view that Kohut is presenting of the Self as the center of psyche "is very close to the view of the self in analytical psychology."[58] Kohut's work was more concentrated on the development of the self in infancy, but his view as to a center is based on the *need* for a concept of a self that exists because of opposites. Opposites must be reconciled or mediated in some form, not only to cope with the vicissitudes of practical day-to-day existence, but also to affirm the fundamental historical foundations of order, peace, and justice. This demand for reconciliation is thus universal in all spiritual traditions.

---

[54] CW 7, § 266
[55] Ewing 1987
[56] Hartmann 1964
[57] Kohut 1977, p. 97
[58] Jacoby 2017, p. 55

According to Jung, reconciliation of the opposites "provides to be the eidos behind the supreme ideas of unity and totality that are inherent in all monotheistic and monistic systems."[59] In whatever way that mediating function comes to be expressed, it is the bedrock for calming upheavals and moral conflicts. The alchemist's idea of a *conjunctio* or union of opposites was thus, as Jung expresses, "based on the view that man, as a result of a loss of his original 'Adamic' state, is divided within himself. He regains his integral nature only when the two powers whose discord has rendered him impotent, are again reconciled with one another."[60]

Opposites yield moral issues causing difficulties in all decision making, and influence thoughts, feelings, attitudes, create hate and division, and are responsible for the political destiny of nations. The need to balance the opposites invokes the requirement to postulate some symbolic expression of *wholeness* to represent their engaged balance or reconciliation. Wholeness is the theoretical goal, the end product if that balance is successful. The Self was chosen by Jung to be the symbolic representation of that ultimate unity, of wholeness, where there is no longer any conflict and the noise of counterdemands is gone.

Opposites suggest that they may be completely reconciled, but as that is not possible, the Self becomes a goal pointing forward, always offering a promise of peace. That promise of peace becomes clearer the closer one gets to wholeness by successful balancing the polarity at a mid-point. Thus, the Self is, as Jung expresses, "the desired 'mid-point' of the personality, that ineffable something betwixt the opposites, or else that which unites them, or the result of conflict, or the product of energic tension...."[61] In citing this passage, Paul Bishop argues correctly that the Self was therefore "underpinned" for Jung by the opposites, the historical and philosophical notion of polarity.[62]

The Self as a representation of wholeness is not only the theoretical idea behind a mid-point but carries more importance because it points forward to the emergence of what Jung refers to as "a new and more solid

[59] *Aion*, § 64
[60] Bradbrook, & Lloyd Thomas 1939, p. 250
[61] CW 7, § 382
[62] Bishop 1999, p. 427

foundation."[63] This is where the feeling value and numinosity of the Self lies, in its orientation in the direction of becoming more whole. The Self idea is then strongest as a concept that wholeness can be achieved so as to settle the conflicts in our minds that we all face as the nature of living. It takes on a meaning similar to the promise of spiritual enlightenment, resting in a transcendent unity. Jung's development of the Self as an answer to the opposites therefore serves two purposes. The first is that as a psychological construct, it offers an immediate means to resolve internal conflict. The second is that it offers a goal, the promise of a more complete or even a fully realized unity in the future, instilling the belief that life does not have to remain so difficult.

Accordingly, it is the mid-point of the opposites where the Self resides *and for which it exists*. It is nothing out of the ordinary as a concept, as it has always been and will always be a necessary ideal. It therefore makes sense that this is considered a prime function within psyche and that it is so innate in all things that it can be observed in symbols. As James Hall expresses it, "The actual functioning of the psyche involves mutual and coordinated interaction of apparent opposites which are, in reality, part of a unified whole that transcends the ego…. When observed by the ego … this underlying unity appears in images of the Self."[64]

The concept of wholeness as a fact and, most importantly, as a future possibility, puts the Jungian concept of the Self beyond controversy. Others may want to call it soul or *Abraxas* or God, but it is a psychological necessity and is the basis for Jung's introduction of the Self. As expressed as a representation of wholeness, it did not need its own concept as it is a universal idea, but it was necessary in Jung's matrix to find a term that made it a regulatory function of psyche. The Self needs to exist or wholeness is not possible and cannot be psychologically realized. The only difficulty is that the Self idea remains abstract and its nature unknowable.

---

[63] CW 7, § 365
[64] Hall 1960, p. 66

Epistemological Basis for the Self

It is clear that as the Self arises entirely by an internal perception of a metaphysical idea, it cannot be expressed as concrete reality in logical terms. To actually know the Self, according to Jung, will occur empirically only by a realization of its existence through absorption of its symbols in the heart and mind. To understand it, it must stand apart from ego consciousness to become its object, and there must be a means whereby the conscious mind can discern it. It was therefore incumbent on Jung to find an underlying theory to allow the ineffable Self to be a fact for consciousness.

By "known" is meant psychologically known, so that it has an effect on the conscious position, rather than it to be known as concrete, tangible realty. As Jung points out, "Psychology does not hypostatize, but considers such ideas as psychological statements about, or models of, essential unconscious factors inaccessible to immediate experience."[65] How then to make such a wisp of an idea as the Self into a known reality to form the basis of his psychology?

The development of Jung's view of the experiential basis of the elements of the unconscious is complex, as could be expected, but as it relates to the Self, there is one specific formational milestone that Paul Bishop explains is the "key notion in the works of Jung."[66] This is based on Jung's need to find the manner in which to unite the polarity of the different realms of being as taken up by Kant.

Immanuel Kant's primary division is of two realms: the *phenomenal*, our day-to-day subjective experiences of the world, and the *noumenal*, the true nature of the actual things the subject of those experiences: concrete reality. The noumenal, which Kant refers to as *Ding an sich*—the thing in itself—stands outside the experience, creating the two different realms as reality is not capable of being known by the experience and therefore remains only a postulate.

In 1898, when Jung was 23, he gave yet another lecture to his medical fraternity, the Zofingiaverein Club, called *Thoughts on the Nature and*

---

[65] CW 19, § 1642
[66] Bishop 2008, p. 2

Value of Speculative Inquiry, which establishes his orientation to the idea of this split between inward experience and concrete reality in light of Kant. Marie-Louise von Franz, in writing the Introduction to these *Zofingia Lectures,* explains the particular significance of this lecture. Jung starts his approach by developing *Ding an sich* into a wider category to include everything that is unknowable, not just Kant's category for the noumenal. Consequently, having expanded the category, it is not only the reality of any outside thing in itself that we cannot know, but also any inner psychic object.[67] However, as it is an object in psyche unlike an external, material object, when it is in fact known by inner experience, Jung concludes that it then ceases to be *Ding an sich.* This was a big leap, but it offered him a way out of philosophical dualism. In a sense, he needed this new bridge, or the Self could never be real. He therefore points out that psychic knowing "turned the unknown into the known, and we have diminished by one term the transcendental domain of the *Ding au sich.*"[68]

Kant was forced to suggest a unity between the two different realms by what he calls a "transcendental apperception" of reality that arises through thought and reason applied to intuitions arising from an "inner sense." This is a convoluted subject matter, as are all of Kant's ideas, but it was his way to create a possible link between subjective experiences and a thing in itself through a cognitive assumption informed by reflection conveyed from our senses that there lies something critical for an individual.[69] In the Zofingia lecture, to solve this, which would otherwise have made it impossible for the Self to be ever really known, Jung proposes that the "absolute realm is not divided into two distinct realms, the *Ding an Sich* on the one hand and phenomenal world of the other. All is One."[70] Von Franz indicates that this joining of the realms in oneness is the precursor to the *unus mundus* or the world-soul that Jung would develop toward the end of his life. This link was essential to his psychology and to the existence of the Self as it provides a means to turn an unknown concept into a subjective experience that renders it a fact.

---

[67] Jung 1983, p. xxi
[68] *Ibid,* p. 76
[69] Explained in detail in Ameriks 1997 p. 57
[70] Jung, 1983, § 197

This approach of Jung to go beyond the use of reason or logic to provide a unity of a preexistent all-oneness is also evident in his consideration of the ancient argument of "ontological proof." This argument, in one of its expressions, is that the proof of the existence of God is found in the *logic* of a necessity for a supreme being that is so overwhelming that it is beyond thought, so it is not possible to think that it does not exist. In finding no basis for this argument, Jung quotes Kant that the idea of God is just that: a mere idea not able to be proved by logical argument that out of absolute necessity it must exist.[71] The specific idea that fixes in Kant and is seized on by Jung is that proof of God cannot be found simply because logic requires it. Jung focuses on this argument because reason and thought can also not be the bases for his psychology of reflection and the existence of the Self. There needed to be a different approach for proof of psychic objects.

Jung uses the weakness of the ontological argument to find a solution for the existence of psychic objects by what he calls *esse in anima.* This is the means he uses to close the gap between the possible existence of a phenomenon that makes sense through the intellectual, logical mind (*esse in intellectu*), and its actual existence, its reality (*esse in re*). The gap between the two realms would never *logically* allow a *tertium,* a third thing, or a bridge joining the two so that a psychic object could never be a reality. Jung therefore postulates that "between *intellectus* and *res* there is still *anima,* and this *esse in anima* makes the whole ontological argument superfluous."[72] It was necessary that Jung take this step in order to justify the Self, a psychic object, as a reality upon realization.

Anima, in this context, is the soul or God, and he therefore explains that from the point of view of Analytical Psychology, *esse in anima* arises from the power of the idea of soul and the divine in an individual: the "God-concept coincides with a particular ideational complex which ... concentrates in itself the maximum amount of libido, or psychic energy."[73] This is best explained as the idea of the soul or God is given the highest psychic value and therefore has the greatest concentration of psychic energy, thereby giving it reality—*res*—in psyche; the psychic object

---

[71] CW 6, § 65
[72] *Ibid,* § 66
[73] *Ibid,* § 67

therefore becomes very much alive as a fact. Logic would not be appropriate as it "strips the objective impression of its vitality and immediacy." He asks, "What would the idea amount to if the psyche did not provide it living value?" "What indeed is reality if it is not a reality in ourselves, an *esse in anima*?"[74] As ideation of the highest value is what produces the libido, psychic energy, it arises by fantasy[75] and imagination that are thus the bases for creating the reality of the Self, because "Only through the specific vital activity of the psyche does the sense-impression attain that intensity, and the idea (of) that effective force, which are the two indispensable constituents of living reality."[76]

The powerful concept of *esse in anima*, derived in a manner to give psychic objects a subjective reality, has the effect that creative imagination is responsible for higher ideation and thus building the bridge between the opposites. In a letter in 1955, Jung explains that it was necessary for him to go his own way in order to create a foundation for this phenomenological approach. This bridge based on creative imagination is the basis for the Self straddling a metaphysical concept and a reality; Jung suggests, "The self is therefore a *borderline* concept,"[77] as it is bridging the phenomenal and the noumenal. The bridge is also reflected in symbols of the Self and synchronistic events that go beyond time and space. For Kant, there was no mediating between the two poles, and Jung's motivation in creating *esse in anima* has been explained in a critique of Jung's reasoning, as his "desire to substantiate the God concept psychologically, which was not Kant's program at all."[78]

As John Dourley points out, this *esse in anima* position means that God can never be understood as actually existent as God can only be known, according to Jung's concept, when experienced in psyche, which is well beyond our capacity. All that can then be known is the experience that is a *reflection* of divinity and will arise from forces in psyche, as Jung explains, "by the impact of numinous archetypal powers, especially of the self, seeking concrete expression in consciousness"[79] Dourley

---

[74] *Ibid,* § 77
[75] The nature of which is explicated in de Voogd 1991
[76] CW 6, § 77
[77] *Letters*, Vol. 2, pp. 258-259
[78] Brooks 2019, p. 126
[79] Dourley 2015, p. 77

explains that this limited experience of divinity can still offer an element of transcendence beyond how it is experienced because "the fontal wealth of the archetypal will never cease the drive to fuller realization and yet will always transcend the degree of its incarnation in individuals and species."[80] The limitation of *esse in anima* explained by Dourley is no doubt the basis for Jung's statement in 1935, as will be discussed, to restrict the Self as embracing "totality" only to the limited extent that it is actually realized.

It can be argued, as suggested by Dourley, that the Self as a reflection of divinity that arises by experience of those archetypal forces contains within it the possibility of a transcendence, so that it can be said to exist beyond its limited recognition. This is a reminder that the many philosophical or metaphysical ideas about what constitutes the Self exceed the dimensions of Jung's approach. He expresses this problem in terms of the attribution to him of the phrase the "*idea* of wholeness" that is often used to describe his approach to the Self: "Concepts play no role whatever with me because I make no philosophical assumptions; hence I never started from the 'idea of wholeness.'"[81]

This statement by Jung means that to think of the Self is not to really know the Self. All concepts about what it might be have limited value, although they must be made because of the significance of the Self. It can only be actually known through *esse in anima* to the extent that it is a psychic object experienced through symbols of the Self appearing in dreams, visions, and fantasies. It can be understood by these symbols, or more directly by mystical or religious experiences. It is also reflected *indirectly* in the *consensus gentium*, the general consensus, not as a matter of logic, but because, as Jung explains, "they crop up again and again and can evidently not be suppressed. This is probably because they represent emotional needs and, as such, are psychological facts that cannot be eliminated, which is how they appear to the empirical mind."[82] The integration of the Self, for it to be truly known then requires, by his epistemological approach, the "creative fantasy" of psyche, defined

---

[80] *Ibid,* p. 78
[81] *Letters,* Vol. 2, p. 294
[82] *Ibid,* pp. 249-250

broadly as a psychological activity of a creative nature,[83] to bring the Self into existence as a reality.

The development of the *esse in anima* idea in order to provide a bridge between experience and reality was an aspect of Jung's earliest thinking and is what moves the Self from a mere intellectual concept to a psychological fact that can alter consciousness. The Self, in accordance with *esse in anima*, exists as an absolute reality to the extent that it is experienced by an individual. If it is not so realized as not yet brought to consciousness by creative fantasy through the activation of psyche and formation of images, then it is a bundle of ideas and does not yet exist in reality. On this reasoning, as the degree of realization increases, it gains substance, gradually comes into form, and will have an effect of altering ego consciousness because of its revelation. Jung explains, "Image and meaning are identical; as the first takes shape, so the latter becomes clear. Actually the pattern needs no interpretation: it portrays its own meaning."[84] It is through this lens of *esse in anima* that images and symbols in dreams and visions are made to come alive in order to bring the Self to the attention of the ego. The bridge is Jung's creation and is not echoed elsewhere, but it arose because of his own revelation that the Self when realized becomes a reality.

---

[83] CW 6, § 84
[84] CW 8, § 204

Chapter 2. Jung's Dream of the Self

In 1927, just after what he describes in his autobiographical revelations *Memories, Dreams, Reflections* as a difficult period unraveling the "process of the unconscious,"[1] Jung had a critical dream where the Self appeared to him in a bleak landscape. It is his first explicit realization of the *reality* of the Self and, as to which, all his future insights correspond. Accordingly, it requires to be analyzed in some detail.

Jung describes the dream as having "depicted the climax of the whole process of development of consciousness" and "Without such a vision I might perhaps have lost my orientation and been compelled to abandon my undertaking."[2] This dream conveys a direct, unobscured message as to the existence of the Self in his psyche.

> ...we found a broad square dimly illuminated by street lights, into which many streets converged. The various quarters of the city were arranged radially around the square. In the center was a round pool and in the middle of it a small island. While everything round about was obscured by rain, fog, smoke, and dimly lit darkness, the little island blazed with sunlight. On it stood a single tree, a magnolia, in a shower of reddish blossoms. It was as though the tree stood in the sunlight and were at the same time the source of light.
> ... I was carried away by the beauty of the flowering tree and the sunlight island....[3]

In the dream he finds himself in Liverpool. He explains that Liverpool is the "pool of life" as the body's liver is the seat of life. The dream structure, in fact, does not relate to the topography and orientation of Liverpool,

---

[1] *Memories*, pp. 193-7
[2] *Ibid*, p. 199
[3] *Ibid*, p. 198

and he never visited the city. The significance of that structure, however, is twofold: It is a geometrical pattern that represents an ordered arrangement, and it has the quality of a magical place. This last impression is expressed when he is informed that another Swiss lived there and, upon being carried away with the beauty of the tree and island, just before he woke, he adds: "I know very well why he has settled here."[4]

The references to the liver and Liverpool are oblique but are examples of how the creative imagination of the unconscious brings symbols into reality. Its origin as the seat of life was verified from a manuscript Jung received in 1928, the year after the dream, of Richard Wilhelm's translation of the *Secret of the Golden Flower*,[5] for which he wrote a commentary. The manuscript contained mandala images that echoed the dream structure and coincided with his fascination with mandalas for some years before the dream. In the course of the manuscript, the importance of the reference to the liver is explained. In the text of the *Secret,* the *animus* is described as the masculine higher soul that needs to be freed from the lower spirit—the body. As relevant to the dream, Jung explains in his commentary, "The animus is in the heavenly heart. ... By day it lives in the eyes [i.e., consciousness]; at night it houses in the liver."[6] It is pointed out by another commentator on the *Secret of the Golden Flower* that in colloquial Chinese usage, liver and heart refer to what are essential to life: "In a human being, the liver is associated with courage and consciousness."[7]

In the dream, Jung finds himself in a dirty, sooty city in winter, walking at night in the rain; it is hard to imagine a more desolate dream environment: "Everything was extremely unpleasant, black and opaque— just as I felt then."[8] Yet, the darkness was illuminated with streetlights. It thus contains a blending of the opposites of darkness and light, and, as Jung points out often,[9] neither the conscious nor unconscious aspects of a person are entirely light or completely dark. Yet, darkness is a necessary precondition for working out a resolution in this dismal city as a bright

---

[4] *Ibid*
[5] Wilhelm 1962
[6] Reproduced in CW 13, § 37
[7] Cleary 1991, p. 83
[8] *Memories*, p. 198
[9] For example, CW 14, § 229

day in summer would probably have made the contrast and realization less.

Significantly, the dream takes place in the setting of a city. Jung's view of cities—a Swiss city—was most likely influenced by Swiss cities as historically and completely self-contained, as each Canton was self-governing with no Swiss state; each Canton was "like a snail in a shell."[10] Western European cities were built as protected, contained areas with an integrated, coherent structure representing a geometric unity, an idea expressed well by its form as an enclosed circle or a quaternion of four segments. Years later in 1935, Jung states: "The city as a synonym for the self, for psychic totality, is an old and well-known image."[11] This is certainly not the case for all Eastern cities, as, for instance, the ancient city of Varanasi in India, oriented around the Ganges. The Western European city was, however, the manner in which the imprint of a mandala on a dream setting could be imposed.

The city in his dream is fundamentally a symbol of a geometric order, taking its strength from the patterning reflected in a mandala of an area, either a circle or square, divided into quadrants. Jung explains, "Experience shows that individual mandalas are symbols of *order*. ... As magic circles they bind and subdue the lawless powers belonging to the world of darkness, and depict or create an order that transforms the chaos into a cosmos."[12] The dream is thus focused on order, orientation, and a stable structure. The use of the expression that order "transforms chaos into a cosmos" reflects the idea that true, esoteric wisdom is found in understanding that the ordered, external macrocosm is the pattern for the internal microcosm,[13] an ancient concept developed, for example, in alchemy.[14]

The emphasis on the microcosm occurs frequently in Jung's writings and is warranted in relation to the Self because the macrocosm is a structure, as Jung expresses it, derived from God's plan for "the creation of the world and the heavenly bodies; *it is the birth of the self,* the latter

---

[10] Cited in Palmer 2014, p. 664
[11] CW18, § 269
[12] *Aion*, § 80
[13] CW 4, § 777
[14] CW 8, § 929

appearing as the microcosm."[15] This transcendental reference is to the patterning of the macrocosm, the grand, ordered plan of the cosmos, as the principle underlying the dream of order suggested by the structure of the city. Jung explains this ordering principle for psyche as a "common intuition ... that the 'total' man is as big as the world, like an Anthropos."[16] The Anthropos, the individual in whom God is indwelling, contains the pattern of the macrocosm as an internal microcosm, so that psyche has within it an innate ordering that is divine. The exact relationship and its analogies are not as important as much as the use of the historic idea of the macrocosm and microcosm, a concept Jung would have found in Aristotle in *Physics*[17] that the order within a person is related to a divine pattern within creation.

Jung indicates that the city in the dream lay above on cliffs on a plateau.[18] When he later describes the city as a synonym for the Self, he also quotes from a saying attributed to Jesus that "A city built upon the top of the high hill and established, can neither fall nor be hid."[19] The location of the city on a plateau in the dream is therefore invulnerable, a fitting metaphor for the Self. On the plateau, he found a "broad square dimly illuminated by street lights, into which the streets converged."[20] The streets are converging into the place for revelation, the illuminated square, indicating that the Self needs to be found by traversing a path toward a central place.

His path to the plateau in the dream is an upward movement that reminds him, he explains, of walking in Basel, coming from the harbor with the market down below, up through the narrow *Totengässchen* alley leading to the plateau above and to *Petersplatz* and the *Peterskirche*. *Totengässchen*, now called *Totengässlein*, is in fact a steep alley coming north from *Marketplatz* with many rising steps up to a higher plateau, wherein lies first the Church *Peterskirche* and then the square *Petersplatz*. This image is clear and illustrative of the need to climb in an upward

---

[15] CW 9.i, § 550
[16] *Ibid*
[17] Aristotle, 1930, 8:2, 252b, pp. 26-7
[18] *Memories,* p. 198
[19] CW 18, § 269
[20] *Memories,* p. 198

direction by a narrow alley to reach a different plane away from the commonality of worldly concerns in the marketplace below.

In terms of this movement, he states: "I had the feeling that we were coming from the harbour, and that the real city was actually on the cliffs. We climbed up there."[21] The harbor as the starting place for a journey offers several meanings. It is at sea level (as it is in Basel), pre-conditioning the need for a higher gradient as one moves away. It also is a place of incipient growth as Jung refers to a city at a later date as a "maternal symbol, a woman who harbours the inhabitants in herself like children."[22] It is thus, if we accept the relevance of this reference, away from the childlike inhabitants and their city to the "real" city, the real meaning of life. The cliff is not just up stairs leading to a plateau, as it was in his comparison to Basel, but it is a reference to a difficult level that specifically requires climbing.

Climbing is necessary to reach what he later refers to as the "mid-point of the personality."[23] This, he states, is "reached by a kind of climb (mountaineering, effort, struggle, etc)."[24] The arrival at the midpoint provides a "point of new equilibrium, a new centering of the total personality, a virtual center which, on account of the focal position between conscious and unconscious, ensures the personality a new and more solid foundation."[25] In explaining a patient's dream two years later in 1929, Jung indicates that in the "old mystery initiations," the flight of steps means "climbing up through the seven (planetary) spheres of your constitution, the complete realization of yourself."[26]

There seems nothing superfluous or ambiguous in the dream except perhaps that he was accompanied by "a number of Swiss—say, half a dozen."[27] Numbers are significant to Jung, and the number six creates "a symbolic circle"[28] with Jung as the seventh, as he is the protagonist.

---

[21] *Ibid*
[22] CW 5, § 303
[23] CW 7, § 365
[24] *Ibid*, § 367
[25] *Ibid*, § 365
[26] Jung 1984, p. 274
[27] *Memories*, p. 198
[28] CW 12, § 287

A "symbolic circle," as pointed out by George Poulet in his *Meta-morphosis of the Circle,* has ancient roots as representing a divine unity consisting of a circumference and a center.[29] Seven corresponds, as well, to the seven stages of Christianity that Jung points out, "symbolize the transformation"[30] and is also an alchemical reference, as he had become familiar with alchemy at this stage and the seven planetary spheres. It is a symbolic circle focused *around* Jung, within a square on a plateau.

Geometry of the Dream

Jung describes the geometry of the city as "The various quarters of the city were arranged radially around the square."[31] "Radially" implies either that the city goes from the center outward or the edges of the city inward. In his description, Jung is pointing to the primacy of the central square as the focal point from which there is an expansion outward. He confirms that the expansion is out from the center when referring to other quarters of the city: "The individual quarters of the city were themselves arranged radially around a central point. The central point in those quarters is formed by a small open square illuminated by a larger street lamp, and with a small replica of the island."[32] He refers to these secondary centers as contained within the remaining three quarters where other Swiss live.[33] Only his center has a main island, which suggests his singular, personal realization. The rationale for these lesser forms of the Self is clearly that the insights are not available generally and were unique to him but offer an opportunity to those who were able to make the climb.

The idea that he had a unique revelation, and that others only had that as potential, is amplified in a mandala he drew a year after the dream. The mandala is found in *The Red Book* and is called the *Window on Eternity*:

---

[29] Poulet 1966, p. xi
[30] CW 12, § 99
[31] *Memories,* p. 198
[32] *Ibid*
[33] *Ibid*

Figure 2: *Window on Eternity* Mandala[34]

In Jung's *Black Books,* his personal diary, he maps the setting for both the dream and this mandala, so as Sonu Shamdasani points out, the "drawing formed the template of Image 159,"[35] the Window on Eternity.

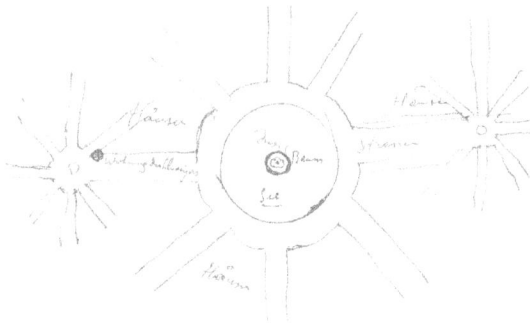

Figure 3: Linking Dream to Mandala[36]

---

[34] *Red Book,* Image, p. 159, From THE RED BOOK by C.G. Jung, edited by Sonu Shamdasani, translated by Mark Kyburz, John Peck, and Sonu Shamdasani. Copyright © 2009 by the Foundation of the Works of C. G. Jung Translation copyright (c) 2009 by Mark Kyburz, John Peck, and Sonu Shamdasani. Used by permission of W. W. Norton & Company, Inc.

[35] *Black Books,* Book 7, p. 240n260

[36] *Ibid,* p. 134. © 2007 Foundation of the Works of C.G. Jung, Zürich. First published by W.W. Norton & Co, published with permission.

This drawing displays the center of the dream as being accessed by eight streets, as is the *Window on Eternity* mandala. The direct connection between the map and the dream can be found in the black dot on the map at the left that refers to the "Dwelling of the Swiss," a reference to the "other Swiss" whom he mentions resides there in the dream setting. The map is not that of Basel that Jung used as an analogy for the city in the dream, but possibly could be related to a town map for Herman Sigg, who was the friend closest to Jung and who died in 1927, the year of the dream. It has, in fact, been suggested that the *Window* mandala was created by Jung grieving that loss.[37] Both the map in the *Black Books,* and the *Window* mandala in *The Red Book* make reference in the legend to the death of Sigg.

Jung includes the *Window on Eternity* mandala in his commentary to *The Secret of the Golden Flower,* and it also appears in the *Collected Works* in an analysis of mandala symbolism.[38] The *Window* mandala was, according to his commentary, a painting of the dream, but "it came out rather different."[39] The difference lies in the complexity of the mandala as connecting up many centers and is also a more defined statement of the reciprocal relationship between his realization and the collective, a theme examined later in this book. In his comments in the *Collected Works* about the mandala, Jung interestingly attributes the dream to a patient, not himself, and adds the patient contemplating that "I noticed that my companions had not seen this miracle ..."[40]

In the mandala, the magnolia tree becomes a rose made of "ruby-coloured glass" that "shone like a four-rayed star." From the square radiate eight main streets and, from each, eight side streets that "meet in a shining red central point." He explains: "The mandala thus combines the classic motifs of flower, star, circle, precinct (temenos), and plan of the city divided into quarters with a citadel." It is a star within a square, expanding out to eight streets and eight side streets, all being a multiple of four that creates a series of tetrads, the basic building blocks of wholeness.[41] He compares the central point of the mandala to the *Étoile* in Paris, now

---

[37] Foundation 2019, pp. 177n124, 175
[38] CW 9.i, Figure 6, after p. 356
[39] *Ibid,* § 655
[40] *Ibid,* § 654
[41] *Ibid*

called the *Place Charles de Gaulle*. It was originally the *Place de Letwal*, translated as the "Square of the Star," the intersection of 12 roads, again a multiple of four.

The addition of a circular pool around the main island, as well as the precincts and protective borders in the mandala, create a "temenos:" a distinct, protected area that emphasizes and defends the center. Temenos is the Greek expression for land that is marked off from common usage as a holy precinct; it "protects or isolates an inner content or process that should not get mixed up with things outside."[42] Gerhard Adler asserts that every mandala in its entirety is a temenos, which he relates to Jung's conversation with a Lamaic Rinpoche.[43] In that discussion, Jung reports that he realizes that the mandala is an inner image built up when "psychic equilibrium is disturbed or when a thought cannot be found and must be sought for."[44] This means that the dream setting and the mandala, by this definition, are the expression of a particular, protected and walled-off inner state that arises for consideration when no external answer can be found.

The re-creation of the dream into this *Window* mandala can be seen, in light of the realization expressed in discussion with the Rinpoche, as a natural progression from what Jung describes as his difficult struggle with his unconscious in the years prior to the dream. He explains, more specifically, that from 1918-19 he would draw a mandala every morning that he describes as "cryptograms concerning the state of the self which was presented to me anew each day."[45] After the dream, he reports, "I gave up drawing or painting mandalas."[46] He found what he was seeking, and the dream becomes a parable of how a continuous struggle for a sense of wholeness will eventually, for those who have made that climb, reveal the Self.

In the dream, the city expresses an ordered pattern: four quarters, a balanced unity that is a mandala. The four quarters of the city and the four sides of the square, each with a central temenos, create a geometric

---

[42] CW 11, § 157
[43] Adler 1979, p. 20
[44] CV 12, § 123
[45] *Memories,* p. 196
[46] *Ibid,* p. 199

arrangement that conveys a sense of order. In analyzing another dream of a patient where there was a square, Jung describes a square or a circle (that can be divided into four quadrants) as "a totality consisting of four parts (four elements)."[47] It is a totality as it contains the entirety of the structure in which the parts are equally balanced.

The setting of the dream is thus within an ordered geometrical structure on a higher level of consciousness, removed from the common marketplace, that emphasizes and is defined by a pattern of containment, geometrical balance, and completeness. This structure is available to anyone but, as can be seen by his companions and their lesser symbols, is not realized by everyone. It is a realization unavailable on the level of the marketplace with its day-to-day consciousness that can only be accessed by traversing a narrow and steep path upward, a climb where one can be eventually encapsulated within the wholeness of the geometrical form.

This geometric structure is the basis of the Self: a center in psyche that is contained in a stable configuration that creates a precise order. This idea of an underlying pattern in psyche is consistent, as will be developed, with Jung's idea of the archetype that is at the heart of his writings: "the word 'archetype' is thoroughly characteristic of the structure forms that underlie consciousness as the crystal lattice underlies the crystallization process."[48] What Jung experiences in this dream is repeated constantly in later works, such as a dream of the city being referred to eight years later as a synonym for the Self. This pattern of order as the crystal lattice that underlies psychological growth is the essence of his opus and the process of individuation.

The existence in psyche of an underlying wholeness is represented by that geometrical formation. The relationship found in that formation is that the stability of the geometric patterning of the square in the circle reflects a psychic resonance of internal order and wholeness. This formation introduces a center point, which is the tree from which the rest of the formation radiates outward. This is a geometric structure that speaks for itself as corresponding to a primal, instinctual pattern, and is best illustrated by Jung's very first mandala that he reports was created in 1916, the *Systema Munditotius* Mandala.

---

[47] CW 12, § 163
[48] *Letters*, Vol. 1, p. 418

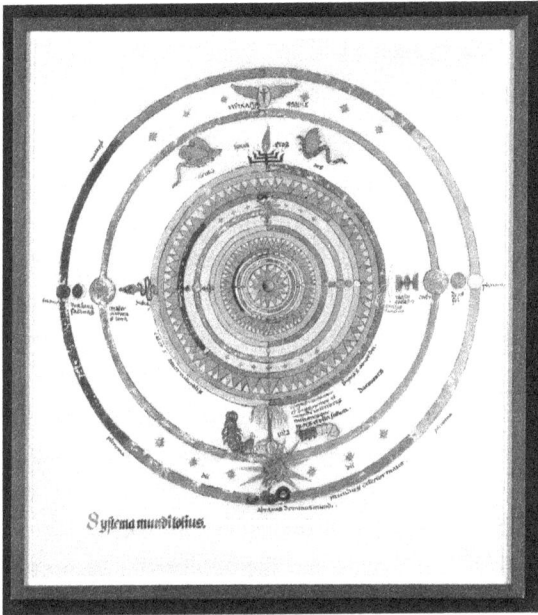

Figure 4: *Systema Munditotius* Mandala[49]

The emphasis on the center in this mandala is powerful as it is the focal point of an extended structure in which it is contained. This mandala holds a very dense center divided into four areas. This image is not only focused on the center point as the key to the structure but is enveloped by other spheres radiating outward. It has been suggested in a detailed analysis of this mandala that geometrically it radiates out by an inverse proportional mean existing between the intensely colored center and the surrounding spheres. This suggests that it will expand in that proportion until it reaches the infinite.[50] This expresses a mandala focused on the four parts of a circle and its center, as well as a transcendent dimension related to the fixed point. The transcendent aspect of the *Window on Eternity* mandala also exists for the same reason, introducing a profound quality to a center,

---

[49] *Red Book,* p. 364. From THE RED BOOK by C.G. Jung, edited by Sonu Shamdasani, translated by Mark Kyburz, John Peck, and Sonu Shamdasani. Copyright © 2009 by the Foundation of the Works of C. G. Jung Translation copyright (c) 2009 by Mark Kyburz, John Peck, and Sonu Shamdasani. Used by permission of W. W. Norton & Company, Inc, Robert Hinshaw, with acceptance by the Foundation of the Works of C.G. Jung.
[50] Harms 2011, p. 148

as Jung hints as to the ruby jeweled star: "The whole thing seemed like a window opening on to eternity."[51]

This means that every mandala, and therefore every constructed geometric pattern of a center and a periphery, is not only a balanced, bounded image, but suggests simultaneously the existence of a center, a circumference, and a transcendent expansion. It is thus, when transposed to the Self, that every expression of the Self assumes a center, a circumference, and transcendence. The relationship in the dream of the center to the surrounding areas of the balanced four quarters of the city is a mandala and is what informs the idea of order and the power of the Self. It is therefore not merely a center, but as the dream indicates, it is a center encased in a square, within an ordered structure that also suggests it is porous and capable of expansion. This intimation that the center includes its transcendence has had great impact on the notion of the psychological Self. It suggests that the center can only be understood in the context of a surrounding structure and that structure is not bound in a static formation and can rise to the heavens. In order for this to have any substance, however, the center must be present, as emphasized in the *Systema* mandala, the dream, and the *Window* mandala.

A center is the focal point in the dream because of the image of a tree at the center of a circle (the round island) located at the center of a square. Most importantly, in carrying its transcendence and importance to psyche, it is more than a normal tree as it is illuminated and is also a source of illumination beyond itself. This focuses all locational aspects toward a tree that becomes a fixed center point as the center of a circle at the center of a square, all within a bounded city that is most akin to the profound ordering of a mandala of four parts.

These are all remarkable structures establishing powerful geometric relationships that derive their effect from the potential of what they evoke; they are dream objects but also exist in and derive purpose from a chain of associations. It is in this context, in that chain, that the center as representing the Self is understood. The chain of connections creates the pattern, and, in this way, the geometric image *speaks for itself*. The significance of such a pattern is nicely understood in the insights of

---

[51] CW 9.i, § 653

Jacques Lacan, the French psychoanalyst, who explains the powerful force that emanates from a chain of associated images. To explain how that force is derived, he calls on the work of the linguist, Ferdinand de Saussure, who proposes that a concept or an image, which he calls a "sign," can be divided into two parts. The first he refers to as the "signifier," the image, name, or actual form such as the tree on an island at the center of a square. The second is the "signified," the meaning given in this chain to which the signifier refers. The leap from signifier, the images, to signified, its meaning, arises from the *impact* of the signifiers, the chain of association, the geometric structure in the dream: "the signifier, by its very nature, always anticipates meaning by deploying its dimension in some sense before it."[52] The chain of signifiers, as well, suggests that dimension by its exactitude, and by conferring a sense of its numinosity, thereby prompting a meaning. In linguistics, the signifier requires a metonym or a metaphor to bring forth the meaning.[53]

This analysis is useful to indicate that the geometric structure of the dream is created by a relationship between a center point and all of the elements of its periphery, and that this chain of signifiers anticipates meaning. This anticipated meaning is wholeness arising from a complete ideographic presentation without the need for description. The Self is then a metaphor, not just for the center, but for the entirety of the structure.

In his essay *The Geometry of Wholeness,* George Hogenson suggests that fractal geometry, which emphasizes recursion where the essential pattern is the basis for the next iteration, explains the geometry of wholeness.[54] The quadratic pattern of the mandala and the city in the dream would, accordingly, reflect the material world that is based on these fractal patterns. Although the attention in the dream is on the revelation of the center, as can be seen by the lesser centers available to the other Swiss, it appears that the sense of wholeness, order, and meaning is derived from the entirety of the geometric structure as a preexistent and recursive pattern in all things.

The pattern is disclosed in the chain of signifiers where each is in relation to each other; every element is therefore necessary for the pattern to

---

[52] Lacan 2006, para. 502
[53] As explained, for example, by Bredin 1984
[54] Horgenson 2020

reflect wholeness. However, it does not have that effect just by the juxtaposition of a center and surrounding structure, but rather because each element has its *own* numinosity, a higher significance of transcendence, and therefore the combined capacity to attract makes the pattern more profound and able to reveal the nature of the Self.

Finding a Center

In translating the chain of signifiers, the structure, to a metonym or metaphor, it is the center that must be privileged as it is responsible for the compelling nature of the image and the dream. In the dream and the mandala, the center *creates* the entire structure of order, the geometric wholeness, and the possibility of transcendence. Jung states very clearly: "The center is the goal, and everything is directed toward that center."[55]

These two aspects, the center and the outward movement that imply a dimension beyond a center, was not how Jung approached the dream. Yet, there is that obvious connection between the center and the surrounding structure that he could have taken up at this juncture as constituting the Self: a center and the wider totality. However, this dream was concerned with the Self only as center and the reasons for that must be explored.

The French philosopher Jacques Derrida agrees that it is the center that is most critical in a structure as it controls the form: "The function of this center was not only to orient: balance and organize the structure ... but above all to make sure the organizing principle of the structure would limit what we might call the *freeplay* of the structure."[56] A center thus dictates and protects the structure from instability, such that "the notion of a structure lacking any center represents the unthinkable itself." He continues, the "center has no natural locus but a function..."[57] The function of the center is that it will not allow for psyche to become uncentered or subject to disintegration; the center is the functional aspect of the structure of the Self.

In Derrida's analysis, the center as primarily functional in creating a containing structure, has no content itself, no intrinsic essence, no

---

[55] *Memories,* p. 198-9
[56] Derrida 1970, p. 1, emphasis supplied.
[57] *Ibid*

substance, and is merely a reference point, perhaps like a stake in the ground. It lacks substance technically as it is derived geometrically by establishing a point equidistant from all points in the circle around it, but mathematically, the circumference alone measured by C=2r, does not yield a center. A center of a circle is therefore only postulated, meaning the center is essentially empty. As Jung explains in relation to a mandala, "Prejudiced by historical analogies, we would expect a deity to occupy the center of the mandala. The center, however, is empty."[58] It is empty as it lacks a form and is *only a function*. However, this does not diminish its significance in its representation of the Self because, Jung explains, "Emptiness in this sense doesn't mean 'absence' or 'vacancy,' but something unknowable which is endowed with the highest intensity."[59]

The center is empty because it is unknowable, without substance, but has great intensity and derives its importance because it is the progenitor of the organized structure. Although divinity or a sense of transcendence was not associated with the surrounding area in the dream, it accounts for the feeling that there is at play a higher organizing power or a numinous revelation when the center is found, as was particularly the case when the tree was visualized.

The illumination of the tree protected by the round island, prevents it from being characterized as an empty center. This particular center is accordingly given a virtue or value by Jung that it does not otherwise have. This value is explained in a commentary on William Blake's *Four Zoas*, where Blake provides that a vortex is responsible for the apocalypse in his constructed world. However, in comparing the vortex to a mandala, it is argued that Blake is suggesting: "While both have empty centres, one (vortex) is associated with fear, chaos, and annihilation, and the other (mandala) with peace, equilibrium, and liberation."[60] By the addition of an illuminated tree to an otherwise empty center, it is a means to convey that the center, although empty theoretically, should be understood as numinous, alive, and a source of that peace.

The addition of a tree to what otherwise would be an empty center was perhaps a cultural necessity for Jung because of the dream setting of a

---

[58] CW 11, § 136
[59] *Letters*, Vol. 2, p. 258
[60] Freeman 1997, p. 99

city. A vital, full center is inherent in the collective European zeitgeist; all European cities have an engaged and defined city center. This cultural phenomenon of attributing a center to the culture of a Western city is illustrated by the Parisian Roland Barthes' essay about Tokyo, *L'Empire des Signes*. He states as to Tokyo: "possede bien un centre, mais ce centre est vide," "it does possess a center but the center is empty."[61] This specific reference draws upon the empty Imperial Palace, a "site both forbidden and indifferent, a residence concealed beneath foliage, protected by moats, inhabited by an empower who is never seen."[62] This "centerlessness," he explains, is in fact the key organizing principle of Japanese food and culture. The content of the center is thus a reflection of a culture's organizing principle. As a European, an empty center is anathema to Barthes, so he sees the Japanese empty center as "decenteredness," rather than an acceptable or culturally appropriate form for Japan. He expresses, therefore, as would any Westerner, and as would Jung, that he is most comfortable with a city to have a vital center to "go to, to return from, a complete site to dream of and in relation to which to advance or retreat, in a word, to invent oneself."[63]

The center is important in any event because the goal is order and orientation, and that would not be possible without a center. That is the importance of the dream and the function of the Self. It is therefore not the Self as center, per se, but the Self as center with an orientation and ordering function in psyche. In the absence of that psychological function, the center would not be important. Derrida, in fact, explains that an empty center is not even part of the structure as it is the geometric structure rising from the center that is important, making the center ultimately irrelevant. The consequence, in Derrida's words is, "The center is not the center."[64] If that is the case, the center in the dream is potentially elsewhere, outside of the structure, confounding orientation, making the entire structure more the key to the Self than the center. This is not, of course, the essence of Jung's dream where the center is functional as the entire focus of psyche.

---

[61] Barthes 1982, p. 30
[62] *Ibid*
[63] *Ibid*
[64] Derrida 1970, p. 1

It does not even matter, as Jung put it in 1928, a year after the dream, that it cannot be located because it is an "unknowable virtual center."[65]

Equating the goal expressly to the center point and not to the entire city or the round island is consistent with the psychological idea of seeking a virtual center in psyche as a means of finding order and therefore relief from the chaos. A center, cast in that light, has a special quality that is more than a function creating the structure, as it is a reflection of a collective yearning about the necessity to seek order. As expressed by Carol Baumann, a participant in several of Jung's seminars:

> "Oh Wilderness! Thy center is not yet!" is the cry of every seeker, whether great or small, who finds that he must wander through an inner chaos; and he feels lost and disoriented until he discovers "the center," or becomes centered. Moreover, contact with that inner center is invariably lost and found many times before he feels assured of its underlying continuity, and realizes that it rests on an indestructible foundation of an eternal order.[66]

The center becomes the essence of the Self as a goal because seeking a center—centering—is the required psychological process of what Jung refers to as "reducing the confusion to order."[67] Orientation to a center, according to Jung, is ingrained in the collective unconscious in order to counteract the disbursement of psychic contents with the resultant loss of ego integration. This counteraction that is so deep within the collective unconscious, he adds, "points unmistakably to a process of centering."[68] Centering is the key as it is the key function in psychological growth, and there is no need to discover the entire structure, although that will always appear symbolically as there is an indelible connection between the center and the structure. The English philosopher Edward Douglas Faucett describes the emphasis on centering as an experiential necessity: "I have to admit that certain events in my Centre point to events which altogether transcend its conscious sphere. I am in touch with a fringe or region of

---

[65] CW 7, § 298
[66] Baumann 1946, p. 52
[67] CW 9.i, § 645
[68] CW16, § 29

the enveloping system, the 'esse' of which certainly does not consist in its being inferred by me."[69]

Another reason for focusing on the virtual, unknowable center and not the periphery that radiates from it is that when the structure is seen as a wider image that embraces the entirety of the geometric structure, it deemphasizes the process of the Self as a centering process, as Giegerich explains clearly:

> Because 'Self' refers to the innermost subjectivity of the subject it cannot be represented. It cannot be symbolized. It can only be experienced, or to be more exact, it is in itself experience. … Since it is experience (has the nature of a process of experience), it cannot be content, not a phenomenon, not something we merely happen to be experiencing. The moment it became a content or image, it would cease to be the Self.[70]

A center points to its function as responsible for a process of orientation. This is the essential theme of psychoanalysis, as it indicates the possibility of being centered. The geometric structure exists, in this viewpoint, to render the center more obvious. Symbolic expressions of a center in a dream or vision are a reassertion of the centering process focused on obtaining internal balance. The centering process then reveals that the center is a reflection of an innate patterning that suggests ordering and that the patterning is preexistent in psyche.

The realization of the patterning in psyche of an innate order is that which offers the potential of attaining more lasting wholeness. The symbols and forms of this patterning will constantly present differently, but all require a center, as it is the source of any ordered structure. The images in dreams, visions, and fantasies that represent the center within a structure are thus symbolic forms of that pattern of a geometric ordering around a center. These symbols, as will be elucidated, can also, interestingly, be an object, a figure, or anything that is symbolic of that pattern or in some other form indicates a new orientation away from chaos. As Ann Ulanov explains, the Self appears in ever-shifting ways, never in the same way twice, and

---

[69] Faucett 1909, p. 107
[70] Giegerich 2001, p. 182

cannot be tied to a specific form: "The Self destroys itself, it will not be reified, stuck fast to one form, it will not be iconized, for it, too, is but a signpost, Jung's God-image, if you will, but not the reality itself."[71]

The Surrounding Structure

Jung concludes, "This dream brought with it a sense of finality. I saw that the goal had been revealed. One would not go beyond the center."[72] There is, in this conclusion, nowhere else to look to find that goal, no further widening of the Self that is necessary other than the existence of a center, making the surrounding circle-square irrelevant except as a structure radiating from and created by a center. The center is a magnet by its mere presence, and this is what creates a process toward it and gradually captures disparate material in a crystal lattice. This is the only result that can be expressed as to the nature of the Self if it is only the center that is being found.

It is the case that the dream displays more than a center, as it is a point that exists within a surrounding context that first has to be reached by climbing. It is necessary to repeat that the center requires a setting to display that it is indeed the midpoint of a larger structure. There is always a larger structure as every center generates the structure as a circumference, the distance once around the center, however near or distant. Plotinus puts it that "the center is the father of the circle."[73] The midpoint must logically create a circumference, and the character of those surroundings therefore can appear to have as much impact as the center. As Dante expresses in *Paradiso* looking into the eyes of Beatrice, "One Point I saw, so radiantly bright, so radiantly bright, so searing to the eyes. … About that point, a ring of fire wheeled."[74] The two—the center and the circle—are, however, *independent* and do not inform each other; the circle exists outside the point, although both are reliant on each other structurally.

Images of roundness, of a circle, are inherent to humanity, so it is natural to speak of the Self as a point that includes its circumference. The

---

[71] Ulanov 2007, p. 207
[72] *Memories,* pp. 198-9
[73] Plotinus 1992, Ennead, IV 3, 17, 12ff
[74] Alighieri 2017, Canto. 1318

roundness of the circumference is a consequence of the center as a point from which expansion outward is uniform. As a manifestation of a center point whose psychological function is order, its expansion carries the emanations of the center outward to the circle, which more accurately reflects the wider nature of wholeness. It therefore can be said, as Gaston Bachelad expresses it in the *Phenomenology of Roundness,* "das Desein ist rund:" being is round.[75]

The attribution of roundness to an individual arises from the transcendent nature of what is suggested by the structure, so that within the circumference lies the potential of each person. This potential of what is contained within the circumference has invoked a long history of transcendent ideation. It was, most likely, during the Byzantine Renaissance that the soul became equated with a center as a microcosm within the circumference of the cosmic macrocosm. The center was used to indicate that the soul was in relationship with what surrounds it as reflecting all that exists in the world.[76] This idea of the relationship of the soul to the world, the individual soul to the macrocosm, naturally suggests by inferring a center drawn from the radii, divine causality. Thus, there is the well-known expression that God is an infinite sphere in which the center is everywhere and whose circumference is nowhere, a formulation attributed to many: St. Augustine, St. Bonaventure, Nicholas of Cusa, Geordino Bruno, Hermes Trismegistus, Aristotle, and for Jung, Alanas de Insulus.[77] Plotinus explains it in a manner that coincides with the center being the soul:

> The soul is not a circle in the sense of the geometric figure but in that it at once contains the Primal Nature (as centre) and is contained by it (as circumference) …. (We) hold through our own centre to the centre of all the centres, just as the centres of the great circles of a sphere coincide with that of the sphere to which all belong. Thus we are secure.[78]

Plotinus made the divine truth, what he calls the Primal Nature, the circle's center that has a relationship with the sphere that contains the

---

[75] Bachelard 1964, p. 386
[76] Spivak 1969
[77] CW 11, § 92; 229
[78] Plotinus 1992, Ennead, 13, VI, 9

divine. It is a relationship of similitude and connection but not a dependent relationship, even though the circumference is generated by the center. It is not, however, possible in this reasoning to say that the soul is the circle; it remains the center, although it has a relationship with the circumference on the transcendent level. Every aspect of the circumference, or every state of being outside the center, however, must trace itself back to the center.

These metaphysical assertions achieve relevancy in terms of psychological totality, the entirety of psyche, that consists of all that is conscious and all that is unconscious. That is the width and breadth of all possible inner, psychic content, its circumference, which can have no boundaries as the unconscious is infinite. In terms of psyche, a claim that the Self as center includes the circumference must therefore always be correct as it is similar to the exhortation that God includes the center as well as the circumference. The connection is affirmed in the reasoning of Plotinus: "each of the (radii) in the circle has a point in (the center), and the radii bring their proper (end point in the circumference) to (the center),"[79] meaning that the circumference has relevance as there is a connection by the radii back to the center. The significant point for the Self is that the circumference, the totality of psyche, is a *manifestation* of the circle's center as its generative form. Plotinus refers to the circumference aptly by the ancient Greek word *kentroeidos* (kentro: master, eidos: form or essence), the center's form.[80]

The surrounding structure in the dream is generated by the center: It is therefore the center's form. It is derived from the virtual, functional center and all aspects of psyche, the totality of an individual, are related back to that center and therefore understood through the center. This is a critical point in understanding the Self as center: When the center is known, its emanations fan out to the circumference so that the center is the source of understanding psyche. Accordingly, the ordering principle derived from knowing the center creates the possibility of ordering the entirety of psyche as its midpoint. The connection of the city, square and island to the center is not made clear in these terms in the dream, but the importance of the center in relation to the whole is expressed by Jung as

---

[79] *Ibid*, V1.11.8-13
[80] *Ibid*

"everything is directed to the center."[81] The idea that the Self in the dream—the center—*includes* the circumference is a necessary conclusion because the nature of a central point is to generate a circle around it, which is the totality of psyche.

In making the statement "One cannot go beyond the center," Jung is stating that the center is expressing the purpose of the Self, as that is the psychological goal of creating order. In this view, the surroundings are only the basis for the presence of the center and are not functional. It then can be in this realization that the structure relates to the center but is not the Self. The structure then becomes relevant in a transcendental formulation of the Self, which naturally arises from its geometric form, as with the soul is a center that is relatable back to the periphery that is God.

The theme that the Self has a transcendent, spiritual, mystical quality is one that Jung was to take up later in ever greater expansions and is responsible for equating the Self with the circumference. It arises naturally because the circumference, as can be seen in the *Systema* mandala, has a potential to reach ever higher and, as Plotinus expresses it, "we hold through our own center to the center of all centers." If we then know the center of our own psyche, then we have the potential to realize not only the circumference at its widest reaches but also the nature of the center in all things.

The Tree and Transcendence

The natural interpretation of the symbol of the tree is that it is so powerful that it is presenting a truth that fixes a center and points to another dimension. It does not anticipate meaning, as that concept is applied to a geometric structure, but immediately confers meaning by its luminescence and being cut off on an island for a singular revelation. The tendency is to think of numinous experiences arising when the ego is overwhelmed, and it is just as likely that the dream can be so categorized when the power of the symbol is in no need of interpretation, as is the situation of his image of this tree on an island.

---

[81] *Memories,* p. 198

It is noted that when Jung wrote about the dream in the *Black Books* entry in 1927, he describes a "small circular lake in a centrally located garden. In the middle of this there is an island." The magnolia tree here is illuminated by "an eternal sun."[82] In interviews conducted by Aniela Jaffe, set out in another of the *Black Books,* Jung adds: "I had the inner vision of this heavenly beauty, and thanks to that one can live.... It was as if the sun shone there, but it was also as if the flowers were self-illuminated. It was as if the tree stood in sunlight. It was a bright day there, and unbelievably beautiful."[83]

Following the descriptions in the interview, he states, "My life would have actually lost its meaning without such a vision."[84] This gives pause to consider that the tree is the *momentum discrimine* for the Self, and the entire process of individuation. The existence of transcendence and numinosity would not have been the case if Jung merely found a center point in the dream without the round pool forming an island and, especially, the magnolia tree.

The tree and island are integral to each other because the entire island "blazed with sunlight" from the tree's self-illumination so the center and its temenos are joined. It is thus made clear that the realization of the Self on the isolated island must be detached from the marketplace. In his description of the dream to Aniela Jaffe, he adds, "I was utterly lonely then. I knew I was occupied by something quite great, but which no one understood."[85] As Shamdasani, the editor of the *Black Books,* explains, "The task now was one of consolidating these insights into his life and science."[86]

The force of the island and the tree in the narration is perhaps understated in terms of its profundity and therefore requires a deeper analysis. The island is a *temenos,* a protected area forming a circle around the tree that, being an island, is separated from and is unique in the surroundings. The dream offers no information as to why there needs to be an island, but Jung, many years later in 1945, refers to an island and a tree in his essay

---

[82] *Black Books*, Book 7, p. 239
[83] *Ibid,* Book 1, p. 98-9, translated by Shamdasani from the German in the Protocols of Aniela Jaffe's interviews with Jung for *Memories, Dreams, Reflections.*
[84] *Ibid*, p. 99
[85] *Ibid*
[86] *Ibid*

on the *Philosophical Tree*, where that tree is a profound symbol of the entire idea of transformation in alchemy.[87] The *Philosophical Tree* is found, mythologically, on an island where it draws on the surrounding life-giving water for its sustenance.[88] Its significance is of a place that is removed from other processes to allow an intense focus and then to protect and nurture the revelation. The island in addition to this significance, has further mythological parallels, as for instance, a place that one can find safety after a night-sea journey, as did Leto, Apollo's mother when she fled to the floating island.

The importance of a tree for Jung seems to have been there in early contemplations. For example, in adding *Abraxas*, the mediator of opposites, into the *Systema* Mandala, the tree of life appears to sprout (Figure 3).[89] At the time of writing his notes for *The Red Book* in this period, he was familiar with Nietzsche's comparison "Of the Tree on the Mountainside" to man. As Nietzsche expressed this connection: "Now it is with men as with this tree. The more it wants to rise into the heights and the light, the more determinedly do its roots strive earthwards, downwards into the darkness, into the depths—into evil."[90]

In 1943, in his work *Alchemical Studies*, Jung explains a tree as having great psychic value because of the "sort of spiritual quintessence abstracted from it, and also (it can) be described as the *principium indivduationis*. The tree would then be the outward and visible sign of the realization of the self."[91] The *principium* of individuation is the truth of psychological growth revealed by its realization. As the tree is connected intimately in the dream with the island, this reinforces that he had a distinct, focused revelation of the temenos of the island protecting the spiritual quintessence of the tree.

The spiritual quintessence of the tree is recognized in mythology, religion, mystical thought, and metaphysical ideas. Some references that proclaim its higher symbolic value in psyche are recited in colorful language by Jacques Lacan. He states that the tree partakes of "signification of strength

---

[87] CW 9.i, § 570
[88] CW 13, § 406
[89] Further description is found in the *Black Books,* Vol 1, p. 130.
[90] Nietzsche, 1961, p. 69
[91] *Ibid,* § 243

and majesty that it takes on in our flora" as the grand expression of nature. He points out that it is used in the Bible in relation to the Cross, where "it erects on a barren hill the shadow of the cross," and it is also, as a "circulatory tree, the *arbor vitae* of the cerebellum."[92]

Marie-Louise von Franz explains the importance of the tree and its numinosity by pointing out that the sun myth, the sun as deity, is connected to the tree myth where it has divine status as the mother of life.[93] The magnolia tree is a fitting symbol for the numinosity of the tree as it has a shower of blossoms that evokes grandeur by the effusive white flowers tinged in red. The magnolia trees in Switzerland are deciduous, and the fragrant blossoms last only for a week or two in spring. The blossoms are tentative and fragile, as John Ashbery's poem indicates: "The wind has stopped, but the magnolia blossoms still Fall with a plop onto the dry, spongy, earth."[94] The suggestion of fragile beauty imposed on the luminescent tree invokes the unknowable reality of nature and the importance of the processes of matter as a source of insight.

The relationship between spirit and matter is a profound theme for Jung that manifests fully in his work *Aion*[95] as the culmination of the realization of the Self. The tree, as majestic yet fragile, finds its strength as a signifier as a primordial image of spirit and matter, as Jung explains in a letter to Father Victor White, where the crucifixion is expressed to be the union of Christ with the tree as a cross.[96] In this profound connection, the tree represents the vegetative, unconscious aspect of a person —matter —that unites with the spirit, as Jung explains:

> The tree brings back all that has been lost through Christ's extreme spiritualization namely the elements of nature. Through its branches and leaves the tree gathers the power of light and air, and through its roots those of the earth and the water.[97]

---

[92] Lacan 2006, para. 504
[93] von Franz 1996, p. 12
[94] Ashbery 1988, p. 24
[95] CW 9ii
[96] *Letters,* Vol 2, page 167
[97] *Ibid,* p. 166

The prime significance of the symbol of the tree in the dream is that it has a place in the collective unconscious as the essence of the natural world and therefore has its own luminescence. Jung notes in a seminar on *Zarathustra*, that *Zarathustra* as the Superman is "an archetype rooted in humanity since eternity—and because he has roots, he is like a tree."[98] The roots of the tree ground the image literally as the bridge between heaven, the spirit, and earth, matter —the ultimate opposites, which it holds. This is the world tree—Yggdrasil—described in the Norse *Poetic Edda* as the "central or holy place of the gods."[99]

The images in the dream, the round island and the tree, are multifocal and serve to emphasize the primacy of the center without the need for adverbs or adjectives. The scene anticipates meaning and brings the symbols to a transcendent level, imparting numinosity on the center. It is, as Bachelard reminds us, "the brilliance of the first openings … it gives the 'I' a non-I that belongs to the I. … For my 'I-dreamer,' it is this '*non-I*' which lets me live my secret of being in the world."[100] The impact of the dream creates the Self for Jung as a living reality that reveals what was hidden from view where it could not be comprehended by the ego. It thus, in his psychology, immediately made the Self a goal, an end result that others were to realize as it is the essence of psychological growth.

The scene is unmistakable in creating the transcendent quality of the tree's self-illumination, radiating over the island and, with mythological antecedents, having a divine or mystical quality. The transcendental imagery is not only to promote the center to a higher plane but also to elevate it as the ideal means to balance opposites. It is the center, but it is also more, and thus has the characteristics that are found in a deity, such as *Abraxas*. The dream, with all its numinous connections is not then just about a geometric center but also a structure that, because of its power and a reflection of macrocosmic order, approaches God. Paul Bishop suggests accordingly, "For Jung the archetype of the 'self' replaces the God in the psychic economy that his system proposes."[101] This must be seen not as an arbitrary leap of the center to a transcendent level, but rather the natural unfolding of the center as attracting a divine

---

[98] *Zarathustra*, Vol II, p. 527
[99] Snorri Sturluson 2005, p. 24
[100] Bachelard 1960, p. 13
[101] Bishop 2009, p. 106

comparison. It was, no doubt, confirmation of his ideas in drawing the *Systema* mandala that a powerful center, as in that image, radiates out to unknown levels. This coexistence of the Self as center with the divine or having divine attributes accounts for many symbols of the Self that he mentions, such as the Anthropos, the man with the indwelling God that he explains is "in psychological terms—the self."[102]

Numinosity, the spiritual or mystical quality of an image or thing, serves the possibility of the realization of the Self as it draws consciousness toward it, as it has magnetic qualities. Numinosity is what is important for the Self because it is a clear route to the possibility that a symbol from the unconscious will alter the existing state of ego consciousness, creating a new foundation. Each aspect of the dream can lead us closer to the overall power of that numinosity. The illumination and self-luminosity will, in Jung's later writings, become the alchemical idea of the *lumen naturae,* the light that illuminates consciousness, along with the *scintillae,* the "germinal luminosities, shining forth from the darkness of the unconscious."[103] The sparks of light arise from that darkness to appear in visions that present to consciousness as dramatic luminosities, so the light and its appearance in a dream will always suggest a divine source. There are other, subtle aspects of that numinosity in the dream, such as the division of the city into four quadrants, and the *Window on Eternity* image (Figure 2) in *The Red Book*, having 30 repetitions of four, as a quaternity is the ancient quintessence of and return to divine wholeness.[104]

This numinosity, enhanced by relating it to transcendence, is critical because it is not enough to just have the dream with its structure, it is only effective if it has the effect of altering the conscious position. The numinous elements of the dream were, indeed, essential for Jung in changing his conscious position so that he much later explains that it "has taken me virtually forty-five years to distill within the vessel of my scientific work the things I experienced and wrote down at that time."[105]

---

[102] *Memories,* p. 221
[103] CW 8, § 389
[104] CW 9i, § 660; CW 18, § 1610-1
[105] *Memories,* p. 199

Chapter 3. The Center as Self

The dream is the concrete starting point for Jung's continued construction of the Self. The dream is relatively straightforward as it speaks for itself, establishing that there is a centering function in psyche. His commentary as to what he derived from the dream confers on the Self a wide range of dimensions that are thereafter reflected in the multiple ways he uses the term such as the "center is the goal,"[1] and that psychic development is "circumambulation of the self."[2] These comments create a cascading effect: As the Self is the center, it is the goal; as it is the numinous goal, the Self is a magnet as it draws us to that goal; the Self is a process to reach the goal; the goal grants us orientation and meaning.

The Self is a polysemy, a word with multiple meanings, and creates a contiguity of the sets of words. The choice of meaning is then largely dependent on the context in which it is used. To take one example, in speaking of extracting the spirit from matter, Jung states, "The 'magnet' that attracts the hidden thing is the self, or in this case the 'theoria' or the symbol representing it …"[3] The Self in this particular context is its process, its power, the idea of it, the symbol for it. He does not in this quote or in his other writings qualify what aspect of the Self he is using and, consequently the term does not permit exactitude, as each reference must be interpreted carefully in its context.

There is one all-embracing meaning of the Self, and that is that it represents wholeness. Wholeness is the *effect* of the Self, and therefore it subsumes all aspects of an orientating center, a process, and an end goal. Even prior to the dream where he had insights from regularly drawing mandalas, he states that the Self should be understood as "the wholeness

---

[1] *Ibid*, p. 198
[2] *Ibid*, p. 196
[3] CW 14, § 700

of the personality."[4] The "personality," in his early writings, consists of the *product* of the entirety of what is conscious and unconscious, the two constituting "psyche."[5] Read in this light, the process and goal are to find the center of psyche, and the *result* is the wholeness of personality. The "personality" is thus expressed as our potential, so the use of the term Self in any derivation is then promoting the possibility of experiencing wholeness. In 1932, in the essay *Development of Personality,* he describes the term "personality" as the "fullness of life"[6] and as "the supreme realization of the innate idiosyncrasy of a living being,"[7] both of which make wholeness an *ideal of a unity* for all conflicting opposites in psyche. He describes that achievement, however, as an "unattainable ideal. But unattainability is no argument against the ideal, for ideals are only signposts, never the goal."[8]

This theme of a potentiality to achieve wholeness, expressed as an ideal of a unity, is prevalent in varying expressions in all his further descriptions of the Self. It does not arise directly from the dream or the commentary but rather from expressing the underlying *product* of the goal. This means that the goal is to reach and realize the center, and the ideal is wholeness of the personality that arises by that realization, even though it is potential, not actual. Whatever touches these two interrelated concepts, such as circumambulating the center and the detailed steps in that process, could also be included in a wider definition of the Self. As a continuum, the Self begins through whatever force commences the search for the Self and extends to wholeness, the effect of complete realization of the Self.

Wholeness and the Center

The dream emphasizes the center but not an idealized possibility of unity or wholeness. It is not excluded from the dream, however, as it indirectly exists as a backdrop in the dream because a center creates the entirety of the structure needed for the goal to be realized. It is, in fact, obvious when viewed from that perspective that revealing a center with a numinous tree on an island within a square on a plateau, creates a dramatic, visual sense

---

[4] *Memories*, p. 196
[5] CW 1, § 87
[6] CW 17, § 284
[7] *Ibid,* § 289
[8] *Ibid*

of a specific central point related to a structured, integrated (whole) framework. Wholeness in this larger sense beyond the center is therefore *implicit* in the visual landscape of the dream, because, as Cicero tells us, "such powers of suggestion do places possess."[9] This raises the possibility that a center always exists within a framework of wholeness, the ideal of unity, so that the two are inextricably bound, even if the ideal is not the focus. From this it can be said that the center is the Self, and the Self is wholeness.

The center and wholeness come together more directly in his dream commentary because Jung there explains that the dream led to the "archetype of orientation and meaning;" the words, incidentally, should be read disjunctively as "archetype of orientation, and meaning," as meaning is not an archetype. He does not mention an "archetype of orientation" again in any other writing, so its natural meaning and usage must be an orientation inward, to a center, to create order. This orientation, critical to his realization, is, in fact, created by the geometric, ordered structure understood as originating and dependent on the center. How this sense of orientation is understood by us, as observers of Jung's dream, is that it is a repetition of a pattern of order that we somehow already know. Therefore, the concept of order immediately throws up wholeness where there is a center that is connected to its surrounding structure in a balanced configuration, even if we are not able to know the margin of the structure.

The relevant question is why, in describing the dream, did Jung not place greater significance on the structure and the ideal of unity and wholeness? The lack was not altered in the *Window on Eternity* mandala (Figure 2), drawn the year after and a representation of the dream. In that mandala, there is an elaborate structure surrounding the center, but the structure reflects a reciprocal relationship with the surrounding areas that still is reliant upon that very large center.

The reason for his initial lack of inclusion of the surrounding periphery and the possibility of wholeness as an equal part of the Self is most likely that it is difficult to understand how far that relationship to the periphery extends. If there is an orientation away from the center to include the periphery, it will eventually become too vague and its boundaries too ill-

---

[9] Cicero 2014, Book V.2

defined to create a sense of order. In that situation, wholeness could not be defined. For instance, would wholeness include the marketplace where he started or the steps up to the plateau? The moment that the periphery is extended beyond a clear boundary, the peripheral structure moves away from being a psychological fact to a transcendent postulate, as was the case with the *Systema* mandala (Figure 3). The Self would then immediately shift from a psychological center to a transcendent idea of God, and it seems this was not the intention in his interpretation of the dream.

Although in later years, Jung was specific that the Self as it relates to the center includes the periphery, in this dream it is only the center that, by its primacy, only hints at wholeness as an ideal. The more limited idea of the Self as center, as that is the most important indicia of the Self, succeeded in creating an alteration in consciousness for Jung because it yielded an orientation toward the center as the goal of his theory and also conveyed a personal meaning as suggesting an internal fixedness in psyche. It is the center that must therefore be honored as Jung's first demonstrative proof that there is, indeed, a definite reference point where one did not previously exist for him, so that his psychology rests on the realization of order that can countermand chaos. It thus is the prime presentation of the Self and any meaning related to an ideal of unity must be assumed, as this is his prior intellectual ideation.

The sense of order is not just his revelation but has its origins in a primordial, geometric pattern in the collective unconscious that depends on a center for protection and safety. He, in fact, proclaims in 1927 what neurobiologists have recently discovered, as will be discussed: that the pattern of wholeness is laid down in the brain of humans and animals. This ancient, preexisting pattern of a center contained within a surrounding periphery is illustrated, for example, in images of early human settlements as explicated by Richard Bradley's analysis. He finds that the use of circular settlements around a center point propagated a sense of order in prehistoric Europe that he traces back to the Neolithic.[10] The purpose of these structures was to create an enclosed space, a center, by use of a surrounding circular arrangement. Bradley quotes a French archaeologist in relation to the power of that enclosing circle: "In the universal language of simple forms, the circle (or the sphere) signifies

---

[10] Bradley 2012

both that which transcends man and remains beyond his reach (the sun, the cosmic totality, 'God'), and also that which, at its own sub-lunar level, relates to germination, to the maternal, to the intimate."[11]

Centering of ourselves is clearly innate and grants us a sense of peace that can be understood as being derived from a center contained within us. When this is understood and appreciated, it allows us to give over to that center and understand that order is always there. A center in a dream reflects the archetypal power of ancient structuring around a center that is a pattern in us all. In explaining archetypes, as is relevant, Jung states how a form, such as a safe orientation, exists in the unconscious substrate of the collective and therefore is not unique or personal:

> ... one seeks in vain for a personalistic causality which would explain their peculiar form and meaning. We must rather suppose that something like universally existent constituents of the unconscious psyche which form, as it were, deeper stratum of a collective nature, in contra-distinction to the personally acquired contents of the more superficial layers, or what one may call the personal unconscious. I consider these archetypal patterns to be the matrix of all mythological statements.[12]

The dream is therefore recollecting and reconstructing this universally existent psychological constituent of centering. He adds that the archetypes are the "conditions for the forming of representations,"[13] so the center in his dream is the representation of the archetype of orientation. It is thus illustrating a patterning as a deeply ingrained, *impersonal* structure directed toward a center. The consequence is that the Self will therefore appear as preexistent, as other than a developed ego. This is the essence of why the dream relies on the center as a means of orientation and does not need to rely upon the ideal of wholeness. We are thereby informed by this impersonal, collective nature of patterning that yields its representations in the form of symbols as in the dream. It is those symbols of the center that, when realized as such, give it numinosity that creates an inner security.

---

[11] Cauvin 2000, p.132
[12] CW 3, § 550
[13] *Ibid*

The Center as Healing

The dream could have included greater consideration of the area around the center, the presence of the water, the process of leaving the marketplace, the fact that it adjoined the harbor, the need for a climb, the narrow alley, and the function of the other Swiss. The reason these are not explicated in the discussion of the dream can only lie in Jung's intense revelation of an orienting function aligning with his continuous engagement in drawing mandalas immediately prior to the dream. It therefore answers his search for an orientation, appearing as a midpoint in psyche, and was not focused on these other possible inclusions for the Self.

Orientation, in its common usage, is a cognitive map of a position held in relation to space, others, and time. As has been shown in neurobiology, there is a highly ordered brain system that controls the processing for that orientation.[14] Orientation in the context of the Self implies that there is an internal place by which one can focus on a still point away from the chaos. This ability to focus creates a shift in emphasis from thoughts and feelings to that point. In meditation, as another example, this can be accomplished by watching the breath or by a mantra, a word or phrase that becomes the primary focus, excluding or quieting the mind. When this is sufficiently realized, the still point will appear in the foreground, diminishing the effect of background chaos. That is a significant shift in one's consciousness, and the dream provided that movement for Jung where it was not a transitory moment but rather one that altered his consciousness permanently. His realization echoes ancient revelations and, when obtained, is an offer for each of us for a peace that is the longing of humanity.

In order for the Self to provide orientation and offer the meaning that he sought, it is clear that it had to set up the center with an overwhelming presence in the context of a geometric structure that leads away from randomness and toward order. If the setting were in a city without a distinct center, such as Bangkok where there is no single, defined center, the dream would be unlikely to have had the same impact. The entire structure of the city is what was important to him as it created his "first

---

[14] Peer, et al. 2015

inkling of my personal myth," of an orientation contained within psyche, as it "allowed me to take an objective view of the things that filled my being." [15] As it is an archetype and came upon him as a numinous dream experience, it thereafter took from the collective unconscious what he needed to establish his sense of order. What is realized by an individual of the collective unconscious can never be lost again.

Jung comes to this dream after a long search driven by an intimation of order and wholeness that resulted in him constantly drawing mandalas: "I no longer remember how many mandalas I drew at this time." [16] This is the specific activation of psyche by his ego consciousness to seek the Self *in that form*. A mandala arrangement alone would not have been sufficient, even though it represents wholeness, nor would a city in the dream without a distinct center. In fact, the dream is not consistent with prior statements he made about the Self as to the need to reconcile the opposites. These were philosophical and metaphysical statements prior to realizing the Self in the dream before it became a psychological fact. It confirms that realization of the center, the Self, is compensatory in a form that is responding to the need of the dreamer. That was his need at that time, and the year after the dream in 1928, he received the *Secret of the Golden Flower*, the mystical Chinese manuscript, and states, "the text gave me an undreamed-of confirmation about the mandala and the circumambulation of the center." [17] This evokes the idea that the Self that appears in a dream or vision is an answer to a question, born from the conflict of opposites, and appearing to the degree to which the question burns in an individual.

The Self displays itself in different ways according to the solution it is providing. As an example, a female artist of 60, having had many deep and sustaining insights about her creativity, revealed this dream:

> I was walking on an island with an ex-lover who held all the characteristics that I lack: wildness and irresponsibility. We were holding hands as we walked on a path that was up a round dome. It was a large smooth dome and was its own island in the middle of an ocean. It was covered by water

---

[15] *Memories,* p. 199
[16] *Ibid,* p. 196
[17] *Ibid,* p. 197

running over its surface. I could see down below that it was suspended above water and there was a zigzag set of stairs going down. There was a big power boat at the bottom of the stairs and the ex wanted me to go with him, but I insisted that I was completely at peace here and did not want to leave.

The joining of the opposite characteristics of dream, the dreamer and ex-lover into a whole, a unity of opposites, presents an image of wholeness that she did not want to leave, having spent so long in the process of psychological growth. The dome, the roundness suggesting wholeness, is there but still covered in a layer of unconsciousness. This was a direct solution to the question of how she maintains and honors her revelation of that hard-to-discover wholeness. It was an answer that arises by the display of the Self not including a specific center or orientation, but rather a solution.

Jung sought his answer intensely, continuously, but this is not the situation of the other Swiss or those in the marketplace, and because of that intense seeking, he found it. Lacan offers an explanation that it is not the center that draws the ego, but rather that the ego seeks the Self because the ego has "the task of answering for reality."[18] Jung explains that the center was an answer as it came after a long period of turmoil, and the Self "gave me stability, and gradually my inner peace returned."[19] The ego, however, has to find the Self by circumambulation, which is the idea that the psychological work of individuation will be carried out by the climb that results in the revelation of the Self to the ego that seeks it. The dream, above all else, confirms that the Self can be found when it is sought and in the form that is necessary. It is this revelation that is implicit in Analytical Psychology as a hope that if he can find it, so can the rest of us.

A dream has the capacity to bring forth the idea of a midpoint whose goal is to hold the opposites and thereby provide healing. Using Jung's dream as an example, finding the midpoint of four quadrants of the city can have that healing function even though the reconciliation of opposites is not

---

[18] Lacan 2006, para. 433
[19] *Memories*, p. 197

made explicit. This is consistent with his sentiment in *Psychologische Typen* in 1921, years before the dream, that "the *self* could be characterized as a kind of compensation for the conflict between inner and outer."[20] The emphasis of the dream, although not directed to reconciliation of opposites, emphasized the "healing function."[21] The dream was therefore about a *starting point* for the Self, an orientation to a center that can eventually lead to reconciling opposites and that healing effect.

This distinction is important as a prelude to understanding how to approach Jung's later comments on aspects of the Self. When the dream is examined in detail, the Self does not convey the idea that is a personal force with agency to reconcile opposites, or that it is guiding each individual, or that it thereby has healing energies that can be employed where there is a loss of ego function, or that it has any religious function. The only component recognized is that it is the center and also a process that occurs as a consequence of the ego's circumambulation of that center and that realization, without more, has a healing effect. Each aspect of the Self is thus *part of its entirety*, so the observation that it is a center also includes it as an ideal of unity and a process to that goal.

A 60-year-old surgeon, struggling with continuing to operate as his eyesight was no longer sharp, had a very direct dream that displayed another form of the Self with an orientation to healing, illustrating that any form of the Self is to be understood as encompassing it in all its aspects:

> I was in an office in the hospital that was on a middle floor. I was sitting at a desk and a man came to the door who was a younger version of myself–about 35. He lifted me from the chair and shook me, saying "you can't be me anymore." Then somehow the building disappeared, and I was still in the office suspended in the air and I noticed that I was in the center of Manhattan, and I could see in every direction. I was not scared of falling. I felt like I was on a magic carpet in fact and felt suddenly optimistic.

---

[20] CW 6, § 405, emphasis supplied
[21] *Memories*, p. 199

Similar to Jung's dream, this was a clear presentation of the Self, not only a confirmation that he cannot continue as a surgeon, but more importantly that he found himself at a center point with a strong hint of numinosity. The center in the form of a middle floor and an absolute center gave him an orientation to another expansive possibility. Its healing function gave him the courage to stop surgery and explore the wider vistas of himself.

In whatever form it appears, the argument that the healing function of the Self includes the process of circumambulation and its realization is accurate because, without it, there is no conscious understanding of the Self, and it is then of no use to the ego. Jung's dream that defines the Self as a numinous center and, as well, a healing process that uses its numinosity to draw the ego closer implies its realization. This is possible because Jung asserts that "everything is directed to that center,"[22] and it could therefore be said that the Self must also include its realization because otherwise that direction is of no consequence. On that basis, the Self is the center, the ongoing process of circumambulation, and its conscious realization.

Extrapolating the Center

The possible realization of the periphery or the totality of psyche as emanating from the center, is not, however, relevant in the dream or for healing. There is no need for that totality—all that is conscious and unconscious —to be called the Self; it is only the center, the process, and its realization that is the Self. This leaves open the question, which will not be resolved by Jung for another seven years, of what is to be said about the structure around the center. How far indeed does the Self extend? It does seem clear that the totality must arise for consideration by him at some point as the center generates a structure out of itself. This structure is related back to the center and therefore suggests that all possible aspects of the Self slide into each other to invoke the archetype of orientation and healing by the creation of meaning. As best explained by Lacan, "it is in the substitution of signifier for signifier that a signification effect is produced that is poetic or creative, in other words, that brings the signification in question into existence."[23] In other terms,

---

[22] *Ibid*, p. 198-9
[23] Lacan 2006, para. 515

it is the endless substitution in describing the Self as having different characteristics—goal, process, totality, God, healing—that extracts the full meaning of how the Self can possibly be envisaged or understood in terms of psychological growth. The use of metonyms, shifting the center into different terms in a widening pattern of associations: "seems to offer itself to our regard ... not as a model of reality, but as a representative *bit* of reality."[24] All of the components of the dream, the entirety of it, "brought with it a sense of finality."[25]

He realized the center in contrast to his companions, who only had a small replica of the center. They were unconscious of the numinosity of the center that was revealed to him. His realization was therefore distinct, *is not our realization*, and arose from for him as the culmination of a continuous, intuitive connection with a center and order through drawing mandalas. He did the difficult work, rose up the steps to a higher level in which the center was revealed. It was not the work of occasional self-analysis of his thoughts, but an intense, internal demand for insight. The dream as the answer to that vast longing has the profound effect of making that journey the central goal of Jungian psychoanalysis. It offers us a glimpse of what we, in the category of the other Swiss, might find should we have the aptitude and fortitude.

Immediately after the dream, as it had not yet been published, it was incumbent on Jung to give the Self a uniqueness in the psychic matrix that included his earlier objective of uniting the opposites; the union of opposites is his philosophical milieu. In the 1928 essay *The Relation between the Ego and the Unconscious*,[26] he first sought to elevate the Self to give it heroic proportions to unite the opposites extending the Self beyond the center.

There is a section of that essay on the "Mana Personality" that describes the nature of magical or great personalities, in which context he makes his first broader, conceptual statements naming the Self as partaking of that great power. A mana personality is described by him as "the well-known archetype of the mighty man in the form of a hero, chief, magician, medicine man, saint, the ruler of men and spirit, the friend of

---

[24] Lodge 1993, p. 109
[25] *Memories*, p. 198
[26] CW 7, Part II

God."[27] This is referring to the possession of such a unique power that, "(we) find ourselves obliged to face the fact that we have learnt more and want more than other people."[28]

Realizing the center when it was invisible to those around left Jung no doubt that he had that trait. This leads us back, as Jung puts it, to the reality of the Self from that mana perspective as more than a center: "it is strange to us and yet so near, wholly ourselves and yet unknowable, a virtual centre of so mysterious a constitution that it can claim anything— kinship with beasts and gods, with crystals and with stars...."[29] He then names this mystery: "I call this centre the *self* ... it might equally well be called 'God within us.'"[30]

Naming the Self as that which is the link to the divine and nature and, as well, the "God within us," is the leap of taking the Self from a luminescent center that performs a healing function to the unlimited dimension behind life, joining the opposites of primal matter with divine power, a realization not explicated in the dream. This is not reduceable alone to the context of the essay about great personalities but rather must be motivated by his separation out from others and a deeper revelation about the nature of the numinous center that he did not express. If one experiences that still point, it becomes the primary orientation thereby permanently altering consciousness so it could indeed become the subject of awe and worship as that which is a bridge to transcendent life forces. This Mana Personality essay is rather inconsistent with the remainder of the topics in the broader essay about the relationship of the ego to the unconscious, and perhaps this is his way of first declaring the glory of what he found and bringing back the ideal of reconciling the opposites by a unity.

He makes a comment the year after, 1929, that perhaps sets the stage for how the Self was to be thereafter examined as it creates a firm basis for granting it such power and scope. In the *Dream Seminars* that Jung presented in that year, he indicates that the "aim of the exercise is to shift the guiding force away from the ego to a non-ego centre in the

---

[27] CW 7, § 377
[28] *Ibid,* § 396
[29] *Ibid,* § 398
[30] *Ibid,* § 399

unconscious. ... I did not invent it but found it to be so."[31] The "aim of the exercise" is that the Self must be cognitively placed outside the ego and have its own unique and separate existence in order for it to be the subject of reflection by ego consciousness. Its realization cannot expand consciousness unless it is concluded that the center is not created by mere cognition but is *a priori* and a different something. This occurred for Jung, as can be seen in the dream, as the center stood out as more than an idea or feeling, but rather as a numinous, unique aspect of being that can overwhelm the ego upon consideration. Separating the Self from the ego allowed him to privilege the Self as having a higher dimension than thought, although this very lofty revelation is unavailable to others, except perhaps a saint or a friend of God.

There is, however, an indirectness in this essay, almost a hesitancy in explaining the Self linked to a mana personality. The conundrum he faced is that as the Self was indeed known to him, to others it was nothing more than a vague hypothesis. Accordingly, there was no other way of explaining its power and the core of his realization except through the vehicle of an essay on extraordinary personalities. It was not possible for Jung to write an essay extolling the divine nature of the Self, as that would, in this early stage of his career, have placed him outside the scientific community. It is therefore likely, as well, that he had to avoid explaining it in terms of it being an actual place in psyche or a little homunculus in our brain. For this reason, in the mana personality essay he expresses it in a way that does not require precision, as "strange" and "near" to us. This allows the Self to remain a mystery so it is more than a vague hypothesis, as we can accept a mystery that stands beyond reason. In fact, many years later in meeting Herman Hesse, he continued this position of the Self as an ideal, allowing it to not be bogged down in logic: "So far, I have found no stable or definite center in the unconscious, and I don't believe such a center exists. I believe that the thing which I call the Self is an ideal center, equidistant between the ego and the unconscious...."[32]

As he knew the Self as a clear reality but yet metaphysical for others, it is probable that he needed to continue to make it understood by more than

---

[31] Jung 1984, p. 105
[32] Serrano 1966, p. 50

a rational narrative describing his own revelation, or otherwise it would fail as a concept. To make the Self more understandable or capable of being realized requires three steps to bring it within an individual's creative imagination. The first step is to acknowledge that the center is not the ego, but rather non-ego, a theme he expresses in a *Dream Seminar,* where Jung accordingly explains that the Self is "not felt or thought of as the ego."[33] The second is that it is necessary to align the Self with the purposefulness of the unconscious, therefore likewise conferring upon the Self a purpose. As he explains, the Self fulfills a "psychological necessity for a transcendental subject of cognition as the counter-pole to an empirical universe, although the postulate of a world-confronting self, at least as a *point of reflection*, is a logical necessity."[34] The third, the subject of the Mana Personality essay, is that the Self is so important and powerful that it must be accorded the highest place in the journey. For this reason, Jung asserts that the Self is not only a psychological construct but also can be called "God within us." How else indeed could he name such an internal mystery that is a non-ego aspect of psyche and is necessary to help us make it the subject of cognition? It needed a numinous, psychological, spiritual, or religious context, or the ego could never envisage what it might be.

The comparison with God is an obvious extrapolation because the ancient idea of a center has a transcendent quality, even more so because of its luminescent numinosity. It should be noted that Jung's use of "God," he consistently explains, is to describe a definitive psychological postulate that there is, as a matter of pure fact, an "independence and sovereignty of certain psychic contents."[35] It is those non-ego psychic contents such as the Self that "thwart our will" and influence our moods and actions, and it is these that he calls God: "Therefore by affixing the 'attribute' divine to the workings of autonomous contents, we are admitting their relatively superior force."[36] This suggests that the Self can always be assumed to partake of the transcendent and thus be a superior force, no matter how practical and grounded it is as the basis for orientation.

---

[33] CW 9.i, § 634
[34] *Ibid,* § 289, emphasis supplied.
[35] CW 7, § 400
[36] *Ibid,* § 403

It has been suggested that the real purpose of the Mana Personality essay was to reveal that the revelation of the contents of the unconscious could be dangerous by inflating the ego and therefore the Self is essential to balance the ego with the unconscious.[37] If this is the case or a possibility as the reason for the essay beyond Jung's need to grant the Self a higher dimension, then it echoes the expression Jung uses of the Self being: "a kind of compensation of the conflict between inside and outside."[38] This is then a reintroduction of the earlier theme of the psychological necessity of the Self as a midpoint that can balance the opposites. He explains in the essay, having been moved by the notion of the mana personality as able to balance the opposites, that a hero can reach the Self, gradually "with much travail."[39] The Self then is given a new role in this essay, taken beyond the dream and modified by the idea of a mana personality, of being a center lying between the conscious and unconscious and balancing the pull of the opposites.

In the course of this extrapolation of the center as being able to balance the opposites, the emphasis shifts to providing the Self with a more specific location. If for his companions in the dream there is no understanding of the existence of a center, it has no location, and the reconciliation of the opposites needed to balance the inflation cannot take place. A realization that locates the Self occurs, Jung states in the essay, through "sensing" the Self, which is seeing the "apperceptive character of the relation between ego and self."[40] The result, he adds, is that the "*individuated ego* senses itself as the object of the unknown and supraordinate subject."[41] This does not give it a fixed or precise location, but makes the realization of the Self the means for its fixedness by the "individuated" ego, one that has achieved full revelation, who then knows they are the object of the Self. The promise of balance in that essay is that realization of the Self creates a point somewhere in psyche that modulates the relationship between the ego and the Self.

As it is only full realization that can give the center an objective appearance and a fixedness, the proposition that it is only an individuated

---

[37] Sorge 2020, p. 372
[38] CW 7, § 404
[39] *Ibid*
[40] *Ibid*, § 405
[41] *Ibid*, emphasis added.

ego that can sense the Self is a very high bar. An individuated ego is rare; Jung describes it as "peculiar,"[42] resulting from the individual "being distinct from the general, collective psychology ..."[43] If it is not realized, the Self cannot be located or explained except as a theoretical, philosophical ideal. It remains for all those who are not individuated a hypothesis with no location, making the idea that it is God within us equally valid but equally obscure.

As Marie-Louise von Franz informs us, Jung explains that "Everything I have written has a double bottom."[44] For those who are individuated and have therefore reached the highest degree of integration, the Self is alive and real and is located in a balance point between the two aspects of the psyche giving it a divine-like presence. The implication is that for all else, it is not real but an *ideal*. Casting the Self as an ideal, phrased by Jung in many ways, such as "the germ of unity is growing within him,"[45] offers the hope and possibility of its eventual realization. The promise that emerges from this Mana Personality essay is that after much travail and psychological development, the developed, individuated ego then senses that there exists a higher divine aspect within the unconscious in the form of the Self. This promise is the *ideal*, a necessary ideal, as it is otherwise too abstract.

The ideal aligns well with the human longing for some peace or orientation but demands much of an individual: a steadfast, continuous development of the whole personality. This can only be obtained if there is some hope for a different state yielding a new guiding principle based on realization found beyond mere self-will and rational intention. That is the true purpose of the introduction of the mana personality, the hero, the wise person in dreams and fantasies, [46] to offer the inspiring hope of an entirely different level of realization that can be currently contemplated.

This extrapolation of the Self as including a promise of that higher state permits of the possibility that there can be a gradual, slowly absorbed "sensing" of the Self. This suggests the power of the Self to be able to

---

[42] CW 6, § 755
[43] *Ibid*, § 757
[44] von Franz 1975, p. 4
[45] CW 10, § 299
[46] CW 6, § 442

arise in consciousness with numinosity to create an incremental awareness of a non-ego aspect of psyche. That is the parallel with the ideal of the mana personality. The mixing of the center with the mana personality changes the nature of the center in the dream from a magnet that attracts and brings order, to a God-given center that seeks deliberately to balance the opposites and therefore will seek its own realization, although this is a root of inflation.

It may be, in fact, that only by a full realization, not available to Jung's companions in the dream, will integration occur of the unconscious and conscious, creating the balance to remove the inflation. The clinical hope is different, and there is, in that setting, no immediate concern for inflation by absorption of the Self. The sought-after formula is instead focused on the proposition that the greater the psychological development of an individual, the more likely that the existence of an orienting principle—the Self as center—will become apparent. However, in that clinical process, the promise of the "individuated ego" or one whose development is substantially advanced along that scale, is an impetus for the work. By creating the ideal, theoretically to deter inflation, Jung has created the Self as the grand construct so that the greatest hope that can be had is that it can be perceived.

Shamdasani asserts that "the assimilation of the encounter of the mana personality led to the self."[47] This refers to the hero or individuated ego "sensing" the "apperceptive" relationship the ego has with that Self.[48] The use of the term "apperceptive" by Jung adds a subtle dimension to the standard necessary for the realizing the Self. It refers to the process of perceiving while, at the same time, being aware of the perception. This is a higher level that derives from the promise of the mana personality and means that realization cannot occur by cognition alone through a dream or vision after the fact; apperception requires that it is understood as the Self *when* it is being perceived. This is overlooked by commentators, and it then makes the realization of the Self a unique case in which it is so perceived where its true effect is immediately evident.

---

[47] *Black Books,* p. 102
[48] *CW* 7, § 404

Jung understood that the dream made the Self out of the reach of most of us. In this Mana Personality essay, as this is first explanation following from the dream, he maintains the center as a foundational structure of the essence of life; in fact, he states, "At the very least, therefore, the self can claim the value of a hypothesis analogous to that of the structure of the atom."[49] He does not go into further explanation of this idea at this stage as he admits in the essay that "an interpretation quite exceeds my power."[50] In this grand expansion of the Self, he appears still in the thrall of the dream, realizing that he had gradually, and after much psychological investigation, found the prize of the Self but, aside from an actual realization that was afforded just to him, it should remain for others only a construct. The construct remains very much in the forefront of his psychology in that it establishes a theoretical goal that is the key to psychological growth so there is no process of that growth without it. It needs to be there in this form as the *ideal* of balancing the opposites, and to offer that it has the capacity, as it did for him, to be the focal point for the ego to connect to the archetypal forces in the unconscious.

Ancient Soundings of a Center

Jung very well could have stopped at this point as he establishes a clear goal for his process. However, in 1928, the year after the dream, he was asked to write a commentary for the *Secret of the Golden Flower*, the ancient Chinese Daoist text attributed to the Tang dynasty. That commentary appeared in print in the autumn of 1929. In his biography, *Memories Dreams Reflections*, he explains that the text of the *Secret* drew him more deeply into the reality of the Self.[51]

In his commentary on that work, in line with its esoteric material, he emphasizes the importance of the mandala structure to understand the center. The text of the *Secret* was replete with mandalas that "become more profound and concentrate themselves gradually around abstract structures."[52] He then describes the Golden Flower, the subject of the text, as a "structure in fiery colours growing out of a bed of darkness,"[53] which

---

[49] *Ibid,* § 505
[50] *Ibid*
[51] *Memories,* p. 197
[52] Jung in Wilhelm 1962, p. 99
[53] *Ibid*

is similar in effect to the luminescent magnolia tree in the dark city in the dream. The mandala symbol, he explains, "works an effect"[54] as it connects to the symbolism arising from ancient folk customs of creating a magic circle. This has a protective function as the mandala draws "a magical furrow around the centre ... to prevent 'flowing out' ... against the deflections through external influences."[55] The magic circle—the mandala—creates a "spell on one's own personality"[56] so that the attention and interest is brought back to the center and is not lost or distracted by other events. All of these comments are, again, consistent with the structure of the dream and the idea of a numinous center, surrounded by a temenos, that draws attention to itself and therefore holds the possibility of attracting everything to it. It was an early confirmation of the ancient derivation of a center as holding the secret of secrets.

In his commentary, he also uses that ancient text to confirm the idea of circumambulation of the center: "There is no linear evolution; there is only circumambulation of the self."[57] The circumambulation, he indicates, is not merely indicative of a circular movement around the Self representing psychological growth, but also, "on the one hand, the marking off of a sacred precinct, and, on the other, fixation and concentration. ... Everything peripheral is subordinated to the command of the centre."[58] This is congruent with the degree to which the Self must be realized by an individuated ego to be integrated; it requires fixation of purpose and hard psychological work to be realized.

In more detail that seems to arise from his analysis of the Daoist text, Jung adds that for the Self to be realized, it is required that the broader unconscious be recognized as a "co-determining quantity" and "lived in such as way" so that unconscious and instinctive demands are recognized. It is not enough, therefore, to have an idea of the Self or to have a dream of a center, but the whole attitude of an individual must be oriented inward, giving priority to unconscious manifestations in order to create a balance.

---

[54] *Ibid*, p. 102
[55] *Ibid*, p. 102-3
[56] *Ibid*
[57] *Memories*, p. 196
[58] CW 13, § 38

This theme of a receptivity—"lived in this way"—is emphasized in order to explain that the nature of the unconscious must be understood so that the Self can be perceived as lying between the opposites of what is conscious and unconscious. Circumambulation, in this formulation, becomes a process of seeking a balance where the unconscious can be understood and then reconciled. That understanding occurs over time as the unconscious reveals itself during the process. This ties in the center in the dream with the idea in the Mana Personality essay that the heroic task of a determined circumambulation also creates a balance, a midpoint, between known opposites.

By this explanation, the Self is made relevant within a larger process of growth. It is not enough, therefore, to merely hypothesize that there is a Self as a theoretical goal or even have dreams of a center or a structure, but for it to create real change, it must indelibly alter consciousness. It accomplishes this task when there is a revelation by a conscious mind of a virtual point between conscious and unconscious, *so both are lived as equally relevant*. The center is then, by its nature, placed within a sacred precinct on the basis that it is or should be protected as necessary for that balance. This alone does not itself necessarily cause this shift, but rather it gives greater credence to the ancient Self, grants it numinosity, and thereby attracts the continued attention of consciousness.

Center Understood as Function

Orientation is a product, a result, of the realization of the center's existence. The structure in which the center is revealed is not important. The dream structure could just as well have been a circle or a square or a form that can be divided into four, like a mandala. There is also no need for others, as in the "other Swiss" in his dream, no requirement that it be a city, that there be steps up to a plateau, that there is darkness or streetlights, or that it is reminiscent of a particular place. What is needed is for the insight to create a healing function as a center comes into focus. There is no requirement for that relationship to be precise but only one that conveys the *idea of a center* through the symmetry of the structure or any notion of it.

A dream or symbol of wholeness as an ordered structure without a center will not have the same impact of providing a healing or balancing function for the chaos of opposites. It can somehow convey that there is an inherent wholeness in psyche, but the realization needs a point of reference, what Jung calls a "point of reflection" as a "logical necessity."[59] This is required for the all-important alteration in consciousness to occur that leads to healing because it offers a refocus away from the background chaos of the mind and body. It becomes an object of cognition, an opportunity to gather consciousness much like a mantra. It is possible, as can occur with a mystical experience, that a realization of all-oneness would allow that insight to become that fixed point or orientation. However, it may not be sufficient when a sense of that all-oneness occurs in a dream or vision as it lacks a psychic object that can be thereafter referred to as that point of reflection.

The healing, the process of moving away from chaos, comes from the ordering function of a center. The center heals to the extent that its *existence* is revealed. This is not as some internal agent or a psychic agent that has healing powers, but rather by the fact that there is, in fact, a patterning in psyche of a center that then alters and widens consciousness by providing an orientation and goal. The center is necessary for individuation to occur.

The gradual *realization* of the center invokes the healing function. This healing is by the easing of the tension of opposites held by the center as it provides a focus away from that tension. This is very much an ideal as the opposites are of such complexity and are so multitudinous that this can never be fully accomplished. The only realistic way that any balance between opposites can be brought about, however, is by a focus away from the opposites, either on a higher plane as an orientation to the divine, for which can be substituted the fully realized Self, or the rare singularity of the overwhelming revelation in a numinous experience. When that occurs in either manner, as they are essentially the same functionally, it is always an approximation of a unity or wholeness in part, so the healing comes from the realization to the extent that has created a new orientation in the conscious mind.

This ideal of a unity can be observed in the *Seven Sermons,* where the center is personified as *Abraxas* as he contains all the opposites of the *Pleroma.* As the midpoint, he is given no function except to be a virtual

---

[59] CW 9.i, § 289

center that can hold those opposites. He exists because there is, conceptually, a need for midpoint between the two opposites that suggests a place where they can meet, share energy perhaps, and ideally be balanced. *Abraxas* is a symbol that has substance and effect as explaining the realization of the center, always with the unexpressed potential healing function to balance the opposites: Jung explains, "It is the effective itself, not any particular event, but effect in general."[60] It has an effect in general by its virtual location. However, this does not confer upon *Abraxas* any effect in healing, nor does it bestow on him a function to direct a life, or even to have a power of integration. He is only an innate, virtual center that has potential because it is the center in which the opposites can be balanced. "It is an unreal reality, because it has no definite effect"[61] in the sense that it performs no task except existing.

The Self in terms of complete healing is the idealized possibility of a fully realized Self. If, however, individuals can redirect their mind in a stable way toward a center in their being, they will begin to move away from the chaos of their lives and partake of some lesser form of healing. This center, as a result of its healing function, is therefore everything we crave, the subject of myth, prayer, longing. We look endlessly for its signs, although find it difficult to understand that it lies as the "God within us." In psychological terms, it need not be considered a God, but when it is realized as a center, it is otherworldly, alien, and will appear as a miracle. Then it is healing as it creates a new orientation so that one's life will change, and that moment of peace will thereafter be always available.

If the primary presentation of the Self is to display a numinous center, and it only has a healing capacity to the extent of that realization as within a structure, its effect is offering an orientation that appears as its function. The Self as *Abraxas* has a general, nonspecific effect because its existence as a midpoint indicates a potential process of uniting the opposites, even though it does not have a specific function. Having an effect can, however, be equated with a function[62] and, therefore, in terms of the Self understood as a center, both its passivity and potentiality yield its function. Accordingly, the center will always have a function as either

---

[60] *Memories*, p. 383
[61] *Ibid*
[62] Cummins 1975

the place of circumambulation, as holding opposites, as being the matrix within which events occur, and as the inspiration for a process of centering. This complex idea may be illustrated better by an example.

A male patient in Sydney, four months into analysis, presented the following dream that recognizes a function for the center:

> I was standing in a park down in Ultimo with a group of mathematicians who had discovered the secret to time travel without violating the Grandfather law so you could go back in time without changing the present. The time machine they had built was a white circle on the ground with a red spotlight in the middle. Passing through the circle would briefly take you to the same physical place but an earlier time and then you could blink to bring yourself back to the present. They warned me that it can be disorienting but I tried it a few times and saw people's hair and clothes change as I jumped between past and present. On one of the jumps, I saw a very young (government leader). He thought I was a rookie reporter and wanted to help show me how to write stories and take photos on an old digital camera before I came back to the present.

"Ultimo" is an actual suburb in Sydney, although it has no real-world significance for him. The Self in this dream is a center where it is possible to go back to an earlier time to observe the past. It suggests a path for this patient to observe past trauma in a nonthreatening way. The center is the red spotlight in a geometric circle, which is where, he explains, he passes through. It points to a way through his dilemma of having to confront a difficult past by an aspect of the Self (the government leader) instructing him in writing stories and taking photos of it. It creates a psychic function that contributes to potential healing because it points to a journey inward as a means to relieve his suffering. It is the center point that is his path to healing, not by a circular journey around it, but by moving through it to the past. The center has functions psychologically as providing both an orientation and the specific effect of contributing to his healing by pointing to a way to the ideal of holding the opposites arising from his trauma.

This dream of the center does not follow a specific geometric structure as did Jung's dream. Ultimo, equated perhaps with the ultimate insight, is not described as a city with quadrants, but it offers a center that has a healing function and orients the patient to the analysis and to the revelation of the past. It had, months later, an interesting effect not related by him to the dream. He explained that he was developing a feeling of something in the middle of his chest like the spot in the circle that he called "the little guy" who was seeking to center him. When reminded of the Ultimo dream, he said, "That's where I got the idea from."

To this extent, the presentation of the center was healing as a focus away from confusion and continued to be healing. In his case, the high degree of trauma required that he find some means to approach it, and the center was his solution. This suggests that the appearance of the center was part of his individuation process, an aid, the beginning of an orientation, a point of reflection, and a theoretical idea that he embraced because of the dream. It was an early approximation of wholeness and indicates that the appearance of the Self as center always has a function to lead to a recognition of it as an ideal.

Chapter 4. Totality as the Self

This relationship between the Self as a center, which is logically clear, and the Self as embracing the wider psyche or even more, which is unclear, is a pivot point in Jungian theory. It resulted in the formation of a different theory of the Self by Michael Fordham because of his rejection of the concept of totality. This led to a split between the adherents to the formal doctrines of Jung and those favoring a developmental orientation. As well, and more importantly, the inclusion of totality has caused confusion as to the possible end goal of the Self in psychological growth, as Jung appears to make totality an aspect of the Self.

The word "totality" immediately hints at a transcendent dimension that is beyond imagination, but which reflects the ancient impetus to seek what is behind existence. Every religion and spiritual practice have eyes pointed upward to discover that which transcends our ego-bound journey in order to offer a connection with the force of creation. If the Self is a center in psyche that exists at the deep instinctual level, then it makes just as much sense that the feeling that it engenders upon realization will also rise higher to the transcendent.

The relationship between the center and the wider psyche was on Jung's mind before the dream. In 1921, he overtly hinted in *Psychologische Typen* that the Self includes all of what is conscious and unconscious— the whole—the totality of psyche.[1] This was not explained in any greater detail in that essay, but it is a reference to his early theme in a Zofingia lecture of the nature of individuality as being ultimately the "whole" person. This is confirmed in his 1928 essay on *Psychology of Religion*:

> When we speak of man we mean the indefinable whole of
> him, an ineffable totality, which can be only be formulated

---

[1] Jung 1921, S. 630

> symbolically. I have chosen the term 'self' to designate the
> totality of man, the sum total of his conscious and
> unconscious contents.[2]

He explains in this essay that he is using the term Self as including
psychic totality in accordance with Eastern philosophy that is concerned
with the "relativity of the gods."[3] This concept, touched on also in the
earlier *Psychologische Typen*, concerns a seemingly reciprocal
relationship between God and man. John Dourley explains the reciprocity
as, "Put succinctly, Jung is contending that only in human consciousness
can God become self-conscious and so relativized, at least, in relation to
a God conceived as an absolute and transcendent self-sufficient divinity
'wholly other' than the human."[4] In both the 1921 and 1928 essays,
totality therefore refers to the width and breadth of psyche, but the manner
in which it embraces the wider dimension contained in Eastern
philosophy is not fully explicated.

At this early stage of development of the notion of totality, its scope is
suggested by Jung's German usage, *Gesamtheit*, meaning wholeness or
the entirety. In that frame, it is consistent with the idea of it being all that
is within psyche, conscious and unconscious, and nothing more.
However, the use of the relativity of the Gods widens the concept
consistent with the phrase "God within us" that he uses in the 1928 Mana
Personality essay.

If there was hesitation in explicitly expanding the Self wider to include
the divine or a mystical level of realization, it may be because he refers
to totality as "a transcendental concept," as it can be "described only in
part and for the other part, remains at present unknowable and
illimitable."[5] However, the sense of a larger dimension is very much
present, as equating it with what is the unknowable unconscious and the
God within us gives the Self a religious function. James Heisig traces the
impact of that thread that runs through Jung's writings as arising from his
revision of Freudian concepts: "Having arrived at (a) positive theory of
the symbol, as a 'life-promoting' and 'redeeming' function of the psyche

---

[2] CW 11, § 140
[3] *Ibid*
[4] Dourley 2006, p. 47
[5] CW 5, § 789

rather than as a merely psychological projection of repressed personal wishes, Jung could hardly fail to alter his attitude to religion as well."[6]

If the Self for Jung is primarily a concrete, psychological postulate that there is and must be a center, then Jung did not need to explain the Self in relation to a wider totality that is anything more than all of what is conscious and unconscious. He could have left it a virtual center that stands, as it is with *Abraxas*, a balancing or midpoint of the opposites. Mario Jacoby, in comparing the Jungian Self to the theories of Heinz Kohut, suggests that they both accepted the Self as a center of psychic activity, but Jung went further because he was informed by the "wealth of imagery flowing from the unconscious" and by the numinous quality of the Self.[7]

The Scope of Totality

Totality can be only on a psychological scale or can be open-ended to include the wider, transcendent cosmic scale. As the former, it is the whole of psyche, all that is conscious and unconscious around the center. As the latter, it is endless as it would mean revealing that which is in the collective unconscious. On the cosmic scale, it would include a divine *conjunctio* and God's purpose. In both cases, in terms of the Self, it would appear by the breakthrough of archetypal collective forces into consciousness, revealing a profound truth and thereby forever altering the conscious mind.

As the psychological scale includes, as it does, the collective unconscious, it is unknowable and limitless and can theoretically include everything. This is a source of confusion about totality. If the Self includes that wider totality, then the Self is much more than a center. However, if the register of Jung's writings is entirely psychological, then it would mean that totality would not move beyond what can be understood by realization. It is not as easy to answer this question as one might hope, and it requires a more detailed investigation of Jung's intentions.

It appears, as a working hypothesis, that totality on the psychological scale is what Jung intended. He explains totality as "consciousness, first

---

[6] Heisig 1979, p. 35
[7] Jacoby 2017, pp. 57-8

of all, then the personal unconscious, and finally and indefinitely large segment of the collective unconscious whose archetypes are common to all mankind."[8] As a concept, this notion of a wider dimension including the collective unconscious is understandable to describe a virtual center point between all that is conscious and all that is unconscious. If there was no psyche to which the center relates, there is no Self.

This form of totality is a logical approach of the inclusion of the periphery, psychic totality, in the notion of the Self. Transcendence is then that which goes beyond the Self to include the realization, *to the extent that it occurs*, of the collective unconscious. This attributes to the center that it generates the periphery and, therefore, realizing the center will point to the realization of aspects of the collective unconscious.

This is not an argument that the Self includes the wider dimension of the cosmic scale of divine knowledge or a mystical level of oneness. If that is to occur, it arises as a realization from the numinous quality of the center that suggests that dimension. There are no pointers in his writings that this dimension is relevant in defining the Self. However, a cosmic scale is not completely excluded, as it exists indirectly on the basis that the individuation process will yield a higher dimension or a religious orientation so it may lead to insights of that nature.

A male patient in psychoanalytic training, who has indeed reached a high level of integration and conceived of the center as a focal point to calm his warring opposites, had this short dream:

> I am to start training in theology. It is a University post-graduate level. I'd no real intention to become a priest so I assume it must be aligned with my psychological studies.

From a centered position, having achieved some degree of integration of the opposites, the religious or transcendent naturally arose for him as a consequence. Instead of merely seeing the world in the way he did before, he is being invited to see its mystery and the transcendence that lies everywhere. This is because he realized the non-ego nature of the Self and was moved by its numinous quality. It may then be seen that

---

[8] CW 9.i, § 634

realization of the wider reaches of the psyche and beyond that another transcendent dimension is entirely possible upon realizing the center.

Jung's reluctance before 1935 to attribute the idea of psychic totality to include a wider transcendent totality is likely because the totality of the psychological universe, conscious and unconscious, may not be capable of being comprehended for three related reasons. The first, mentioned in the previous chapter in relation to the geometric structure of the Self, is that the extent of the periphery is not able to be determined; the example of this is the *Systema* mandala, which shows the limit is always indeterminable. The second is that as the unconscious includes all that is unknown, it is unfathomable, so it would be dangerous to traverse that territory as it contains good and evil. The third is that the unconscious also includes that which is not able to be brought into consciousness at all, material that cannot be held by the center, so it is confusing to extend totality too far. In terms of the psyche, this unavailable area is the psychoid region, as Jung calls it, the "ultraviolet end of the psychic spectrum,"[9] that includes the archaic tendencies of humanity, the archetypes, and primitive instincts.

The logical consequence of postulating the Self as including transcendent totality beyond the psyche would be to raise the critical question of whether this enhances the primary purpose of the Self as advancing psychological growth. This growth is a result of struggling with the opposites of what is conscious and unconscious by, theoretically, bringing them to a union. Holding the opposites contained within totality means that the Self, to be realized, must discriminate those unknown opposites. If totality includes the far reaches of what is unknown that are distant from consciousness and beyond imagination, it seems meaningless to equate the goal of the Self with that which is never going to be realized.

The only reason for inclusion of a wider, cosmic totality may be that discrimination of those opposites and their reconciliation is the endless task of the Self, even though that seems irrational. In responding to a question by an Anglican priest about the union of opposites, Jung explains that it is *God or the Self* that seeks *disruption* of a potential union in order to spark consideration and discrimination of opposites, a process

---

[9] CW 8, § 417

necessary for the perpetual expansion of consciousness: "... the self does indeed seek such issues because it seeks *consciousness,* which cannot exist without discrimination."[10]

The nature of a Self that instigates and promotes the clash of opposites makes the Self the *source* of the revelation of itself so it can include whatever is necessary. To do so, it must manifest symbols: "The Self is a numinous wholeness, which can be expressed only by symbols (e.g., mandala, tree, etc.)."[11] This line of reasoning makes the Self responsible for its own manifestation, for which it creates symbols that indicate its purpose and operation, and it is not possible to understand its full mission. This, as will be discussed, is an "agency model" of the Self, where it is taking the active role in its realization. In the context of totality, the Self can then be understood as carrying out a purpose of discriminating the unfathomable opposites. If it is operating in that way, then an individual realizing totality on a cosmic scale by holding the entirety of the opposites is not possible. This conceptual difficulty creates a natural hesitancy to easily equate the Self with the widest reaches of totality and a dilemma as to how that form of totality may be included.

These metaphysical complexities do not exist with the Self as center but only flow from the idea that the Self embraces totality. The lack of clarity appears to be a result of Jung's personal realization of higher levels of totality in the Self but an inability for him to publicly claim it as a transcendent idea. The evidence for this is that Jung, later in life, continues to avoid explaining the nature of the Self in a way that would cause it to be regarded merely as a transcendent postulate because "What it is in its transcendental condition, we do not know."[12]

A decision to open the Self to a wider, cosmic, transcendent dimension can be made because that totality can clearly exist empirically to the degree it becomes the subject matter of the ego. The realization of an aspect of that form of totality in a numinous experience makes it concrete, real and vital: a psychological fact. Underlying this vitality is that upon that form of realization, it yields meaning. To deny that would be a

---

[10] CW 18, § 1630, emphasis supplied.
[11] *Ibid,* § 1567
[12] *Ibid,* § 1630

fundamental rejection of Jung's emphasis on *esse in anima* and the ability to make an inner experience real by its realization.

Clinically, there is no psychological process to experience that cosmic totality, as it arises only by an archetypal irruption into consciousness that comes unbidden. It is, therefore, not the subject of psychoanalysis, as the greater, primary proclivity is to direct the search for the center, a preestablished harmony, that is a primordial force that reconciles inconsistencies. This proclivity can be deduced by the presentation of unifying symbols for the Self, as well as by the varied processes of and tendency toward centering and homeostasis. Those processes easily translate to establishing a structure with a center, which also accords with the principle of natural symmetry; for the physicist Wolfgang Pauli, "symmetry was the archetypal structure of matter."[13]

The need to realize totality is not a psychological need. However, the need for centering of oneself in the face of chaos, both internal and external, is always an underlying impetus or instinctive tendency. Freud calls the tendency toward stability the principle of *Nirvana*, the desire to return to a uroboric, primordial place.[14] It arises for him theoretically because of a conflict between the idea of satisfaction and the pleasure principle and, on the other hand, the need to abandon that principle for the sake of reality. *Nirvana* does not include the desire for centering as it takes away all interest in attainment. It becomes closest to the development of what Freud calls the "oceanic feeling"[15] that he uses to describe the state reached in a mystical experience.

Clinically, the incomprehensibility of the Self as inclusive of all that is conscious and all that is unconscious is ameliorated when the Self is realized as the center. The effect of this realization of the center is to create a clear marker of a specific place in the wide ocean of the unconscious because it is otherwise not possible to give a form or structure to the unconscious. The unconscious is formless as it is all that is unknown and can never be fully understood: "Our consciousness is a small circle contained within a wider circle of our unconsciousness. The smaller

---

[13] Zabriskie 2001, p. xxxvii
[14] Freud 1920
[15] Freud 1930

cannot understand the greater ..."[16] At least a center provides an orientation in what cannot be understood.

The need to include totality is not critical to understanding the Self. In 1941, Jung gave a lecture to Swiss psychiatrists at the Swiss *Kommission für Psychotherapie* in Zürich where he explains the Self as center but does not even hint at the inclusion of totality. It is possible that the lecture would not have been received well by an audience of psychiatrists if he speculated about totality. This lecture made its way to the English-speaking world in the 1942 *Spring* journal.[17] This presentation is interesting because, as will be detailed, from 1935 on, he expands the notion of the Self as embracing totality. However, in this essay, he explains the essential nature of the Self as only a center:

> In opposition to the dangerous disintegration–tendency there arises out of the same unconscious a counter effect in the shape of a centralizing process characterized by unequivocal symbols. This process creates nothing less than a new personality center, which through its symbols is hallmarked as superior to the ego, that later proves its superiority empirically.[18]

In this lecture, he also raises yoga as an example of the experience and realization of that center.[19] This is an easy, practical summary of the Self, devoid of any mention of notions of the Self as totality. It would have been apparent to this audience that beyond the centering function of the Self that can be grasped, the realization of all that is conscious and unconscious, the totality of all, would be the ultimate summit of human achievement, although impossible to imagine. It not only would require a mana personality, but one that goes beyond the current understanding of human evolution. Such a realization would obviate the need for realization of the center if the individual were merged in the infinite. This would have been confusing for the assembled psychiatrists, as it is indeed for the rest of us now, because totality is indeed the entirety of all that is unknown, as the unconscious has no limits. He would not then have been

---

[16] Jung 2019, p. 160
[17] Jung 1942; in CW 16 as *Psychology Today*
[18] *Ibid*, p. 6
[19] *Ibid*

able to keep totality in the psychological box although in natural language it will always cleave to the absolute, widest definition embracing the *Pleroma*, the preexisting formlessness. In this view, it could not be contemplated as the *Pleroma* is, as Jung explains, fullness and nothingness, "endless, eternal, and entire."[20] It is therefore with caution that the Self as totality needed to be unraveled and understood in order for it to be capable of being manifested at all.

The 1935 Eranos Lecture

1935 is highly significant in understanding the nature of the Self as totality. Jung presented a lecture in that year at the Eranos conference in Switzerland that specifically extended the Self as including totality, and it became a turning point in the concept of the Self. However, its incorrect translation into English thereafter in the *Collected Works* is responsible for most of the confusion as to its scope and meaning. The translation is the source of conflicting contemporary commentary, ungrounded transcendent statements about the Self, and speculation about what is expected in the realization of the Self.

A high degree of speculation is understandable in any event, even without the translation error. The idea of the Self embracing literally everything, complete totality and not just psychic wholeness, was perhaps seized on so readily because it aligns with Jung's view of the powerful arcane forces lying in the unconscious. This idea was often applied by him as the cause of great events as, for example, in his statement in the September-October 1935 lecture at the Tavistock Clinic in London of the power of the archetypes that are "the great decisive forces, they bring about the real events, and not our personal reasoning and practical intellect."[21] This was a statement about National Socialism that invoked the daimon Wotan in the unconscious, elevated by Jung to a god-image.[22] When there is an attribution of such forces to the Self, it too can be transposed to be in the category of "great decisive forces."

In February 1935, in a Zarathustra lecture, Jung presented a preliminary idea of his thinking about totality, which was to be amplified in the critical

---

[20] *Memories,* p. 379
[21] CW 18, § 371
[22] CW 9.i, § 442

Eranos conference lecture six months later in August 1935. In the Zarathustra lecture, Jung explains,

> But to say we know the unconscious is going too far, we only know *of* it. The unconscious has an extension that can reach anywhere; we have absolutely no means of establishing a definite frontier. We cannot say where the world ends, so we cannot say where the unconscious ends, or whether it ends anywhere.[23]

As the Self is to include the broadest sweep of the unconscious, it then became in that lecture as Jung recognizes, "metaphysical in its nature *per definition*: it overreaches itself."[24] To say that the Self may contain totality in this manner is a testament to the Self as an unimaginable concept, as it includes all that is unconscious. All that is unconscious, defined in that way, can exist, as mentioned, on a cosmic scale so that totality cannot ever be comprehended. As a prelude to the Eranos lecture, this statement leaves his ideas of totality as including that which can extend beyond the known psyche to a different transcendent realm.

The Eranos lecture was titled *Traumsymbole Des Individuationprozesses* (Dream Symbols and the Process of Individuation)[25] and interpreted a series of patients' dreams for the purpose of explaining stages in the individuation process. At the very start of the lecture, he references his comments about the Self in the Mana Personality essay. The ideas contained in the Mana Personality essay in 1928, as discussed, yield some insight into a connection between the Self and totality by his comments about the Self having kinship with "beasts and gods, with crystals and stars."[26] In this light, it is an initial statement in this essay that the center consists of more than a reference point in psyche and is therefore a limitless phenomenon. This is because, as mentioned, a mana personality such as the hero and savior, adds that extraordinary dimension to the Self and was congruent with the numinosity and importance of the center in the dream, verifying his prior intimations in drawing mandalas.

---

[23] *Zarathustra,* Vol 1, p. 414, emphasis supplied.
[24] *Ibid*
[25] Jung 1935
[26] CW 7, § 398

It is important to set out the actual statement in the Eranos lecture:

> *Aus gewissen dort erwähnten Grunden bezeichne ich dieses*
> *Zentrum auch als das „Selbst", worunter die Totalität des*
> *Psychischen uberhaupt verstanden sein soll, n. b. insofern*
> *such dieses in einem Individuum manifestiert.*[27]

The German is set out here because statements in that lecture are the primary basis for the contemporary characterization of the Self not only as a center *but also* as totality. The German passage reads in direct translation,

> *(that for the reasons set out in that Mana Personality essay),*
> *I also refer to the center as the Self by which the totality of*
> *the psyche is to be understood at all, n.b. insofar as this is*
> *manifested in an individual.*

The German quote places emphasis on the word "understood," *verstanden,* which occurs in terms of totality by realizing the Self *as center.* There are four gradations of explanations of how it occurs that realizing the center yields totality. The first is that, by realizing a center point of psyche it is theoretically possible to understand the width and breadth of psyche because you look outward from the center point. The second, more cogent argument is that it is so numinous as a center that this brings in the transcendent realm that can then be realized. The third is that if you truly realize the Self as the center, you then understand it as the preexistent center of a wider dimension of psychic space, so that realization of the center confers insight into the true nature of aspects of the Self beyond the center. The fourth, and most important is that the center contains all the opposites including those in the vast collective unconscious, and when those opposites are reconciled, totality is understood to that degree.

Totality, in this statement in the Eranos lecture, is a function of realizing the center, but the indescribable vastness of totality, cosmic totality, does not necessary follow from establishing a midpoint of psyche. Instead, and most importantly as the key to the passage are his words that it is "understood at all," "*insofar as this is manifested.*" Totality is so vast on

---

[27] Jung, 1935, p. 13

a psychological scale or even on a cosmic scale with no boundaries that it can only be realized, if at all, as to only a limited part. This is the essence of understanding totality as the Self because Jung adds "n.b.," *nota bene*, meaning that the emphasis must be placed on totality being understood *only* to the extent that this insight is reached; *n.b.* is the critical qualifier that holds back a more generous explanation of the Self embracing totality.

The consequence is that to the degree totality is not manifested or understood, the concept of the Self as totality is, at most, a vague hypothesis. It is accordingly not appropriate to say, more generally, that as an empirical fact the Self is the center *and* totality. The crucial limitation on that statement is the Self as totality is relevant for psychological growth only to the extent it is realized by consciousness.

The next sentence of the German 1935 lecture complicates the issue further by a reference to the Self as including the circumference, the *Umfang*:

> *Das Selbst ist nicht nur der Mittelplunkt, <u>sondern auch jener</u> Umfang, der Bewußsein und Unbewußtges einschließt; es ist das Zentrum dieser Totalitat, wie das Ich das Bewußt-seingszentrum ist.*[28]

The literal and effective translation of this passage is:

> the Self is not just the center point but is also that circumference, which includes conscious and unconscious; it is the center of this totality as the ego is the center of consciousness.

This provides that the Self is the center and also the *psychic* totality, the whole of psyche, as the circumference around it. Reading these two German quotes together, explains the proper meaning relationship of the Self to totality. The Self, when realized as the center, offers the possibility of realization of psychic totality because the Self as center *contains the whole of psyche within itself.* However, that circumference around the entirety of psyche—the width and breadth of psyche that is endless—can only be said to exist *empirically* as a psychological fact, to the extent *it*

---

[28] *Ibid*

is manifested: realized by an individual. The Self does include totality as well as the center, but this is only understood through realization of totality (the opposites in the collective unconscious) held in the center and then, critically, to the extent that it is realized.

These are confusing sentences and can easily be read to make the Self *at all times* both the center and totality. Its proper interpretation is that the Self is a hypothesis until realized, and although a center can be realized fully, totality is more abstract, and only a small part of it can also be realized. The transcendent part flows out of the Self as he expresses in the Mana Personality essay, so that it is possible for that to be given some form in psyche by which it can be recognized and, thereby, can be seen as connected to and originating from the center.

It is important to repeat that if totality is *not manifested*, then the nature of the totality of psyche is not to be understood, and the relationship between the totality of psyche and the center remains only a hypothesis. That *hypothesis* is always there, and, in that light, the Self is *theoretically* (and not empirically) both center and totality as Jung sets out later in the same lecture, *Das Selbst ist per definitionem die Mitte und der Umfang des bewußten und des unbewußten Systems*;[29] in translation: "The self is by definition the center and the circumference of the conscious and unconscious system." This is the hypothesis and a metaphysical explanation that is the structure of the Self, but it becomes more than a hypothesis when the center is first realized, and from that revelation, the further reaches of psychic totality can then be understood to an extent it also is realized.

In June 1936, in another Zarathustra lecture following the *Eranos* lecture by almost a year, he speaks of the missing link of how a connection between a center and everything unknown, the wide, never-ending unconscious, can possibly be understood at all. The Self, he states in that lecture, is "trying to manifest in space and time, but since it consists of so many elements that have neither space nor time qualities, it cannot bring them altogether into space and time. ... So much of the Self remains outside, it doesn't enter the three-dimensional world."[30] Totality as

---

[29] *Ibid*, p. 120
[30] *Zarathustra*, Vol. 2, p. 977

psychic totality, therefore, can never be realized in full, so it is not proper to speak of the Self as totality without the qualifier of it being as is manifested. Jung admits this limitation on a wider proposition: "the term *self* is often mixed up with the idea of God. I would not do that. I would say the term *self* should be reserved for that sphere which is within the reach of human experience ..."[31]

This last statement means that the Self should be properly reserved for what may possibly be realized. It is of no use to define it as including a distant galaxy in the universe, the dimension that may exit after death, or the unrevealed secrets of the Higgs boson particle. Totality is incorporated in the psychological matrix of his ideas because the Self is the endpoint of individuation, where realizations may comprehend the farther reaches of the unconscious. If this is accurate and the way he intends it to be understood, then totality is only relevant in defining the Self when it is understood through the realization of the center. To say that the Self is the center and totality without more is misleading and inconsistent with the purpose of the Self in individuation.

It is a difficult idea, in any event, to propose the hypothesis that the center and the totality are both the Self. This would mean in interpreting his 1927 dream that the entire city would be the Self, not just the center. This is not what Jung directly implies in the dream but perhaps can be argued to be the case because the city is the backdrop that creates a structure in which the tree is geometrically the center. There is no direct hint in the dream, however, that there is more involved. If this is all that Jung meant, it is somewhat confusing to speak of the Self as totality, and at the same time to speak of it as the center. Conceptually, a circumference and its center are not related either mathematically or practically. It would be the same as saying a central area in Basel (the market) is not only the center of Basel but is the center of the world or the universe; the psychic totality would then extend into the cosmic totality.

This interesting conundrum was refined in the June 1936 Zarathustra seminar. In this seminar, he recast totality in the widest possible terms, making it clearly a transcendent postulate beyond human understanding: "So you can say everything of the self; you can say it is a devil, a god,

---

[31] *Ibid*

nothing but nature ... It is just everything—the totality"[32] He explains that totality is found by realizing the center because *the center holds within it the unlimited contents of psyche* that extends to any dimension. He calls it the ultimate "great secret that has to be worked out" that exists in man and in nature, that holds every mystery and every aspect of creation. By this reasoning, it is indeed a center as well as the circumference that includes the entirety of psychic contents, which is all that exists psychologically, and therefore extends to the complete unknown. The statement that it is the center and the circumference means, therefore, that the center is *all things within itself*, so it can be both at the same time. However, most critically, it must be manifested for this to be relevant and understood empirically, because as center and totality, he explains, it is "specific yet universal. It is a restricted universality or a universal restrictedness, a paradox. ..."[33] This can be read as the universality being restricted in humankind, because "our consciousness is always restricted, no matter how extended it is."[34] The Self therefore is restricted in relation to totality only to the extent it is manifested in an individual.

As can be seen in these convoluted quotes and especially the limitation of totality to what is manifested, it makes no sense to speak of the Self as totality in the abstract. An assertion that the Self should be understood as totality is not correct. What indeed could that mean? A center can be found, but the endless reaches of psychic totality cannot. A piece of it may be manifested, brought into realization, such as having a numinous experience of oneness or experiencing the presence of the divine.

This Eranos lecture was presented in August 1935 and, the following year, Jung traveled to the United States to give a series of lectures on the same topic, *Dream Symbols of the Individuation Process*, that clarifies some of his Eranos statements. In analyzing a dream of the physicist Wolfgang Pauli about the world clock, an image that suggests totality, Jung explains that there are aspects of psyche that we cannot at all grasp and that the "unconscious mind covers an area of indefinite expanse while our conscious is very limited." An individual "cannot grasp the whole of

---

[32] *Ibid,* p. 979
[33] *Ibid,* p. 978
[34] Jung 2019, p. 161

human consciousness." The Self as center is then the "compound" of conscious and unconscious, "which holds the whole thing together."[35] This reaffirms the primacy of the Self as center and as *manifested* totality as forming a psychological postulate, excluding that which is totality but not able to be grasped.

Aligning totality, transcendent, eternal universality, with the Self could only have arisen out of Jung's own realization of the center; it is no wonder therefore that he had no need after the dream to draw mandalas. The center's numinosity of self-illumination would have been one factor that brought Jung to the experience of it having an ordering effect and also containing the vast unknown that becomes the psychological Self as it was manifested in him.

This actual realization of the Self as both a psychological center as well as a transcendent miracle, should that occur, is the only underpinning for allowing it to be both the center and the totality. If the Self is interpreted as merely a psychological center, the full nature of the Self that holds all of the opposites is not found. If it is interpreted as relating to totality without any manifestation, then it is only a hypothesis. Any manifestation of the totality, as Jung must have had, would provide an individual with a sense that there is a force that guides us, a *spiritus rector*, that is responsible for our lives. "But the totality of our conscious and unconscious contains all: it is the thinker of our thoughts, the doer of our deeds, the feeler of our feelings."[36]

This can only mean that Jung realized, manifested, aspects of totality prior to or as a result of the dream in a form that he never directly explained.[37] It was material, he states, that "burst forth from the unconscious, and at first swamped me,"[38] which is a description of a numinous experience as that which breaks through unbidden. A numinous experience he had is referenced in the *Black Books,* his personal notebooks, where Jung first states in 1914 that "Through uniting with the self we reach the God, who unites heaven and hell within himself."[39] He then adds in 1917, "I must

---

[35] *Ibid*
[36] Jung 2019, p. 161
[37] Stein 2015
[38] *Memories*, p. 199
[39] *Black Books,* Vol 5, p. 239

say this not with reference to the opinion of the ancients or that authority, but because I have experienced it."[40] Sonu Shamdasani, the editor and a translator of the *Black Books,* concludes, "This unshakable experience was nothing less than the experience of God."[41] Shamdasani also relates a letter Jung wrote to Emma Jung that he indeed had, in 1917, that numinous experience: "I had a most remarkable, mystical experience, a feeling of connection of many millennia. It was like a transfiguration."[42]

The offer of realization of a center makes complete sense but so does totality to the few to whom the insight is revealed. Once again, Jung was explaining *his* realization, not that of the "other Swiss" or us, unless we have that realization. This is so mystical that it was bound to be misunderstood, as it has been.

The Incorrect Translation

The German original underwent two English translations. The first, published in 1939, *The Integration of the Personality,*[43] is a direct, literal English translation of the 1935 statements and maintains the meaning correctly. The second was a retranslation some 20 years later for the current English edition of the *Collected Works* where the proper characterization of the Self was distorted, changing its meaning, having a profound effect on how it thereafter was understood.

The 1939 first English translation is true to the literal meaning of the 1935 statements:

> (the Self is) *a term that is meant to include the totality of psyche in so far as this manifests in an individual.* The self is not only the centre, but the circumference that encloses consciousness and the unconscious; it is the centre of totality, as the ego is the center of consciousness.[44]

The idea that the Self is "meant to" include the totality of psyche is perceptive, although it is not found in the German, as it gives significance

---

[40] *Ibid,* Vol 1, p. 68
[41] *Ibid*
[42] *Ibid*
[43] Jung 1939
[44] *Ibid*, p. 96, emphasis added.

to what Jung requires as the realization of totality: only in so far as it is manifested. This is consistent with the German original and means that the existence of the Self as totality only occurs for psychological growth when aspects of it are manifested. Until that time, it cannot be understood as having these qualities, and perhaps then the idea that it is "meant to" makes sense as suggesting a hypothesis.

The translation in the *Collected Works* provides a radically different and incorrect emphasis to what is in the original German as well as the prior 1939 English translation. It states:

> I call this center, the 'self' which should be understood as the totality of the psyche. The Self is not only the center, but also the whole circumference which embraces both conscious and unconscious; it is the centre of this totality, as the ego is the centre of consciousness.[45]

The clear error in translation arises from what is missing from the *Collected Works*: the fundamental proposition that the center includes totality *only* to the extent it is manifested in an individual. The Eranos original lecture and the 1939 translation both indicate that the Self as totality can be understood *insofar as it is manifested in an individual* (that phrase Jung marked with *nota bene*: "*n. b. insofern such dieses in einem Individuum manifestiert*"), but this phrase is not found in the *Collected Works*, nor does the translation hint at this critical concept. It is the case that the Self includes totality within it, but this cannot be a blanket statement as it only exists as a reality when realized. It does not reach the fundamental principle of *esse in anima* until it is absorbed into and alters consciousness. As a hypothesis alone, it means nothing of psychological significance, and the translation deteriorates the essence of the experience of the Self.

The phase (insofar as it is manifested) has great significance because the Self has to be realized experientially to remove it from a mere hypothesis before its complete depth and importance as totality can be understood. Another way of explaining these complex ideas and to understand the problem with the translation is to return to the *Seven Sermons,* where totality implies that the Pleroma, which contains all of the opposites, all

---

[45] CW 12, § 44

that is conscious and unconscious, lies within an individual. In each person lies that totality but it must be the subject of discrimination, *Creatura*: It must be discriminated, manifested, in the individual. This idea of the Self in the 1935 Eranos passage is no different from the *Seven Sermons* in that the potential of each individual is to discriminate these opposites within them, and to carry out this difficult journey to realize the Self. There appears no basis for this translation omission that excludes the need to realize the Self before it is a reality, thereby altering the nature of such a significant essence of Jung's opus.

The retranslation was of the 2ⁿᵈ Swiss edition of the *Gasammelte Werke* that *did contain* the important phrase. It was Jung who nominally approved the English version of the *Collected Works*, although this translation appears in the essay in Volume 12, *Psychology and Alchemy,* that had several editors (including Michael Fordham and Gerhard Adler). Sonu Shamdasani indicates that "Jung basically did not involve himself much in translations" and that manuscripts were not always accurately reproduced.[46]

A reason that the requirement that the Self as totality exists insofar as it is manifested in an individual was removed could also have been, if Jung was involved in taking it out, that it was in line with the reality that totality is not likely to be manifested, so it is merely a metaphysical statement. Returning to his September 1936 lecture in America that mentions totality, he indicates that not much of totality is realizable in drawing a comparison to the contents of the unconscious with a public library,

> You can only contain a very small amount, and even if you read and read and heap up knowledge, only a few things remain at all you have read; it has influenced you, but you could not for the world reproduce it, though you might get it back in a dream, or in the fantasy of psychological condition. But to your consciousness, it is extinct.[47]

What we are left with is that the Self is the focal or midpoint of the opposites as it contains the *Pleroma*, the entirety of opposites—the totality—within us. Therefore, we can know the center as a psychological

---

[46] Personal Communication, 16 June 2020.
[47] Jung 2019, p. 161

goal and construct, but we cannot know the totality within us until we discriminate the opposites by fully realizing the nature and extent of the center. This is as far as we can go, and there is thus the hope that if we can realize the Self as center, that may lead us to some image of totality. To go any further is of no psychological use and would be a metaphysical statement of little worth. As Jung recognizes: "But it transcends our power of imagination to form a clear picture of what we are as a self, for in this operation the part would have to comprehend the whole." It has, as he expresses it, a "supraordinate quantity" because it can never be fully known by consciousness.[48]

In this understanding, the process of individuation leads us closer to totality, the realization of the entirety of psyche, as the circumambulation around the goal continuously reconciles the opposites drawn from those contained in the totality—the *Pleroma*—that are within us. The Self as a virtual center makes perfect sense as the conflict of opposites seeks a point of balance. The Self is therefore, to summarize, that revealed as a center that is capable of holding all opposites in balance and which also includes, through a revelation if it occurs, some of the contents of the collective unconscious which the center also holds.

Influences Pointing to Totality

The realization that the Self includes totality when manifested, establishing that vague, uncertain aspect as the higher reaches of the goal of an individual's life, requires a context. It may simply be, as already suggested, that Jung perceived the transcendent totality because he had numinous, mystical experiences that had been building in intensity and then broke through. They constituted unique, individual revelations as it was not, at that time, a view shared by his companions in the dream of the Self or those occupying the surrounding regions in the *Window on Eternity* image in *The Red Book*.

The experience of the center in the dream may also have been interpreted to thereafter include totality because Jung was entwined in a deep philosophical thread that was particularly alive in the 1930s. It is a thread interwoven with the influence of the German Romanticism of Johann

---

[48] CW 7, § 274

Gottlieb Fichte and Friedrich Schiller that struggled with the implications of the right relationship an individual is to have with the opposites and how they can be reconciled. This reconciliation, to be possible in any form, must have the capacity to hold the opposites, and the self promoted by Fichte was of a totality resting or self-contained in itself.[49] This orientation to a transcendent self echoed Kant's reflections on holding the opposites by an inner sense of "transcendental apperception," to which he made the object of that apperception the soul.[50] Jung took this further in a natural way by the creation of the Self as not only an ideal of unity but also a reality created by apperception. Bishop argues that Jung inappropriately conflated the Platonic Ideal (of preexistent universals) to Kant's idea of apperception that gave him the "licence for such claims about a transcendent realm," offering him an easier way, perhaps, to leave open a concept of the Self as real and also transcendent.[51]

Whether Jung was influenced in this way, or he had a mystical experience that perceived totality in the Self, or he interpreted the numinosity of the center as revealing totality is not, of course, known. Jung did acknowledge the vastness of the Self in his commentary in the *Secret of the Golden Flower* but did not expand the Self in that instance as representing totality as well as the center. However, in 1932, Jung gave two seminars in which he focused on the relationship of the Self to Hindu Vedanta philosophy and the concept of the *Atman,* the indwelling of the divine in an individual. These two seminars indicate that the idea of the Self as totality was very much in his mind only a few years after the dream.

In the first of these two seminars, the *Visions* seminars in February 1932, when he mentions the Self, his reference to totality is present but only tangentially as a parallel to Hindu Philosophy where the *Atman* is an aspect of the indwelling ultimate Brahman.[52] This was echoed again in the second seminar, the 1932 *Kundalini Yoga Seminar,* where he equates the Self with the middle chakra: *Anahata,* the critical bridge between the realms of upper and lower chakras.[53] Neither the *Vision* nor the *Kundalini*

---

[49] Bonhoeffer 2009, p. 215
[50] Kant 1798/1974, Ak, VII: 161
[51] Bishop 1996
[52] Jung 1997, Vol. 1, p. 555
[53] Jung 1996, p. 40

seminars explicitly explains that the Self is not only the center but also totality, although both are a clear recognition that he was reaching further beyond the center for that apperception.

The inclusion of the essence of the Self as encompassing a transcendent totality in these seminars may, however, have been influenced by concurrent events in the 1930s. Eranos, where Jung in 1935 announced the relationship of the Self to totality, was then an environment where the connection of psychic phenomena, such as the concept of the Self and mystical ideas, was the orientation. In 1933, Jung gave an earlier lecture at an Eranos meeting amongst a concentration of presentations by others on mysticism, such as Heinrich Zimmer on Tantra Yoga. In a 1934 lecture at Eranos, the German Indologist Professor Hauer set the stage for Jung's 1935 statements about totality with his extensive paper *Symbole und Erfahrung des Selbstes in der indoarabischen Mystik*,[54] (*Symbols and Experiencing of the Self in Indo-Arabian Mysticism, Exploring the Concept of the Self as Atman*). This and other papers in that period framed the theme of what he presented at Eranos and the relationship of the Self to the transcendent, so the assertion that there was a Self that contained totality was at home at Eranos in 1935.

Paul Bishop explains, more precisely, that the underlying idea for Jung's view of the Self as totality is derived from his reading of Nietzche's *Thus Spake Zarathustra*.[55] Bishop suggests that Nietzsche's concept of *Eternal Recurrence*, the infinite repetition of one's life, raised for Jung the symbolism of a never-ending circumference. Jung, in the Zarathustra Seminars in 1937, states that "the ring is the idea of totality and it is the idea of individuation naturally, an individuation symbol."[56] This, Bishop argues, "culminated in the totality of the Self" because the goal of the endless circularity of the individuation process is the Self.[57] As Bishop also explains, Nietzsche calls "your own true self" something concealed within a person, but of a higher order that can be encountered and, under the name of "virtue," can recognize itself.[58] Examining Jung's margin notes in his copy of Zarathustra, Bishop points out that Jung was thinking

---

[54] Hauer 1935, pp. 35-96
[55] Bishop 1995, p. 341
[56] *Zarathustra*, Vol 2, p. 1044
[57] Bishop 1995, p. 341
[58] *Ibid*, p. 347

with a transcendent orientation as he marked the line offered by Nietzsche that Goethe had the "discipline to shape himself into a totality and to *create himself*."[59]

Deidre Bair, one of his biographers, adds the historical context, "But as the 1930s began, he saw his 'main task' as one in which he needed to put the experiences he had gathered, of himself as well as his patients, onto 'firm ground.'"[60] This can be seen in terms of the Self repeatedly being invoked in all his writings in that period as a center. However, in 1934, shortly after the dream and just prior to Jung going to Eranos to explain the nature of the Self, he was also involved in the political upheaval of that time. This is apparent in the material he presented in the *Berlin Seminar* about "cultural identity," as he was under intense pressure about his position in relation to National Socialism.[61] This led him to a wider view of the Self in the particular context of "identity" that can be seen in letters exchanged with Erich Neumann about previous comments Jung had made on the consciousness of Jews. It required Jung in 1934 to address the relationship of the individual, the idea of individuation, and the Self in relation to the community. Jung states in that letter:

> The more the center of the personality moves in the direction from the ego toward the Self, the more "unindividual" does the personality become in a certain sense, and the more a center appears in the place of the ego that stands in close connection with the collective. Indeed the Self is in a certain sense a *center in the collective*....[62]

Making the Self a center in the collective means that it is an aspect of the collective unconscious and is not personal to an individual. It therefore expands the center to include the entire psyche of all humanity. As well, it introduces the idea of the Self expanding out in order to give it a transcendent connection where totality can be experienced by all. This statement coincides with his first major exposition of the archetypes of the collective unconscious in another Eranos lecture in 1934.[63] These

---

[59] *Ibid,* p. 351, emphasis supplied.
[60] Bair 2004, p. 397
[61] Jorg 2012; Stein, et al. 2012
[62] Jung & Neumann 2015, pp. 43-44
[63] Jung 1934, pp. 179-239, revised and in CW 9.i.

ideas all preceded his explanation the year after of the Self in relation to totality and, again, had to be an insight he had that the Self is more vast than individual experience of a personal, psychic center.

In the 1935 lecture, "totality" is a *déctic,* where the word triggers a different meaning for the Self. This was not a deviation from his ideas because totality is a concept that is indeed congruent with the idea of the Self because it theoretically includes all that is conscious and the unconscious, personal and collective. What can be known of that psychic totality is limited, but aspects of the collective unconscious can be realized and can break through into consciousness to become the highest form of knowledge. The Self as a center therefore clearly generates a circumference that expands out to an unknown point, approximating the idea of the unconscious and, whatever is realized then is known as part of the Self. Totality is the factual description of all that we are, and it can be realized in part through perceiving the center or by a numinous experience. His numinous experiences, the influence of the German Romantics and Nietzsche, his orientation to explain his experience, the mystical themes at Eranos, all combined to make totality essential to the Self.

There are many aspects of totality that Jung may have realized. An example of an aspect or part of totality would be sensing the Self in others and in matter, or being aware of a divine presence by an inner voice, or a realization that Sri Aurobindo provides is having found "that which endures and is imperishable in us, from birth to birth, untouched by death, decay or corruption, an indestructible spark of the Divine."[64] If this occurred for Jung, then the Self is seen as that spark that is akin to the indwelling *Atman,* a comparison he would later make. Totality cannot be refused a place in the concept of the Self, but it means nothing if not realized. One can only write about it from their degree of realization, and it does not at all submit to its content being the subject of logic.

Fordham and Totality

Starting from this period in the mid-1930s, Jung kept expanding the idea of the Self in his writings, widening its scope and finding further

---

[64] Aurobindo 2005, p. 238

refinements in both Alchemy and Gnosticism. In none of these later writings was the conundrum of the Self being the center as well as the circumference—at once a center point and the totality—ever modified or redefined.

There was a lacuna in the logic that as the Self as totality includes all that is conscious and unconscious, it is not possible for the conscious ego to observe the totality which it is within. This breaches the concept of Jung's that nothing can be realized without the ego. This appears as a logical paradox, but it can be said at the outset that there is nothing logical about totality as a concept, nothing at all. However, an early student of Jung's, Michael Fordham, used this paradox to reject Jung's notion of realization of totality and to establish a different orientation to the Self.

In 1963, Fordham's analysis of Jung's concept of the Self was published: *The Empirical Foundation and Theories of the Self in Jung's Works.* He indicates that the Self as center and the Self as totality are incompatible and "Jung clearly tried to resolve the incompatibility he noticed."[65] To ground this assessment, Fordham first seizes on inconsistencies in Jung's work, *Psychology and Alchemy*, that contains various mandala images that arose in the dreams of two patients that reflect the center and totality. Fordham argues that the imagery of a circle and a center, such as in a dream of a snake in a circle around the dreamer, a blue flower and a globe, and further examples where Jung uses 54 pictures from 22 patients, were not a random sample but were from people with a well-developed inner life. He therefore questions the use of this sample to make totality statements about the Self[66] and otherwise doubts the veracity of the incorporation of other cultural material, such as Hinduism or Daoism.

The difficulty with this criticism is that Jung's statements were never intended to be read as providing proof of the Self by a significant sampling. If that was the case, so many of his concepts would fail the test of reliability. The Self is developed out of Jung's realizations that are apparently not those of Fordham's. In fact, Jung states that in his analysis of the patients' dreams, these are his associations: "I proceed rather as if

---

[65] Fordham 1963, p. 15
[66] *Ibid*, p. 19

I had had the dreams myself and were therefore in a position to supply the context."[67]

Fordham then specifically rejects the Self as totality. He starts by quoting Jung's statement in *Psychologische Typen* in 1921 that self is "my totality." This phrase is not in fact in the original German, but that sentiment is contained in the definition of the "*Ich*," the German for "ego," where the Self is mentioned as distinguished from the ego. The original German explains the Self as the "*Subjekt meiner gesamten, also auch der unbewussten Psyche ist,*" the subject of my entire psyche.[68] This statement, it should be noted, is not referring to a "totality" in the sense that it was expressed in 1935, but rather in 1921, at this early stage, that the Self is the *subject* of the psyche, meaning it is a manifestation of psyche; its realization comes from the activity of psyche. This is consistent with the idea that it contains all of psyche within it, but that it also is the center.

Fordham argues from this incorrect viewpoint: "If the self is the whole psyche, then it cannot be observed as such, since the ego is contained in it as a part and there is therefore no observer."[69] This is, as mentioned, his proposition that logically there is a mistake. This leads him to postulate a means by which the ego can step out of totality to know it, found in his idea that only when the unity of the conscious and unconscious is deintegrated "and when some part of ego stands separate from or only participates up to a point is the rest of the whole that data about the self can be collected."[70]

This seems an odd conclusion and is unsustainable because Jung was quite clear that "it transcends our powers of imagination to form a clear picture of what we are as a self, for in this operation the part would have to comprehend the whole."[71] The 1935 Eranos statement was accordingly that the totality is *understood* by realizing the center, implying that full realization will reveal to the ego that the Self holds all opposites. The ego does not observe totality, but it is understood when the real essence of

---

[67] CW 12, § 49
[68] Jung 1921, S. 630
[69] Fordham 1963, p. 11
[70] *Ibid*
[71] CW 7, § 274

the center is grasped. More importantly, totality arises for the ego when it is overwhelmed and supplanted by the revelation. This is how an archetype or primordial force reaches a breakthrough into consciousness. In writing about his experience of mandalas, Jung states about such symbols, "And they are convincing for a very old-fashion reasons: They are *overwhelming,* which is precisely what the Latin word *convincere* means."[72]

Fordham's argument was first published in 1963. At that time, the interpretation of the 1935 lecture had been translated correctly in 1939, explaining the notion of totality only as realized and arising from realizing the center. It appears that Fordham derived his notion of totality from the incorrect translation in the *Collected Works.* It is noted that Fordham did not speak German and, when he became an editor of the *Collected Works* in the 1950s, it was Gerhard Adler who was given the responsibility to check the translation.[73] It is possible that if he had read the 1939 correct translation, he could have avoided that error in misunderstanding the idea of the whole of psyche, totality.

These criticisms of the Self were expanded by Fordham in *Explorations into the Self* in 1985 on the basis of including Jung's writings on alchemy, which were published after Fordham's earlier article. Significantly, as he had his own theory of the Self now embedded in the London School, he adds, "I am persuaded that Jung's method of presentation stems from his attempt to find ways of expressing the wholeness of the self. In doing so he ran up against the lack of inadequate language for so doing."[74] He accepts in this statement that Jung had an experience of the Self but then uses his own language to form an argument against pure interiority as proof of the Self:

> The difficulties in taking the primordial experience to represent the totality of the psyche are many, but the greatest so far considered is that experiences in solitude, however important in themselves, leave out the organism's adaptation to external objects whether personal or otherwise.[75]

---

[72] CW 11, § 167, emphasis supplied.
[73] Astor 1995, p. 19
[74] Fordham 1985, p. 8
[75] *Ibid, p. 22*

This is a proposition that the experience of totality that is a mystical, numinous experience, does not consider adaptation to the environment. The influence of such external events may in fact be relevant, as discussed in my previous work in terms of receptivity to the mystical experience and the context in which the experience is interpreted.[76] There does not, however, appear to be any statement by Jung that such experiences do not reflect environmental issues. This is because it is always the buildup of moral conflicts generated by external experiences that eventually lead to the breakthrough of the primordial, as Paul witnessed on the road to Damascus. For such experiences, Jung states: "In reality the irruption has been preparing for many years, often for half a lifetime, and already in childhood all sorts of remarkable signs could have been detected which, in more or less symbolic fashion, hinted at abnormal future development."[77]

The influence of Fordham's view is profound and is now indelible. The basis of his argument turns on the separation of the ego and the Self so that as the ego is contained in the totality that is the Self, the ego cannot stand outside to observe the Self. However, the deficiency of this argument is he approached totality logically when it can only be "understood at all," as stated in the 1935 Eranos lecture: "*uberhaupt verstanden sein soll,*" by realization. Following this logic destroys the extent of the Self so it is no longer even an abstract concept and, as Fordham puts it, it is, "not as a vivid metaphor."[78]

In his 1985 revision, Fordham argues against the proposition that comparative material provides evidence of totality, as he asserts that Jung essentially "derived the concept of the self from Eastern mysticism."[79] Eastern mysticism was not the source of his revelation; it was his intuition about mandalas and his 1927 dream. Eastern references arose when he received *The Secret of the Golden Flower* after the dream. It is also to be noted that Eastern references are to a *religion*, not mystical statements. A follower of Buddhism or Daoism or one who holds a belief in the *Atman* is not a mystic. It is clear that Fordham found these statements unverifiable and not of great worth as he did not engage with the nature

---

[76] Stein 2019a, Chap. 5
[77] CW 7, § 270
[78] Fordham 1985, p. 18
[79] *Ibid,* p. 20

of these religions. In picking an example, he quotes from the *Laws of Manu*, which Jung mentions in *Psychological Types*: "He who has in this manner gradually given up attachment and is free from all pairs of opposites reposes in Brahman alone."[80] Fordham asserts, "This frame of reference makes the self the wholeness of the personality outside time space and desire."[81] The quote relates to what is outside time, space, and desire *only* when the entirety of totality is realized, which Jung said is not possible.

Yet another basis for Fordham's criticism of Jung's expression of the Self is Jung's 1916 essay on the *Transcendent Function*, where the tension between opposites brings about a new situation, a "living third." Fordham states that this is "little if at all different from the self."[82] The Self *is* the coincidence of opposites, not because it arises from the tension as does the transcendent function, but rather because it contains all opposites within it. The Self is not its product as is the transcendent function, as the Self is preexistent. As well, although the reconciliation of the opposites is indeed a platform of philosophical thought, the transcendent function is a personal manifestation of the clash of opposites, while the Self is an aspect of the collective as Jung pointed out in the letter to Neumann in 1934.[83]

It is apparent that Fordham did not himself have a revelation of the Self but was approaching his subject matter with a refined logic. In the 1985 work, after reviewing Jung's use of *Atman* and other parallels, he adds, "It now must be apparent that the self is not only manifested in mysticism, the concept is mystical."[84] This seems the real point of departure from Jung. In 1960, prior to his critique of the Self, Fordham indicates his orientation when he examines the relevance of Analytical Psychology to alchemy, mysticism, and theology. He approaches it, as he does the analysis of the Self, on the basis that Jung proceeds by first proposing a model and then testing it, but adds, "A theory does not exist in the sense of empirical material, whether it be a dream, fantasy, everyday talk about

---

[80] CW 6, § 328
[81] *Ibid*, p. 20
[82] Fordham 1985, p. 18
[83] Jung & Neumann 2015, pp. 43-4
[84] Fordham 1985, p. 22

events in the outer world, or any text under consideration ..."[85] In comparing Jung's model to mysticism, he evokes experiences of St. John of the Cross and asks, "Why is this kind of mysticism so removed from everyday life?"[86] He explains that St. John had these experiences because he was in a religious order that "gave form to the archetypal energies."[87] He summarizes his attitude to a mystical revelation as "The theologian needs to assume the existence of a transcendent metaphysical Godhead, the psychologist needs to assume the existence of psyche."[88]

Mysticism for Jung was concerned not with abstract possibilities of visions or a metaphysical Godhead but only those numinous experiences that came upon a person unbidden and, *critically*, affected conscious-ness.[89] They were phenomena that needed to be included in the context of any psychology as they exist for patients and analysts. The visions in *The Red Book* and the revelations in the *Seven Sermons* were essentially experiences that Jung had that changed him; the dream of the center was also just that experience. We can only understand these by our own experiences and not by logic; mystical experiences certainly are beyond logic. When experienced, they are psychic facts that indicated to Jung that the Self embraced totality. For the rest of us, totality is only relevant, as he pointed out in 1935 in his Eranos lecture, to the extent that it is manifested. This understanding that is left out of the translation in the *Collected Works* and possibly not available to Fordham, was that the totality is a hypothesis—nothing more—until realized by an individual. To this, Jung added *nota bene*, to indicate it is real *to the extent* it is realized. To Fordham, who did not have that revelation, he surmises, "a concept of the totality is particularly difficult to construct. ... Indeed it is impossible."[90]

Elizabeth Urban offers a "re-examination" of Fordham's contribution to the Self, starting with Fordham's view that a totality is impossible to construct. She makes the statement, "The totality definition, (is) derived

---

[85] Fordham, 1960, p. 113
[86] *Ibid*, p. 123
[87] *Ibid*
[88] *Ibid*, p. 124
[89] Stein 2019a, Chapter 2
[90] Fordham 1985, p. 21

from references in Eastern mysticism to states of at-one-ness."[91] This directly follows Fordham's approach to the concept of totality, but totality does not need states of oneness to be realized nor is that implied by Jung. This ultimate state of the winking out of consciousness in *samadhi* that is being inferred would indeed be a glimpse into totality but is certainly not essential as totality from the 1935 definition is to realize a part, not the whole. The "at-one-ness" experience certainly cannot be used as a definition of totality. Again, these are parallels from another *religion*, in the same way the Holy Ghost is a construct of Catholicism.

Urban states, "Jung seemed to regard experiences of wholeness *as if* they were actually totality, ignoring that the whole is beyond experience."[92] "Experiences" of wholeness are never equated by Jung as "the whole," and this comment makes little sense because Jung explains that it exists only *to the extent* realized by an individual. There is no need to experience complete wholeness or totality in order for totality to become an aspect of the Self. Wholeness occurs through realization of the center and to that *extent*.

Urban makes another observation, that "Jung had conceived of the self as a way of accounting for certain, particularly mystical, phenomena in childhood."[93] This is certainly not the case, as the Self arose in him through an ever-increasing set of insights from drawing mandalas to having a dream. Mystical phenomena in childhood are certainly not the source of the Self. As a primordial, *a priori* patterning, an archetype, it would explain its early presentation, but the Self was not conceived by that insight.

Fordham spoke in terms of a "primary self" as a postulate that exists in a neonate for the eventual integration for the child. To this observation of Fordham, no objection can be taken, and it would not be at odds with the idea of a structural pattern of incipient wholeness existing from birth, as suggested by the *Pleroma* in the *Seven Sermons* and Jung's statement that symbols of wholeness appear in infants.[94] What Fordham suggests is that the Self is active and develops through a process of deintegration and

---

[91] Urban 2005, pp. 573-4
[92] *Ibid*, p. 575
[93] *Ibid*
[94] CW 9.i, § 278

reintegration. The idea that the Self so described is as an active force, as Urban states: "As the earliest period in development, the primary self is assumed to operate from before birth.[95]" This corresponds with findings in neurobiology, as will be discussed.

The exclusion from the 1935 lecture proviso that totality is the Self to the extent that it is manifested has led to the repeated, incorrect discounting of the Self as totality. The Self is fundamentally the patterning of a center that, by its structure, offers an orientation for us and a goal of psychological growth to become more whole. As it is a numinous presentation and carries with it transcendent parallels, it theoretically is more than just a center. The totality exists as a potential to hold the opposites and, when that is realized, rather than just in theory, it is the Self.

---

[95] Urban 2005, p. 576

Chapter 5. The Self as Psychic Object

The glorification of the Self as the numinous center of psychological growth that embraces what is realized as totality elevates it in Analytical Psychology to become the essence of a life's journey. This confers upon it a distinct role and a purpose as the cornerstone of the evolution of psyche for every individual so that unconscious revelations or psychological processes can be ascribed to the guidance of the Self. There are two issues that arise from this profundity to be able to contemplate its nature. The first is whether the Self can be considered a fundamental aspect of the mental apparatus of every individual. The second is whether, by having a role in psychological development, it should be considered, at least, a preexisting entity or personality in psyche.

The two issues arise in this formulation because if any aspect of the mind or the brain is ascribed a role, it immediately steps out of the normal, continuous, interplay of psychic interactions and is isolated as a substance, a thing-in-itself, *Ding an sich*. As a thing, it is given a name and then becomes a goal, as well as establishing a consequent process for attainment. When the name accords with it being the highest goal of psychological development, the locus of manifestation is the individual, and its attainment is divided into a path and stages. This has a direct parallel with the use of the term Self in Sufism, where the Self (*nafs*) offers stages of perfection and, "By traversing these stages it moves ever closer to God and further from its fallen nature."[1] It then draws to it parallels, prototypes, and the promise of perfection, so that in the Sufism of Ibn 'Arabi, "The Perfect Man is precisely the human self at its final stage of perfection and completion."[2]

---

[1] Chittick 1979, p. 136
[2] *Ibid*, p. 137

When it is named, has a role and a goal, it is then required to be understood as a substance in the sense that is corporeal, or it has another form of existence. As it is not possible to know exactly what it is, these creations are seen as necessary for explanatory purposes or are convenient for psychic orientation. It is no wonder that Wolfgang Giegerich points out that Jung created the Self as a "substance," even though throughout his works, he expresses psychic phenomena as having non-substance interiority. Giegerich asks, accordingly, "Why could he not stay true to it without?"[3] He points out, astutely, that seeing the Self as a substance of the mind, rather than just an evolving process of what he more generally calls soul phenomena, means that wholeness, the Self, and individuation "had to become for this theorizing hard-to-achieve future *goals*, i.e., utopian."[4]

A role and a future goal are indeed coupled: There cannot be one without the other. A role emerges only because the Self is perceived as having a purpose as a goal and possibly a will to accomplish that purpose; it thus contains an ideology. That ideology is that the unconscious is purposeful as is the Self. The passivization approach, the use of syntax to neutralize an active role and to make it obscure, is not warranted with the Self and an explanation of that active role must be formed.

The exact starting point for Jung rendering the psyche and the Self purposeful is not clear. In an early, 1897 Zofingia lecture when he was 22, Jung refers to the soul as intelligent, and states, "The criterion of intelligence is the purposefulness of its acts."[5] He explains that this grants the soul entelechy, the vital principle that guides an individual. He follows this viewpoint to ascribe purposefulness to the instincts[6] and insists on the idea that "a notion of purpose must exist prior to every action intended to have a purposeful character."[7] It is therefore fundamental to Jung and the idea of the Self that it has a purpose. He states, framing it differently as an urge to realization:

---

[3] Giegerich 2012, p. 296
[4] *Ibid*, p. 306n231
[5] Jung 1983, § 97
[6] *Ibid*, § 177
[7] *Ibid*, § 176

> Yet it would, in my view, be wrong to suppose that in such cases the unconscious is working to a deliberate and concerted plan and is striving to realize certain definite ends. I have found nothing to support this assumption. The driving force, so far as it is possible for us to grasp it, seems to be in essence only an urge towards self-realization.[8]

As it has no finite purpose itself, Jung provides, "all our highest and ultimate purposes seem to be striving towards it,"[9] and "it has somewhat the character of a result, of a goal obtained, something that has come to pass very gradually and is experienced with much travail."[10] This idea Jung repeats as conclusive so that even if the existence of a psychic substance having an active role may be called an illusion, it "may be for the psyche an extremely important life-factor, something as indispensable as oxygen for the body—a psychic actuality of over-whelming significance."[11]

It is therefore possible to state that the nature of the Self relies upon the proposition that as a psychic object, it pursues an *active role* in psychological growth. At least one inescapable influence on Jung's philosophical orientation toward the Self having such a role is his interest in Schopenhauer. The unconscious, according to Schopenhauer, is activated by the primordial force of will: "The will is the substance of man, the intellect the accident; the will is the matter, the intellect is the form; the will is warmth, the intellect is light."[12] This influence recognizes the will as a primordial force that bestows a purpose lying in the unconscious.[13]

The connection between an underlying purposefulness and the dynamism of the Self has become the manner in which the Self is explained, rather than as a passive center with no purpose. This arises because Jung accepts "will" as the primary cause of any form of creation, as he embraces Schopenhauer's will as a "Primal Will" that created the world,[14] and, more

---

[8] CW 7, § 291
[9] *Ibid*, § 399
[10] *Ibid*, § 404
[11] CW 16, § 111
[12] Schopenhauer 1958, p. 201
[13] Jarrett 1981
[14] CW 5, § 591

importantly, as that which is the basis for libido or psychic energy that is in a "ceaseless forward movement."[15] The analysis of the nature of the Self therefore requires that the Self be considered as containing a dynamic principle that leads to its multiple functions and makes it a *substance*. This is verified in Jung's statement that the "will then has the self as a possible aim."[16]

Self as a Brain Function

The tendency that naturally arises from assigning will or purpose to a psychic phenomenon in the mind is to raise the possibility that it may be an aspect of brain functioning. This evokes the structural problem that Freud highlighted in his *Project for a Scientific Psychology*[17] that assigning any aspect of mind to the brain, creating it as a corporeal substance, would make it a function that requires it to be stimulated by the sense organs. In the case of the Self, this cannot occur as it is entirely internal and is not activated by other than itself. Jung, however, suggests that the Self may be of such central importance for mankind that it is in the brainstem:

> I have long thought that, if there is any analogy between psychic and physiological processes, the organizing system of the brain must lie subcortically in the brain-stem. ... The reason that led me to conjecture a localization of a physiological basis for the archetype in the brain stem was the psychological fact that besides being specifically characterized by the ordering and orienting role, its uniting properties are predominately affective. I would conjecture that such a subcortical system might somehow reflect characteristics of the archetypal form of the unconscious.[18]

This statement reflected earlier comments Jung made when analyzing the transcendent function as a form of unity: "The meaning and purpose of the realization, in all aspects, of the personality originally hidden away in the embryonic germ-plasm, the production and unfolding of the

---

[15] *Ibid,* § 680
[16] CW 6, § 183
[17] Freud 1895
[18] CW 3, § 582

original, potential wholeness."[19] In a letter written in 1955, he was more specific that the Self archetype is "embedded in the brain structure and is physiologically verifiable: through electrical stimulation of a certain area of the brain-stem of an epileptic it is possible to produce mandala visions (*quadrature circuli*)."[20]

Using this suggestion from Jung, neurobiologists tested this proposition through a meta-analysis of research into subjectivity and the brain and conclude that the Self is inherited as an "instinctual archaic action-foundation" of the brain that expressly confirms Jung's view. They explain "that before reflective self-consciousness is developmentally acquired by an infant, a primordial affect form of Self already exists, expressing itself in the form of affective-psychic intentionality that interacts effectively, in an evaluative way, with the material, deterministic world."[21] Affective-psychic intentionality refers to the emotional dynamics that spring from the core.

This significant finding of a Self as a primordial human response to the need for ordering explains why it appears as preexistent. The symbols of the Self therefore appear, as Jung puts it, to "arise in the depths of the body."[22] It suggests many possibilities that arise from it being a brain function, such as that it may mediate the relation between brain functions and the manner in which the psyche develops and functions. As it is thereby an archetype, it then manifests involuntary in consciousness,[23] so that it creates itself as an intrapsychic center by invoking a process of circumambulation that seeks its own realization.

This mechanistic description of the Self as setting the structure or pattern for the activities of the brain is what Jung probably intended, as can be seen in a letter to Aniela Jaffe, his secretary and collaborator. He was responding to her dream where a copper pot first was vibrating from electrical wires and then by an external, atmospheric electric oscillation. Jung proposes the pot as a symbol of the Self and makes other relevant, but somewhat obscure references:

---

[19] CW 7, § 186
[20] *Letters,* Vol. 2, pp. 258-9
[21] Alcaro, et. al. 2017, p. 10
[22] CW 9.i, § 291
[23] *Ibid*, § 260

> What is so peculiar is the symbolization of the Self as an
> apparatus. A 'machine' is always something thought up,
> deliberately put together for a definite purpose. Who has
> invented this machine? The Tantrists say that things
> represent the distinctness of God's *thoughts.* The machine
> is a microcosm, what Paracelsus called the 'star in man'.[24]

In these terms, the Self is being described as an apparatus because it has
a definite purpose of imposing a predetermined pattern and a process to
advance its orienting functions. His use of "apparatus" and "machine" is
as a mechanism that yields a purposeful result, such as in his describing
how a dream is created: "Nature has an apparatus that makes an extract
of complexes and brings them to consciousness in an unrecognizable and
therefore harmless form: this is the *dream.*"[25]

The references to Tantra and Paracelsus in the quote expand this
patterning as an underlying structure emerging from God's will that
requires that humanity live in accordance with that pattern. The reference
to Tantrist ideas is of all things reflecting God's thoughts, and thus the
pattern is of the divine macrocosm. This arises in a Tantrist text that
contains directions for the use of fixing on images in a mandala structure
that can reveal the macrocosm,[26] implying that these are prescribed
structures set by God. More clearly, the reference to Paracelsus, the 15th-
century philosopher, is of a mechanistic structure he proposes that is the
microcosm, so and individual "carries the stars within himself" of the
macrocosm.[27]

The Self as a brain function is the originator of an ordained pattern, and
psyche is the receiver of the core pattern as constituting a core Self, which
then creates symbols to be transmitted to consciousness. In speaking of
the soul as psyche in 1912, prior to his formulation and use of the term
the Self, he sets out this important structure:

> The determining force (God) operating from the depths is
> reflected by the soul, that is, it creates symbols and images,
> and is itself only an image. By means of these images the

---

[24] *Letters,* Vol 1, p. 326
[25] CW2, § 822, emphasis supplied.
[26] CW 12, § 123
[27] Paracelsus 1952, p. 154

soul conveys the forces of the unconscious to consciousness, it is both receiver and transmitter, an organ for perceiving unconscious contents… But symbols are shaped energies, determining ideas whose affective power is just as great as their spiritual value.[28]

Self as Entity

The Self is not only a brain function but, when projected, becomes an aspect of *mind*. The projected core Self then becomes an apparent entity that has a role in psyche. This entitic creation of an inner being in the mind space, of no certain location, is similar to Freud's idea of a dream censor as a psychic entity that prevents dreams from emerging when it is necessary to protect sleep. The inevitable consequence of making an aspect of psyche an entity was clear to Freud when he said of it that it is not a "little manikin or spirit living in a closet in the brain."[29]

From a functional point of view, the existence of the Self as an entity in psyche is psychologically necessary. It is more important for it to be an entity than merely concluding that it is in the brain because, as an entity, it initiates a process for its realization. The Brazilian psychologist Walter Trinca explains that the formation of an inner, active object is responsible for our experience of existence as an individual. This occurs because it allows us to sense ourselves, as he puts it, "united with ourselves in an indivisible presence experienced in the intimacy and essence of our personal life."[30] It is, in his beneficent interpretation, necessary to declare the Self as an entity in psyche as it is what "puts in order the processes involved in living" because, "Although the various parts of the personality are discordant among themselves, a fundamental and single nucleus serves as their reference point, which has the basic function of integration."[31] This is certainly the benefit that Jung realized in his dream of the Self of a center as an ordering principle that fosters meaning.

---

[28] CW 5, § 425
[29] Freud 1915-1916, p. 140
[30] Trinca 2001, p. 565
[31] *Ibid,* p. 566

If it is useful that the Self is to be regarded as an entity, it will then have numinosity as it can only be of relevance *if it has an effect*. The essence of all numinous experiences or psychic objects is that they have the potential to alter consciousness. In the *Terry Lectures*, Jung explains that the experience of the numinous, which would arise by an overwhelming manifestation of the Self, "causes a particular alteration of consciousness."[32] It is therefore necessary for there to be numinosity to bring it the attention of consciousness where it can be realized. It is the creation of the Self as an entity that gives it numinosity and increases the opportunity for it to have an ordering role.

It is perhaps appropriate to say that whatever may direct or give coherence to our lives is functionally present for the purposes of psychology as an inner being, an entity with agency. If it is ascribed agency, as is likely if an entity is declared to exist or else its significance is indeterminable, then it also follows that is not acting randomly but is directed to a goal. The goal in the case of the Self is to orient consciousness and move the individual toward its realization so when it so manifests, its capacity to orient and confer meaning increases.

The inclusion of the Self as the critical agent has the immediate consequence that it is not just envisaged as an inner entity but becomes idealized as the living center of psyche and thus the most important goal. This results from a linguistic declination where the points of entity, agency, and goal come together to enforce an ontological proof that also implies a process. It then must be given form and content once it is a process even more than when it is a mere entity, as first explained by Freud when writing about Thanatos, the death instinct:

> We need not feel greatly disturbed in judging our speculation
> upon the life and death instincts by the fact that so many
> bewildering and obscure processes occur in it – such as one
> instinct being driven out by another or an instinct turning
> from the ego to an object and so on. This is merely due to
> our being obliged to operate with the scientific terms, that
> is to say with the figurative language, peculiar to
> psychology. We could not otherwise describe the processes
> in question at all, and indeed we could not have become
> aware of them.[33]

---

[32] CW 11, § 6
[33] Freud 1920, p. 60

Once the entity and process are named, it impacts the psychological process. Robyn Ferrell indicates that the consequence of naming a psychic object is an induction into the reality of the unconscious, as it gives the ego something substantial to relate to and to possibly integrate.[34] Integration is then desired because it aligns with the innate push to recognize one's self in contrast to reliance on the ego, which is marked by its unreliability, tensions, and contradictions, and cannot be the source of stability.

The benefits of naming and isolating an internal object, however, blurs the understanding of its true nature and its contents. The difficulty, to quote from Pierre Bourdieu, a critic of Freud, is that named objects become "camouflage through form…(and) remain misrecognized in practice; though present as substance they are absent as form; like a face hidden in a bush."[35] Their true nature is hard to discover because acknowledging the named object creates it as a singularity that forces acceptance of every one of its traits in full and in all its various forms and appearances, conferring endless explanations of its function based on hope and potential. When named, however, these complications in analyzing its functions or theoretical bases in the end have little impact on its overall purpose.

A useful means to examine the Self as a brain function as well as an entity in psyche is to understand the nature of the agency in psyche that it creates. In her analysis of the alchemical work *Aurora Consurgens*, von Franz explains the role of the soul as expressed by St. Thomas. The soul, he asserted, does not create things directly, *it has no agency*, but as a "second cause" it has functions which "flow from the essence of the soul as from their principle…."[36] It is, using this idea, that the Self as brain function does not have agency but is responsible for the *principle* that it encompasses, its essence. That principle is centering of the being, an orientation in life's journey as having a center in order to reduce the chaos through uniting the opposites. This creates the potential for unity hinted at by the Self through symbols, and it is then the psyche that realizes that possibility. The Self as an entity then appears best as the progenitor of a principle emerging from its patterning, rather than an entity that has deliberate agency in all manner of a person's life.

---

[34] Ferrell 1996
[35] Bourdieu 1991, p. 142-3
[36] von Franz 2000, p. 173-4

The Self as brain function is not yet conclusive. It is still a working hypothesis that, as preexistent patterning, dovetails well with the idea of the Self as archetype. The possibility of it being a brain function or an archetype is not as important as the phenomenon that indeed there is an innate pattern of the Self that can be projected onto psyche. It is this, as the center or central principle presented in psyche, that governs psychological growth. It does not matter if the originating Self is seen as brain function, God, an entity, a personality, or an archetypal force: What is critical to its existence is the manner in which the individual becomes aware of what is projected. The Self can thus be said to an intrapsychic function that originates and projects the principle of order and therefore is manifested as a process of both the originating patterning and the projection onto psyche as the means by which symbols of the Self lead to its realization.

Self as Archetype

When Jung reported his dream of the Self in *Memories, Dreams Reflections*, it was referred to by him as leading to "the principle and archetype of orientation and meaning."[37] He did not then claim the Self as an archetype but rather only a center he had come upon in the context of an ordered city. The archetype he found was one of *orientation* that has one common meaning as an archetype responsible for compensating for disorientation, as Jung explains: "Mandala symbols appear very frequently in moments of psychic disorientation."[38] It is the center that represents the emergence of a principle that appears to be an archetype. In this way, the Self as the center is, at least, a *representation* of the archetype. The transposition of a concept of wholeness to the term "Self" raises the question of whether it can be said that there is a separate archetype of the Self.

There are several bases upon which the Self can be considered an archetype. The first is that it is the representation of an innate underlying pattern that provides an orientation for psyche. Jung constantly confirms that the term archetype coincides "with the biological concept of the

---

[37] *Memories,* p.199
[38] CW3, § 582

'pattern of behaviour.'"[39] In a lecture on schizophrenia in 1958, he refers specifically to a mandala, and that suggests an archetype arising by the localization or patterning of wholeness in the brainstem.[40] This aspect of the Self, the patterning, fits the characteristic of an archetype because an archetype is a "congenital and pre-existent instinctual model."[41] It appears therefore as an archetype, more specifically because as a model it has a functional "disposition to produce the same, or very similar, ideas."[42] Here the fit is clear, and the patterning is a firm basis for the Self to be considered an archetype.

Another basis is that the archetype of the Self exists because it has numinosity as a center and is that which reflects the ideal of wholeness. The Self, especially as an ideal, points to its potential transcendent quality, what Jung calls, "transcendent wholeness."[43] In speaking in another context of a hero with "more than human stature," Jung confirms that "psychologically (he is) an archetype of the self, his divinity only confirms the self is numinous, a god, or having some share in divine nature."[44] Christ is thus said to represent "this most important and most central of archetypes" and this archetype of the Self "as symbol of wholeness" becomes, as an elevated quality, the "ruler of the inner world."[45]

The archetype of the Self is not suggested as a God and is not intended to postulate a God,[46] but the archetype is similar, "an analogy,"[47] as it displays profound numinosity. The existence of the Self as an archetype is therefore persuasive because its numinosity raises the level of a generated symbolic image that then, because of that power, "seizes hold of the psyche."[48] These symbolic images are, he states, "archaic, mythological images"[49] that provide a "*dynamism* which makes itself felt

---

[39] CW 3, § 565
[40] *Ibid*, § 582
[41] *Ibid*, § 729
[42] CW 5, § 155
[43] CW 3, § 498
[44] *Ibid*, § 612
[45] *Ibid*, § 576
[46] *Ibid*, § 89n29
[47] *Aion*, § 79
[48] CW 7, § 110
[49] *Ibid*, § 188

in the numinosity and fascinating power of the archetypal image."[50] It is therefore a collective image[51] shared by all of humanity of an "instinctual pattern"[52] and an "organizing schema."[53] In this way, the patterning and the numinosity combine so as to express the archetypal nature of the Self that is the representative and holder of both.

Jung clarifies that the archetypal representations of Self are in images and ideas, such as the center as an image, and wholeness as an ideal. These are symbols coming from the unconscious but "should not be confused with the archetype as such," because the archetype is "irrepresentable."[54] Thus, it could be said that the Self is an archetype primarily because it is an unknown instinctual pattern that exists but cannot be fully represented, and also because it is so numinous that it can be conflated with Christ or a God image.

Ultimately, it is the similarity to the Christ image that confirms for Jung that there is an archetype of the Self.[55] The comparison is awkward as the realization of the Self will always be imperfect and can never reach perfect roundness, so it does not accord with an archetype forged from the perfection of the Christ. It creates a paradox as we are otherwise drawn to completeness, but it cannot be attained. As will be discussed, Jung does explain that Christ is imperfect as a symbol of the Self because it does not contain the necessary quality for completeness: evil. However, the practical effect of the comparison is that the Self can always be suggested as an unreachable "ideal," as it will produce incomplete symbolization of perfected wholeness.

The best answer of why the Self should be considered an archetype arises by combining all of those aspects derived from its innate nature that are functional in relation to its realization. Each of these aspects are intertwined; for example, when the Self is equated with the idea of the God-image, it draws on that comparison and *points* to an archetype. This concatenation with the God-image creates the Self as having numinosity, fascination, and transcendental potential. It is then functional as

---

[50] *Ibid,* § 414
[51] CW 8, § 722
[52] *Ibid,* § 856
[53] CW 11, § 281
[54] CW 8, § 417
[55] *Aion,* § 123

combining and drawing in other aspects of the archetype that offer the realization of wholeness by consciousness. In addition, it derives the category of archetype, without any comparison, as offering the opportunity for order in psyche because it provides an "instinctual pattern" of wholeness repeatedly, one of the "definite forms in the psyche which seems to present always and everywhere."[56]

The archetype of the Self is psychologically the basis for the pattern that, in turn, determines the symbols that are projected. Until projected, the patterning is in, as Jung explains, a "quiescent, unprojected state,"[57] which then becomes, because of the fascinating and transcendent qualities, a projected state when psyche is activated. This suggests the realistic view that as an archetype, the Self should be considered primarily a pattern of wholeness, a primordial image, that creates in psyche an atmosphere that when psyche is activated, causes psyche to produce symbols of the underlying pattern of wholeness. It creates what Jung refers to as a "circumambient atmosphere."[58]

The Self as archetype, as combining all its aspects, appears as the *primary force of existence*, so that it will "relate other archetypes to the centre."[59] All aspects of psyche are drawn into the atmosphere of the center and, if those images cannot be integrated into consciousness, they are, because it is an archetype, still "forced to manifest itself directly in the form of spontaneous projections."[60] These can be projections of power onto a mana personality or a feeling of calm in a setting of a peaceful location that have arisen to serve the patterning. It is not every symbol that is relevant when projected but only those that carry with it numinosity that approaches the force of an archetype. This is what occurs in an archetypal presentation because, although the nature of the patterning cannot be comprehended, a symbol that is projected "possesses a transcendence"[61] because of its numinosity;[62] when it is so constellated by symbols, its power lies in its ongoing fascination.[63]

---

[56] CW 9.i, § 89
[57] *Ibid*, § 142
[58] *Aion*, § 257
[59] CW 11§ 757
[60] CW 10, § 635
[61] *Ibid*, § 854
[62] *Ibid*, § 10
[63] *Ibid*, § 224

Michael Fordham, writing about archetypes, suggests that there is a wide gap between psychology and neurophysiology so the issue of the biological, instinctual nature of the archetype as a patterning of wholeness is unclear as a matter of psychological fact.[64] In a review of the issues surrounding the debate about the nature of archetypes, John Merchant addresses the specific question of whether archetypes such as the Self are related to their biologically inherited structures. He turns to genetics to conclude that there is a reciprocal relationship between genes and developmental growth arising from the external environment. "In this approach, it is acknowledged that genetic starting points do exist but critically, final outcomes are not predetermined."[65] This is sufficient in terms of the Self to postulate that the primal idea or principle of wholeness as a genetic starting point arises as an initial schema presented to an infant, but the form it takes is influenced by developmental factors. In this way, the core Self, in this contemporary analysis of archetypes in terms of developing neurobiology, is that starting point, so the symbols of the Self come from environmental interactions.

Stages of the Self

The symbols presented in dreams and visions are reflections of those image schemas but require a constellated or activated psyche in order to appear. This constellation, or concentrated gathering together of thoughts and feelings, can be activated by a complex[66] and a feeling tone.[67] The constellation then creates symbols that have to be interpreted in a "meaningful and appropriate manner" for any transformation to take place.[68] The presence of the Self as an archetype and principle suggests five connected stages:

> 1. *Patterning*: The first stage is the unconscious presence of the primordial, archetypal patterning of order, the core Self, carrying the principle of wholeness.

---

[64] Fordham 1957, Chap 1
[65] Merchant 2019, p. 798
[66] CW 3, § 558
[67] *Ibid*, § 606
[68] CW 5, § 351

2. *Activation of Psyche:* The second stage is that this patterning is activated in psyche by a strong feeling tone.

3. *Symbolization:* The third stage is that the patterning of the Self, once activated, gives rise to symbols.

4. *Reflection:* The fourth stage is that the symbols are the subject of projections in psyche, revealing the inner patterning to consciousness.

5. *Realization:* The fifth stage is that consciousness—the ego— realizes the Self as a center and, to the extent manifested, totality.

The Self is (at least) this five-part process as the originator of a patterning of wholeness that is activated in psyche, that forms symbols as its way of presenting the underlying pattern, as a connection being made with the symbols and an inner orientation by way of projection, and is possibly fully realized in consciousness. The first three stages remain in the unconscious while the last two specifically require the direct engagement of consciousness.

The stages repeat endlessly but cannot be said to be linear, but rather recursive and repetitive. George Horgenson proposes that the Self experiences different periods where it is engaged but then is disrupted yet improves by constant reorganization: "From this point of view, it seems to me that we cannot posit that the self exists as some stable state of affairs that, in theory can be attained."[69] It does not, in this analysis, need a progressive, linear system of stages for it to be realized; it is a circumambulation around a center that is sometimes engaged and is often disengaged. There are also no necessary times between stages; all stages can manifest instantly as in a numinous experience, can be spread out over only a short time, or develop gradually over a lifetime.

Horgenson suggests that the instability of the process means that it cannot, in theory, ever be attained. There is clearly no completed state of the Self that appears to be attainable in contemporary society; the claimed experience of others is no guarantee of individual realization of the Self. For every person, there is only an innate pattern of wholeness, and there

---

[69] Horgenson 2004, p. 76

will always be times when there is an activation of psyche and symbol formation. This is a process carried out within what Jung calls "an impersonal psyche,"[70] common to all, but that varies in its expression for each individual in terms of recollection and realization.

---

[70] CW 9.i, § 314

Chapter 6. The Self as Pattern

Jung's emphasis is to present that there is an innate pattern of wholeness that exists in the unconscious on the psychoid level, what Jung calls "quasi-psychic."[1] It is therefore akin to an instinct that is below the threshold of awareness and therefore cannot be known directly by consciousness. When it is realized experientially through symbols in dreams, visions, and fantasies, it reveals itself, but it feels alien, as not us. As he explains, as it is unknown in that psychoid level, "wholeness is thus an objective factor that confronts the subject independently of him."[2] When confronted with an objective factor, it will always seem prior to consciousness, as if it has always been there.

The dimension, substance, and blueprint of that pattern contained within the archetype of wholeness cannot be understood. Wholeness as a term for the archetype is therefore only a conceptual category as its forms can arise by an infinite variety of patterns; it is not possible to indicate how it will express itself for each individual. Jung only implicitly recognized the surrounding structure in his 1927 dream by concentrating just on the center. Accordingly, one symbol of that patterning can just be a center, another can include the close periphery, yet another can extend out to the heavens. The archetype varies in its form and presentation because, according to Jung, "everything archetypal which is perceived by consciousness seems to represent a set of variations on a ground theme."[3] Jung confirms this specifically in relation to the mandala, his prime reference for wholeness, where he calls it the "structure of a center" and adds, "although it looks like the structure of a center, it is still uncertain

---

[1] CW 8, § 368; 380
[2] *Aion*, § 59
[3] CW 8, § 417

whether within the structure the centre or periphery, division or non-division, is more accentuated."[4]

The archetypal nature of the pattern of wholeness is perhaps best illustrated not through dreams but by its revelation through numinous experiences where it is arises by direct perception. A numinous experience, which includes mystical and religious experiences, is where the ego is overwhelmed by a non-ego, archetypal force that yields a truth that has the effect of altering consciousness. In its highest form as a "unitive" experience that implies merger with the Godhead or nothingness, realization occurs where the ego is suspended and wholeness is perceived as the interconnectedness of all things. This intimation is the ultimate goal of the archetype as interconnection means a complete unity of opposites. The extent of that unity that is revealed is then translated differently through the individual's tradition and capacity to be receptive.

From a psychological viewpoint, a numinous experience is indeed the most direct revelation of the archetypal pattern of wholeness. For this reason, Jung was clear that "the approach to the numinous is the real therapy and inasmuch as you attain to the numinous experiences you are released from the curse of pathology."[5] This makes the patterning that is revealed as that which is buried at the core of being that echoes the paradigmatic ideal, oneness. Accordingly, when it is displayed symbolically outside a numinous experience, it is only an approximation but, as such, conveys the tendency toward oneness.

As a tendency, the archetype can be seen to be a force as well as a function in psyche. Jung explains that "there are archetypal forces in the background which have existed for an indefinitely long time as preformative psychic forces."[6] He uses "preformative" in relation to archetypal forces suggesting a "preconscious psychic tendency," independent of time and space, that as a function, "continually causes similar statements to be made, as is the case with mythologems, folklore motifs, and the individual formation of symbols."[7]

---

[4] *Ibid*
[5] *Letters*, Vol. 1, p. 377
[6] CW 11, § 459
[7] *Ibid*

The Emergent Pattern

Although the archetype of wholeness appears as a psychic force, Jung divides up the force as instinct and archetype respectively: "The inborn mode of *acting* has long been known as an *instinct,* and for the inborn mode of psychic apprehension I have proposed the term *archetype.*"[8] The instinct is thus the mode of acting, the tendency that contains the force, and the archetype is the manner in which it appears in psyche. The distinction is unnecessary as they work as a pair to operationalize the archetype and promote the appearance of the pattern. The activation of the archetype of wholeness is therefore that which is innate in psyche and its symbolic representation, so that its appearances "frequently occur at the beginning of the individuation process, indeed they can often be observed in the first dreams of infancy."[9] Gerhard Adler records visions of wholeness in a child of 5,[10] and the existence of a primary Self in infants is the basis of Michael Fordham's thesis about the Primary Self.

Jean Knox points out that genes do not encode mental images, such as the pattern of wholeness, "but instead act as initial catalysts for developmental processes out of which early psychic structures emerge."[11] The innate archetypal patterns are then dynamic, "emergent structures" resulting from the interaction of genetic coding with the environment and, therefore, how they manifest cannot be predetermined. She explains that the structures are underscored and fostered by a "self-organizing" principle that arises out of psyche's ongoing process of reanalyzing material that is then recoded into more complex representations.[12] This dynamic view of the creation of patterned structures suggests that the processes begin with a primary structure, a core Self, that is developed by ongoing self-organizing seeking of order in psyche. Psyche then is in constant flux as it is emergent and which is accordingly subject to different manifestations.

Most importantly in understanding the Self, Knox proposes that the underlying structures create "image schemas" that operate at a primitive

---

[8] CW 6, § 624, emphasis supplied.
[9] CW 9.i, § 278
[10] Adler 1979, p. 5
[11] Knox 2004, p.4
[12] *Ibid,* p. 6

level for infants, including fundamental locational and structural distinctions such as "part-whole."[13] This would make the whole a primal structure that brings together the parts, a primitive aspect of the simplest image schema at the core of being. She calls the "image schema" a "mental gestalt:" "the mental structures which underpin our experience of discernible order, both in the physical and in the world of imagination and metaphor."[14] This accords with the Self being a mental structure that is emergent by an ongoing self-organizing psyche. It is a variation in the theme that the archetype of wholeness as a pattern also embraces the instinct toward wholeness, although nothing turns on the distinction.

This precognitive image schema forming a primitive psychic structure is the pattern that unites the parts, not by a full blueprint of wholeness, but rather by a gestalt or principle of the ideal of a whole. If this is the case, there is nothing to prevent that early gestalt becoming a more complete pattern as it emerges from necessity because of conflict or by aspiration due to the success of self-organizing. It is the *principle* of the ideal of a unity that is breaking through in a numinous experience because the revelations are mostly associated with feelings of oneness and interconnection. Following her reasoning, emergence is of the proteiform parts that are combined and reflect the principle of wholeness, the core foundation of which is deeply embedded in the infant psyche. The early image schema does not require a complex patterning as it is the preformative principle of unity. When it is projected onto psyche, the incomplete geometric structures are what Jung calls the "most important" symbols.[15] The symbols are, most significantly, *echoes* of the principle of unity, always implicit but not actualized in the preformative structures. This reinforces the idea that the early patterning is not a schema of center and circumference or a complete unity, but rather the existence in whatever form, of the principle of the whole and its parts.

The emergence of all-oneness in a numinous experience, the ultimate shared ideal, brings into question the theory of an "emergent" archetype that is a core Self that changes and matures by the manner in which it interacts with the environment. If this is the case, the emergence of the

---

[13] *Ibid*, p. 8
[14] *Ibid*, p. 9
[15] *Aion*, § 351

primal archetype that overwhelms the ego in that experience would be, in its ultimate realization, varied. The ultimate experience is the truth of interconnectedness and an absolute unity that is complete wholeness and only varies in its interpretation in a tradition. It is not an emergent core that varies by environmental influences but the original form of all-oneness. It suggests that the archetype as the *principle* of wholeness never varies, and that is what is realized both as a numinous experience and the realization of the Self through individuation. As a principle or ideal, its symbols will always vary and be altered by developmental influences.

This analysis highlights that the Self, as far as neurobiological insights can take us, exists in the first stage as a basic pattern, a "scaffolding," as Knox calls it,[16] of an early psychic structure, an image schema, that is emergent and always echoes the principle of a unity. She asserts, and her arguments are persuasive, that this is the "most developmentally sound model for the emergent nature of concepts and the earliest form they take, that of image schemas …"[17] In commenting on Knox's findings, John Merchant adds that image schemas are laid down in an infant due to the full range of all developmental experience.[18] In a later commentary, Merchant provides clinical vignettes to conclude that there must be, at least, a developmental starting point that accords with the image schema model of Knox.[19]

Patterning and Transcendence

There is a starting point of a core Self as an instinctual patterning that generates a principle that points to wholeness and is effective in early psychological development. Research on the primary images of whole-ness, summarized in a meta-analysis of neuro-archetypal perspectives, confirms that the core patterning of the Self, its primordial form, is a non-cognitive but affective state so that "*before* reflexive self-consciousness is developmentally acquired by infants, a primordial-instinctual form of Self already exists …"[20] This conclusion follows from the 2010 work of Antonio Damasio that there is, what he calls, a "protoself" that gathers

---

[16] Knox 2003, p. 9
[17] Knox 2010, p. 529
[18] Merchant 2006
[19] Merchant 2016, p. 71
[20] Alcaro, et al. 2017, p. 10, emphasis supplied.

images and generates feelings about the body, orienting to the principle of wholeness, and, thereafter, a "core self," where there is interaction between the organism, represented by the protoself, "and any part of the brain that represents an *object-to-be-known*."[21] In this manner, there is a buildup of the core Self over time as it interacts with other psychic elements and is developed and shaped by environmental influences, always with the formative protoself as an organizing principle that reflects the ideal, the principle of unity.

The neurobiological research suggests the possibility that there may be a wider dimension to the core Self than is apparent by its interaction with the environment and other elements of psyche. This wider dimension arises because its preexistence leads to the specific question of whether it arises from an evolutionary or transcendent source. The issue of the driving force behind the emergent Self arises in Analytical Psychology because Jung describes that we all have an *urge* to self-reflection, and therefore individuation operates by gathering "what is scattered and multifarious" and returning it to its original form.[22] This original form is beyond time and space, as it is the "Primordial Man," an inherent unity prior to differentiation. Consequently, the urge, he asserts, is to return to undifferentiated unity, which existed before time and is what he calls an "approximation of the Self."[23] It is, therefore, both evolutionary *and* transcendent because, as the Self is eternal, or at least appears as eternal as preexistent to consciousness, it suggests a way forward for psyche, operating in the guise of an instinct. Jung calls this primal urge and orientation a "repristination" or "apocatastasis," both signifying a restoration back to an *original* condition or a reconstitution.

This dimension places the core Self as an undifferentiated unity to which we seek to return. It does not arise from a mechanistic image schema that is emergent. Instead, Jung is referring, in evoking repristination or apocatastasis, to a return to the *cosmic* pattern of primal wholeness; in alchemical terms, it is the idea of restoration of the macrocosm through an individual's realization of the microcosm,[24] the force behind the pattern of the Self and also the ultimate revelation for the Self. This transcendent

---

[21] Domasio 2010, pp 180-1, emphasis supplied.
[22] CW 11, § 401
[23] *Ibid*
[24] CW 13, § 372

quality is a point of difference from the Self as image schema, instinct, archetype, or archetypal force because, as Jung also refers to it, it is the "original state of oneness" associated with the God-image that bridges the split in the personality caused by conflicting instincts.[25] He therefore refers to the Self as an "original propensity to wholeness" found in the power of the transcendent that he compares to the Zen *satori* experience of "show me your original face."[26] In this transcendental formulation, it is not the presentation of the Self as a pattern produced by the brain or as an archetype, although that still exists, but rather by the idea to achieve unity through realizing the cosmic oneness. This oneness is a *psychic germ* patterned on the macrocosm, that has, Jung states, a "static character," as it is not a force that acts on anything but is the true foundational substrate.[27]

Reducing this theoretical complexity to a functional idea, the macrocosm is order on a cosmic scale, and therefore the microcosm reveals that principle of order on a psychic level. That would suggest that the archetype of wholeness is no more or less than *order in psyche,* and it can be evidenced by the protoself and the core Self, the early appearance of symbols of order, and the urge to have it restored. Any symbol or intimation of order is, *ipso facto,* the Self.

Eric Neumann supports this view of the Self having an underlying archaic existence, but from a different position that links it to a function. In his 1949 work, *The Origins and History of Consciousness,* he employs "centroversion" as the term for "the innate tendency of a whole to create a unity within its parts and to synthesise their differences in unified systems."[28] This is consistent with the idea of the pattern of the archetype representing the principle of order in psyche, as well as the neuro-biological emphasis on wholeness as an image schema, a self-organizing principle, or an innate, preconscious tendency. The process of the whole seeking to unite the parts, Neumann adds, "manifests itself as a directive center,"[29] upon its realization as the center of psyche. The directive center,

---

[25] *Aion*, § 73
[26] *Ibid*, § 263
[27] CW 8, § 70
[28] Neumann 1954, p. 286
[29] *Ibid*, p. 287

as Jung found in his dream of 1927, is then the most prominent symbol of order in psyche.

In a later 1953 Eranos lecture, Neumann goes further and postulates that the Self "during centroversion, directs the ego's development and individuation, and in large measure fatefully guides the unified whole of the individual life processes and of his or her way of coming to terms with the world."[30] This gives the Self the character of an entity that has a primordial function of directing centroversion through a preexistent tendency. The *urge* to return to the original order may arise by the self-organizing function in psyche, by the Self as an entity that is the possible manifestation of that function, or by God's will. It is just as clear to say that the original starting point of order, the *principle* of order, is the foundation upon which the infrastructure of psyche is built and therefore psyche is always oriented to that order.

The innate tendency, the urge, represented by a process Neumann terms centroversion, is born and activated out of the primordial soup, the *Pleroma* in the *Seven Sermons,* which Neumann calls the "uroboros," a circle of chaos and amorphousness.[31] This is again consistent with the Self consisting of a principle reflecting order that is the counterbalance to that chaos and amorphousness, in order to move away from that uroboros state toward a unity. This places the pattern of wholeness at the beginning of time as an innate tendency, the nature of which can never be understood. In the section called "Retrospect" in *Memories, Dreams, Reflections*, Jung lays it bare: "I exist on the foundation of something I do not know."[32] This something, Neumann makes the Self. It is the original *prime mover*, a phrase used by Aristotle, that directs life by presentation of an ordering out of chaos, leading Neumann to the conclusion that the Self is "as godhead."[33]

The attribution of the Self as the origin of consciousness rather than invoking other forces such as the divine spirit, the soul, or that developed in various creation myths, will occur because it matches the idea of the Self that Jung promotes as the unknowable metaphysical answer to the

---

[30] Neumann 1989, p. 46
[31] *Ibid,* p. 281
[32] *Memories,* p. 358
[33] Neumann 1989, p. 47

mystery of existence. In that case, it can be said that the patterning exists to present the principle of order based on the macrocosm, the cosmic design echoed in our being. Neumann's leap of assigning to the concept of wholeness that it *seeks* a unity perhaps takes it too far. As well, it creates an inconsistency because, as the germ of consciousness, it has no identifiable energy to carry out its function. It was therefore necessary for Neumann to find a source of energy by creating a link with the innate tendency found in nature and biology, postulating that the power derives from matter.[34]

The individuating energies or agency Neumann suggests do not appear to arise from psychic energy because the Self's archetypal pattern is a substrate in the psychoid region with no direct energy. Jung refers to that which lies in the psychoid as "form"[35] *as well as* a function,[36] suggesting it may include the tendency for wholeness as just another aspect of the substrate. Ann Addison argues that Jung did not confine the psychoid to a single orientation, and it could indeed embrace a primordial form as well as a purposeful intent.[37] On the other hand, it could be said that it has an intent only in the limited sense that it is a primitive structure as are other image schemas that have a function of creating the infrastructure upon which psychological and biological processes build.

This idea of reaching for purpose for the core Self is a consequence of its empirical presentation. When the Self appears in the form of symbols in dreams and visions, it certainly can be linked with an apparent purpose as a reason for its appearance. It could be looked at then as a necessary process, or otherwise it would fail to reach the principle of ordering, for as Jung points out, the Self is only known through its symbolization and not by it being a psychoid pattern.[38]

The pattern is therefore the first stage (or state) of the Self that cannot be known, but yet is the primary basis of its existence; the neurobiological research offers emerging proof that it exists in that form. As a consequence, when looked at as a step in the process moving toward

---

[34] *Ibid,* p. 49
[35] CW 13, § 350
[36] CW 8, § 382
[37] Addison 2018
[38] CW 9ii, § 351

wholeness, it is that which stands behind the pattern and forms the pattern. In a study of the issues around the psychological self that relate to the integration of the ego, it was explained in another, just as accurate way, that there is a "radar toward a Gestalt-like whole that cannot yet be delineated in a clear-cut circumference but that displays its contours ..."[39]

Patterning and Purposefulness

It is hard to logically deny that the core Self pattern has a purpose, an intention to present the principle of wholeness. The psychologist Ira Progoff describes a psychic, protoplasmic image "moving towards a purpose."[40] To propose a purpose, the pattern must also include an impetus for its realization as containing a biological need. This will occur if the definition of the archetype is expanded, as suggested by Knox and Merchant, as a process interreacting with the external, social environment for the purpose of developmental growth. This purpose continues because, as Merchant suggests, the nature of that Self is then activated in that process by intense affective experiences, which accounts for the engagement of psyche with the patterning of the Self.[41] An express purpose or the inherent purpose emerging from that process of an emergent Self suggests an underlying force directed to its realization.

The alternative analysis suggests that the images are glimpses of wholeness, but there is no directed intention. Michael Fordham states that when the images are considered the Self, which may have a purpose, it is only hypothesization:

> The images, Jung often makes clear, cannot be the *actual self*, at best they are representatives of it. They are approximations representing states of relative wholeness which alone are possible, while bits of ego are split off and function as observers. Therefore, when the images are referred to as *the* self, this is not theoretical but a metaphorical statement—or hypothesized thinking.[42]

---

[39] Weger & Herberg 2019, p. 259
[40] Progoff 1959, p. 121
[41] Merchant 2012, pp. 156-7
[42] Neumann 1985, p. 22, emphasis supplied.

The arguments for the Self having intention and purpose have weight if it is perceived as an entity or it is suggested that it generates a process. This is not true, however, if the Self is seen instead as having different stages, not necessarily connected. For example, the first stage of the basic imprinting of a pattern of geometrical order does not require ego consciousness, and there is no evident purpose yet emerging. This incipient wholeness can create order only when the symbols are integrated by realization of a center. Before then, it can remain indefinitely as unconscious, psychoid, and archetypal through its primordial preexistence without intention.

It is also not a definite process that can be assigned purpose because it is not realized by the collective; it requires a long process of individuation or a numinous experience that may be assumed to be rare. It is not significant that what follows from the first stage may evoke the possibility of wholeness, as it is just a pattern that may not be realized. If it has a purpose, it should always reveal itself for its own realization, which is not the case.

This is not the end of the analysis, as this takes away the Self's potential and disconnects the patterning from the result. It ignores the nature of the Self as a hope, a goal, a life's work, a principle, and a salvation. It is true that these end-states are very distant from the primal patterning, but can the two ends of the Self, primordial image schemas and achievement of wholeness, still not be reflective of each other?

Fordham makes the claim that wholeness achieved is complete oneness without the presence of ego.[43] The achievement of that perfect wholeness is, except in rare cases, by a profound mystical experience that alters consciousness. It will never be perfectly achieved in any event as it includes the far reaches of totality and instincts, as Jung indicates: "We know that a man can never be everything at once, never quite complete. He always develops certain qualities at the expense of others, and wholeness is never attained;"[44] Wholeness is "an ideal goal that had never been reached."[45] In alchemy, the perfect wholeness, the rotundum, is never attained. This suggests that the purposefulness of the Self is not in

---

[43] Fordham 1985, p. 22
[44] CW 6, § 955
[45] CW 8, § 366

the primal patterning or the end state but as a process, as it is able to display itself and achieve some presentation resulting in greater adaptation toward wholeness. Therefore, it is the sum of all of the stages that defines the purpose of the Self.

It is clear that perfect wholeness is not the underlying nature of the core of the Self as the primal image schema. What is in us, instead, is the principle of a pattern of order where disparate parts, the opposites, can be brought together to some degree. It then evokes a *tendency* toward order that is represented by the patterning and the possibility of realization of some connection with wholeness. It is both the metaphysical principle of the macrocosm and primitive patterning within all beings that are the two pillars of the Self. The Self, Jung explains in accordance with this proposition, is "both God and animal ... the totality of his being, which is rooted in his animal nature and reaches out beyond the merely human towards the divine."[46] The tendency and the ensuing process to achieve ordering are the bases of purposefulness as the wholeness that is within us already at the animal, instinctual level as the patterning and that which is also the idea of the macrocosm being realized as the individual's microcosm. Jung explains this again when he quotes the statement of Schiller: "we must be at liberty to restore by means of a higher Art this wholeness in our nature which Art has destroyed."[47] Therefore, the principle of wholeness in the core Self includes the patterning *and* the metaphysical idea of the macrocosm, not as an entity or a force, but rather as hidden in the "embryonic germ plasm, the production and unfolding of the original, potential wholeness." There is thus, according to Jung, "instinctive wholeness"[48] that reflects the tendency of the core Self and its process that may be said to appear as a purpose.

If this view is correct, then there is no need to assign any agency to this first stage of the Self. It is a primitive pattern of the structure and idea of wholeness that, because it exists, joins with other image schemas to form an infrastructure for developmental changes initiated by an emergent personality. Mario Jacoby, in analyzing Heinz Kohut's view of the Self, indicates that Kohut asserts that there is a point of origin of the Self for

---

[46] CW 5, § 460
[47] CW 6, § 113
[48] CW 8, § 190

an infant: a primal, rudimentary Self, based on the infant's innate potentialities. He compares this to Neumann's idea that the Self exists as a substrate; in Neumann's terms, an underlying preexistent *field* that directs the growth of consciousness.[49] It is the clay out of which the individual is formed and progresses. For Kohut and Neumann, it is indeed the prime mover, not because it is imbued with energy by the tension of opposites or is an entity with purpose, but because of the miracle contained in the germ of its existence of the innate tendency toward a principle of wholeness or a unity.

Michael Fordham, in *Explorations into the Self,* explains his ideas of the Self in a way that confirms a purpose for the Self as the basis for psychic integration. He poses a "primary state of integration" in an infant that must then deintegrate to come into relation with the external environment, still carrying with it the elements of that original wholeness. Accordingly, states of integration and deintegration define the development of the individual. Fordham explains, "The deintegration postulate is thus useful because it provides a bridge between wholeness and its expression in relatively formed archetypes referring to it."[50] The deintegration derives from the primary integration that he refers to as wholeness, so developmentally, "it will be a number of small nuclei the result of deintegration, which soon become linked together so that one can speak of a center of consciousness as in Jung's writings." He concludes, "In that process the integrating function of the self plays an essential part," and "In progressing from unknowing to knowing, it can be understood the self has a powerful influence in the formation of mental structures whilst still remaining unknown and unknowable."[51]

In this view of the Self, the existence of an integrating function, perhaps what Neumann would call an innate tendency, is responsible for the process of development because of the unity from which all is born. In terms of expression of that wholeness, Fordham states, "the central archetype, with its clear relation to the central ego, expresses it best in that is (sic) transcends and unites opposites."[52] Fordham adds that not only does it have the integrative function, but because it unites the

---

[49] Jacoby 2017, p.55
[50] Fordham 1985, p. 32
[51] *Ibid,* p. 32
[52] *Ibid,* p. 33

opposites, it is more likely to manifest itself. This conceptualization of the Self is that it derives its significance as a primal, fundamental tendency to integration caused by the potential for order as wholeness or unity. The Self, in his interpretation, is a mental structure or what influences that structure as it is initial wholeness out of which the process of individuation begins, initially by deintegration. Fordham's approach is consistent with the emerging neurobiological findings and the contemporary ideas of archetypes being emergent.

All of these categorizations of the Self establish that it is, in its first stage, order through imprinting as well as fostering the principle of it aiming for "completeness and perfection."[53] It is a preconscious wholeness that exits as instinct, potentially to become a symbol projected by psyche, and that raises the possibility that it may be realized empirically through the principle it contains. The symbols of the Self are the empirical proof of the "*a priori* existence of potential wholeness."[54] It is the wholeness as imprinted and as a tendency and principle that is the first stage or aspect of the Self.

---

[53] CW 7, § 186
[54] CW 9i, § 278

Chapter 7. Activation of the Pattern

The patterning of the Self as constructed, varied, and as a principle of order and orientation is a product of an archaic brain function. Psychologically, it is an archetype that it is emergent, presenting in varied forms according to its interaction with the environment. This is an activity that takes place at the unconscious level, not understandable by consciousness. The processes by which it appears are speculative; when Jung spoke of the idea of how the virtual center is found, he concludes, "I have no theory as to what constitutes the nature of these processes."[1] However, there are conditions that evoke the process that leads to the presentation of the Self to consciousness.

The means by which the Self is presented to consciousness is primarily twofold. The first is by a numinous experience where the pattern pushes past the resistance of the ego and overwhelms the conscious mind with sufficient affect that it alters consciousness. This is not a psychological path that can be replicated through psychoanalysis, but one where the wholeness in the form of interconnectedness arises unbidden. The second is by the archetype of orientation displaying itself through symbols that arise in dreams, fantasies, visions, and all of the other ways that the unconscious reveals itself.

The fact that the symbols of wholeness are found in the dreams of young children does not suggest that the patterning requires any particular level of conscious awareness in order to present symbols. In an adult, the patterning can lay dormant throughout a lifetime, or the symbols may be so vague as to never be noted. In the context of psychoanalysis and the discovery of the Self, there is one possibility as to what may give rise to symbols that are of such significance that they can break through and become apparent. This is the idea of the psyche being activated or in a

---

[1] CW 7, § 365

state of excitation by the occurrence of strong affect. The basis of this idea is that order and orientation are then the intrapsychic solution to the disorientation that evokes that affect.

This idea of strong affect initiating an increased concentration on the Self is speculative, and its appearance could be just as well assigned to God's will or the interplay of unknown processes and forces in psyche. However, the concept that the Self is purposeful, drawing us to a center in the midst of chaos, suggests that that purpose can only be achieved by the presence of strong affect. This is an idea that Jung supports.

Strong Affect and Psyche

The Self is a solution, an evolutionary answer to chaos and disorientation, so it a sound idea that it will arise when there is a conflict in psyche that needs resolution. When affect seeks a solution, the numinosity of the Self as center and the ideal of wholeness respond. Until psyche is activated, the Self is "asleep," as Jung describes it in a Kundalini Seminar. It is lost in the conscious world of day-to-day activity, in the mundane, the victim of "instincts, unconsciousness, of participation mystique, where we are in a dark and unconscious place."[2] There needs to be an awakening, a breakthrough by the activation of psyche, and this occurs practically when there is strong affect that leads to the psyche being enlivened so that which is non-ego, the Self, appears.[3]

The manner in which strong affect awakens the psyche to provide a solution is a subject matter of neurobiology. Jaak Panksepp argues that there is a primitive, self-centered awareness in the brain that is an aspect of the core Self, and strong affect in waking consciousness results in brain stimulation of that Self.[4] This research as to the connection between affective states and the stimulation of the deep, evolutionary layer of a primal self-organizing structure is augmented by more recent research that the link begins "only when intense enough to mandate deliberate actions."[5] In the absence of that intensity, background emotions such as feeling warmth upon greeting a friend, does not begin that connection.

---

[2] Jung 1996, p. 14-5
[3] *Ibid*, p. 39
[4] Pankseep 1998
[5] Vandekerckhove 2014, p. 3

The core Self is confirmed in later research as revealing itself when there are "intense affective feelings" because they correspond to the brain's microwaves.[6] The activation of psyche by strong affect occurs, in neurological terms, because "affects may be viewed as transpersonal forms of experience pervading a primal subjective field that is not yet individually conscious (or self-conscious), since it lives within an undifferentiated organism/environment continuum."[7]

In Jung's theories concerning synchronicity (acausal, meaningful occurrences), he provides several similar insights in a psychological frame as to how the psyche becomes activated by strong affect. One insight he provides is that strong affect narrows consciousness, so focus is lost, and this strengthens the unconscious so then an individual "comes under the influence of unconscious instinctual impulses and contents."[8] When psyche is intensely disturbed, the Self as both patterning and promise of unity arises because it offers the intimation of a solution. In explaining how these instinctual contents are brought to bear on psyche, Jung states, "we are finally compelled to assume that there is in the unconscious something like an *a priori* knowledge or an 'immediacy' of events which lack any causal basis."[9] This refers, when applied to the Self, to the possibility that the activation of psyche by strong affect caused by events and circumstances, draws on the underlying pattern of wholeness to resolve a situation because the solution is there already as *a priori* knowledge.

The method of activation is explained in both neurological and psychological terms, but the question arises as to why the affect must be intense to activate psyche, thereby bringing the archetype into play. Evoking the patterning in the face of affect may not normally occur because, on reflection, it will be intimidating to confront the powerful impact of the Self on the ego as an *a priori* "other" in psyche; psyche does not want to be overwhelmed by such unconscious, primordial contents. As well, when there is only a hint of the Self that begins to vaguely come into focus for the ego, the danger is that the ego may begin to identify itself with the Self as it is desperately seeking a solution. This

---

[6] Alcaro, et al. 2017, p. 7-8
[7] *Ibid,* p. 8
[8] CW 8, § 856
[9] *Ibid*

can become a critical situation because it is impossible then for the Self to project symbols or to be realized by the ego, when the ego is "dissolved in identification with the self."[10] An individual can lose the steadfastness of the ego by the introduction of the Self that results, as Jung puts it in relation to the Self, in a "blurring or darkening of ego-consciousness and its identification with a preconscious wholeness."[11] This is a warning that Jung makes clear in relation to the process of activation of the psyche where the true Self may be prevented from prematurely appearing or the individual will be a "nebulous superman with a puffed-up ego and a deflated self" that loses the *scintilla*, the soul-spark.[12]

Strong, perhaps overwhelming affect is, however, necessary for the activation of psyche to usher in a solution. It will not necessarily overwhelm the ego because it is likely that this activation creates a non-cognitive, *anoetic* state, where the core-Self experiences its own sense of itself, a "reflexivity … applied to the psychoid patterning process …"[13] It has not come into consciousness in that situation but still becomes known by a sense of itself. It has little psychic energy initially, so it appears, as Jung calls it, as a "hunch," or a "spontaneously arising presentation."[14] This form of non-cognitive self-awareness can be attributed to the reflective instinct of turning inward for a solution so that "there ensues a succession of derivative contents or states which may be termed reflection or deliberation."[15] The consequence is that an activation of psyche by strong affect can be considered to manifest in an early form of knowing, a presentation, that is necessary for the psyche to then make the Self known further by symbols and then realization because "Reflection re-enacts the process of excitation and carries the stimulus over into a series of images, which if the impetus is strong enough, are reproduced in some form of expression."[16]

The activation of psyche that calls upon the Self yields an indirect but immediate knowing that arises at the time of the strong affect. This is

---

[10] *Ibid,* § 430
[11] *Ibid*
[12] *Ibid*
[13] Alcaro, et al. 2017, p. 5n6
[14] CW 6, § 180
[15] CW 8, § 241
[16] *Ibid,* § 242

consistent with the theories of the 18th-century philosopher and theologian Friedrich Schleiermacher, who emphasizes that knowing must be an *immediate experience*, a link between the problem and the Self as solution. Later deliberation about the Self arising from its symbolization will offer a discourse, but it is initial feeling or hunch that creates the connection with the non-ego by immediate self-consciousness and an "immediate affective state of being certain that a particular representation is beyond dispute." It is that feeling that "best expresses the way that the subject has and knows its own being as unity."[17] This suggests that the activation of the psyche, where the Self can be awakened, is because it is presented as of immediate significance as a hunch or perception that causes its significance, numinosity, and continued evolution.

It is strong affect that can be said to *begin* the process of the core Self interacting with the higher cognitive processes that evoke that core because of the presence of new instances of affect in consciousness. It is finally through consciousness that the Self is seen to exist because is realized by the ego, but it starts with strong affect, as Jung explains in relation to the mandala as one of the symbols of order: "they occur in patients principally during times of psychic disorientation or re-orientation."[18]

This idea of the core Self activated because of strong affect is consistent with future stages of the process of individuation. This occurs because its initial presentation sets it up as a magnet that pulls consciousness toward it so that further affective circumstances move the stages along toward the goal. Its nature as a primordial instinct, suggested by neurobiology, expresses that when it is presented initially at the level of an unconscious hunch through instinctual reflectivity or self-noticing, it must then start a process of symbolic representation and realization.

Formation of Self Symbols

The next stage or component of the operation of the Self, approaching this as having a logical sequence, is where psyche, activated by strong affect, brings forth symbols that are modeled on the underlying patterning

---

[17] Klemm 1997, p. 175
[18] *Aion*, § 60

of order. The formation of symbols is a process that takes place entirely in the unconscious, most likely producing endless symbols that reflect the pattern of wholeness, but it is only those symbols that are *realized by the ego* that have psychological significance. According to Fordham, the Self will "function mostly in the unconscious until it gets realized,"[19] suggesting that it will possibly be productive in many ways once psyche is enlivened.

The symbols come forth from an activated psyche that already has embedded within it the instinctual, primal ground of a core Self with its archaic patterning. A symbol, according to Jung, derives its "motive power" from just such primal instinctual processes, although he admits its appearance can be also explained metaphysically from the unknown "spiritual side."[20] The mechanism of symbol presentation is a complex topic that he explicates throughout his writings and is most easily observed experientially in relation to the Self. Jung explains that every symbol "does not of its own accord step into the breach" until it "acquires a higher value than the unconscious."[21] As the Self is the most profound of archetypes, the *central* archetype, as Jung calls it,[22] its symbols have a higher value than those generated by other archetypal foundations. This concept is also suggested in neurobiological research where the appearance of symbols invoke higher order representations over a large portion of the cortex,[23] perhaps giving those that offer an orientation greater significance than the pull of other symbols or processes.

The strong affect that activates psyche is not only for the production of symbols, but also for the Self being ultimately realized by the ego as "only in moments of affectivity can fragments of the unconscious come to the surface in the form of thoughts and images."[24] It may also be that in times of distress, the potential for unity or the mere idea of it, commences a process for "differentiation of the self from the opposites."[25] The symbol

---

[19] Fordham 1985, p. 31-3

[20] CW 5, § 338

[21] CW 6, § 182

[22] CW 10, § 771

[23] Borghesani & Piazza 2017

[24] CW 7, § 323

[25] CW 6, § 183

that then appears of the Self is one that accordingly "rises to the surface"[26] in response to the intimation that there is a basis for orientation in psyche.

Energy for Symbol Formation

The creation of symbols in psyche does require some quantum of energy, a point Jung explains in his discussion of the importance of Schiller's idea of the effect resulting from extracting the Self from the opposites. This is the basis for Self symbols and the ego's involvement with those symbols. The energy, according to Schiller, arises when the warring instincts are held apart from the ideal of unity, a process which then enlivens the possibility of a potential solution. In Jung's terms, the patterning itself contains the tendency, ideal, or principle of a potential unity, thus that incipient wholeness is the source of that discrimination, and therefore it creates the needed energy for symbol formation. This proposition explains that the possible ideal of a unity, when it arises in the chaos of daily life, then creates libido, psychic energy, as the Self begins to be detached from both the opposites (and the conflict) and psyche then is directed inward to seek that ideal. It then "sinks into the unconscious, where it automatically takes possession of waiting fantasy material, which it thereupon activates and forces to the surface."[27]

This approach of energy for symbolization arising from seeking the ideal or principle of unity is tied into Schiller's concept of the will, which Jung refers to as "God's will." This is a concept frequently encountered when Jung speaks of the Self; the Self, in fact, is considered by Jung as an act of "God's will,"[28] which "does not decide between the opposites, but purely for the self."[29] In this approach, the psychic energy, generated by the tension between opposites, is introverted and employed by the Self as an ideal of unity where it is used for the creation of symbols. The power of that "will," Jung assumes, is "by an antecedent psychic process which through intellectual or an emotional judgment, or a sensuous desire, provides the will with a content and an aim."[30] As a result, the strong affect and the will that seeks a solution combine in ego consciousness as

---

[26] *Ibid*
[27] *Ibid*
[28] CW 11, § 237
[29] CW 6, § 183
[30] *Ibid*, § 178

a longing to find a unity that then activates the formation of symbols of the Self.

It is reasonable to assume that the longing for order in the face of chaos can build to a point where a solution is a highly charged imperative. At that point, that longing is introverted, powerful and seeks wholeness, not as something known, but rather as an ideal. The buildup of the libido that is necessary to bring forth the symbols arises from the continued, unresolved tension of opposites as there may be no initial hope that there is a solution. A moral decision between good and evil, to give an example, creates enormous internal tension that produces energy in one's psyche, without orientation to an ideal or principle. This needs some form of unity that offers a new approach, a new thing that Jung expresses as not necessarily following rationally from the conflict:

> In practice, opposites can be united only in the form of a compromise, or *irrationality*, some new thing arising between them which, although different from both, yet has the power to take up their energies in equal measure as an expression of both or neither.[31]

The accumulation of libido that comes from the tension of opposites fosters an introversion, as one turns within for an answer, as he explained in relation to more austere, spiritual solutions in Indian practices of self-denial. These practices, called *tapas*, are where the complete detachment from all affective ties to objects takes form as an "inner self an equivalent of objective reality, or a complete inside and outside."[32] As objective reality, this makes the Self equivalent to a "third thing," some unknown, perhaps irrational ideal of unity, activated by the tension of opposites, deriving energy from the conflict and the ideal of a solution, that activates psyche to produce symbols.

In practical terms, a possible unity is always able to be imagined, even though it is not able to be understood conceptually, because it exists in the mind as a hope, as we all strive to live our potential by removing conflict. That potential calls on the psyche because of the compelling need to somehow balance the tension of opposing forces that then fosters

---

[31] CW 6, § 169, emphasis supplied
[32] *Ibid*, § 189

a premonition and thus enlivens the desire for a balancing place within us—a center—or a third thing. Jung expresses it clearly in relation to mandalas and the geometric symbol of the Self of squaring of the circle:

> Their basic motif is the premonition of a centre of personality, a kind of central point within the psyche, to which everything is related, by which everything is arranged, and which is itself a source of energy. The energy of the central point is manifested in the almost irresistible compulsion and urge to become what one is, just as every organism is driven to assume the form that is characteristic of its nature, no matter what the circumstances.[33]

In terms of the derivation of the energy for the production of symbols of wholeness, this is a critical passage to understand. The source of energy can be said to be the power arising from the mere existence of a center (the ideal of a unity) that when presented as a premonition or a hint that can arise from its activation in psyche, *manifests* in an individual through a desire to reach a solution. This is the principle of order that is the Self arising by the mere possibility of its existence and by an early presentation of some form of order in psyche that is the energy and directed will that activates the psyche. This occurs because that hint aligns with the drive to become what one can be.

To become *what one can be*, as an underlying drive in every individual and in nature, is echoed by Jung in the idea that the Self is "green," as proposed by the 12th-century mystic Hildegard of Bingen, whom Jung calls an "outstanding personality."[34] He quotes Hildegard to say that the Holy Spirit she proffered as coming from God is a cause of "greenness," the presence of spontaneous growth and productivity in nature.[35] The green, which she calls *veriditas,* is also a state of being where one is receptive to the ideal of unity as that is consistent with what one can be.

Light plays a part in the greening as she declares, "I have always seen a light in my soul."[36] This is a relevant reference as to what specifically is

---

[33] CW 9.i, § 634
[34] CW 13, § 42
[35] CW 11, § 151
[36] CW 13, § 42

providing energy. This elevates light to a role in the nature of the Self as an incorporeal force that enlivens a symbol, as it did for the tree in Jung's dream and thus the source of energy for the Self. Light, luminosities as Jung calls them, are also associated by him with complexes that inhabit the unconscious that have "a luminosity of their own."[37] He does not directly associate light as the source of energy for the Self, but it is included as it is relevant to the idea of greenness.

The characteristic of greenness and the push of becoming what one can be are useful in reflecting the importance of the ideal of unity that, according to Jung, has "the highest significance of the unconscious."[38] It has this importance because it brings into focus that the unconscious is productive, the fundamental theme of psychoanalysis. This positivist ideal of the existence of a productive Self is what grants it the highest content of psychic energy. This is, in practical observation, the situation that accounts for the appearance of the Self when there is strong affect where the need to find some balance is because the conflict is agonizing. Day to day, as Jung proposes, it is always the subjective feeling value *in consciousness* brought on by the affect such as powerful emotions that have the highest affective rank in the ego; "the affective value increases the higher up the scale you go: ego-consciousness, shadow, anima, self."[39] This approach grants to the Self, *upon ego recognition* even as a premonition, the highest affective value so that it can be an object of consciousness. It reinforces the idea that an ideal of unity based on the hunch or presentation of wholeness aligns with the will to become what one can be as the source of energy for the formation of symbols, so the Self can present itself to consciousness.

It, therefore, in this expression of the Self as an ideal, means that the energy contained in the Self is either derived indirectly from the tension of opposites, or the corresponding compulsion to seek a balance, or most likely both. It may be that either is called upon for energy at different times or are part of the same expression because the idea of a unity is derived from the tension of opposites. In either form, the creation of symbols of the Self results from the oppression of the conflict caused by

---

[37] CW 14, § 270
[38] *Aion,* § 57
[39] *Ibid,* § 53

the opposites; "they generally appear in time of psychic disorientation in order to compensate a chaotic state."[40]

This energy from the tension of opposites and a premonition of a solution activates the psyche that then creates symbols for the Self's realization to realize that unity, to make it a psychological fact that provides orientation and meaning. As Jung puts it in discussing the Hindu deity Lord Shiva and the energy of the *Pleroma*, "Creation therefore begins with an act of division of the opposites that are united in the deity. From their splitting arises, in a gigantic explosion of energy, the multiplicity of the world."[41] The opposites hold that energy, that tension, to the point where something new is bursting forth to hold that division and not before, so then the psyche can take up the patterning and display the symbols.

The idea of the opposites clashing to create energy is embedded in Jung's work and can be traced back primarily to the idea of the "transcendent function," which Jung first wrote about in 1916 in similar terms:

> The shuttling to and fro of arguments and affects represents the transcendent function of opposites. The confrontation of the two positions generates a tension charged with energy and creates a living, third thing ...a movement out of the suspension between opposites, a living birth that leads to a new level of being, a new situation.[42]

This is his starting point, reaching back to his Zofingia lectures, the *Seven Sermons,* and thereafter as an explanation for all psychological development. The Self as an ideal of unity, coincidentally a third thing, is therefore its innate pattern, as well as a process in that direction, and finally as the healing solution.

---

[40] CW 8, § 870
[41] *Ibid,* § 632
[42] CW 8, § 189

Chapter 8. Symbols of the Self

The activation of the psyche by strong affect is the catalyst for the formation of symbols of wholeness. The symbols may vary depending on the emergent archetype's interaction with the environment and, in any event, only receive significance when they are the focus of ego consciousness. Jung explains when this occurs: "the self is felt empirically not as subject but as object, and this by reason of its unconscious component, which can only come to consciousness indirectly, by way of projection."[1]

The Self is an object because it is seen as other than consciousness, it is numinous, and is preexistent. It becomes an object at its earliest presentation as an intimation or hunch, even before it arrives for conscious reflection. It comes to conscious reflection because, as Jung explains, it achieves significance as its symbols receive a projection of unconscious patterning and the ideal of unity. The realization of that match between these unconscious aspects and the symbols makes those symbols profound and likely to alter consciousness. Projection is the most important means by which a symbol becomes a symbol of the Self because it is a mirror reflection of the unconscious patterning of order and the principle of wholeness.

There are those symbols that appear to be direct representations of order and orientation. Jung states, "when the Self emerges from the unconscious, for example, in dreams, it is always pictured as a *center*."[2] It is so revealed because it is closest to our thoughts and sentiments, as a centering process is consistent with the instinctual orientation to homeostasis. When the symbol is a center, the projection of the ideal of unity is a tight fit, and the bridge to conscious realization is patent.

---

[1] CW 9.i, § 315
[2] Jung 2014b, p. 99, emphasis supplied.

As the Self is completely other to the ego, Jung explains, "Because of its unconscious component the self is so far removed from the conscious mind that it can only be partially expressed by human figures; the other part of it has to be expressed by objective, abstract symbols."[3] In the essay *The Psychological Aspects of the Kore,* Jung lists examples of those human figures that can be considered as symbols of the Self. The examples are of figures as pairs to suggest that they are a coincidence of opposites and that which create the ideal of unity: father and son, mother and daughter, king and queen, god and goddess.[4] King and queen, god and goddess strongly suggest a possible *conjunctio* or the ideal of unity. The same is not true of "parent and child," which he also lists, but they are of the same effect as he explains in the case of Demeter and Kore. They were mother and daughter (only in the sense that Kore was her maiden form), so they are the opposites of older and younger that adds the dimension of a more integrated personality.[5] This adds potential relevancy to the quality of any symbol that provides meaning and orientation and therefore is sufficient to be a symbol of the Self. In the case of Demeter and Kore, they provide a wider outlook that shares in the "eternal course of things" and also that their recognition confirms the connection of generations, providing meaning in life.[6] None of these figures relate to a center but require a deeper interpretation with an eye on the empirical goal of the Self to assess their relevancy.

Jung explains why these figures and not only the symbol of a center, are sufficient, "At first, the Self is always something simple, something little or cheap." This could reflect, as the statement is made no clearer in its context, that the center is a simple, direct symbol that so fits into that category. As well, the figures suggesting a unity are the precursors to a center. In discussing a king appearing in a dream, one of the figures that he lists, he states, the "king, the crown, the phoenix, the saint, the savior, even the deity" are the "center toward which everything is oriented."[7] These symbols suggest a center but are second order, as their significance is oblique. They do add a numinous dimension as supraordinate

---

[3] *Ibid*
[4] *Ibid*, § 315
[5] *Ibid*, § 316
[6] *Ibid*
[7] Jung 2014b, p. 100

personalities, as in the case of a king. The importance of the phoenix that appears different from the others, is explained in an analysis of a child's dream where Jung points out that the phoenix burns itself every 500 years and therefore represents immortality,[8] so it contains the ever-present concept of the Self. This last idea, although obscure, addresses another aspect of the Self as immortal and raises the possibility that if any symbol does not address the particular aspects for the Self's realization directly as a center, it can still do so if it evokes other qualities of the Self, such as preexistence. The symbol will not necessarily be the simple display of the Self as center but is reliant upon that superadded quality of numinosity.

The symbols are, accordingly, of a wide range and are relevant if they can lead to a projection arising out of the unconscious patterning to respond to the ideal of order and orientation. The tendency for projection, as Marie-Louise von Franz so clearly expresses, is that that an archetypal structure appears in two forms: "on the one hand, as an inwardly experienced flare-up of emotions and affects and, on the other, as a fascinating image that is, however, regarded as belonging to the outer object."[9] This accounts for the wide range of symbols that serve as Self-symbols on the basis that they draw on the inner patterning that has been activated to seek a solution and are a numinous presentation of a symbol that can hold the projection.

The next category he lists in the *Kore* essay are animals as theomorphic symbols. "Theomorphic" is that which is imbued with a divine aspect that thus includes "powerful animals," such as the dragon, snake, elephant, lion, bear, and "the spider, crab, butterfly, beetle, worm, etc."[10] These symbols are not directed to a center but rather to the primal power of the Self in terms of its numinosity. This creates the Self, properly understood as having that power, as supraordinate, reflected in its symbols and echoing the ideal of unity. He also includes plant symbols that are particular flowers that carry some aspect of that transcendent power, such as the lotus and rose. He explains the effect of these arises because "the unconscious supplements the picture with living figures ranging from the

---

[8] Jung 2008, p. 198
[9] von Franz 1995, p. 33
[10] CW 9.i, § 315

animal to the divine, as the two extremes outside man, and rounds out the animal extreme, through the addition of vegetable and inorganic abstractions, into a microcosm."[11] In this explanation, the symbols are pointing to transcendent level that suggests the patterns in the animal and vegetable layers as a microcosm, a key theme of order and orientation, and that also corresponds with the existence of spirit as well as matter, joined as the ultimate unity.

These animal and plant symbols of the Self are rather indeterminant and require deduction, rather than offering a clear, direct presentation, as Jung had in his dream of a geometric structure and a center. It means that many symbols can be expanded into a narrative about the Self as any surroundings or the presence of others can be taken to increase the idea of a microcosm. These are, however, not as helpful or direct as symbols that create order by the more profound symbols of a "mathematical structure," because they do not appear to carry out the function of the Self to "compensate a chaotic state or as formulations of numinous experiences."[12] Mathematical structures can be seen in a numinous experience, the highest form of realization of the Self, by a clear orientation to the whole, a connection with the cosmos, and the indelible truth of interconnectedness. These ideal mathematical or geometrical structures are, he adds, "as a rule," quaternities, arrangements of four, the primary symbolic expression of wholeness.[13]

The symbols that are indirect and require amplification should indeed be considered as possible symbols of the Self but may not have the gravitas that is needed for the difficult translation into a psychic fact. If everything is considered a symbol of the Self, that is theoretically correct because the Self includes all of what is conscious and unconscious. However, what Jung is seeking by these symbols is empirical proof, a psychological fact, by making them attract consciousness to seek its realization and therefore there may be caution necessary in making symbols into more than they convey.

Among mathematical structures, a quaternity appears the most important as it is used in his most detailed work on the Self, *Aion,* as the perfect

---

[11] *Ibid*
[12] CW 8, § 870
[13] *Ibid*

balance that is the basis of the ultimate *conjunctio* of spirit and matter.[14] This serves the theme of symbols that suggest the great unity between the fundamental opposites of inside and outside, of spirit and matter, that is also repeated in his mention of the microcosm. He refers to symbols that are a quaternity or directly suggest a microcosm as joining psyche with "extremes outside man,"[15] to present that the Self holds within itself the primal opposites of inside/outside and spirit/matter.

It does seem that aside from human figures of importance that have unique attributes approximating the idea of the Self, such as the capacity to guide or be of transcendent significance, other figures, to be relevant, must have a numinous quality. By having numinosity, making it stand out from the background of all the material that is revealed from the unconscious, a symbol must at least point to the principle that is the ideal of unity. This is the most appropriate test as it fulfills the possibility that it can then be translated into a movement toward order in psyche.

The attributes of the human figure that are most likely to elevate it to a symbol of the Self, and give it numinosity, are those that imply that it has agency in guiding the hand of fate. It is too abstract to extrapolate that such a figure is then a center but rather it can become important as it offers an orientation. Those symbols are therefore an adjunct to the symbol of the center. The idea of a human figure having power to orient that gives it numinosity suggests that it would be benevolent by that association and would lead one in the right direction. However, this may not always be the case because the Self can produce figures as symbols that may seem benevolent but instead are negative and destructive.

A dream figure appearing as a symbol of the Self but having dark or sinister attributes is explained by Jung in discussing the spirit in fairytales. He refers to the frequency of the spirit-type symbol of an old man who performs a "spiritual function or an endopsychic autonomous action of some kind."[16] The "endopsychic autonomous function," the opposite of a spiritual function, derives its scope from Jung's analysis of the phrase in the Tavistock Lectures in 1941. He describes it as that which is responsible for fostering a negative, subjective reaction because of dark,

---

[14] Stein 2012, p. 30
[15] CW 9.i, § 315
[16] CW 9.i, § 403

unconscious forces that are not available to the ego.[17] It can cause an *invasion,* as he calls it, where the Shadow side rules the conscious condition. In terms of the spirit, and equally for the figures of the Self, this can create a disturbing figure that is evil.

The role of this endopsychic autonomous function in establishing a possible figure for the Self, although unpleasant and difficult to amplify into a center or ideal of unity, is not to be underestimated. As will be mentioned in discussing the dangers of totality, the Self holds all opposites that necessarily include all that is dark and evil; the dark figure therefore can be a symbol of the Self. The origin of the concept of the endopsychic function comes from Freud, who phrases it as the "obscure recognition (the endopsychic perception, as it were) of psychical factors and relations in the unconscious (that) is mirrored—it is difficult to express in other terms (in the external world)."[18] This, for Freud, explains paranoia as the projection of delusional representations on the world. Endopsychic functions are clear illustrations of the internalization of those objects and probably were influential in the psychoanalytic theories of object relations.[19] This means that the Self can be found in negative projections brought about by the symbol of a dark figure. This is not a comfortable place to expand the notion of the Self in order for it to be realized, but it indicates that a Self-symbol is not restricted to the center and can include any characteristic of the Self in whatever form it arrives in consciousness.

Dark figures as Self-symbols require that the Self be described as a process whereby Shadow figures emerge in order to create the conflict of opposites that suggest the ideal of unity. They arise because the Self as emergent has created this form, such as when trauma has recast the orientation of psyche. They can easily be subsumed under the idea that the Self has agency and has engendered this form to create a clarifying effect on psyche. All of those explanations require the advancement of an intermediate argument as to the Self's operation and may not be the best symbols upon which the operation of the Self should be based.

---

[17] CW 18, § 37- 43
[18] Freud 1901, p. 258-9
[19] Fairburn 1944

If Self-symbols are cast so widely, there is an argument that all dreams are indirectly pointing to the Self, as it is a process initiated by the activation of psyche, or they are possibly created by the Self for its own realization. Consequently, it has been proposed by a commentator that each dream is a mandala, and the contents of the dream are therefore within a circle, irrespective of the symbolism.[20] Jung is, however, specific about symbols that are important and therefore have a higher value in psyche because of the Self fundamentally being focused on offering an orientation. In the Definition section that is attached to the *Psychological Types* essays, he provides a definition of a "Symbol" as "the best description or formulation of a relatively unknown fact, which is none the less known to exist or is postulated as existing."[21] Therefore, it is only the symbols that can convey the unknown fact of the Self as order and orientation that are relevant, and it is not possible to extrapolate from every symbol or the existence of a dream.

Symbols of the Self can be relevant if they reflect the key elements of the Self where order or an orientation is significant and there is a basis for a linkage with the ideal of unity. The main symbols are therefore what Jung calls the "organizing dominants" that suggest a geometric form such as a center, a circle, and a quaternity, the last being a perfect balance.[22] They are the most appropriate symbols to receive a projection of the core Self. What follows for him in this preference for the dominants is the existence of lesser forms but with the same structuring basis, such as a cross or square or a radial arrangement.[23] It is the geometric design that makes a symbol one that is providing orientation and order, such as any sphere or a clock. The geometric symbols are the most important because they align directly with the archetype of orientation that brings a new foundation to psyche as they directly draw consciousness into an ordering schema. They then become empirical, practical symbols, as Jung expresses that they become important in the processes of realization: "Its empirical symbols … very often possess a distinct *numinosity,* i.e., an *a priori* emotional value, as in the case of a mandala."[24] The high emotional value of order

---

[20] Bogart 2009
[21] CW 6, § 814
[22] *Ibid,* § 611
[23] CW 7, § 401
[24] CW 6, § 791

and orientation, giving those symbols profound valence in psyche, leads to their numinosity because they are the "same as those mankind has always used to express wholeness, completeness, and perfection."[25] The wider idea of wholeness attracts other, more transcendent symbols if they also suggest the ideal of a unifying force, such as a magician, a priest, a quadrangle, a ring, and the like.

Symbols of Totality

The introduction by Jung of the term "totality" is the single most confusing aspect for symbolization because of the incorrect or incomplete translation of the 1935 Eranos lecture. This confusion is also due to the continuous use in expressing totality of transcendent parallels with their own dimensions and significance, such as the Hindu *Atman*, wherein the term totality is used or presupposed. There is also the natural thirst for widening the term, seeking the deity, echoed in every prayer and meditation. In her book, *Dreams of Totality,* Sherry Salman extensively explores the images of totality in dreams. As she explains, these images are a "living record of symbols that have left traces of the evolutionary path of the human mind and heart."[26]

Salman is using totality in its transcendent, cosmic sense, and therefore she naturally equates symbols of totality with mythopoetic images.[27] Symbols of this kind suggest totality with no boundaries, but this is not, however, how Jung uses the term in relation to symbols of the Self. In his Definition of the Self, he states, "the self appears in dreams, myths and fairytales in the figure of a 'supraordinate personality' such as a king, hero, prophet, saviour, etc., *or in the form of a totality symbol,* such as the circle, square, *quadratura circuli,* cross, etc."[28] These latter symbols must be understood on the basis that totality for Jung was the totality *of psyche* that is understood *via the center*, as he explained in his 1935 Eranos lecture. This suggests that the revelation of a situated center will possibly allow the realization of the totality of psyche, to the extent that it is manifested. The literal translation from the 1935 lecture is: "*I also refer to the center as the Self by which the totality of the psyche is to be*

---

[25] CW 7, § 186
[26] Salmon 2013, p. 17
[27] *Ibid,* p. 21
[28] CW 6, § 790, emphasis added.

understood at all." This totality expressed in this manner is all that is conscious and unconscious contained within the center that is described in that lecture as the circumference of the circle and does not suggest directly or indirectly any connection with the cosmic or supraordinate transcendence.

A symbol of totality, it is noted in the Definition, is distinguished from symbols of a supraordinate personality; it is only a geometrical structure that suggests an orientation to a center which has a circumference that is the extent of psyche: conscious and unconscious. These images have a specific function, different to those personalities, to invoke the idea of an entire structure with a virtual center as the midpoint of the contents of psyche. Jung found this in his 1927 dream in which there was a center, the tree, located in a geometric structure. This serves the more precise definition of the Self as a center whereby it is possible to realize its function as an ideal of unity for the opposites of the conscious and unconscious contents.

Symbols of totality, according to the Definition, are not directly about transcendence beyond psyche but rather are directed to a more practical effect for psychoanalysis of conveying a principle of unity and an orientation that offers meaning. Transcendent ideations or cosmic visions may be responsible for strong affect that may activate the psyche; they do not, however, become a symbol of totality unless they somehow express a geometric structure that points to order and balance. Transcendent dreams or visions may indeed imply by deduction or seem to intimate psychic totality but are not the symbols Jung uses to illustrate the function of symbols of totality. This distinction is necessary in order to make the symbols of the Self understandable. If it is primarily a center, as was his realization in 1927, totality must be understood in relation to that center within a surrounding structure. If that center is realized, it then must be the center of something and that may give way to a realization that it is the center of all that is conscious and unconscious, the psychic totality, the circumference of that center.

Totality is not about what can be conjured by the imagination or can be assumed by religious figures in a dream, but rather is concerned with bringing an individual to an even greater still point, where it can be understood that the opposites can indeed by held ideally by that center, the ideal of unity. This realization allows one to pivot to that ideal of unity, providing a psychic strength of character and a resilience not otherwise available. It is the center that has *psychic weight,* and totality opens up the idea that the center that has been realized is *also* the midpoint of psyche. That indeed can be realized, to the extent that it is manifested in an individual.

Use of Transcendent Symbols

The possible transcendent cosmic dimension of the Self as more than a center, somehow beyond the realm of psyche, is hinted at by figures such as the hero, king, savior, and others of similar quality. They all suggest the possibility of a superadded quality of individuality and transcendence, what Jung calls the "supraordinate personality." That phrase is used by Jung specifically to make a figure an "ideal entity," or ideal personality beyond the ego, and to indicate that the Self is supraordinate because it has a greater function than the subordinate ego.[29] The purpose of these types of symbols is that transcendence gives the Self numinosity and points to it having higher value in psyche than the ego, thus creating a magnet for continuous psychological growth.

When totality is realized, to the extent it is manifested, it would in fact lead to an understanding that goes beyond the center and a simple view that there are conscious and unconscious contents. The circle, square, and the *quadratura circuli,* the squaring of the circle being a circle coterminous with a square, create a recognition that there is a vast totality in psyche that offers the possibility of a wider view of a life. In one of his deconstructions of a mandala, Jung proposes the squaring of the circle as a symbol of the entire alchemical opus because it contains the insoluble mystery of the different dimensions of the square and the circle, suggesting a transcendent level.[30] The circle alone he describes as a symbol of totality,[31] but the squaring of the circle, like the realization of cosmic totality, suggests a different level, one in which a transcendent involution appears to flow.

The list of symbols of totality is not exhaustive (it ends with *etc.*), leaving room for similar symbols. The question of which are relevant appears to

---

[29] CW 7, § 274
[30] CW 12, § 165
[31] CW 13, § 272

be limited to those that have a geometrical structure. For other symbols of the Self, even of supraordinate figures, it is not easily solved as to which may also be significant in terms of totality. If they can appear indirectly as referring to a center or the ideal of a unity, such as a dream with a round building or a midpoint in a connection of roads, this may not be enough to translate the symbols into an empirical experience of the Self as totality. These images lack the power of transcendence in the greater sense that here lies a pointer to the highest realm of realization. It is true that such symbols may suggest that the qualities of the Self as center and the ideal of unity are met, but a high degree of numinosity is not there, so the opportunity for reception by the ego is diminished.

The supraordinate quality of a figure has possible significance as a symbol of totality at most when it is suggesting a guide, or it is innately numinous from mythological associations. As a guide, it is a projection of the qualities of the Self as a process so that an individual can climb higher, finding a path through the miasma. These figures still are direct symbols as Jung put forward specifically for the Self (but not totality), and the category would include any symbol that allows the ego to match the feelings created by the possibility of wholeness, such as a guide, a hero, or a historic figure like Saint Paul or a guru. The symbol can therefore perhaps serve the dual purpose that includes totality. As a possible instance, the presence of a wise, spiritual teacher may indicate a transcendent, supraordinate personality that is a guide to a higher dimension, or an orienting function of the Self. This succeeds as a symbol of the Self because it evokes the idea that there is an internal personality that will take one beyond current limitations, suggesting totality, and the possibility that the ideal of unity exists, suggesting orientation.

The distinction between symbols of totality and those of orientation is not clinically necessary. As a starting point to determine the relevance of any symbol as a symbol of the Self, a distinction between significant symbols and others that are doubtful can be made. This is possible by discovering the manner in which it promotes advancement of the realization of the Self as orienting principle, as numinous, and as suggesting unity. Acceptable variations in the types of symbols are those that are consistent with these three themes. For example, a dream concentrating on a physical body part, such as the center of the chest, or a dream or vision of energy coming from the body, suggest the possible assistance of a personality within psyche to find an orientation to an ideal unity, as well as possibly being numinous. It is numinous because it seeks to help, to orient, and to assist in the journey. In examining a dream of a treasure in the sea, Jung states: "I conjecture that the treasure is also the 'companion,' the one who goes through life at our side—in all probability a close analogy to the lonely ego who finds a mate in the self, for at first the self is the strange non-ego." [32]

The choice of symbols for totality, if that distinction is made theoretically, suggests that they must include all the elements for a symbol of the Self *as well as* a geometric structure. There are then four elements: the structure, a center, the ideal of wholeness, and a numinous quality that gives it the highest value in psyche; its standards exceed those of the center alone or an ideal personality.

The phrasing of the Definition of the symbols of totality suggests that the possible realization of the Self as totality does not, in fact, entirely depend upon the emergence of these forms of totality symbols, as they are rather particular. The emphasis in the 1935 Eranos lecture is on the realization of the center as, from that location, there is a suggestion of a structure, numinosity, and the ideal of unity that can be grasped as pertaining to the totality of psyche. It is here, in centering, that one must look to find the Self as totality, and the other symbols are only pointers that require amplification to reach the same end. Jung confirms this in the essay, *On the Nature of Psyche* in 1947, where he states, "the centering process is, in my experience, the never-to-be-surpassed climax of the whole development and is characterized as such by the fact that it brings with it the greatest possible therapeutic effect."[33]

All of these symbols of the center and totality carry an element of transcendence to some extent, as they always point to a spiritual or religious realm. This element of numinosity, apparent at the time of a dream or on reflection, draws us higher and allows the symbols to resonate with our longing. This aids greatly in the receptivity to what is revealed and the manner in which it is analyzed. The symbols that contain numinosity come upon an individual unbidden and have sufficient value

---

[32] CW12, § 155
[33] CW 8, § 401

to be recalled and then to hold interest. The required level of numinosity is nonspecific but is effective at any level where they come into relief against the background of the vast chaos of the conscious mind. The non-ego and numinous quality of the symbols and their effect in offering a sense of wholeness portends that symbols have a universal, collective nature, thus adding to their numinosity. It is not therefore necessary for the Self to realize itself as totality, but if it does, it can only do so through numinous experiences, global symbols of geometric structures, or by an insight of psychic totality gathered by realization of the center.

The *source* of numinosity in a symbol of the Self does not, in fact, need to be examined because a sense of its essence arises naturally as a consequence of seeking wholeness. Psychologically, the tension of opposites suggests unity as a possible solution, what Jung calls the "'irrational third' *tao*."[34] It is that irrational, transcendent level, contained in psyche, that can "end the conflict between mind and matter, spirit and nature, as contradictory explanatory principles."[35] This ultimately creates in the collective imagination the all-encompassing *unus mundus,* the location theoretically of a complete "non-differentiated unity,"[36] complete wholeness.

Wholeness or some form of unity is, of course, fundamental to Jung's formulation in *The Red Book* of the "supreme meaning,"[37] which thereby points to a transcendent nature. The symbol of the "divine child" is the symbol of that *conjunctio,* as the innocent, primordial, nondiscriminating holder of the opposites. If the Self is considered the center and mediator of the opposites, its highest form of symbolization is wholeness. Thus, Jung explains that the child motif can be "expressed by roundness, the circle or sphere, or else by the quaternity as another form of wholeness."[38]

Any sense of wholeness, the ultimate ideal and principle of unity, exists "below the threshold of consciousness"[39] and all concepts of it are therefore of a "nascent whole; it is on the way to wholeness."[40] This

---

[34] CW 6, § 369
[35] CW 8, § 681
[36] CW 9.i, § 660
[37] *Red Book,* pp. 229-230
[38] CW 9.i, § 278
[39] CW 8, § 856
[40] CW 9i, § 285

means that there never needs to be a realization of complete wholeness because the underlying ideal evokes "holism," expressed as a superadded truth that can imagine the full extent of the whole from the parts so that it exists firmly as an ideal and will have the requisite effect of healing, as Jung explains: "The meaning of 'whole' or 'wholeness' is to make holy or to heal."[41]

Wholeness, when symbolized, will always have a transcendent aspect that hints at it as a symbol of totality: "A symbol does not define or explain; it points beyond to a meaning that is darkly divined yet still beyond our grasp, and cannot be adequately expressed in the familiar words of our language."[42] Every symbol that *could be* one of wholeness is a representation of that primordial innate tendency to become what one can be. It is *ipso facto* numinous in that it carries a transcendent quality as it is reaching back to a primordial archetype of wholeness that has broken through into consciousness. It is therefore useful that any sense of wholeness in a dream or vision, any structural symbol, will be considered a symbol of that wholeness, no matter how incomplete, as what it evokes is that ideal, even if objectively inadequate.

Clinical Vignettes of Self Symbols

A dream of a center point, as was in Jung's 1927 dream, or a circle or a clear guiding spirit all can do the work of being obvious symbols of the Self. This is not always the case, and the unconscious does not necessarily comply. It may be that in determining a symbol of relevance, a question of whether what we understand to be the Self, the components of the Self, is being addressed by the symbols at all in the context of a dream or a vision where there is no clear or specific mathematical structure and none of the exact symbols suggested by Jung.

Vignette 1: Dream of the Center

A dream of a 41-year-old male patient, who had no deep connection with self-reflection, illustrates how less than clear symbolism may be interpreted as a revelation of the Self:

---

[41] CW 18, § 270
[42] CW 8, § 644

I am in beautiful and peaceful New Zealand in our New Zealand office and they were having tech problems they wanted help with. The office had 6 people in it, men and women. As well, Jacinda Ardern (the current Prime Minister) and Judith Collins (the leader of the opposition) were both there. As soon as I arrived people kept jokingly asking if the Wi-Fi was working now. Someone had put a USB cable in back to front. I saw these big microphones setup and sound recording software was installed on the computers. Someone said it was so audio would work in the car. I couldn't stay long but asked them to put together a list of everything they wanted me to fix and I could always come back for a few days if needed. As we were finishing up at night, I saw a big black spider/bat/bug type creature walking on the outside of the window. One of the guys opened the door, I pulled up a sheet as protection because I thought it was going to leap through the open door but then someone got some bug spray and it fell and crashed into a wooden table.

The setting of the dream is a beautiful and peaceful place where the coincidence of the opposites—Prime Minister and opposition—are present. The patient had never been to New Zealand, but it represents to him an idyllic place where he then finds the primary opposites. The coincidence of opposites suggests an ideal of unity: one symbol of the Self. The presence of a total of eight people is a doubling of four, a quaternity and a pointer to wholeness. There is no circle or square, but the setting speaks to the primary characteristics of the Self: the peace and beauty it provides, the opposites, and wholeness.

The images can fit into the possibility of Self symbols made up of the Self's various aspects. They do not directly indicate the three essential qualities of a center, numinosity, and an ideal of unity. The ideal of unity is, however, expressed and is capable of providing significance, although not the excitement of numinosity. The peace and beauty do not indicate a center.

The dream goes on to communicate that it is necessary to fix the Wi-Fi for the message to reach his psyche, to reverse the connection to the cable to make it work, to have big microphones, and to record it and bring it to his ego. The unconscious is presenting the Self and wants it to be embodied, to be connected to all aspects of the psyche, and to be heard. He is willing to come back more to fix whatever is necessary for better communication.

The spider is specifically identified by Jung as a "powerful animal," as no doubt would be the bat, especially with the dream occurring in the time of the pandemic where the virus is possibly linked to a bat. The powerful animals Jung identifies become a focal point in the dream and have the effect of moving from the confusion in the background to the foreground, even though that symbol is a threat and is destroyed. It does not seem possible to transpose the bat to a center, and this illustrates well that when some elements of the dream appear to be pointing to the Self, there may be a tendency to make the dream work too hard.

There are, of course, other amplifications such as the bat being a creature coming as a surprise from the darkness. As well, the animal is part of an individual's connection with the microcosm that is used by Jung in explaining theomorphic images of animals that indicates a connection with the presence in psyche of that higher ordering.

The question that arises is how these symbols—eight people, the presence of opposites, the powerful animals—should be translated into symbols of the Self in this case, or should they be viewed as trying to break through to his consciousness, although he is not yet ready? There is an inkling here of the Self, viewed from another perspective. The symbols embrace the idea of the Self as a peaceful place in which the opposites are held, the need for this to be heard, the geometric or mathematical setting of the eight people of which he is not yet a part, and the power of the connection with matter. Looked at from the point of view of the Self, these are indeed *incipient* Self-symbols, and, at most, this is an early presentation of the Self at the beginning of analysis that indicates a capacity in the dreamer for further revelation.

Vignette 2: Dream of Totality

A patient who has had a long analysis, revealed this dream:

> I am in (an alternative community in the hinterland). I am managing the delivery of a large goldfish within a firm

sphere with a soft and clear membrane, similar to a yoga ball, but about 1.5 m in diameter. Some of the townsfolk are helping me carry this ball overland toward a new pool or sanctuary. The goldfish is pregnant with the hermaphrodite child. I can see its form and movements in the translucent belly of a goldfish. The problem is that the dam is no longer suitable for the goldfish as the council was planning to put some chemicals in the water supply to stop the frogs from breeding (maybe alumina oxide). For its pregnancy, the goldfish needs a pool of water guaranteed to be clear and fresh. So, I'm taking precautions.

What is significant about this dream is the cascading images of the Self. There are four distinct Self-symbols presented: gold, fish, round container, child, forming together a quaternity. These four aspects of the symbols of the Self are undoubtedly of a wholeness in an ordered pattern: the source of wholeness of the fish, the container for the source, the mention of the round ball, the presence of the opposites to be held as the child and its androgyny, and the ultimate goal of the gold. These are the principles of the Self that form a quaternity, a whole, holism as a dynamic consequence, and the splitting of the Self into two as a hermaphrodite, because the split into opposites is the process of the Self; as Jung expresses, "These structures not only express order, they also create it."[43] The quaternity of four interrelated symbols is structural and represents totality because it "forms a real and not merely postulated symbol of totality."[44] This is because it is arranged as a stable and complete configuration as it has no missing elements, such as in the Trinity that does not include the devil.

More particularly in this alternative setting in the dream, known for its interest in matters spiritual, the fish is a metonym for Christ and therefore the Self. Jung extensively explores the ancient symbol of the fish in this context in *Aion* that is found in paganism, Christianity, and alchemy. The fish is "gold," the prize of alchemy that symbolizes the attainment of the *conjunctio* that is contained within the perfect roundness of the membrane, compared in the dream to that used in the eastern practice of

---

[43] CW 8, § 870
[44] CW 13, § 127.

yoga to attain a state of equanimity. The fish is developing in the *vas*, the contained vessel of alchemical change. The significance of the number is not clear, but it can be hypothesized that a 1.5 meters diameter is just under five meters in circumference and the fifth is symbolically the center of four, a midpoint in the stability of four. The forthcoming birth is self-evident, the child being the primary unity before differentiation that is contained within the Self and is the product of the Self as revealing that potential joining of opposites. For that reason, the *Atman*, a powerful representation of the Self, is therefore considered hermaphroditic, as it was initially alone and needed to create another for discrimination.[45] The notion of androgyny is also connected with Christ,[46] and thus the Self. The associations and amplifications in respect of orientation and order abound in this dream.

The patient is anticipating the Self that is being realized as the creator of the hermaphroditic child, the personal manifestation of the Self in him. It has all the elements for a symbol of totality, a structure of roundness, an implied center, unity itself, as well as the end goal of individuation as the gold. The dream indicates that it needs protection, a *temenos*, in order to manifest. Aluminium oxide is an abrasive that is insoluble in water and does affect humans in high concentrations. The lysis of the dream is therefore to get away from this contamination and to protect the treasure. Jung reminds us, "When such symbols (guarding the treasure) occur in individual dreams, they will be found on examination to be pointing to something like a centre of the total personality, of the psychic totality which consists of both conscious and unconscious."[47]

This dream is concentrated on the pregnancy: what is emergent. This may be the nature of dreams that suggest totality as conveying a *process* leading to wholeness or symbols standing for wholeness, rather than a single, stand-alone symbol of the complete picture of conscious and unconscious. It is an intimation of wholeness in every aspect, but not a completion or the realization of the unity. As such, it is about the elements of the process: the substance or force, the effulgent nature of that source, the manner in which it is in movement, the orientation and direction, and

---

[45] CW 5, § 227n35
[46] CW 9.i, § 293
[47] CW 5, § 569

the need for a *temenos*. As an example of dynamic movement, Jung points to springs and fountains as symbols of totality.[48] This reveals that totality can be symbolized as a never-ending force that brings forth itself, and that carries the *aqua doctrinae,* the Gnostic idea of the magnetic quality of the Self that gathers around it what it needs.

This patient, by the revelations in this dream, is ripe for the realization that he is in a process where an unconscious non-ego part of psyche, the Self, is present as a supraordinate personality. The need to protect its birth is so that the Self emerges from the mire to be moved safely to clear water. It was accompanied in the analytic session by a clear moment in the field where the sense of wholeness became patent, and little had to be explained. It led to the question of whether it then required more work, the work of a lifetime, to refine and seek greater realization when the Self had presented itself so clearly. It appeared to have an indelible effect as became evident by continued analytic work with a greater longing. This is best explained by the Alchemist Morienus: "And when you experience this, the love and desire for it will be increased in you. And you shall know that this thing subsists truly and beyond all doubt."[49]

Vignette 3: Dangerous Center

A female patient in her late 30s, an accomplished dancer who is in the limelight, had the following dream:

> I was walking down a gorge or pit by myself, and it was very steep, and I kept on worrying that I might fall. The walls were white and sheer so there was nothing I could hold onto. I kept walking further and I saw what looked like a crater that perhaps was formed by a meteor. It was a dark color except for a yellow or yellowing ring around the center. I walked to the center, which was red as I thought I could get a better look around from that position. I stood on the center and the earth gave way and I found myself falling and spinning from right to left as I sensed there was no bottom and I forced myself awake.

---

[48] *Ibid,* § 624n16
[49] *Aion,* § 529

In her analysis, she had opened up to some painful although not traumatic memories and was willing to pursue their origins and effect. However, there appeared to be, through other dreams and her projections, some deeper trauma that had not yet arrived in the consulting room at the time of the dream. In each session, she required assurance and support, and to be assured that there was no expectation that she exposes anything.

The meteor is alone in its travels, as she is, and comes upon one in a possibly disastrous and shocking way. It presented to her as a journey that contained all of the original colors of the Alchemical process—black, white, yellow, and red. This is an intimation, vague and uncertain, of a unity of four and a process toward the Self. The black is the disturbed material but was subject to a yellowing. The yellowing in alchemy is that which can be used to wash the eyes so as to understand the secrets.[50] It is the bridge to the dawning of greater consciousness that would suit the concept of the Self. The reddening is a stage toward the eventual integration in the *Lapis*, the symbol of wholeness *par excellence*. However, in this dream, the colors are out of order and suggest that the process of the Self is not proceeding as it might.

The collapse of the center is reminiscent of Yeats' 1919 poem, *The Second Coming*, "Things fall apart; the centre cannot hold."[51] Anarchy and chaos are the result in the poem awaiting the second coming, although not of Christ. It has an apocalyptic narrative, as does the memoir of Elyn Saks, *The Center Cannot Hold: My Journey Through Madness*.[52] It is noteworthy as pointing to the possibility of a psychic collapse, although there were no diagnosable conditions that were apparent at that time. Jung spoke of this form of collapse in his enunciation of the concept of the regressive restoration of the persona. When there is a collapse of the conscious attitude and there is an inflated ego, the possibility of some power of conviction arising from the unconscious may break through.[53] The inflation was observable from her stardom but the spinning from consciousness (the right side) to the unconsciousness (the left side) indicates that there is a is corresponding process occurring in psyche that is ongoing.

---

[50] *Ibid*, § 195
[51] Yeats 1989, p. 187
[52] Saks 2007
[53] CW 7, § 254-265

The spinning into an abyss is paramount in William Blake's contrast between the mandala as a symbol of wholeness, and a vortex as a downward spiral "coiling inward toward a perpetually vanishing center and outward toward a never attained boundary."[54] The center or the symbols of wholeness can only hold with the help of the Self breaking through from the unconscious and offering realization. The dream does have the elements that reflect the Self as setting out the stages of the alchemical process, allowing for a deep descent, and offering a movement to the unconscious that is the origin of revelation, but it is very much premature as there are other issues to be resolved. It is a reminder that the Self consists of light and dark, consciousness and unconsciousness, and if it is viewed as having agency, it can author a collapse for its own purposes, opening up a regression.

---

[54] Michell 1982, pp. 126-7, cited in Freeman 1997, p. 101.

Chapter 9. Realizing the Self

The importance of the Self in the therapeutic journey, individuation, is not that there is an acceptance that it theoretically exists or there is an understanding of Jung's ideas, as it is then merely a theory and a hypothesis, but rather that it must be realized by consciousness to have an effect on psychological growth. This occurs when the ego, the conscious mind, has a revelation of the existence of an aspect of psyche, previously unconscious, that establishes order and creates life's meaning.

It is the ego function, consciousness, an aware mind, that must have the revelation of the Self, as "nothing can be conscious without an ego to which it refers."[1] In that revelation, the purpose of individuation is carried out as it satisfies a need to discover a unity to stand against the chaos. Realization will thus expand the state of consciousness to profoundly embrace and give vitality to the wider perspective of the numinous existence of the non-ego Self that has a centering effect on the ego. Jolande Jacobi explains, "Only when it has become conscious of it as a living thing is the reciprocal action between ego and Self established."[2]

The revelation, to qualify as a realization of the Self, must alter the conscious attitude, our worldview, in a manner that is indelible. In speaking of the realization of the Self in these terms, Jung explains that it "acts upon the ego like an *objective occurrence* which free will can do very little to alter."[3] For this to occur, the revelation must have such a high degree of numinosity that it partakes of a transcendent quality, making it so attractive that it offers consciousness a new foundation and overwhelms ego's resistance to what otherwise appears as alien. This need to *overwhelm* the ego draws its significance from the statement by Jung

---

[1] CW 18, § 17
[2] Jacobi 1967, p. 53
[3] *Aion,* § 9

that when an alien psychic state of the highest value and that is transcendent comes upon an individual spontaneously, "The unconscious God-image can therefore alter the state of consciousness."[4]

Revelation can occur in any form, but it is important to repeat that it must have an overwhelming, lasting effect on the existing conscious position, which it accomplishes by its numinosity, its intensity, and an inherent capacity in the individual to be receptive. The receptivity occurs by individual predilection and cannot be foreseen but, to occur at all, the process of individuation must reveal the Self with sufficient intensity to allow consciousness to become aware of its presence. The importance of intensity is highlighted by Jung in relation to dreaming: "Only when a dream is very impressive, or repeats itself often, do interpretation and conscious understanding become desirable."[5]

Jung's own revelation, reported in his dream of 1927, indicates that prior to the dream he was made aware, consciously and intellectually, of the need for a unity of opposites, as he had an ongoing intuition of wholeness as he was compelled to drew mandalas. This led to a dream that broke through and confirmed for his conscious mind the manner in which the center exists. It was cumulative and, upon waking from the dream and only then, he *realized* the existence of the center as a psychological fact. Thereafter, he obviously had further realizations about the width and breadth of the Self. This explains that there is nothing to restrict realization to a single instance and there can be *continued buildup* and multiple realizations of the Self as more aspects of it are revealed to consciousness.

Common Goal

Realization of the Self is greatly assisted in that buildup by the fact that wholeness is a common, understandable goal of all psychological and spiritual growth. Although phrased in this work as an element within a complex psychoanalytic theory, the Self as an idea is a common, practical goal that is a response to inward and outward chaos and confusion. All growth is therefore explained as a journey, a process, an unfolding, all

---

[4] *Ibid,* § 303
[5] CW 18, § 476

the time gradually purifying or progressing. Ibn 'Arabi, the 18th-century Sufi mystic, explains this constant movement in another context, using the term "immanencing" for the involution of the divine in the material world:

> ... creation, bringing about, inventing, making and immanencing, all point to the same meaning. Even if each of these have a slight difference of meaning, they all come to the same. What is meant by all these is the manifestation and revelation of God.[6]

Jung, of course, recognizes this common longing for the ultimate delivery from strife. What we seek, he states, is the "high heart," that appeared for him in the form of a "mandala divided into four, the *imago Dei*, or self."[7] The consequence of seeking the Self because of a profound longing, as shared by Jung, is that there must be a journey undertaken to that goal, originating from a deep resonance in our being to a process that enhances the possibility of a still point. This is what brings each patient to analysis.

The journey to the realization of the Self is the common process of psychological growth. This arises in all therapeutic modalities, because wholeness represented by the Self is defined widely in terms of healing, a cure, making the unconscious conscious, bringing about structural change, peace, a healthy mind, or even Freud's early suggestion of "much will be gained if we succeed in transforming your hysterical misery into common unhappiness."[8] This makes the Self and the individuation process much more than a Jungian theory as that which is implicit in all of us, regardless of the school of thought.

The operation of the longing is by the psychological work moving in a continuous circumambulation toward a virtual center in the unconscious. That occurs because every interpretation of a dream, analysis of childhood issues, unraveling projections, and, in fact, every revelation of unconscious forces, are sought and achieved by the pull toward integration and unity, the innate tendency that is the core patterning in all beings. The idea of a center as a point of orientation brought about by the

---

[6] Ibn 'Arabi 2016, p. 45
[7] CW 13, § 301n16
[8] Freud 1893-1895, p. 308

centering process, is also a common goal, even if the psychological process has different theoretical orientations, alternative terms, or varying aims at each phase of the process. The center in this uncomplicated, straightforward idea of an inner goal suggests that success in analysis is achieved by stepping out of the chaos, a reduction at least in internal conflict by mutual negotiation, a disassembling of barriers to align with the longing of the human striving for harmony.

The center is only an idea, a virtual not actual point that does not need to be found as such, as it is theoretically only a dot within the wider circumference of being. It is only the reality of the center that needs to be recognized. The idea of a dot at the center has been recognized as serving the discovery of the ancient monad, as called by the Pythagoreans, which is the extreme point of oneness. Jung describes it in *Memories, Dreams, Reflections* as "'The unity,' the One, All-oneness, individuality and non-duality—not a numeral but a philosophical concept, an attribute of the archetype of God."[9] The monad cannot be found, as it has no dimension as a dot, although, according to the *Kuiha Upanishad,* it is "finer than the fine, huger than the huge."[10] The idea of the Self or the goal of centering as one focused point, a dot that holds everything as a metaphysical goal of unity, if expressed in that manner, orients the individual to an inward journey that by definition culminates in that point.

The Self is well understood clinically as a centering process but not a virtual center in a wider psyche. However, the process of psychological growth will imply necessarily that there is a center in our being, even if not made explicit. Jung was not suggesting that the center be located, but rather that there should be recognized that there can be an inner mediator and balancing between consciousness and the unconscious, "a new centering of the total personality, a virtual center ... a focal position between conscious and unconscious."[11] It is the realization that the focal position in the centering process suggests a center, even though it cannot be located, and that there is a mediating function, which is more important than locating the monad.

---

[9] *Memories,* p. 310
[10] Aurobindo 1996, p. 224
[11] CW 7, § 365

Understanding centering as universal as in "a new centering of the total personality," as well as accepting that a point of balance can be reached, requires those insights to be made personal for each individual as a goal that justifies the work of individuation and points to a future direction. The realization of the Self in all instances must therefore align with and be explained in accordance with this common goal of centering and also seeking a unity for it to have sufficient affect to alter consciousness. It has this higher value because it is also logical to accept that the potential unity is a worthwhile goal. Thereafter, the lasting recognition by the ego may occur because the Self has great value, which arises by the centering process and the potential unity. The archetype of orientation, hinted at by any concept of the Self, offers centering as a meaning arising from that process. This is enhanced as it creates an emerging sense of wholeness or integration by a premonition or early presentation, unrelated to any mental construct. This felt sense, which is consistent with the cognitive understanding of centering and a unity, arises naturally in the course of individuation, as it is enhanced by the emergence of symbols of integration and wholeness in dreams, fantasies, and visual expressions. Jung states that the insights "occur whenever the individuation process becomes the object of conscious scrutiny."[12]

The images that arise must be translated into a form that can be understood by the conscious mind as consistent with the common elements of centering and unity. The sense of wholeness can be felt but needs to be the subject of the ego's continuous and deeper cognitive understanding. If the images or sense are not translated to accord with the common elements, they may lose some of their force and effect. They must then be presented to the conscious mind preferably in a dialogue, because naming the process and the unity as the Self creates a narrative of how the process has progressed and is meant to continue. The idea of the Self puts the process into a structure that, as it aligns with common longing for peace and unity, becomes a means of containment for the content of dreams, projections, and fantasies.

The theorem suggested is that the commonality of the goal of centering will elevate the symbolic objects that point to a structure and center as having value when there is scrutiny by the conscious mind. This view of

---

[12] CW 16, § 474

the whole picture of the purpose of the Self, its centering orientation, makes the Self an empirical reality because it then becomes a psychic fact that is universal. In this way, any form of analysis is justified as adding to the centering process because buried complexes come to the surface and "The surfacing collapses the tension of opposites that normally exist between the ego and the archetypal core of complexes, and it releases the potential energy buried in this dynamism."[13] The task of individuation is then to release this energy contained in the tension of opposites so as to bring the Self to psyche and present its importance as the common goal of all.

Requirements of Realization

The initial sense or intuition of the Self, as mentioned, is what Jung refers to as a "presentation," a hunch or premonition, where the undifferentiated material of the unconscious is activated so the underlying patterning of the Self begins to come into focus. The entire quote is, "it then rises above the threshold of consciousness, and it can do this only by virtue of the energy accruing to it. It becomes a 'lucky idea' or 'hunch,' or, as Herbart calls it, a 'spontaneously arising presentation.'"[14]

A hunch or a presentation is the way the intuition or the sense of the Self is initially manifested, but, although it is a form of revelation, it is not the ego's *realization* of the Self. Realization of the Self has three essential components, all of which appear as necessary for the alteration and expansion of consciousness. If any of the three are not present, then there will be no realization of the Self. This is not in a strict order, but all three must occur at one time or as a product of multiple realizations.

> 1. *Self as Non-ego.* The ego must experience the Self as "other" and therefore not a product of the ego. If it is perceived as possibly a product of the ego, it ceases to be numinous, unique, and worthy of concentration, losing its higher value.

---

[13] Sandner & Beebe 1992, p. 66
[14] CW 6, § 180

2. *Center as Significant.* The experience of the Self, however it arises, must be understood as a significant, meaning event because of the discovery of a centralizing power in psyche.

3. *Ideal of Unity.* The Self must be perceived as having the potential to hold the opposites, the ideal of unity. This is in two related parts: the existence of opposites, and the ideal solution that they can be unified.

The first, experiencing the Self as other than ego, is clear and needs no explanation. The second is necessary for the establishment of some higher feeling-value, thus conferring meaning on a revelation. The third arises because the essence of the Self is that it has the capacity to hold the opposites, making the *ideal* of unity critical to its essence. The ideal of a possible unity arises because there is a tension arising from the conflict of opposites suggesting the critical importance of the Self as it offers that ideal of a unity.

In speaking about the integration by the ego of unconscious contents, Jung states there must always be an awareness of its opposite: "a content can only be integrated when its double aspect has become conscious."[15] This theme is the reason why the Self must be seen as non-ego in contrast to the conscious mind. This is an essential aspect of realization, as Jung explains, because an individual must "come to grips with the anima/animus problem in order to open the way for a higher union, a *coniunctio oppositorum.* This is an *indispensable prerequisite for wholeness.*"[16] Anima/animus, the context for the particular quote, are primal psychic opposites and therefore represent the split that requires a union. The feeling-value arises from the need for the ideal of a unity triggered by the "problem," with the resultant strong affect. This feeling-value and the need for unity then become stronger than the conflict: "wholeness claims a value superior to the szergy" (anima and animus).[17]

The ideal of unity, of becoming centered, the powerful feeling tone of the revelation, and the otherness of the Self are the goals of individuation. In Jung's 1927 dream of the center, the meaning was derived from the

---

[15] *Aion,* § 58
[16] *Ibid,* emphasis added.
[17] *Ibid,* § 59

archetype of orientation that had the effect of bringing peace from the conflict of opposites that existed before the dream. It also had the highest feeling tone, perhaps best illustrated by the enormity of the center in his *Window on Eternity* mandala, drawn after and in relation to the dream. If all three do not exist as *interrelated* realizations, as occurred for Jung, there can be no peace. Peace, internal certainty, a sense of concentrated power, a transcendence that is a wider opening to life, require an understanding that one has an innate, inner focal point that is a uniqueness, and the place that will withstand the swirling chaos that surrounds us.

Each of these three aspects, however, may easily fail to occur. The realization of a potential non-ego aspect may be ignored by the ego out of fear or other issues that cause a lack of receptivity. The existence of an "other" in psyche may not be given any meaning, and the non-ego may just be perceived as an instance of the activity of the unconscious and not carry the possibility of orientation or unity. It is also highly possible that the numinous presence of the Self may be of such force that it is rejected as too overwhelming for the ego. The Self may not be merely accepted as an endpoint on the continuum of consciousness but could be received as an attack on the ego. The ego has its own sense of self, an ever-changing self-representation, and it is that which has to make room for the larger Self. Fichte states, "It is all one consciousness, but a consciousness that involves an absolute self, on the one hand, and a divisible, limited self on the other."[18]

These considerations make the essence of human life the *triumph* of the Self. It naturally made it for Jung the highest peak that is fundamentally transcendental. From this lofty height, the importance given to realizing the Self unfortunately carries the implication that failure to reach the highest state suggests an immaturity, knotted complexes, or some limiting issue such as trauma. In the grip of trauma, as an example, the ego lacks the necessary acuity to become aware of the objects of the unconscious, so the realization of the Self is not likely, and the lack of the realization is made part of the disorder. As well, as Jung warns, "But if this opportunity is overlooked or not used, the situation does not remain the

---

[18] Fichte, et al. 2003, p. 109

same as before but gives rise to a repression coupled with dissociation of the personality."[19]

If an individual is able to discriminate between the ego and the Self, observing the Self as non-ego, the decision to accept it is not then an intellectual one "but is primarily a moral one," as otherwise it is refusing "a task that has been laid upon them by fate."[20] Turning away from realization is thus a moral failure, but with psychological consequences that are significant. This approach naturally leads to a never-ending hunt for symbols that might reveal the Self or finding some sense of integration, a presentation, that is at least a signpost for its emergence. It results, as could be expected, in many symbols being pressed into service to represent the goal. Realization of the Self can then be seen inappropriately as a scale of how far along an individual is from the bluntness of the ego-oriented conscious mind to the rarified state of being absorbed in the Self.

As realization of all three aspects is made so difficult and idealistic, it is perhaps best clinically to view the Self as an entity with agency, a distinct personality, or a substrate with psychic energy to progress individuation. In this way, the failures are the Self's own process and thus directed to greater awareness at the service of the Self. In the morass of complexes and in the vertical climb out from the Shadow, realization seems a distant goal without the promise of this intrapsychic assistance. The Self can then be called in aid in the therapeutic process because it is needed. The argument is never advanced, however, that the Self can do it all on its own and no psychoanalysis is needed. There is no expressed school of Jungian thought that the Self specifically will do its own work in its own time because it seeks its own realization for its own sake, although that is a convenient approach.

Approximating the Goal

In his commentary on the *Secret of the Golden Flower* about those who can progress, Jung states it does not have to do with their desire, "In no case was it conjured into existence intentionally or by conscious willing,

---

[19] CW 13, § 332
[20] *Ibid*

but rather seemed to be borne along on the stream of time." He asks, "What did these people do…?", and he answers: "As far as I can see they did nothing … but let things happen."[21] This is a logical possibility that the primal patterning of wholeness will be evoked by itself in times of disorientation and strong affect and will activate psyche, bringing forth symbols to aid the individual to find a center. It is not then a matter of agency but the natural development and the tendency of the innate patterning. Yet, with the idea of the ego being reluctant and needing therapy to peer out of the chaos and see the Self, it must be postulated that it requires specialist skills to extract it from the mire. This leads inevitably to a rational, logical path that the Self does not naturally possess.

The characterization of the Self as an achievable goal is logical but not aligned with how Jung viewed realization. The realization of all three aspects of otherness, a center, and the ideal of unity essentially means, in his view, an integration of the world outside with the world inside, the extraordinary realization of the Self in all things. The last phase of realization, Jung suggests in *Aion*, is perceiving the Self that is realized in an individual as also in matter, so that psyche and matter are perceived as one and a person can experience the absolute integration of all. This realization of the Self elevates it to the very highest form of experience, as will be discussed. He accepts that this is the level of a unitive mystical experience that is "always connected with the feeling of timelessness, 'eternity,' or immortality."[22] Thus, the biblical idea of the resurrection "represents an indirect realization of the self"[23] as the complete alteration of an individual's state and the overcoming of death, the entropy of matter. He goes even further and adds that "The realization of the self also means a re-establishment of Man as the microcosm, i.e., man's cosmic relatedness,"[24] a concept echoed by him on several occasions to reflect that innate patterning that repeats that of the cosmos.

These mystical allusions are why the idea of realization is made the loftiest goal, invoking comparisons to enlightenment, but yet are practically unattainable. If this level is required for realization, the goal

---

[21] In Wilhelm 1962, p. 18.
[22] CW 18, § 1567
[23] *Ibid*
[24] *Ibid*, § 1573

is clinically an illusion that is not going to be found in the analytic encounter. Once again, this is Jung taking the ideal to its logical end, its transcendent state beyond psychological knowing. The explanation could well stay simpler so that every time we cleave towards a center we are living in harmony with the Self and therefore have a continuous realization of it uniting the opposites, although not in those exact terms. The idea of enantiodromia of the psyche, of moving from one opposite to another, suggests that the pendulum is seeking some balance and that can be used as equal proof of the Self as an innate, pre-existent center that is purposeful, and a full realization of what it is.

Jung, in making these mystical statements, is not writing to place realization as a state of perfection but bringing the Self in line with the idea that it has a higher, evolutionary purpose as it is "inborn in man as a peculiarity that provides civilization with one of its strongest roots."[25] Having made these claims for the Self, he also perceives that this level of realization has no practical use. In drawing a comparison with the archetype of the Self and the Christ-image, he points out that it should not be expanded to be a complete state of divinity because there is considerable difference between perfection and completeness. The Self as realized, at most, is only completeness but "is far from perfect."[26] The level of completeness, he adds, is only an "approximate state of wholeness that lacks perfection."[27] It is fulfilled for the purpose of realization and becomes the root of civilization, not by perfection, but an approximation.

The goal of the Self as an approximation and not a perfected completeness, leaves open the question of to what extent it must be realized. As an approximation, it suggests that the search for realization can never reach an end, in line with Zeno's Achilles paradox. The word "approximation" is understood more accurately in the context of the idea of the assimilation of psychic contents into consciousness. Jung defines this assimilation as "approximation of a new content of consciousness to already constellated subjective material, the similarity of the new content to this material especially accentuated in the process."[28] This makes

---

[25] *Aion,* § 123
[26] *Ibid*
[27] *Ibid*
[28] CW 6, § 685

approximation an accumulation of realizations relating to the content of existing material that has been assimilated. This approximation is the manner in which the Self is assimilated,

> as a kind of approximation of conscious and unconscious where the center of total personality no longer coincides the ego, but with the point midway between the conscious and unconscious. This would be the point of a new equilibrium, a new centering of the total personality, a virtual center which, on account of its focal position between conscious-ness and unconscious ensures for the personality a new and more solid foundation.[29]

He adds that this is describing a *psychological fact,* which means it has become known to the ego. Here he is accepting that the realization of the Self is an approximation by a build-up over time of psychological facts that have the three elements, the Self as non-ego, the Self as a center, and that center suggesting the ideal of unity. It is proved by a new and more solid foundation, although that is not a final goal, but always a work-in-progress.

The level of revelation that seats the Self in psyche is best understood by the fact that Jung makes the specific goal of realization of the Self as that achieved through the process of individuation. He was clear that "the more numerous and the more significant the unconscious contents which are assimilated to the ego, the closer approximation of the ego to the self, even though approximation must be a never-ending process."[30] This is to "the extent that the integrated contents are *parts of the self.*"[31] This points to an ongoing process concentrated upon the three aspects of realization, the parts of the Self, to achieve that approximation.

The method of integration of the parts of the Self requires the conscious mind to reveal the Self by projection of the inner patterning on symbols arising from the unconscious, as Jung put it, the "symbol *per se.*"[32] The Self speaks about this process in a variety of overt ways, in dreams, fantasies, visions, but also by providing a gradual sense of wholeness, a

---

[29] CW 7, § 365
[30] *Aion,* § 44
[31] *Ibid,* § 43
[32] CW 10, § 24

feeling of centering or integration. This arises and expands through a process of being directed to the parts of the Self by symbols in the overall process of individuation. Those symbols do not create the Self as other, but rather create the Self as a center and a potential unity that makes it the "other" upon realization of the significance of those aspects.

Realization and Individuation

The revelation of a center holding the opposites, the ideal of unity, is the level of realization that is necessary as it then fulfills the three requirements. This is confirmed when Jung discusses the spirit *Mercurius* as representing "on the one hand the self and on the other the individuation process."[33] In the second part of an Eranos lecture in 1942, *Der Geist Mercurius*, he first explains the link between the Self and individuation by conceiving of *Mercurius* as consisting of all opposites and also as a unity where the opposites are held. It indicates that individuation is a process derived from the conflict of opposites with an idealized goal.[34] *Mercurius*, as is the Self, is thus given an active agency because it unites the opposites that it holds within it to create the unity and, thereby, carries out the process of turning the lower, material to the higher, spiritual. Like *Abraxas*, *Mercurius* obtains significance as holding all opposites, and for that reason, is "a representation of the Self."[35] Those opposites, such as for example, good and evil, spirit and matter, are the *complexio oppositorium,* and when held, ideally achieve unity so the Self in this characterization is the animating principle, the process. This makes the Self as a potential unity not only the end point, but also the process of uniting the warring opposites in equal measure.

This is the process of individuation. The focus of Jung's invocation of *Mercurius*, this alchemical figure, is directed at conceiving it as both that which contains all of the opposites, the starting point, and also the end state (unity), so that it explains individuation as the process for the realization of the Self. His comparison with alchemy is appropriate because that process is dependent upon working through the opposites for the creation of the imperfect *Lapis*: "Through the study of these

---

[33] CW 13, § 284
[34] Jung 1942a, p. 211
[35] von Franz 1975, p. 209

collective transformation processes and through understanding alchemical symbolism I arrived at the central concept of my psychology: the process of individuation."[36]

The *ideal of unity* is therefore the underlying basis for all Self-symbols to realize the Self. The relevant symbols suggest that ideal by establishing in the individuation process that there is a center that is an orientation within the psyche; the center is what points to the ideal of unity. The Self is therefore realized by the symbolization and revelation of the reality of its end point, even though only a glimpse of it is possible; at most, an approximation. Accordingly, as both the alchemical and individuation process are concerned with the uniting of the duality of opposites, the objects and figures that represent the Self are symbols of unity, such as the Philosophers' Stone of alchemy. The end goal must be symbolized because that is the only road to peace: "Alchemically, the duplicity of Mercurius (ego-consciousness as Sol and unconscious as Luna) is thus cancelled out in the unity of the stone."[37] Realizing and orienting to the ideal of unity is the realization of the Self.

Measuring Realization

In 1960, Edward Edinger proposed an ego-self axis. He divides the life of the Self in relation to the ego into two phases, the first half of life is primarily ego-Self separation, and the second half is ego-Self reunion. The alternation between the two phases continues to take place in some form during the entirety of life. The shift between the two he designates the ego-self axis, what he calls a "vital connection" between the ego and the Self.[38] He suggests that psychological development is characterized by the two processes occurring simultaneously forming one process.

Edinger makes the statement that "Clinical observation leads one to the conclusion that the integrity and stability of the ego depend in all stages of development on a living connection with the Self."[39] The axis, in his terms, is that connection, and if that axis is damaged, it causes ego-self alienation: "Since ego cannot exist without the support of the self and the

---

[36] *Memories*, p. 209
[37] Mather 2014, p. 156
[38] Edinger 1960, p. 8
[39] *Ibid*, p. 7

self apparently needs the ego to *realize* it, psychic development can be considered a continuous process of dialectic between ego and self leading paradoxically to both greater separation and greater intimacy."[40]

It is clear that the ego and the Self are independent, yet also inter-dependent in terms of a process. The Self in Edinger's terms, at any one time, can be found on a connecting line so that the Self may be suppressed or lost, a "break in the path of connection,"[41] and there needs to be a way for ego and Self to be reunited through the individuation process. Edinger does not suggest that the Self can become non-existent but that an individual at any point in time is located closer to the ego or the Self. The axis is then a measuring scale of where an individual is in relation to an adjusted ego-Self identity. It is a form of locating the Self in terms of its loss of connection with the ego, where there is ego-Self alienation or, instead, the existence of a clear unblocked, connected link between the two. As Edinger identifies, the exact connection will always be uncertain.[42]

The effect of Edinger's approach is to classify progress in individuation at a point in time that reveals the ego-Self identity. It is possible that this cannot really be understood except in extreme terms, such as complex trauma or catatonic schizophrenia, the latter mentioned by Edinger.[43] It downgrades as well the dynamism of the primal patterning that is still there in all circumstances as a magnet, continuously drawing the contents of psyche to itself unconsciously. The axis, instead, indicates that when the link is broken or blocked, an individual is stuck in one place and then the Self exists outside of a dynamic centroversion process. This occurs in his theory because the Self is being treated as an entity with which one has a relationship, as opposed to it being a dynamic, emergent, pattern of wholeness that is always there where the primal patterning is operating unconsciously in a never-ending manner.

It will be impossible to try to locate a point in psyche where an individual is situated in terms of psychological growth; the Self can never be a fixed

---

[40] *Ibid*, p. 17
[41] *Ibid,* p. 12
[42] *Ibid*
[43] *Ibid*

point. It has not been localized by neuroscience[44] and it only becomes artificially located as a specific entity within psyche in two ways. The first is that because it is experienced subjectively through visions, symbols and dreams, it has the appearance of a specific psychic fact that indicates that it is "absolutely other." When so experienced, it appears to have a personality and therefore loses its otherness because, as Hegel explains, it "receives back its own self, because by superseding its otherness, it again becomes equal to itself."[45] The second is that when it is realized, not as an object or a pre-existing otherness, but as a centering or ordering function, it has a role in human development and is then located as a specific entity in psyche. Consequently, the ego-Self axis as expressed by Edinger is not relevant to these two ways of locating the Self as a clear entity and therefore his axis can only be used, at most, as a general expression that an individual is blocked apparently in their process but can be unblocked through symbolization and realization.

Degrees of Realization

A critical question is what effect the revelation of a center and a potential unity will have on the ego. An individual could have the same dream as Jung did in 1927 but with no apparent impact. There could be a mystical experience of complete oneness, but it may be discounted or ignored. There are many psychological reasons why this could occur in both instances. It could be, as one example, that the strong affect activating psyche is too overwhelming for the ego to be able to contemplate a non-ego psychic entity or force. On the other hand, it could have an entirely different result so that even a glimpse of wholeness, a hunch, can cause a rapid, powerful, sustaining, re-orientation of consciousness. It is therefore the case that realization of the Self is resolved by the *degree* to which consciousness is altered by the indicia of the experience of a non-ego presence that exposes a center in psyche and the ideal of a unity. It may not be correct, however, to speak of realization of the Self only in terms of the degree of progress even measured by an alteration of consciousness. This is because the Self is always evolving and being integrated into consciousness, although this process may not be apparent.

---

[44] Bob & Laker 2016, p. 11
[45] Hegel 1977, p. 121

As primal patterning, the Self operates in the unconscious where it shapes development and also it conveys symbols of wholeness as it enters dreams and visions, as well as being part of the human story forever present in myths and fairy tales. It may not be correct then to say that it there is no degree of progress until realized, because, according to Jung, the Self anticipates more. He states that "there seems to reign a dim fore-knowledge not only of the pattern but its meaning."[46] He elaborates this point further to explain that archetypal patterning is formative and operates "with seeming foreknowledge, or as though it were in possession of the goal to be circumscribed by the centering process."[47] The Self is therefore always seeking its revelation and is in constant motion in the unconscious, creating a buildup that may break through. Symbols always offer a hint, sometimes vague or obscure, that this pattern is always there and working in some way for realization. There is no means to draw a distinction between different forms of realization to explain the progress of the Self, even when it appears dormant or blocked.

The essence of realization, psychoanalytically, has been focused on an individual removing the blocks and barriers in the waking ego in order for realization to occur. This is a result of the ego being associated with stubborn complexes and therefore buffeted by opposites. It is then considered not enough to merely wait until the Self reveals itself by way of symbols or through unconscious processes, but rather it is thought necessary to mine the unconscious to bring the Self forth for examination. As well, as the Self is conceived by Jung as a goal, all insight in psychoanalysis is oriented to encouraging revelation of what previously was hidden. These accepted psychoanalytic processes have the effect of establishing a series of markers along the path of individuation, when to do so ignores the operation of the Self in the unconscious.

The idea that the Self is a process in the unconscious that is ongoing should diminish the concept of the requirement at any point of a high degree of realization. The only appropriate test is the alteration of consciousness over time. This allows for the process to be always an unfolding series of realizations rather than an unreachable goal. This brings up the sentiment of Hannah Arendt, "What the thinking ego senses in 'his' dual antagonists are time itself and the constant change it implies,

---

[46] CW 8, § 402
[47] *Ibid*, § 411

the relentless motion that transforms all Being into becoming instead of letting it *be*, and thus incessantly destroys it being present."[48] This suggests that the Self's natural development is preferable to an insistence on attainment that can destroy it as a concept. As expressed by Jolande Jacobi, development is a consequence of the self-regulating mechanism of the psyche responding to the occasion of a too one-sided ego.[49] Realization of the Self to some degree is therefore a natural aspect of that self-regulating mechanism as a continuous, unceasing process where unconscious tendencies work, in their own time, to achieve a return to wholeness. This process will continually bring up symbols of wholeness or intimations of peace because it is seeking to express itself. This is a psychological fact as there is always a return to some centering position, some self-awareness of peace, some cleaving to order. It may be ignored or unreachable where there is pathology, but the potential for some form of realization is a constant possibility.

The degree of realization will appear in different forms that cannot be categorized as levels or made explicit. The Self can be realized as a continuous approximation by intimations of wholeness that appear spontaneously, a presentation or a hunch, by symbols arising by an activated psyche, and also by another neglected category of self-awareness through observation. Although a presentation or premonition is not a fully conscious interaction of the ego in relation to the Self, it is not given prominence as it appears as insufficient to alter consciousness. However, it may be able to have that effect when it is considered that the Self is making itself known, so as to constitute one form of realization. It may be difficult to rely on this intimation because it can be formed by other processes of an integration of disparate parts of the personality, or it could be fleeting, or may suggest as does Kohut that it is crystallized largely by the "interplay of inherited and environmental factors."[50] All of these are realizations of the Self in different forms of the Self as self-disclosing, unrelated to effort, but attuned to the manner in which it is most effectively revealed at a point in time. As an approximation, there are no degrees of realization except the manner in which consciousness is altered.

---

[48] Arendt 1978, Vol. 1, p. 206, emphasis supplied.
[49] Jacobi 1967, p. 31
[50] Kohut & Wolf 1978, p. 414

Self-Observation as Realization

A form of self-observation may be more aligned with the Self's natural unfoldment and has profound potential to alter consciousness. Jung never addressed this form and it is closer to the practices of *Advaita Vedanta* that he did not discuss. Its basis is that there is, empirically, a "watcher" that is constantly observing all experience. It is not part of the ego as it is an observer of ego functioning. Its existence is not able to be explained as a product of cognition. It lies passively behind conscious awareness and does not rely on integration of conscious experience and sensory input to achieve a state of wholeness; it just is. Individuation is irrelevant to its existence. It is closer to the so-called, speculative "Cartesian Theatre,"[51] suggested as the place in the brain where there is awareness of what is happening, and which is there even if not made conscious. That "Theatre," however, is not sufficiently helpful as an answer to its nature, as it can imply that it has awareness because it is an active inference engine that translates sensory evidence.[52]

The concept of the self-observing watcher arises best from the examination of the experience of pure subjectivity[53] that requires the existence of an underlying observer that is able to observe itself perceiving. This makes perception a reflexive case of the watcher representing itself at the same time as it represents the environment. Elaborating on this idea, Perera, commenting on the notion of the Cartesian Theatre,[54] speculates that this underlying agent works on an inferential basis to know the world and therefore it is an "audience" agent that can observe itself perceiving. In this way, it has intention and therefore "gives rise to an 'audience,' not an inner homunculus whose power of vision is the source of our power of vision, but rather a self-simulating agent who can not only see but can appreciate that it sees, and is thus able to become its own audience." Thus, "we watch ourselves watching the world."[55]

---

[51] Dennett 1991, p. 107
[52] Hobson, 2014
[53] Metzinger, 2003
[54] Perera 2019
[55] *Ibid,* p. 152

This watcher can be observed self-reflexively, but is, critically, outside normal ego consciousness. It is therefore an underlying substrate or at least a non-ego "other" of our existence. Altmanspacher employs this idea of it as a substrate as one possible theory to reconcile the mind-matter split by an approach, promoted by Spinoza, that there exists a "distinction-free, unseparated underlying realm."[56] Altmanspacher later relates this realm to the Jungian "*unus mundus.*"[57] This ties the watcher to the Self as the *unus mundus*, the ultimate ideal of unity. He quotes the physicist, Wolfgang Pauli in an unpublished letter to Jung that expresses in terms of the unconscious, "the 'observed system' would, from the viewpoint of psychology, not only consist of physical objects, but rather comprise the unconscious as well, whereas the role of the 'observing device' would be ascribed to consciousness."[58] This leads to Altmanspacher's model that there is the neutral *unus mundus* at the bottom, the mental and physical on top, and intermediate levels in between.[59]

Regardless of these theories, the background watcher as a matter of fact is always there, even when we are not aware of it, and can observe the centering process and therefore offers a central point and the ideal of unity. There is no reason to think it disappears with loss of consciousness even during sleep where it is there to observe the realm of images. Its existence is apparent without a long process of self-reflective enquiry or a marked out path of individuation. There is also no particular reason to accord it an intention or a purpose or the capacity to work to a goal. If, however, it *appears* that way as having a goal or purpose, it is because the realization of its existence and its numinosity make it an object of fascination, attracting interest.

Although this is not a concept developed by Jung, it is closest to his use of the *Atman* of Hindu Vedanta that he often invokes as a parallel to the Self. The significant aspect of the *Atman* as Self is that it is a witness; Jung quotes from one of the Upanishads: "There is no seeing but he, no other hearer but he, no other perceiver but he."[60] This leads to the

---

[56] Altmanspacher 2014
[57] Altmanspacher 2018
[58] *Ibid*, p. 64
[59] *Ibid*, p. 66
[60] *Aion*, § 349

intimation that a form of realization of the Self is the revelation of the watcher as it can be considered a function of the Self or indeed a proper characterization of the Self. This is because the realization of it is obvious as it is a recognizable observer, a non-ego identity in psyche that offers a unity above the chaos and increases its scope and depth by greater awareness of itself. In terms of the *Atman*, it is said "the experience of the phenomenal world is altered by a deeper understanding of the way things are."[61] This comes from self-reflection that points to the watcher so as to better understand the nature of psyche.

This is giving the realization of the Self a greater scope than Jung hints at by symbols and by numinous experiences. The watcher or a sense of wholeness or even a hunch offer a greater centering capacity in clinical settings than expecting the Self to be fully understood by a patient. In terms of the "sense of wholeness," it is observable in clinical practice that the most common form of centering appears as a felt sense. Jung, in his early speculations explains that a sense impression is either received unconsciously, below the threshold of consciousness, or it is received consciously but does not enter the "speech route" because of distraction.[62] The "sense of wholeness" or "sense of Self" are not, in fact, terms used by Jung. However, the sense will constantly arise, as Roger Brooke expresses it, with the idea of a center that yields "a sense of rightness and inner coherence. It can also occasion a sacred sense of one's place in the wider scheme of things."[63] The sense of order follows from the possibility that the intimation of a center can fill our minds, be the subject of self-observation, and thereafter we may give it a linguistic reference. It was explained by Kant in relation to the soul that it is "stuff" with which we fill our mind prior to thinking.[64] The watcher offers the sense of order and unity, thus appearing to have the characteristics of the Self.

Totality and Realization

The German 1935 Eranos lecture left no doubt that the idea of the Self embraces the realization of the Self as center, *and* the realization of totality, but only to the extent that it is manifested in an individual.

---

[61] Anderson 2012, p. 279
[62] CW 1, § 73
[63] Brooke 2009, p. 613
[64] Kant 1965, p. 67

However, this statement was expressed during a period in which the Self had not been yet fully explicated by Jung and was an expression of his own realization that was not yet integrated into his theory. How then is totality to be realized? In his Tavistock lecture in the same year, he only briefly mentions the Self and, after expressing that the dimension of the Self is as big as the universe, he explains that this is a philosophical question that only the "special mind of the philosopher" should conceive, but "It is not good for patients, nor the doctors ..."[65]

Two years later, in 1937, Jung delivered the Terry Lectures in English at Yale University. He makes the point in these lectures that he does not enjoy philosophical arguments, and when we speak of totality, it can only refer to the conscious part of it that we can know, and therefore it is not a reference to absolute totality that contains another part that is not experienced. The view that there can only be a part that is manifested confirms the reality of only manifesting, making conscious, a very small part of the vastness of totality that is an aspect of the Self. He continues with the idea that the possibility of such a dimension can be presented by psyche as an intuition or hunch that "has come of itself, and you only catch it if you are clever or quick enough."[66]

To be clever or quick enough and to reduce totality to an intuition or hunch did not provide clarification of what are the elements of totality that can be realized. That same year, 1937, marked Jung's journey to India, and in 1940, the influence of that journey became clearer when he published *Essays on the Science of Mythology* with Carl Kerenyi. In these essays, there are references to the Hindu *Atman* as a parallel to the Self's possible realization of a transcendent dimension of the indwelling deity. In the essays, the *Atman* in Hindu thought is expressed as introverted to the point that it is an illusion as it is not made conscious, therefore reducing the chance of its manifestation. He then explains that, *in contrast*, for the Western mind, it is still useful to define a transcendent subject as an express, cognitive counter-pole to the day-to-day empirical universe, which is dominant at the expense of the Self. Therefore, the ego "confronting self" is a logical necessity for its realization by the ego; it is a psychological postulate necessary for realization rather than a

---

[65] CW 18, § 120
[66] CW 11, § 69

transcendent entity. This psychological idea is made possible because the unconscious will always "produce a symbol of the self in its cosmic significance."[67]

This is not a statement about realizing cosmic totality or describing how totality may be perceived and therefore revelation of the wider dimension remained unanswered in these essays. It is providing a utilitarian response that totality is to be seen as a practical counter for mundanity. The greater expression of totality and its possible realization may have failed to find expression because of Jung's early concept, suggested in 1936, that an archetype, of which the Self is one, has no "determinable form but is in itself an indefinite structure, which can assume definite forms only by projection."[68] There was thus no idea of how to make totality a form, as is the center. The idea of the *Atman* was at least useful because it gives the Self a form for the first time, not as a center, but in relation to a wider dimension that could be the subject of projection of an indwelling force. The mention in 1935 of totality and the concordance with the *Atman* in 1940 at least establishes a prevailing sentiment of totality having transcendent dimensions but, at this stage, without a point of reflection whereby it can be realized.

In the Zarathustra lecture of 3 June 1936, Jung did add new dimensions to the Self but also caused further doubt as to what constitutes realization, especially of totality. In these lectures, he explains that the Self, being outside time and space, is "dimly visible" by the ego and, under favorable conditions, an individual would get "a fair idea of it through the ego— not a very true picture, yet it is an attempt."[69] What are the favorable conditions for it to be visible is not mentioned but hinted at: "The success is that it could manifest in space and time, that it could break through into existence and appear to the world; and whenever you suffer or enjoy such a victory you have succeeded in giving wide space to the existence of the self."[70] There is nothing here that suggests that an individual will be able to, by his or her own efforts through the individuation process, get the Self to break through or to realize that the Self embraces totality. It may

[67] CW 9.i, § 289
[68] *Ibid,* § 142
[69] *Zarathustra*, Vol 2, p. 977
[70] *Ibid,* p. 979

break through, or it may not, so as Jung puts it, it wants to exist and appear and "Whether we know it or not doesn't matter."[71]

The position that totality indicates a higher dimension that could be realized was hinted at but never developed in this period. It was left up in the air because of how it was mentioned in 1935 and 1940 and the obvious doubt of how it is to be realized expressed in the Zarathustra seminar. This unanswered issue required other possibilities, as well illustrated by Jung's early student Gerhard Adler. In his 1948 work, *Studies in Analytical Psychology,* he argues that the goal of individuation is the Self and therefore "This goal can only be attained by an ever-increasing consciousness which, through constant application and a corresponding awareness of the psychic process, tries to find its way back to its own sources."[72] This allusion to the "source" can be read as an extrapolation of a divine totality that, at this point, was not consistent with the limited treatment of totality in the 1935 Eranos lecture. It appears to possibly be a means to bring in the transcendent in a particular form to explain that higher dimension.

The emphasis of the Self as including totality, especially because the original German Eranos lecture in 1935 was improperly translated into English, turned the realization of the Self into an abstract concept with no anchor as an object. As well, to say the Self presents itself only vaguely, and is "dimly visible," also makes its realization particularly unclear. Furthermore, when the Self is linked to transcendent qualities through actually realizing totality, it becomes an experience that few would ever grasp:

> Anyone who has experienced (numinous experiences that have a totality character) anything of the sort will know what I mean, and anyone who has not had the experience will not be satisfied by any amount of descriptions. Moreover there are countless descriptions of it in world literature. But I know of no case in which the bare description conveyed the experience.[73]

---

[71] *Ibid,* p. 980
[72] Adler 1948, p. 14
[73] CW 14, § 779

This statement, written in his last work, *Mysterium Coniuntionis,* is what Jung really means by realization of totality as that which has the character of a numinous experience where the archetype of wholeness overpowers the ego and thereby alters consciousness and conveys an indelible fact. For most, it will only be what Jung refers to as a "dream of totality."[74] That is why realization of the center cannot imply that there must also be realization of totality in order to say that the Self has been realized. The Self is fundamentally the center of psyche and when that is realized as in Jung's dream in 1927, it is fulfilling the goal of individuation.

The Self as a mere dream of totality therefore does not demand that it must be realized to its full extent as all that is conscious and unconscious, the psychic totality, but it does suggest the center as having a greater dimension. This is because the existence of a center suggests the *ideal* of unity that is an essential ingredient for the alteration of consciousness. The requirement of realization is therefore that the centering process is of high, even transcendent value because it offers the possibility of a unity where the opposites are held. This is the extent of a transcendent aspect of the Self that must be the subject of realization to alter consciousness and create a new foundation. A center in a dream or vision must be understood as having a purpose that must be interpreted, as Jung did in his dream, as offering an orientation. It is only then that it has meaning and is of sufficient impact to create an orientation in what otherwise is confusion and chaos.

Jung could just as easily have said that the Self is a complete mystery that is behind psychological development and does not include totality, leaving the center alone to be realized. William James approaches the self as that which is constructed by the ego, but he states in recognition of its other dimension, "… it involves a real belonging to a real Owner, to a pure spiritual entity of some kind. Relation to this entity is what makes the self's constituents stick together as they do for thought."[75] It appears that totality was made part of the Self for Jung as it was a psychological fact from his own numinous experiences that he never explained. This also arose from his finding the center in a geometric pattern, thus predicting the Self as having a wider dimension of a midpoint between

---

[74] Serrano 1966, p 50
[75] James 1890/2007, p. 337

the conscious and unconscious, where the latter has no known limit, and also his movement to equate the Self with a transcendent hero or deity.

The most significant result of a transcendent dimension of the Self, equated with totality, is that it gives the Self the appearance of agency. We can understand the idea of centering or a center, but not the wider dimension, so the consequence as Jung explains is that "if it transcends our cognition, we are its objects or slaves or children or sheep that cannot but obey the shepherd,"[76] If consciousness cannot understand totality, it will appear to create our lives. The sense arises that we must follow it as it appears to be a guide that speaks to us and so, Jung asks, must we then fulfill "the primordial instinct of obedience?"[77]

If the proposition is advanced that there exists a totality through the center where all the opposites unite, can this *ever* be rationally understood or ever realized? Sanford Drob explains that Hegel's proposition that the reconciliation of opposites yields an understandable principle has been irrevocably rejected, and a complete unity of opposites is an idea that can never be understood logically.[78] Drob suggests that we can attain some non-cognitive insight into totality only as an "echo of the non-differentiated state that pre-exists logic, language, and representation … "[79] It is then the sounding of the Pleroma, its echo, that may make itself known, if only barely. If a small echo is heard, it would be difficult to conflate that reverberation with the whole, making it always a truth that can never be realized, outside perhaps of a mystical experience. This was an explained well in the Foreword to Drob's extensive unraveling of the opposites and their unity, where Paul Bishop[80] extracts a quote from Goethe that is apt: "People say that between two opposed opinions truth lies in the middle. Not at all! A problem lies in-between: invisible, eternally active life, contemplated in peace."[81]

The Self existing as a totality capable of being realized is only a hypothesis, although psychologically it can become a psychic fact to the extent that echo can be manifested in part through a numinous experience.

---

[76] CW18, § 1630
[77] *Ibid*
[78] Drob 2018, p. 306
[79] *Ibid,* p. 308
[80] *Ibid,* p. 21
[81] Goethe 1986, p. 83

It then becomes empirical, offering irrefutable proof of that aspect of psyche. As it cannot be understood by logic, it cannot otherwise be made the subject of ego consciousness; it is then "manifested" in a numinous experience that overwhelms the ego, as far as the laws of the unconscious permit. This is the basis for Jung's comment in the 1935 Eranos lecture (in the original German), that the Self will be understood as totality "insofar as this is manifested in an individual."

If the Self as totality is not manifested in an individual, it remains a metaphysical idea, although the Self as center can still be revealed and *realized* as the goal of psychological growth. They are not dependent on each other to attain realization of the Self, but they may be realized at the same time as a link between inside and the wider dimension of outside. The process of individuation, of circumambulation of the center, centering, will more likely lead to the Self having symbolic representation or being experienced as a goal, and it is less likely the Self as totality will ever be revealed.

Why does the Self not give us all an illuminated tree at the symbolic center of our psyche? Why do we not have a numinous experience that displays totality? The answer lies in Jung's dream that his companions, although in the presence of the tree with Jung, did not notice its existence. This is a result of the one-sidedness of consciousness that requires inner work to be done to make room for the substrate of wholeness. Jung did that work, as proved by the dream, and others must find it anywhere possible such as the recesses of the body. As Jung explains "In psychological terms ... the self has its roots in the body, indeed in the body's chemical elements"[82] and, therefore, the journey is not only glimpsing the Self from afar as a possibility but embodying the Self as the secret that was always there.

The Dangers of Totality

Totality as a transcendent postulate, where the Self is equated with divinity or a cosmic dimension, encourages speculation about its nature. When interpreting images in visions and dreams suggesting totality, the symbols must be analyzed to determine their essence. The nature of totality is not able to be perceived but may suggest an idea to be

---

[82] CW 13, § 242

212 THE SELF IN JUNGIAN PSYCHOLOGY

contemplated in depth by the conscious mind. It is the case that in the absence of a numinous experience, we cannot grasp the nature or extent of totality, yet we must attempt to make sense of it. Contemplation is indeed the means to create a fixedness on revelations of the Self.

As totality contains everything that is conscious and unconscious, it embraces *all* opposites including the darkness of evil. The Self, therefore, as Jung recognizes, can have "unpleasant qualities."[83] Evil is therefore essential to realizing totality and cannot be excluded even though it is not able to be understood. The Self, Jung reminds us, "even creates esteem and contempt for itself."[84] As its existence includes both light and dark, what follows when we touch the light can cause grandiosity and esteem, or the dark can invoke a great fear so it can be the subject of hate. Jung compares this, without explanation unfortunately, to Eastern beliefs where "love of God and the hatred of God are essentially the same."[85]

Mircea Eliade explains a center as an instance of "architectonic symbolism," such as the sacred city or temple, but this is to be conceived of as the meeting point of all opposites: heaven, earth and hell.[86] Heaven and hell therefore exist on the same axis and the center is the midpoint of not only all that is conscious and unconscious, but its contents of good and evil. It is therefore naïve to think that the revelation of the Self will only draw one closer to the center, always creating a positive integration of healing aspects of psyche.

In 1948 in *Transformation Symbolism in the Mass*, Jung explains, "Anything that a man postulates as being of greater totality than himself can become a symbol of the self. For this reason, the symbol of the self is not always as total as the definition would require."[87] Only seeking positive symbols or turning a dark symbol into a benevolent entity is missing the point of totality. As Jung explains, the Christ figure is not one of totality because it lacks the darkness of the spirit so that, "Without the integration of evil there is no totality."[88] Somehow, evil must be integrated for any realization of the Self including totality.

---

[83] *Letters*, Vol. 1, p. 529
[84] *Zarathustra*, Vol. 1, p. 397
[85] *Ibid*
[86] Eliade 1959, p. 12
[87] CW 11, § 232
[88] *Ibid*

Concerns about the negative effects of darkness within the Self may not, at first glance, appear problematic clinically because confronting the Shadow and depressive states are expected and may be considered positive markers of psychological growth. However, evil is not necessarily just a bad image or feeling but can create an overpowering terror, negative annihilating thoughts, or be manifested in illness, injury, or death. The darkness of the Self, however, may contain much more. How then can it be approached?

The underlying proposition is that evil cannot be ignored or interpreted out of existence. It must be approached as it is a necessary counterpoint for the conscious mind, as Jung points out: "Consciousness requires as its necessary counterpart a dark, latent, non-manifest side, the unconscious, whose presence can be known only by the light of consciousness."[89] The surfacing of evil and accepting its presence is possible as an aspect of the Self, but this is *vastly different* from the cognitive examination of totality through its contemplation, getting closer to what it contains, thinking about it, digging for its source.

In the beginning of 1944, Jung had a thrombosis and cardiac infarct and then had a vision he describes in *Memories, Dreams, Reflections*.[90] In summary, he was high in space and saw the blue globe of the Earth, and directly in front of him was India. A tremendous block of dark, granite stone entered his field of vision. In an antechamber on the stone, to the right of the entrance he was facing, "a black Hindu sat silently in a lotus position upon a stone bench. He wore a white gown, and I knew he expected me." As he approached the entrance, he had the feeling that everything was being "sloughed away." Yet something remained of his own history and everything he had ever experienced, leading him to feel that he existed in objective form. As he approached a temple in the antechamber, there was a sense that he would enter a room in that temple and be told all the answers to his life. At that moment, he was distracted by his personal doctor in his primal form surrounded by a gold laurel wreath. The doctor gave him a message that he must return to Earth.

This vision offers insight into the actual reality of darkness. The "black" Hindu man in the vision was sitting to the right of the entrance, a

---

[89] CW 14, § 117
[90] *Memories*, Chap. X

locational point within the vision. To enter the Temple, where revelations were sought, it was necessary to enter the antechamber. Within the antechamber, looking back to the entrance, the Hindu man was sitting to the left. This specific location could very well be an allusion to the "left-handed" position or path in Hinduism (*Vamacara*), as it fits the description well. In relating the *Rosarium Philosophorum* pictures in his essays on Transference, Jung is familiar with the "left-handed path" when describing the first stage of the King and Queen holding left hands.

> This gesture points to a closely guarded secret, to the 'left handed path' as the Indian Tantrists call their Shiva and Shakti worship. The left-handed (sinister) side is the dark, the unconscious side. The left is inauspicious and awkward; also it is the side of the heart, from which comes not only love but all evil thoughts connected with it ... [91]

Tantrism contains extremely unorthodox sects that include the *Kalmuckhas*, called "black-faced." They hold mystical powers and are considered black magicians as they use magical amulets and occupy charnel grounds,[92] where human ashes are used to draw mandalas.[93] Although there are different sects within that lineage, they all cover themselves in fire bleached, funeral pyre ash, so they appear white.

The "left-handed (sinister) side" is a recognition that in the search for ultimate answers in the Temple, there are also sinister forces, and it is better not to inquire too deeply as to their nature or source. In *Memories, Dreams, Reflections,* Jung adds, "Granted what I experienced in my 1944 visions ... gave me the deepest bliss. Nevertheless, there was darkness too, and a strange cessation of human warmth. Remember the black rock to which I came! It was dark and of the hardest granite. What does that mean?"[94]

The possibility of encountering evil in a vision is not in itself harmful, as Jung explains when he analyzes the terrifying vision of Brother Klaus and suggests, "I know that it takes a complete and a brave man to stand

---

[91] CW 16, § 410
[92] Lorenzen 1972
[93] Dyczkowski 1989, p. 6
[94] *Memories* 1989, p. 321

up to it."[95] This actual confrontation with evil is repelling the destructive effects of darkness; it is a personal journey for each of us to make. However, *contemplating* evil, rather than standing up to it, may lead to the manifestation of that darkness. Jung asks, "what does that mean?" because he expressly is not inquiring into its source but leaves it as a mystery. The process of contemplating its source is where the danger arises as it can then overwhelm the ego. As Jung explains it: "It is of no importance whether evil is here or there, but one can deal only with the evil in oneself, because it is within reach, elsewhere one trespasses."[96]

It may be that an error that evokes destructiveness is committed because, in contemplation of totality, too much of evil will be revealed as stated in the *Idra Zuta* section in the Zohar: "Perhaps, God forbid, it has been decreed that we should be punished because matters have been revealed through us that had not been previously revealed since Moses stood at Mount Sinai."[97] The entry into darkness therefore comes from contemplating the nature of totality in which it is revealed in all its dimensions, not from a personal confrontation with evil. If one manages to stand up to its manifestation personally and be that "complete and brave man" who can survive the darkness, it will bring bliss because it is the *conjunctio* of the primordial opposites of good and evil.

When one has personally survived evil, it can be spoken about but only then. The Zohar also speaks of a duty for such an individual to disclose the secret knowledge *after* it is obtained. In the following year after his vision, 1946, Jung had a second cardiac arrest and, in the period that followed, he concentrated on writing *Aion*, a book concerning the Self, as will be discussed. He explained about this period:

> Before my illness I had often asked myself if I was permitted
> to publish or even speak of my secret knowledge. I later set
> it all down in *Aion*. I realized it was my duty to communicate
> these thoughts, yet I doubted whether I was allowed to give
> expression to them. During my illness I received
> confirmation …[98]

---

[95] CW 11, § 42
[96] Jung, et al. 1982, p. 56
[97] Giller 2000, p. 6
[98] Ostrowski-Sachs 1971, p. 68

It may be that when the unconscious, as Jung explains for a patient, "had to give him a hard knock and roll him in the dirt to pull him out of his infantilism and make him more mature,"[99] the presence of evil was necessary and understandable and was a personal confrontation. When one, however, deliberately inserts oneself into totality by contemplating its width and breadth, it is to submit to its contents that are potentially unfiltered, so that the darkness is then ripe and immediate. It, accordingly, can be asserted that an examination of totality is inherently dangerous, and it is better that it be understood for an individual by the symbols that the unconscious provides. Thus, the Self is realized in terms of totality "to the extent that it manifests in an individual," as Jung explained in the 1935 lecture.

Jung's early thinking on this conundrum of how to address the darkness in totality appears most specifically in two places in *The Red Book*. In *The Gift of Magic,* he states that "the gifts of darkness are full of riddles" and the "way is open to whomever can continue in spite of the riddles."[100] His advice is to submit to the riddles as they are "the bridges over the eternally deep abyss." In *The Anchorite,* he explains, "If you comprehend the darkness, it seizes you," but "Silence and peace come over you if you begin to comprehend the darkness."[101] It appears that, in this context, the riddles are the symbols, consistent with knowing totality by what comes from the unconscious, and it is important to "begin" to comprehend the darkness in the sense of understanding its riddles *for an individual*. However, that indirect revelation of totality through symbols is different in kind to seeking to understand the darkness through contemplation.

The notion that the Self includes totality is that it can manifest symbolically or, more likely, through a numinous experience. In this way, one can personally "begin" to comprehend the darkness that is within totality and therefore the Self. If the choice is made to be absorbed in the darkness and to make that one's focus as in the left-handed path, the rewards would be great, but the danger is inherent and likely to require a mana-personality or an individuated ego, neither of which is easily found.

---

[99] CW 10, § 867
[100] *Red Book,* 128/130
[101] *Ibid,* 21/22

In referring to the striving for individuation, Jung points out that recognition of the archetype of the Self, if carried out by a "binding personal commitment," contains a warning:

> If he takes the burden of completeness on himself, he need not find it 'happening' to him against his will in a negative form. This is as much to say that anyone who is destined to descend into a deep pit had better set about with all necessary precautions rather than risk falling into the hole backwards.[102]

The danger within totality therefore suggests that it must be approached with great caution and only through symbols (or a numinous experience). Colman suggests that contemplation of the center may yield some insight into totality, "so more I can develop the image of the self as centre, the more it is also possible for me to contemplate and allow for the totality of my being."[103] This is a sound proposition because from the center, theoretically, one can safely look out. However, contemplating the nature of totality is to seek a confrontation in which we may not be able to contain the consequences.

Enlightenment or Wholeness

Clinically, the approximation to the ideal of the Self or becoming centered by psychological work is a welcome development. It does not, however, echo Jung's ideas for the realization of the Self. Gradual realization is recognized as an early presentation, but the emphasis lying behind his ideas is on a full realization of the Self wherein the archetype of orientation is apparent, and meaning is established in a conclusive, indelible manner. Gradual centering with the consequence of some form of healing is not to be discounted, however, because of Jung's insistence on full realization. The impossible goal was necessary for his theoretical matrix as the ultimate endpoint of individuation, no less than Buddhism requires *Nirvana*.

The full realization of the Self defines the ultimate goal of individuation; it is the *difficilis exitus* of the entire Jungian opus. There are two

---

[102] *Aion*, § 125
[103] Colman 2008, p. 364

possibilities as to the nature of this end state. The first is what can be called the absorption into "all-oneness." It is then indeed a rarified state found, at most, by a sage who lives in the oneness of all, or, as one of the modern *Advaita Vedanta* masters, Sri Nisaragadatta Maharaj, calls it, dwelling in "the limitless, universal consciousness."[104] The second possibility is of resting in and surrendering to the center, so the opposites are held and will create what Jung calls "the four-squared man who 'remains himself' come weal come woe."[105] It is this that is the practical completed achievement of psychological wholeness by producing the unflappable, centered individual. In this second view, this is as far as realization needs to go, as the Self as all one-ness—complete totality—can never be grasped except in very small part.

It must be immediately accepted that it is the introduction of the word "totality" that creates the problem in understanding the nature of the end state. In the abstract, totality hints at knowledge of all things, connection with the mind of God, not just an understanding of the nature of a center in psyche but also the inconceivable oneness. If this is the goal, there are stories, endless stories, of saints and mystics who have achieved that state, but little modern presentation.

This degree to which totality must be realized is answered in the 1935 Eranos lecture wherein Jung, properly translated, states: "I also refer to the center as the Self by which the totality of the psyche is to be understood at all, n.b. insofar as this is manifested in an individual." Jung is referring to totality as being understood (at all) through the existence of a center because it can be seen as an *ideal* that can hold opposites as it is a mid-point between the conscious and unconscious. It is used in that lecture only in that sense and does not imply that it extends to the totality in any wider sense, such as merging with the divine.

Jung uses the term "totality" over 400 times in his writings, and no reference is directed to realization of oneness but, instead, all are pointing to *psychic totality*. The use of "totality" is therefore best limited to the totality of psychic functions, the contents of what is conscious and what is unconscious. The idea that realization of the Self is a state way beyond

---

[104] Nisaragadatta 1996, p. 41
[105] *Aion,* § 418

a center that has to do with cosmic knowledge is not warranted. There is only one sentence where Jung appears to tilt in the opposite direction. In referring to Zen satori, a mystical experience, he states that "enlightenment implies an insight into the nature of the self."[106] This is best understood on the basis that enlightenment, all-oneness, would illuminate the interrelatedness of all things, the ideal of unity, and that would be an *effect* of enlightenment. He does not suggest that enlightenment, realization of totality in its cosmic sense, is necessary as the goal of individuation.

In a letter to a Jungian Analyst in 1954, Jung explains the relationship more clearly. This is a lengthy quote, but it brings his view of enlightenment and the Self into an understandable proposition:

> If the self could be wholly experienced, it would be a limited experience whereas in reality its experience is unlimited and endless. It is our ego consciousness, that is capable only of limited experience. We can *say* that the self is limitless, but we cannot *experience* its infinity. … What does a grain know of the whole mountain, although it is visibly a part of it? If I were one with the self, I would have knowledge of everything. I would speak Sanskrit, read cuneiform script, know the events that took place in prehistory, be acquainted with life on other planets, etc. There is unfortunately nothing of the kind. … You should not mix up your own enlightenment with the self revelation of the self. When you recognize yourself, you have not necessarily recognized the self but perhaps only an infinitesimal part of it, though the self has given you the light.[107]

Jung may appear to be reflecting, although not clearly, that a mystical state embraces full realization when he discusses the Self as integrated with transcendence in four other instances. The first is the statement that the realization of the Self by an individuated ego will perceive that the Self is "incorruptible" and has an "eternal character,"[108] which suggests perhaps that it is realization beyond time and space. The second is in *Aion*

---

[106] CW 11, § 884
[107] *Letters*, Vol 2, p. 195, emphasis supplied.
[108] *Ibid,* § 400

to the effect that a theoretical stage in realization of the Self is the return to an "original state of wholeness"[109] that may imply a mystical revelation. This state is not obtainable, as expressed by Marie-Louise von Franz: "The original Oneness, the original unit of your personality—your Self—is still different from and greater than even the most individuated form of the Self."[110] The third is in Jung's last work, *Mysterium Coniuntionis,* which concerns the union of opposites, where totality is equated with symbols of wholeness, and he refers to "the Microcosm, the mystical Adam bisexual Original Man."[111] The microcosm is the patterning of the Self, and the reference to Adam implies that the original man holds the capacity of uniting the opposites. Finally, at another point in that work, he refers to totality that is beyond the bounds of knowledge, but he inserts a specific footnote that the totality he is referring to is the sum of conscious and unconscious.[112]

When explaining other mystical or religious works, there are references in that context of a totality that includes the transcendent and oneness. However, when Jung speaks particularly of his view of the Self, it is consistently the same: "I have defined the self as the totality of the conscious and unconscious psyche … when we want to lay emphasis on the psychic totality it is better to use the term 'self.'"[113] Totality does not imply in this and all other statements about the Self that its ultimate realization approaches a mystical state.

Mystical or religious experiences, where there is full realization of that oneness, are of course possible, so that Jung, in speaking of the stages of the alchemical opus described by the alchemist Gerhard Dorn, expresses that we must completely accept those experiences:

> To the Westerner this view appears not at all realistic and all too mystic. … I would therefore counsel the critical reader to put aside his prejudices and for once try to experience on himself the effects of the process I have described, or else to suspend judgment and admit that he understands nothing. For thirty years I have studied these psychic processes under

---

[109] *Aion,* § 410
[110] von Franz 1992, p. 148
[111] CW 14, § 8
[112] *Ibid,* § 63n145
[113] *Ibid,* § 133

all possible conditions and have assured myself that the
alchemists as well as the great philosophies of the East are
referring to just such experiences, and it is chiefly our
ignorance of the psyche if these experiences appear
'mystic.'[114]

Individuals can have these experiences to a lesser or greater extent, but
enlightenment belongs to the great Arhat who has continued, ongoing
insight into the nature of existence. In the *Mundaka Upanishad*, it is
written: "He strives by these means and has the knowledge in him this
spirit enters into its supreme status. ... Satisfied in knowledge, having
built up their spiritual being, the Wise, in union with the spiritual self,
reach the Omnipresent everywhere and enter into the All."[115] Sri
Aurobindo, who is such a being, as his writings evidence, argues that
humanity does not have the capacity to absorb all of the mystery and it
requires a new species that is sufficiently evolved to hold that higher
consciousness: "If then man is incapable of exceeding mentality, he must
be surpassed ..."[116] Jung, in his statement about Gerhard Dorn, refers to
having respect for "experiences," and indeed these experiences may be a
connection, a numinous experience of a transcendent quality of the union
of opposites in the Self, but this is not the manner in which he uses the
term totality. He does not at any point relate the Self to these numinous
experiences of totality.

The *Collected Works* error in translation appears responsible for that
transposition and has often obscured the apparent meaning of totality and
the goal of the Self. The conflation of mystical experiences with totality
can lead to statements that elevate wholeness or centering to a level that
was not intended. A statement by Eric Neumann illustrates this problem:

> the centered person appears as creative spontaneity which
> has attained form, as one numinously grasping and grasped,
> as well as one enlightened and knowing, in whom the
> world's luminosity apprehends itself, in the center of the
> world.[117]

---

[114] CW 14, § 762
[115] Aurobindo 2005, p. 880-1
[116] *Ibid*, p. 879
[117] Neumann 1989, p. 62

This statement occurs in his discussion of Zen masters who are, he says, "no longer 'normal' individuals,"[118] and thus he combines enlightenment with centering. This conflation of mystical terms with concepts of the Self can be seen as a great pull that is subtle and seductive as it elevates the ideal of unity with the all-oneness of a mystical experience. When speaking of the oneness experience of the mystic, the complete union that is enlightenment, it enriches the language of the Self and appears to support it as the central archetype. However, this is not how Jung explained it, so it is a mistake that makes it an impossible and untenable goal if that is to stand for realization of the Self. This form of error leads to a contemporary failure to describe the true nature of the realization of the Self. This can be seen in the expression of realization of the Self by Warren Colman:

> The self-directing ego disciplines itself to function in a very special way so that it not waylaid by the ordinary contents of consciousness, far less by powerful affective states of desire, but is able to abstract and distil an experience where consciousness is able to focus entirely on itself—to observe itself being without content. These states of mind require an extremely high level of self-reflective consciousness so that act of knowing is abstracted from the contents of what it knows and become itself something to be known.[119]

This is a statement of a state of mind that has reached a profound, enlightened level of a complete Self-absorption that approaches a unitive experience, which is relevant only in the context of mystical experience. It makes the end point of individuation, expressed in this way, as a union with the totality of the infinite, or a form of samadhi that Jung explains is not suitable for the West as in the East; it is "nothing but a meaningless dream-state."[120] This may be taking Colman's comments too far and obviously are a testament to his own realization, but it is illustrative of the fact that casting the realization of the Self in that unitive form as the goal of individuation thereby gives too much weight to an end state that is not the nature of the Self and is not going to be obtained.

[118] *Ibid*
[119] Colman 2008, pp. 361-2
[120] CW 11, § 785

This approach of conflating esoteric or mystical states of consciousness melds the Self into a process and a goal reserved for Eastern lineages. In this realm, where the ideal adherent is directed to go beyond duality, consciousness, to use Colman's words "is able to focus entirely on itself." *There are very few, if any, current Western or Jungian examples of this state that have been reported,* although it is possible that there are individuated egos that are so realized somewhere behind closed doors. If full realization is to embrace this mystic totality, that would require an individual who has dedicated his or her life to opening up to the mystery in a supportive culture, not one who goes about the daily requirements of Western life.

In 1959, in another letter, Jung refers specifically to the Eastern notion of enlightenment:

> But this whole is too big for the ego to grasp. I can only be divined, but his is not a cognition. I can become conscious neither of the whole of myself nor the whole of the world. I know that the East believes in a consciousness without a subject and says the personal *atman* is capable of encompassing the knowledge of the whole. Nevertheless the East also says that dreamless sleep in the highest stage of cognition. For us that is an inconceivable paradox because dreamless sleep is, for us, the epitome of an unconscious state in which no consciousness exists, as we understand it. … Perhaps there is a transcendental consciousness of the self which cognizes the self. But since I am a mere mortal and an empiricist to boot, I cannot assert that I am this self which is capable of such cognition.[121]

A reflection on this statement is that the dreamless sleep is not, in fact, the final goal of Eastern forms of enlightenment. It is instead the result of the truth revealed as the dreamless sleep ends and cognition surfaces. Enlightenment is not the dreamless state but the truth that has been understood, most likely as interpreted in the context of the mystical practices of the individual.[122]

---

[121] *Ibid,* p. 524
[122] Stein 2019b, pp. 68-9.

The fact that that unity is an ideal, a *principle*, is where the comparison with Eastern enlightenment has purchase. Murray Stein compares individuation with Eastern enlightenment using quotes of Gerhard Dorn's states of union. Stein explains, "The thought Dorn expresses by the third stage of conjunctio is universal: it is the relation or identity of the personal with the suprapersonal atman, and of the individual *tao* with the universal *tao*." Stein concludes that there are indeed similarities because there is a "stage of individuation in which ego-consciousness and the collective unconscious are united and synthesized."[123] This can certainly be said to be accurate, if that occurs, in that *conjunctio* of all of the opposites in psyche is that *ideal* and is therefore a theoretical endpoint of the concept of the Self. It does not seem, however, to be the focus of Jung's concept of the Self, which is more limited. Jung suggests that the merging state may be found by a different route that includes such practices as solitude, fasting, and meditation, where that, in his view, opens up to a numinous experience.[124] The ideal in Eastern religion is that an enlightened person does not remain in samadhi that is a permanent merging with the collective unconscious, but their whole being has been informed by that experience so they retain an equanimity that approximates a unity of opposites. If enlightenment is observed in this manner, there is no inconsistency between that end state of identity with the widest sense of totality and realization of the Self. A mystical experience of the oneness of all things would provide the understanding of unity as the *unus mundus* rather than a continuous merged state except in the rarest individual where that is supported by the culture.

Enlightenment indicates a permanent alteration in consciousness by one or, more likely, many mystical experiences that lead to a knowing of the nature of reality. The only basis of combining the experience of all-oneness with the end state of the Self is that psychic totality includes the collective unconscious, which, by definition, spans all that exists. This theoretically removes any boundaries for the Self so that it could become, as Jung expresses, that "indescribable totality" that is "inconceivable and 'irrepresentable.'"[125] However, this idea of totality being indescribable and related to the realization of the entirety of the collective unconscious

---

[123] Stein 2019b, p. 18
[124] CW 5, § 519
[125] CW 14, § 181

was never given a functional role by Jung in realizing the Self, as it cannot be made the subject of the ego, except in a case that is so rare that it would never present itself in analysis. The main function for his psychology was given to the center and the *ideal* of unity, an understanding that evokes the orientation of order, which is what brings forward the idea into focus. It was never suggested by Jung that the view of the Self as realized, by including the indescribable totality, was necessary for realization of the Self.

The closest but yet relatively obscure statement by Jung that realization *does not require* a higher, all-oneness state as the goal of the Self, arises in his analysis of the alchemical view of Ezekiel's vision of the chariot with four wheels and four seraphim. The vision represents wholeness amplified by the earliest depiction of God as a man. In this context, Jung explains what can be known of the Self; he speaks of how the four elements are integrated with consciousness where the "state of totality has *almost been attained.*"[126] This is a statement of almost realizing wholeness, the state contained in the alchemical idea of *albedo,* where conflicts disappear and one feels peace for the first time. Beyond this, he explains, there is indeed a *further state* but that is not able to be reached.

In describing the psychological nature of the vision of the chariot, he adds that only one function can be reached at the human level, "whereas the others are still in an unconscious or animal state."[127] The wholeness can only be completed by some other action of entering into the transcendent, making the vision "the true psychological foundation of the God-concept."[128] This relationship of realization with the God-concept, makes the Self concerned with not only that which is human but also that which is related to its transcendence. Accordingly, in this difficult reasoning, totality is both the human level of wholeness in terms of the Self but also the divine level of transcendence that is a level beyond the Self that is indeed an aspect of the Self to the *extent that it is manifested.* However, and most importantly in terms of the Self, it is only the human level that can be realized, the center and its significance as an orienting function toward the ideal of unity, and there is no writ to go further, although the

---

[126] *Ibid,* § 265, emphasis added.
[127] *Ibid,* § 269
[128] *Ibid,* § 273

Self *can* touch totality if the transcendent realm is manifested and then only to that extent.

Holding up that endpoint that exists for a sage as the realization of the Jungian Self makes it an impossible goal, even though there are putative examples that others, outside the process of psychoanalysis, have reached that stage. The clinical disadvantage of holding up realization in the transcendent sense as the goal is that each patient (and analyst) will be seen to fall short of that target. It may be best to create more useful expressions of realization than that available to the sage where that state will be so rare that there are no proximate examples.

A way into a better expression of the Self in order to understand the nature of realization of the Self is hinted at by Colman. He raises the possibility that the Self as totality may indeed manifest itself as part of a natural progression. This is because numinous, archetypal images of the Self occur naturally through the tendency of the Self toward integration, as evidenced by Fordham describing a child drawing a circle. Colman adds that this occurs—this push to a higher integration—where "the existing images of the self needs to be transcended."[129]

This emergent view of the Self implies that the ego's understanding of the Self is not fixed but is constantly evolving and could, as a natural progression, embrace the transcendent. This is probably the situation where the Self as center has been attained but is then attended by a push for further integration. That implies that the transcendent is implicit in the Self so that it will always seek its highest form. It accords with the idea of Deleuze that "the soul is not a body in a point but is itself a higher point and of another nature, which corresponds with that point of view."[130] Is it enough then to present realization of the Self as the center and the ideal and leave the transcendent quality to rare manifestation or future development?

Wholeness as the Goal

The answer of the end goal of realizing the Self may lie in referring to the goal of the individuation process as the *creation of wholeness* rather

---

[129] Colman 2008, p. 362
[130] Deleuze 1993, p. 23

than the realization of the Self. Jung states, "I have called the wholeness that transcends consciousness the 'self.'"[131] Wholeness is the actual goal; the Self is its name. In referring to the effect of a continued reference to "God," Jung adds, "Though our choice characterizes and defines 'God,' it is always man-made, and the definition it gives is therefore finite and imperfect." The same holds true of the "Self," as conflicts in the definition abound as this work certainly shows. Wholeness is more clearly defined as the totality of an individual's being that incorporates the ideal of a unity[132] and suggests, by its structure, a center. More specifically, wholeness is not a complete state of oneness that must be reached, but one where it can be seen in an individual that "His wholeness implies a tremendous tension of opposites paradoxically at one with themselves."[133] If an individual is at peace, the individuation process has been successful. That individual has realized a central point and has become whole; there is no need to have realized any level of transcendent totality, even though that level certainly exists.

In Jung's 1935 Eranos lecture, in referring to the Self's realization, he aligns the process of individuation with the "creation of wholeness" (*Die Herstellung der Ganzheit*),[134] translated accurately as the "production of wholeness" in the *Collected Works*.[135] That link between "production of wholeness" and the Self is most apparent in his 1940 analysis of the nature of the child archetype. That discussion suggests the possibility of psychological growth arising from the pure, undisturbed, potentiality of uniting the opposites—making them whole. Thus, that child is symbolized as roundness, of the ordering qualities of the circle or the square, and other allusions to wholeness.[136] The reasoning is not that the child is complete roundness, but that the *potential* within the child for uniting of the opposites is what produces wholeness. This then speaks of the goal or manifestation of the Self as the representation and realization of potential wholeness.

---

[131] CW 9.i, § 278
[132] CW 5, § 460
[133] *Ibid*
[134] Jung, 1935, p. 116
[135] CW 12, § 295
[136] CW 9.i, § 278

Transposing the child motif or any symbol of wholeness to the Self occurs because the beginning state (the core Self) carries in it the future end state; the symbols when activated thus anticipate a potential unity. This is made somewhat clearer in Jung's statement that "The goal of the individuation process is the synthesis of the self."[137] He indicates, as is most relevant, that the term "entelechy," "might be preferable to 'synthesis,'"[138] so it would read that the goal of the individuation process is the entelechy of the Self. Entelechy is used philosophically to mean the realization of what is *in potentia*. Leibnitz, the 17th-century Enlightenment philosopher, refers to it as a manifestation of a vital force that directs life through a preestablished harmony, similar to the idea of a preexistent Self[139] and, in this way, is the potential for that harmony. That is why entelechy is preferable to synthesis, as Jung explains, because "the symbols of wholeness frequently occur at the beginning of the individuation process, indeed they can often be observed in the first dreams of early infancy."[140] The wholeness anticipates itself and it is the starting place, and its potential is the end goal. The realization is of *the potential for wholeness*, the ideal or principle of unity, a numinous center. That is what is to be realized.

The appearance of a symbol of wholeness raises the ideal of the uniting of opposites, which is the realization of what was already there because of the preexisting coincidence of opposites. Phrased in terms of the Self, to the extent that there are symbols of wholeness, those are the expressions of the Self *in potentia*. Although these symbols of wholeness appear more frequently in infancy, the process of individuation and the integration of the Self "arises in the second half of life."[141] These symbols of wholeness are directed to an end state possible in the second half of life by the realization of the ideal of uniting opposites in psyche.

The emphasis of realization of the ideal of unity, the potential for wholeness, is completely consistent with finding the existence of a center in psyche, as that also anticipates the possible unity. The center, when understood as significant, confers the highest value in psyche as it offers

---

[137] *Ibid*
[138] *Ibid*
[139] Cambray 2005
[140] CW 9i, § 278
[141] CW 16, § 474

the hint that there can be a unity, the quiescence of the conflict of the opposites. As expressed by von Franz, "The goal of individuation, as pictured in unconscious images, represents a kind of mid-point or center in which the supreme value and the greatest life-intensity are concentrated."[142] This reflects Jung's dream, the creation of the center as a goal that anticipates order, that is the nature of wholeness and realization of the Self.

The more grandiose idea of direct realization of the Self as transcendent totality is, outside a numinous experience, more of a fantasy and not relevant. It is not available to the patient in the consulting room so that holding out hope of its realization to that extent may be an injustice. However, the concentration on the center leads, at least partly, to the possibility of glimpsing the magnitude or numinosity of the Self. This may or may not lead eventually to a numinous experience, but that is secondary to realizing the center and recognizing the potential for wholeness. This may make the symbols of the center far more important than others because the center, as von Franz explains, "brings a feeling of standing on solid ground inside oneself, on a patch of inner eternity which even physical death cannot touch."[143]

Individuation is thus the process of circling the center until the Self reveals itself as that center and provides the possibility of wholeness, best expressed as the "ideal of unity." The potential of wholeness, the ideal of unity, evolving from realization of the center is the real goal of individuation, and it is that and only that which points to the concept of realization of the Self. This is not a difficult concept to grasp intellectually because the idea of centering is accessible. This does not deny that the Self as totality can be the subject of unconscious images, but that realization is not gainsaid by the individuation process.

Thoughts on the Work of a Lifetime

In simple terms, it seems to follow that a realization of wholeness and, as well, a partial realization of the transcendent totality may be earned by inner work. The Self is always there to be realized so, as Jung puts it,

---

[142] von Franz 1975, p. 73
[143] *Ibid*, p. 74

"Regardless of philosophy's perpetual attitude of dissent or only half-hearted assent, there is always the compensating tendency of our unconscious psyche to produce a symbol of the self in its cosmic significance."[144] If it is not produced by a numinous experience that overwhelms the ego, the realization comes through the process of individuation. The circumambulation of the center is the process of individuation that creates an interrelationship between the ego and the unconscious, and this makes the unconscious more receptive to the symbols of the Self that may arise. These symbols may hint at something but require the process of analysis to make them more apparent. The notion of the individuation process does not support that the Self will eventually be realized as a totality, but it leaves open that it could yield that dimension to some extent, so it becomes, as Jung expresses in a Zarathustra Seminar, an "attempt."

Murray Stein asks, "Does the Self change as a result of lifelong individuation?"[145] and answers, "Emergence of the Self is a lifelong process, continuing into old age and especially so if the work of making it conscious is deliberately undertaken."[146] The editors of the *Collected Works* surmise from Jung's work, "The inference would seem to be that every individual, by virtue of having, or being a psyche, is potentially the self. It is only a question of 'realizing' it. But the realization, if ever achieved, is the work of a lifetime."[147]

The level of accomplishment to fully realize the Self, even as a wholeness, remains a dream, and that dream finds its way into the expression of the Self. Esther Harding describes it as:

> In order to find the Self ... one must be freed from ego desirousness and from the conflict of opposites. (First), the possibilities of ego consciousness must be fully explored, then it will be possible to perhaps to go a step beyond the accepted cultural level of the day and bring up from the depths of the unconscious a value that will produce an enlargement and transformation of consciousness itself.[148]

---

[144] CW 9.i, § 289
[145] Stein 2008, p. 319
[146] *Ibid,* p. 320
[147] CW 7, p. 460n
[148] Harding 1973, p. 235

She does not reserve this possibility for only a mana-personality but rather someone who has completed the needs of the ego and is no longer struggling for reputation and cultural approval; this may be rarer than a mana-personality. Thus, the individuation process, or the *Principium Individuationis* as Jung calls it in the *Severn Sermons*, appears as the lifelong development toward greater consciousness by having completed the journey to calm the chaos of the opposites. It is not, therefore, final realization of the Self that is the practical goal of individuation, but rather it is an endless, continuous circumambulation of the center, expanding the ego, strengthening it, and then shifting the emphasis away from its vicissitudes over time. In the course of that process, an intimation of the Self may arise, deepening the process by giving the ego an expanding revelation.

It is then fair to say that some may, due to their receptivity and persistent longing, come to an accommodation where they reach a level of finite calm, but realization of the Self *as a clinical idea* is the gradual development of *some indicia* of the potential of wholeness. To say that an individual has realized the Self is to present an idea that the personality is characterized by a presence, a congealed calm, that approaches equanimity. This can be accomplished in a lifetime and is not evidenced by intellectual explanations, positions of power, or achievements, but by the subjective sense of the individual. There is no proof required.

If the work of a lifetime was to be the transcendent realization of the higher or divine nature of the Self, individuation will not likely produce that result, indicating a failure of the process. An unbidden numinous experience must be received in consciousness to create an indelible alteration in consciousness, and only then can it be said that the work on that transcendent level is accomplished. However, at different stages of life, there are progressive levels of working more deeply to approach wholeness and the peace that ensues. Murray Stein reminds us, speaking of the states of a man's individuation, "Beyond simply reflecting on their personal lives, men in old age turn philosophical and consider the meaning of human life itself."[149] This he calls the "age of the sage," and this may be when the reality of wholeness can be reached as the culmination of a found orientation and a taste of unity and, in some cases, by a direct knowing of the all-oneness.

---

[149] Stein 2019b, p. 88

232 THE SELF IN JUNGIAN PSYCHOLOGY

Jung's Formal Definition

Jung published a specific definition of the Self very late in life, wherein he explains that the concept of the Self "is in part, only *potentially* empirical and is to that extent a postulate." For the Self as totality, he adds, it is a "postulate, it is a *transcendental* concept, for it presupposes the existence of unconscious factors on empirical grounds and thus characterizes an entity that can only be described only in part but for the other part, remains at present unknowable and illimitable."[150] Both of these hold out hope that the center and totality of the Self can be realized as empirical even though, for the latter, it is very much a part realization.

The realization he emphasizes is possible only through the symbols projected by psyche that offer the chance to bring the center and totality into conscious awareness. He is not referencing numinous experiences. This is consistent with his earliest comments in relating to dream symbols that the Self is an idea that "in empirical ways, (is) constantly elucidating itself" as dream images show.[151] The "empirical ways" are the never-ending production of symbols that are framed in a manner that can thereafter be extrapolated to a center of a geometric structure or as a union of opposites that comes from the transcendent possibility of the symbol. These symbols are, as the definition suggests, constantly presenting themselves when psyche is activated, almost as a hint or suggestion as to the center and the ideal of a unity.

The translation in the *Collected Works* as to the Self that Jung first presented in the 1935 Eranos lecture is, however, inaccurate in explaining the nature of this continuous process of symbolization. It states that the Self is "a concept that grows steadily with experience."[152] The original German is:

> *Es is zwar eine empirisch sich beständig verdentlichende Idee, we unsere Träume dartun, obne aber darum von threr Transzendenz einzübußen.*[153]

---

[150] CW 7, § 489, emphasis supplied.
[151] Jung 1935, p. 176
[152] CW 12, § 247
[153] Jung 1935, p. 104

It can be literally translated as an *empirically evolving idea*, and there is no mention that it grows steadily from "experience." In the context of the dream to which this phrase relates, the Self is brought into psyche by the continuous production of dream symbols, not from experience. The empirical proof arises from the nature of the symbols as being realized as a center and, possibly, a part of totality, as the definition explains, and not in a linear way by life experience, assuming that is what the translation implies.

It is through this objectification of the center and totality as symbols that the revelation of the Self becomes at all possible because the ego needs a means to relate to the Self for it to be manifested in the individual. It is not at all critical, however, for the Self as center to always be symbolized, as it could also be personified through the idea of a centering process that is natural and in the collective, or a feeling of wholeness. Symbolization is clearly more empirical as it offers a firm image that attracts a projection and conscious scrutiny. What appears to be the priority is that the symbols, as in Jung's 1927 dream, are evocative, such as the geometric pattern evoking an archetype of orientation by establishing a virtual center for the chaos by a geometric structure. The meaning is not derived from the symbol but by the orientation it suggests.

It will remain a mystery why Jung did not use the formal definition to clarify further the nature of realization of the Self and what he meant by totality. It could not be assumed that he believed that totality was understood by the community of those interested in his work, as Fordham had already published his dismissal of totality when the definition was framed and published. It is also not a sufficient explanation that we had to figure it out ourselves because it is the centerpiece of individuation. The only explanation could be that as an idea it needed to remain hypothetical until it is realized, and then the definition can be read clearly and with no missing explanation.

Chapter 10. The Self as Agent

The most difficult aspect in understanding the operation of the Self is the issue of whether the Self is responsible for creating its own realization or, instead, the mere numinosity of its existence draws one to it. Is it best understood as having its own agency or as having magnetism that attracts? As it holds opposites at a center point and appears to produce symbols for its consideration, it may seem a guiding spirit, so there is a tendency to give it agency. It is indeed approached most often in the Jungian literature as a *substance* with distinct, self-directed functions, and, because all psychological growth can be assigned to the process of centering, the Self is considered an independent actor.

If the Self is an active entity with its own goal of wholeness, it takes on the characteristics of a perennial companion, so that an individual may find solace in its existence as a guiding spirit. If the Self is conceived, instead, as a core Self or patterning in the psychoid region that attracts the ego when there is strong affect, then it is not a substance, and the meaning of its existence is derived instead from knowing that psyche cleaves to a center. In the latter case, the energy for psychological growth does not come from the Self, but from the broader individuation process where the movement forward is derived from an unknown source, such as archetypal forces in the unconscious, "God's will," or libido stored from the tension of opposites.

The issue is, to be more specific, whether "individuating energies" flow from the Self in order to create both symbols of itself and its ultimate realization. If it does, then those energies arise from an innate self-agency of the Self to bring an individual to its realization, and therefore it will purposefully project the symbols that are needed. If there are, instead, no "individuating energies" flowing from the Self, then the patterning comes forward to be symbolized in accordance with the emergent archetype, affective activation of psyche, and the magnetic power of the numinosity of the Self. In this case it is up to circumstance that the ego, in an affective state, will grow dim enough to fall back into the unconscious and be gripped by the patterning of the Self. This creates two models of the Self that weave their way through the ideas of Jung, that the Self either appears to have agency, thus an "agency model," or the Self as a center is numinous and attracts the ego, the "magnet model." This is perhaps the most difficult inquiry that can be made of the Self as there are many statements Jung made that can be interpreted on their face as supporting one or the other model. The only way it can be approached is by a close, logical examination of a very illogical subject matter to try to come to terms with what is the preferred view.

The Agency Model

A useful starting point arises from the basic proposition that the ego must realize the Self for it to have any psychological significance. This offers an effective entry into investigating the different models because it opens an inquiry of whether a very weak ego or one damaged by trauma or psychosis can have that realization. Can the Self as an entity in an agency model still carry out its goal as realization will fail in terms of the magnet model as the Self will be effectively dormant, asleep, as there is no effective ego to be drawn by its magnetism?

In his analysis of the relationship of the Self to the multiplying effect of a trauma complex in psyche, Donald Kalsched suggests that there are two aspects of the Self: the "survival" Self that remains after severe trauma, and the "individuating" Self that can be invoked at a future point for psychological growth: "The survival Self seems to be taken by the Self when its otherwise *individuating energies* have been diverted to earlier developmental task (sic), i.e. assuring the individual's survival."[1] In his later writing, he describes how this leads to a self-care system that develops in the individual for the purpose of protecting "soul."[2] He relies for this latter assertion on an active agency for that system by relying on Jung's statement that behind a regression "slumbers the 'divine child' … the germ of wholeness."[3] … "It is these inherent possibilities of 'spiritual'

---

[1] Kalsched 1996, p. 97, emphasis added.
[2] Kalsched, 2013
[3] CW 5, § 508

or 'symbolic' life and of progress which form the ultimate, though unconscious, goal of regression."[4] This idea expresses that there is something behind or underlying psyche, a *germ* of wholeness, a dormant entity, so Kalsched adds: "Behind the clash of opposites there seems to be something else 'waiting' for us to make a choice—or not."[5]

The idea of a "germ" is a powerful concept for Jung as he also speaks of the *Golden Germ* in Indian philosophy, whereby the protagonist creates himself from the one that he is to become many out of his own womb, implying the ultimate agency of self-propagation.[6] The protagonist is Prajapati, the Lord of Creation, who "propagates himself" and his own "son," whom he has birthed, and practices austerities to create the universe.[7] In the reference to the "germ" quoted by Kalsched, he uses the analogy of a regression back to an individual's creation, the mother. This regression is to the original germ that suggests the very moment of creation where the "divine child," the innocent unity of opposites, sleeps. In this self-propagating, complete unity, the moment of creation, lies a germ of wholeness as the "seed" of knowledge,[8] and this is an excellent image that Kalsched invokes to describe the core Self or the patterning being the formational elements of human life. The idea of a germ in the contexts in which it is used by Kalsched and Jung *implies* agency but could also be explained as a reference to the archaic core Self that is part of the structure of the brain that is only functional psychologically when it is activated.

Kalsched moves more deliberately in the direction of an agency model from the "germ" idea by pointing out how commentators have tended to see the Self as "nudging" the resisting ego "toward its prespecified 'plan' of individual wholeness."[9] This agency, as he points out, can be manifested in positive and negative forms to accomplish what is ultimately best for the ego. The negative forms are in conflict with a beneficent agency model, requiring him to revert to more subtle reasoning. In answer to how the agency of the Self can be squared with

---

[4] *Ibid*, § 510
[5] Kalsched 2013, p. 157
[6] CW 5, § 589
[7] *Ibid*, § 388
[8] *Ibid*, § 590
[9] Kalsched 1996, p. 96

"axe-murders, shotgunners, and zombie-doctors," he places this dark side of the Self as an aspect of a primordial survival Self affected by trauma. This survival Self is then an unconscious remnant of the larger Self, but this makes it a difficult proposition. The individuating energies, he therefore asserts, can only come later when the ego is relatively well established.[10] With trauma, he states "for reasons that are not altogether clear, horrific and destructive imagery of the Self predominates."[11]

It is hard to understand how the primitive, core Self, viewed only as a patterning of order and orientation that is the basis for the development of psyche, suggests destructive imagery. When, at a later stage, psyche is activated by strong affect, there are other archetypal forces that can account for dark images; there is, Jung explains, a "dark creative power in the unconscious,"[12] and there is also the Shadow, the "dark half of the personality."[13] The darkness that exists is always part of the Self as it holds, by definition, the preexisting warring opposites: "The self is made manifest in the opposites and in the conflict between them; it is a *coincidental oppositorum*. Hence the way to the Self begins with conflict."[14] It is not possible then to assign the darkness to a survival Self, the core Self, and then benevolence to a more integrated ego and its individuating energies.

Kalsched was forced logically into that position once he accepts the views of commentators who suggest the Self is positively nudging its way to realization. The better position would have been the magnet model, wherein the Self as patterning is dormant and, even if activated in psyche, would be unable to create symbols. When the ego strengthens, it will be drawn to the numinosity of the Self as it begins to sense its existence. The reason to give the Self individuating energies in Kalsched's explanation is not found, but it does indicate that the powerful place of the Self in psychoanalysis can strongly suggest that it is moving psyche along, a nudge in a particular direction, bringing up tragedy and triumph for its own realization.

---

[10] *Ibid*, pp. 96-7
[11] *Ibid*
[12] CW 5, § 182
[13] CW 12, § 37
[14] *Ibid*, § 259

The strongest sentiment for the agency model is created by the association of the Self with transcendence. This can be found in Kalsched's idea that when by regression or otherwise the ego drops its defenses and becomes, as he calls it, a "sacralized ego" that holds the link between human and divine because of the sacrifice of the ego.[15] It is here that the agency model is born again because of a shift in emphasis to a transcendent potential. This idea follows easily by the language that Jung uses when he writes about the Self as joining transcendent ideas with psychological facts. However, these are Jung's realizations, and the problem comes when those insights are called into the service of a theme of agency he did not suggest.

The largest impediment to the agency model is that the Self as agent must have the capacity to move the process along by somehow activating the ego by strong affect, even though this is not logically possible, as the ego is not the Self. If indeed the Self can direct the ego, it must move consciousness to come to the aid of the Self to effect realization. Jung offers a possible solution that the Self "takes the ego into its service."[16] He does not use this idea to claim agency for the Self but explains that, by enclosing the ego in the totality of the psyche, it is within the Self: "the 'self,' by which I understand a psychic totality and at the same time a centre, neither of which coincides with the ego but includes it, just as a larger circle encloses a smaller one."[17] How this might work is not explained and does not follow from the Self enclosing the ego, as how the Self acts on the ego is not able to be understood.

This critical link between the ego and the Self that is required for an argument of agency is best explained on the basis that the Self contains the powerful and determinative patterning of the core Self that will establish the future development of the ego. It then recruits the ego to its patterning. Jung puts it this way: "My consciousness is like an eye that penetrates to the most distant spaces, yet it is the psychic non-ego that fills them with non-spatial images ... tremendously powerful psychic factors."[18] The manner in which the ego is filled by psychic factors is from the non-spatial images or primitive image schemas proposed by

---

[15] Kalsched 1996, p. 177
[16] CW 11, § 390
[17] CW 9.i, § 248
[18] CW 4, § 763

Knox, Merchant, and others. This would mean that the primordial patterning accounts for the influence it will have over the ego when it is formed and develops by environmental factors. This creates the vision that the Self directs the development of the ego to include all steps needed for its realization. Again, this is not able to be understood.

The ego and the Self only have a direct connection when the Self is *realized* and then it is, Jung explains, "the lonely ego who finds a mate in the self, for at first the self is the strange non-ego."[19] Until then, if agency is postulated, the only manner in which the Self can control the ego is through its transcendent power: "A religious terminology comes naturally, as the only adequate one in the circumstances, when we are faced with the tragic fate that is the unavoidable concomitant of wholeness."[20] It is, therefore, to a transcendent dimension that Jung and others turn to confer agency on the Self. This is how the "agency model" must be found at all: in the transcendent aspect of that divine energy that is in the Self. In a footnote, Jung makes this transposition the source of individuating energies: "The divine dynamism of the self, which is identical with the dynamism of the cosmos, is then placed at the service of the ego   ."[21] This is not a proposition that the stages of the Self are motivated by the dynamism of the cosmos, or God's will, but rather that the Self has its *own* divine dynamism. If this is the case, then the agency of the Self must exist psychologically as an internal, intra-psychic presence and not just an idea. This is because, on many occasions, Jung warns of the arrogant "metaphysical assertion that seeks to make a God outside the range of our own experience responsible for our psychic states."[22]

There are other concepts presented in his last work, *Mysterium Coniunctionis*, that suggest agency through the divine as the essence of the Self. The first is that symbols have, he proposes, a "transconscious character" that arises from the effect of a transposition from theriomorphic (animal) forms to human figures, such as a king or a representative of divinity.[23] Jung uses "transconscious" often, for instance to explain how mandalas come about from a quality that is more than just

---

[19] CW 12, § 155
[20] *Ibid*, § 36n17
[21] CW 13, § 373n5
[22] *Ibid*, § 75
[23] CW 14, § 4

consciousness.[24] This superadded aspect of consciousness, a transpositional, transcendent quality, corresponds to the movement toward the ideal of unity that is the Self and that can be equated with that which rises above the finite capacity of the ego.

These are Jung's realization that there lies within us higher capacities than what is evident, such as the capacity to hold the opposites and to find orientation in the chaos that has the effect of elevating the center to a more transcendent reality. It is certainly true that many seek this higher level and partake of a greater possibility for the Self as offering an ideal unity to mediate the conflict of opposites. This makes Jung's statement understandable as the reason why the Self is elevated as having divine attributes: "The pairs of opposites constitute the phenomenology of the paradoxical self, man's totality."[25]

There are counterapproaches that could suggest that the ego and not the Self has agency, or it exists when the Self and the ego combine. One approach is that the ego supplies the agency as it is, as Jung explains it, a *"relative constant personification of the unconscious itself,"*[26] so that the ego lives out the patterning of the Self and is what wakes up the Self. Another is that the split between ego and Self, it could be argued, is only a Western problem where God and the ego are "worlds apart," as Jung puts it, and instead, as viewed in India, the ego and Self are a combined, world-creating power.[27]

The only downside of the agency model is that it ignores the importance and impact of strong affect that comes upon an individual circumstantially and not necessarily from the common pattern of the core Self. If that is ignored, it would mean that the Self causes the chaos that leads to strong affect, and this is not an idea promoted by Jung. It is also the case that the ego may not make use of the symbols that are projected, which is a real and observable possibility, so that the ego cannot realize the Self. If the Self presses the ego into service, it will then often fail, as the Self is not realized.

[24] CW 9.i, § 711
[25] CW 14, § 4
[26] *Ibid,* § 129, emphasis supplied
[27] *Ibid,* § 130

Warren Colman points to research that the brain initiates action before a decision is made as a prelude to his statement, "It is not the ego that is agent of our lives but the self ..."[28] This could provide an answer, as it suggests that the Self, as a preexistent entity, prefigures how the ego will move toward individuation once it activates psyche. This is the idea that the decision to act follows the established primal pattern of wholeness once psyche is activated, that then means that the pattern may be determinative of the manner in which it operates, including strong affect from a clash of opposites.

This approach of agency and individuating energies concatenates the pattern of wholeness with the activation of psyche and the projection of symbols of wholeness. The pattern influences the nature of individuation as an imprint determining how the psyche gets activated and the symbols that are projected. This requires the patterning to have an added intelligence of when to activate the psyche, under what circumstances, and which symbols to project. Colman explains it this way:

> The idea of an intentional self is probably due to a linking of these deeply convincing inner experiences with Jung's more abstract ideas of a self-regulating, homeostatic psyche which has an urge to individuate and throws up images, dreams and even behaviours which act as compensation to a one-sided consciousness.[29]

There is indeed a linking of Jung's experiences with the importance of individuation, but that does not justify the idea of the Self having a specific role in the day-to-day progress toward its revelation. Therefore, in order for Colman to press his argument of the Self having agency, he cites Jung's comments in *The Secret of the Golden Flower* that once the illusion of consciousness is shattered by the recognition of the unconscious, "the unconscious will appear as something objective in which the ego is included."[30] In relation to the Self, it is objective only if the symbols are realized and its role then will be clear. Colman combines this idea with statements by Jung that there arises a feeling that Christ is born within us "as if the guidance of life has passed over to an invisible

---

[28] Colman 2008, p. 356
[29] Colman 2006, p. 164
[30] CW 13, § 76

centre."[31] This appears correct but only when he moves to a transcendent position because it is not possible otherwise to suggest a power that is so particularly directive.

It is apparent that the recognition of the existence of the unconscious has the effect of introducing something new to consciousness, and this allows a release from the burdens of the conscious mind and the *masa confusa* of the collective. It highlights why Kalsched, Colman, and so many others treat the Self as having individuating energies, but it is only by resort to a transcendent argument that it has that nature. There needs to be a better explanation that does not rely on comparisons with a higher power as to how the Self operates behind the scenes in effecting psychological growth.

The Magnet Model

It is the case that the Self as attractor, as magnet, does not need individuating energies but rather its existence as the non-ego *fascinates* and, by that factor alone, draws every aspect to it to create a sense of Self. The mere fact that it is there as a numinous center is the basis for the attraction and will trigger the *Logos* to a greater or lesser extent. It "works" only by it being observed, which then indicates that there is a non-ego aspect that is unconscious, leading to a glimpse of the potential for a unity of both consciousness and the unconscious. The Self remains completely passive in this interpretation and is an attractor because it is sensed as existing as a non-ego presence.

Jung explains that there is, indeed, a form of energy created from the attraction qualities of all archetypes. An archetype, as is the Self, is energic in the sense that it contains a primal patterning that influences the formation of symbols of the Self that can be realized by the ego: "The energy of an archetype communicates itself to the ego only when the latter has been influenced or gripped by an autonomous action of the archetype."[32] This means that the archetype is persuasive at the level of image creation that "seizes hold of the psyche."[33] These symbols are

---

[31] Colman 2008, p. 356
[32] CW 5, § 101
[33] CW 7, § 110

"archaic, mythological images"[34] that provide a "*dynamism* which makes itself felt in the numinosity and fascinating power of the archetypal image."[35]

This dynamism is understood by Jung's discussion about instinct and instinctual images. The archetype is in the psychoid region and is irrepresentable, but the images are its effects, "which make visualizations of it possible."[36] As such, psychoid instincts and their resultant images are opposites, and that tension between them produces psychic energy.[37] This is the "dynamism" that suggests the numinosity of the Self and its images, leading to what Jung calls, a "spiritual goal."[38] He refers to it as like a "spirit" because its nature is transcendent.[39] The tension of opposites between the irrepresentable instincts and its images gives the archetype its numinosity, but it does not imply that it is an entity with agency. Rather, it is a presence that, because it is numinous, attracts like a magnet, drawing to it the underlying pattern in the form of images when consciousness is activated.

The power of the Self is as an archetype that creates our basic structures. In an interview with Marie-Louse von Franz, she is asked if life itself is a manifestation of the original archetype. She replies, "Yes. Jung does not dare say that, but we can infer it from what he says. (They are) world creating structures as well. That is, they are not only structures of our unconscious but are structures of the whole universe."[40] She adds, "I would say that the archetype of the Self is what starts and regulates the process of individuation."[41] Regulation comes from the degree of dynamism of the archetype of the Self that makes it sufficiently numinous to attract the ego.

This "magnet model" accounts, as one example, for a numinous experience where an individual is gripped by the wholeness archetype that has overwhelmed the ego and altered consciousness. It also can be

---

[34] *Ibid*, § 188
[35] CW 8, § 414
[36] *Ibid*, § 417
[37] *Ibid*, § 414
[38] *Ibid*, § 415
[39] *Ibid*, § 420
[40] Hannah & von Franz, 2004, p. 152
[41] *Ibid*, p. 204

said that the numinosity has the appearance of a form of energy because it is an attractor that brings psyche to it. Jung confirms that an archetype, which is numinous, is said to possess a certain energy because it will attract to itself the contents of consciousness, "conscious ideas that render it perceptible and hence capable of conscious realization."[42] The image schema or patterning of wholeness, the psychoid archetype, will attract to itself conscious ideas as it stands as a significant force in psyche and therefore has energy, but not directed intention.

In *Aion: Researches into the Phenomenology of the Self,* Jung suggests a magnet approach based on an examination of Gnostic symbols of the Self. He introduces specifically the notion that the Self acts as a magnet that is *passive without intentionality* yet draws to it what it needs for its recognition. He explains this in a discussion of the Gnostic Nassene doctrine of *Paradise,* a stage that is reached in the process of psychological growth where there is a quietude brought on by the dawning realization of the Self. There are four rivers of Paradise, as conceived by the Gnostic sect of the Nassenes, and the river Euphrates is the most significant, as it yields totality as the fourth, the universal number that is a symbol of wholeness. The Euphrates as the fourth is said to be the "living water" that draws forth what is relevant to it as a magnet.[43] This power exists because of the *aqua doctrinae,* a property of this special water that *attracts.* Jung explains that a magnet "attracts to itself that which is proper to it … everything that pertains to the original and unalterable character of the individual ground plan."[44]

The magnetic attraction, Jung adds, also comes from the idea of sonship, whereby Christ is symbolized by the serpent that is carried down from heaven so that it is "a magnet that draws to itself those parts or substances in man which are of divine origin …"[45] He extends this directly to the Self by comparing this magnetic effect to the *Lapis,* the goal of alchemy, that is the conscious realization of the spirit hidden in matter, a symbol of the uniting of those opposites and therefore a symbol of the Self.[46] In speaking of the magnet quality of the Euphrates, he adds, "the doctrine

---

[42] CW 5, § 450
[43] *Aion,* § 288
[44] *Ibid,* § 297
[45] *Ibid,* § 291
[46] CW 9.i, § 651

is the magnet that makes possible the integration of man as well as the *lapis*."[47] The existence of the *Lapis* can be said to prove that the Self is there, sleeping in the stone until realized.[48]

This makes the Self, or rather the core or schema of wholeness, able to suggest eventual integration as it is a magnet that draws in psyche for it to be recognized. He makes this clearer by saying that "… the magnetic attraction comes from the *Logos*. This denotes a thought or idea that has been formulated and articulated, hence a content and a product of consciousness."[49] Consciousness, seeking wholeness, is drawn to the unconscious, which contains that pattern. In that way, the Self activates psyche, projects symbols of itself by attracting consciousness to then be realized by a magnet model and not agency.

This is a good reason to assume that consciousness seeks the Self by the magnetic presence of the patterning of wholeness that is at the psychoid, instinctual level. Jung goes on to describe the three aspects of the magnet: It is passive, it fascinates, and is a philosophical idea.[50] He concludes: "This magnetic process revolutionizes the ego-oriented psyche by setting up, in contradistinction to the ego, another goal or centre," which therefore leads to the two—the sum of conscious and unconscious processes and this "objective whole … is what I called the self …"[51]

The fascination lies not only because of its numinous quality, but because it also is the "fertile soil from which all future life will spring" that leads to the idea of "immortality."[52] As with the agency model, the magnet model benefits from the transcendent images. It is, in this wider view, the manner in which we touch wholeness that not only carries orientation and meaning, but the possibility of future psychological growth. It thus has spiritual value and contains "the deposit and totality of all past life."[53]

The analysis of Gnostic doctrine is complex, but in this orientation of the Self as a passive magnet presented to consciousness by the activation of

---

[47] *Aion*, § 289
[48] CW 9.i, § 541
[49] *Ibid,* § 295
[50] *Ibid,* § 293
[51] *Ibid*
[52] CW 7, § 303
[53] *Ibid*

psyche by strong affect, the Self does not have intentionality. It is effective because of its magnetic qualities that indicate that it is a non-ego aspect of psyche and therefore it has capacity as an ideal of unity to hold the opposites. If a comparison of the process of the Self can be made with the Gnostic reasoning, it is the first stage of the patterning, the *aqua doctrinae*, where the Self is passive, which moves to the second stage of the activation of the psyche because consciousness is drawn to it and, by reflection, sets up the formation of symbols. This is the Gnostic recognition of the passive numinosity of the Self and the fascination with the passive patterning that engages psyche. This engagement is necessary because ultimately the symbols produced by psyche lead to the realization of that non-ego force in psyche that widens consciousness and is healing as it shifts the emphasis away from the ego.

The idea of a magnet is that it contains a magnetic field and offers the opposite poles of attraction and repulsion, the latter accounting for disinterest in the Self. Accordingly, there is no need for agency; as Jung explains about the *aqua doctrinae*, it is "an inanimate and in itself passive substance, *water.*"[54] He compares it specifically to the serpent as a symbol of Christ that as "an animate, autonomous being …. It fascinates" by its glance, and it is the *Logos,* consciousness, that is the "agent" as it is a philosophical idea as well as a "dynamic power."[55]

The magnetism is not the same as the Self having specific agency to determine the destiny of an individual. It does, as an archetype, have substance in the psychoid region and at the time of activation of psyche by a complex or feeling tone, there will be a drawing closer to that primordial ordering that offers protection from chaos. In this way, it does influence the manner in which an individual will move toward wholeness as a result of its numinosity.

The consequence of the center, Jung emphatically explains in a manner that defines its energy, is that it "acts like a magnet on the disparate material and process of the unconscious, and gradually captures them as in a crystal lattice."[56] This leaves no doubt that the center creates a process by being recognized due to its *mere existence.* It does not do anything

---

[54] *Aion*, § 293
[55] *Ibid*
[56] CW 12, § 325

itself, such as having particular power or being the subject of a drive or instinct, but it draws other processes to itself. A symbol such as squaring the circle, in terms of magnetism, therefore creates a *"premonition* of a centre of personality, a kind of central point within psyche ..."[57] because the center appears.

On this reasoning, the ever-effulgent, numinous quality of a symbol carries out the function for its recognition, as Jung explains, "the central symbol, constantly renewing itself, will steadily and consistently force its way through the apparent chaos of the personal psyche and its dramatic entanglements."[58] Polly Young-Eisendrath explains how quotes of this type can suggest the Self as an entity like a person, but she observes: "This way of speaking conflates the interpretative stance of a human subject with the role of an organizing principle in such a way that sounds as though the Self is acting on a motive of its own ..."[59] Instead, she maintains that Jung clarifies that the Self is an archetype and therefore it is the unconscious that provides a predisposition to form an image so that it is then an organizing principle "that provides an enduring tendency for the whole personality to *cohere,* and an underlying potential (which may or may not be actualized) for greater integration and differentiation of the individual over time."[60]

The full force of the Self and its usefulness lies in discovering the numinosity of the central symbol, centering and the ideal of finding shelter from chaos. Jung speculates that that the Self is a "dynamic process" that consists of it renewing *itself,*[61] which accounts for its numinosity and for its appearance in all things (the "Lapis"). The idea of "renewing itself" is mentioned by him as an ongoing process because when "a rearranging of personality is involved (there is) a kind of new centering."[62] It is the realization of a center that changes and renews or recreates itself as individuation takes place; he is making a reference to renewal as the Self becomes realized and not to a form of agency.

---

[57] CW 9.i, § 634, emphasis added.
[58] CW 12, §135
[59] Young-Eisendrath 1997, p. 161
[60] *Ibid*
[61] CW 12, § 411
[62] CW 9.i, § 645

The central symbol, the innate patterning, presents itself as a natural orientation as the hope for a center and balance, so it is innate and ontological. The Self, insofar as it is the psychic center, will always be sought because it is a primordial archetype of a life's journey toward consciousness, lying in the collective. It exists on every level in different forms, constantly changing in whatever way it is understood, from wanting to heal any psychological wound to finding the ultimate oneness. Paul Bishop, in his analysis of the effect of Goethe on Jung, explains this concretely with a reference to Nietzsche:

> The Jungian 'self' is a Dionysian self, inasmuch as it is born, dies, and is reborn, again and again, ceaselessly reconfiguring itself between its polar boundaries and, by means of specification, approximating the potential totality that lies in the coordination of all its facilities.[63]

It is the projection of the central principle in the symbols of an *Imago-dei,* the conflation with God, that makes it, according to Bishop, "a *point of reflection* ... a logical necessity."[64] When its numinosity is sensed, it is natural that it will be equated with the transcendent divine so that its realization will bring about a movement in psyche to a higher level, increasing its magnetism. Even with psyche evolving toward seeing the connection of the inward center with divinity, so often used by commentators as the springboard to create an agency model, the Self *does not individuate*, but the center point, by its numinous presence as transcendent, is a point of reflection. As Jung expresses, the need for the Self to be connected to the God-image is that "the visualization of the self is a 'window' into eternity, which gave medieval man, like the Oriental, an opportunity to escape from the stifling grasp of a one-sided view of the world or to hold out against it."[65]

That connection with the divine must absolutely follow, even if it does not throw up a specific God-image. The desire for that transcendence is in all our hearts, whether we give effect to it or not. However, the center need not always be taken to that level and can remain, as it did in Jung's 1927 dream, as a principle of orientation. It may still become a point of

---

[63] Bishop 2009, p. 168
[64] *Ibid,* emphasis supplied.
[65] CW 14, § 763

reflection even if the transcendent possibilities are not initially brought into awareness. However, this level of realization takes hold where it is found that the Self is distinct from the ego as a non-ego central aspect of psyche. Most importantly, it does not, however, lie within a person as a bundle of individuating energies, but only becomes dynamic from reflection on the level of a God-image or a centralizing non-ego function, and therefore it only has healing effects (as Jung indicated for the center in his dream of 1927) by pointing to the resultant archetypes, such as orientation, brought about by its existence.

It is therefore doubtful that the Self, *as defined by Jung*, is acting in the best interests of an individual as a personal guide, manipulating every move and direction. However, we are ascribing to the Self a definition and operation when it is beyond a definition and is a manifestation perhaps of something else, a soul, divine intervention, the complete unknown. This is an analysis of the Jungian idea of the Self that has parameters and a definition and, from that basis, does not appear to carry individuating energies. In terms of Analytical Psychology, the most convenient theory is that it operates as a magnet of a powerful, numinous, center of psyche and has the greatest effect when it is realized as being distinct from the ego, a psychological "other."

It is appropriate, if the sentiment of Jung's quotes is followed, to assign a sense of individuating energies when it is equated with transcendent or special qualities and, as well, appears as purposive on the basis that that it is needed to balance opposites. It then achieves this by logic that there must be a center between the opposites that holds the potential for a unity, and that is what has special qualities that approach that of the divinity. It becomes a psychic fact in the agency model only when it is confirmed by images that appear from the unconscious that equate with a center as a unity or a divinity. The fact that the images are dim, as Jung suggests, means that the psychic existence of the Self is then explained by contemplation and thoughts, emphasizing that before it is realized, it only has a passive quality and an inability to direct the conscious mind. Individuating energies upon realizing the Self may appear to confer upon it a capacity it otherwise does not deserve in fact, but only in theory as a hope or ideal.

From a clinical viewpoint, the Self as center does not need transcendence to be effective in its effect and in creating a deep connection with oneself.

It is not necessary to rush to add the transcendent, even though the words have that uplifting quality as an ideal related to God that always is joyful. A good example of providing qualities of the Self by unnecessary extrapolation to the transcendent is in the writing on the Self by the object relations psychoanalyst James Grotstein. This illustrates the form of words that must be then employed when that transposition is made. He sees the important numinous images as radiating from an inner divinity becoming "incarnate in the clinical setting." It is the inner divinity, what he calls the "ineffable state of *Being* (in the Heideggerian sense)," that is the "voiceless initiator" that "is doomed like Cassandra to prophesy without being believed and like Hermes to be voiceless in announcing the message."[66] If this connection between a voiceless initiator and dynamics that produce images of the Self is considered, then his ideas lead quickly to the conclusion that the Self has agency and healing energies because it is manifesting and responsible for a larger process.

Grotstein quotes from Jung's extensive August 1941 Eranos lecture *"Das Wandlungssymbol In Der Messe"* that appears to give agency to the Self as the "mover:"

> The term 'self' seemed to me a suitable one for this un-conscious substrate, whose actual exponent in consciousness is the ego. The ego stands to the self as the moved to the mover, or as object to subject, because the determining factors which radiate out from the self surround the ego on all sides and are therefore supraordinate to it. The self, like the unconscious, is an a priori existent out of which the ego evolves. It is, so to speak, an unconscious prefiguration of the ego. It is not I who create myself, rather I happen to myself.[67]

This quote, which appears as an agency model, changes its "model" to a magnet model when examined in context. It is explaining an ego that is unable to embrace the totality of conscious and unconscious and therefore must be less than totality, contained "like a smaller circle within a larger circle."[68] The ego is formed from the core Self, the primal, emergent

---

[66] Grotstein 1998, p. 43
[67] CW 11, § 391
[68] *Ibid*, § 258

patterning, so that one appears to happen to oneself. It becomes "the moved" *when realized,* where it changes the orientation of the ego. Until it is realized, it is an idea but is not a psychological fact. It is not at all a statement of agency but rather that, when the Self is realized, the ego will serve it because the revelation will change consciousness. This does not suggest that the Self actually does anything other than being preexistent as the primordial substance out of which the personality develops, and the ego is the means of its self-expression only when it is realized.

This position of a passive Self that stands as the moved because it attracts consciousness and the ego is formed from the patterning substrate, easily suggests the idea of agency, implying as a result that there is energy that must therefore exist in the Self. Gerhard Adler was strongly of the view that the Self was a *dynamis,* "the power which sets it in motion."[69] His argument is constructed on the basis of a quote by Jung that:

> Human nature has an inevitable dread of becoming more conscious of itself. What nevertheless drives us to it is the self. ... Conscious realization ... is in one sense an act of the ego's will, but in another sense it is a spontaneous manifestation of the self, which was always there.[70]

It could be said that, following this quote, we are driven to have a conscious realization of the Self. As well, this can be interpreted that the manifestation comes spontaneously out of the primal patterning, a magnet that attracts us to it; there is no need for an agency model. Conscious realization of the magnetic Self is, in fact, a spontaneous manifestation of the wholeness patterning of the Self because the symbols are projected in an enlivened psyche, the generator of which is conscious affect.

Adler provides two case studies to make the point that the "self is always a result of the action of the non-ego on the ego."[71] This leads him to a singular view that childhood development is "directed by the self."[72] This may be explained equally by the innate core Self as emergent and that has influence on childhood development.

---

[69] Adler 1979, p. 14
[70] CW 11, § 400
[71] Adler, 1979, p. 16
[72] *Ibid,* p. 17

There are many instances where the Self can be explained in either model. The Self, therefore, may also appear to be both, especially as it will always have a dynamic dimension in its transcendent state. It is noteworthy to observe how the choice of model dictates the manner in which the Self is viewed in a particular context. The theme of the Gnostic Basilides may hold an approach that allows for the two models to be used interchangeably. His theme is that there is a "universal seed" that rises out of creation: "God made the world out of nonentities, casting and depositing some one Seed that contained in itself a conglomeration of the germs of the world."[73] This one Seed produced by God contained a triple "filiality," or offspring, that then entered all other realms, material and transcendent, and produced Christ.[74] The Self, by analogy, can be said to have multiple derivations, as agent, as spirit, as world-soul, as magnet, and therefore there is no necessary inconsistency in it being both agent that seeks its own realization *for its own sake,* and magnet, where it is an attractor to its existence that enhances the consciousness of an individual by such an awareness.

It is perhaps best to say that there is no preferred view and the Self can exist in any formulation, such as Christ, the Holy Ghost, a guiding spirit, the Hindu *Atman*, the instinctual push to be what one can become, an archetypal force in the unconscious, a presence like a homunculus lodged in our being controlling our decisions, or that perfect unity that is the Dao. Read in this way, Jung's exposition of the Self exhibits a single-minded orientation for the Self to reveal itself as that which is the core of our human nature. It is the essential spiritual drive, the search for order, but also embraces the divine that does not operate in a linear way but rather in a manner that speaks to its profundity. To seek oneself requires the aid of energy, magnetism, and the involution of divine energy.

Multiplicity of the Self accounts for its presence in myths and fairytales that differ in emphasis. The presence in those forms makes the Self always transcendent and beyond space and time, the general position of all that lies in the deep unconscious.[75] Its practical operation is in space, so that, as Jung explains: "Wholeness, empirically speaking, is therefore

---

[73] Hippolytus 1868, Book VII, p. 275
[74] Quispel 1969/1948, pp. 218-20
[75] CW 7, § 912

of immeasurable extent, older and younger than consciousness and enfolding it in time and space."[76] In understanding the Self as a multiplicity of functions, all derived from the infinite, however conceived, allows it to be understood that the multiplicity yields the one—the monad that is a single point that contains totality.

Jung on the Agency Model

It is important to restate what has been implied, that Jung did not argue for proof of the agency of the Self, that it has individuating energies, or that it was a magnet, or that it otherwise could be hypostasized because "The self is not a philosophical idea, since it does not predicate its own existence, i.e., does not hypostatize itself. From the intellectual point of view, it is only a working hypothesis." It leads to symbols but remains an "archetypal idea."[77] His expressions that can point to a specific "model" vary, depending on the context of how he was evolving other ideas and his many statements about the source of psychological change, such as God's will or becoming what one can be. Perhaps this is to be expected because the Self can never move away from the fact that it is a hypothesis and is only made an understood psychological fact in rare instances.

There appears only one reference to offer up the concept of the Self as a reality and not just a psychological idea. Jung states, "If we hypostasize the self and derive from it (as from a kind of pre-existent personality) the ego and the shadow, then these would appear as the empirical aspects of the opposites that are preformed in the self," although Jung then states, "I set no particular store by these reflections."[78] This is a common-sense idea that the proof of the opposites in psyche can be found as a matter of reality by observing the constant struggle of the ego with the Shadow that is the working out of a fundamental pattern. His rejection of his own statement was made because it was contrary to his initial position on psychic objects and the evaluative method of *esse in anima* as the way of making a psychic object into a psychological fact.

---

[76] CW 9.i, § 299
[77] CW 6, § 791
[78] CW 14, § 129n.66

It is useful to explore whether Jung, even though not explicitly, tended toward an agency model or were his relevant statements more focused on a magnet model. As can be expected, the answer is not clear, but some direction and the reasons for that direction can be ascertained. The only way to explain a trend is to unravel the way he expresses himself over time and how the direction was formed. There is no definitive answer that emerges as to the appropriate model, but there are ideas that were developed that suggest, although inconclusively, his preferred model of the Self.

When Jung had the dream of the center in 1927, his first full realization of the Self, it was the existence of the center as an established psychological fact that evoked an orientation and a meaning. There was nothing there said in the telling of the dream that gave that center agency as an active, purposive participant in his life. It was a center around which one circumambulates and that acts as a magnet, the luminescent tree, drawing the other aspects of psyche closer. He maintains the idea of circumambulation around a center thereafter and never varies from its formulation. For example, in a letter in 1955 speaking of the Self, he explains, "The goal of this approximation seems to be anticipated by archetypal symbols which represent something like the circumambulation of a centre ..."[79] In terms of a center in psyche, this would mean that there is no need for there to be agency as the realization of its existence is, as Jung also adds in that letter, "a confrontation of the ego" with the center, when its existence will be revealed.[80]

In *Symbols of Transformation* in 1912, there was an early hint that he was then oriented to the Self as more than a passive, numinous center. He analyzes the religious image of the sun and how in ancient reflections, it exists as both a soul and a center. In this comparison, he provides the Self, although at this time he was using the term soul for Self, with a higher, divine aspect. He calls in aid the *Bihadaranyaka Upanishad*, which states, "It is by the light of the Self that a man rests, goes forth, does his work and returns."[81] In this quote, the Self has a directive, divine nature that is

---

[79] *Letters*, Vol. 2, p. 258
[80] *Ibid,* p. 259
[81] CW 5, § 230

within in an individual and the light of the sun, its emanation, confers on it a transcendent, guiding influence.

The nature of the Self as containing an inborn aspect of divinity is ultimately the basis for any reading of Jung in favor of the Self having agency. As with all transcendent assertions as to the Self, it elevates the center to a creative, transformative role that is beyond human endeavor. This appears to be his earliest idea and was clarified in the Mana Personality essay in 1928 specifically in terms of the Self. In that essay, the Self coincides not only with divinity but with those same characteristics that can be found in figures that have a superhuman capacity, such as a hero or Christ. The reason those figures become a representation of the Self is that psychologically they reflect the impact on consciousness of introducing a new aspect of a higher form of being that is an ideal. A figure such as the hero or Christ therefore share the same archetype of the explosive power of the non-ego that becomes a structural dominant. The comparison is not meant by Jung to be precise in this regard as it is never explained as agency, but rather it goes to promote a sentiment that the Self as wholeness is numinous and, as well, a dominant, archetype because it takes an individual away from the collective.

There is no statement being made in this 1928 essay that the Self is carrying out the individuation process. It is rather that it has characteristics of the hero that seems superhuman when realized and is representing an ideal of unity. A hero in the earlier *Symbols of Transformation* is therefore explained as beyond and above who we are: "The hero himself appears a being of more than human stature"[82] and in myth, the hero is tied in with unity as representing an "organizing dominant"[83] and a new foundation as it "personifies the world-creating power." [84]

A figure representing the Self of such power can easily be translated as the Self having these powers. However, he is referring to it as a "dominant" when it is realized, as that is when it has a psychological effect and creates a new foundation. The furthest he goes in elevating the Self to this dominant is to say that the Self "is numinous, a sort of god,

---

[82] *Ibid*, § 612
[83] *Ibid*
[84] *Ibid*, § 592

or having some shares in the divine nature."[85] This statement then requires Jung to immediately consider the problem of "homoousia" in relation to the Self, the ancient issue of whether Jesus is the same as God, for him to answer the issue of whether the Self is the same as God or, instead, only has some small share in the divine *nature* or is an emanation of God. Jung pauses in the text to answer this question but never does. He only suggests that in the hero myth "may lie the root of the argument in favour of the 'homoousia.'"[86] However, he turns to the psychological point of view instead to indicate that Christ is only a manifestation of the Self, a generated symbol, but they appear the same *empirically*. It is critical to his phrasing that it will appear empirically *only* when it is realized. Until then, nothing is being said that it has a role as an agent.

Psychologically, the Self and Christ are of the "same nature."[87] This is not from the viewpoint of Christianity, he adds, as that religion is incapable of understanding the idea of an inner aspect of God that is personal. That psychological nature, the critical comparison, is what led him also to invoke the hero as representing the "protagonist of God's transformation in man."[88] This is a wider view that is consistent with a theme, not yet expressed by him but that will later become important in *Aion* and *Answer to Job,* that man is essential to God's transformation. The best we can extract is that God and the Self have the same nature where *upon realization* (empirically) its revelation has a similar effect of altering consciousness to provide a new orientation and meaning. The hero and Christ bring transformation, but only when the Self is realized, so those transcendent qualities that would imply agency are relevant when the ego is overwhelmed by the existence of the Self. The power of transcendence does not seem to be applied by him as pertaining to the Self *before* realization. It is not a hidden power behind the scenes with agency but is the product of realization.

In all statements that give the Self agency, it is because they are equated with a transcendent power. This is the case *once the Self is realized* as that power of the Self become evident. It is then understood as the prime

---

[85] *Ibid,* § 612
[86] *Ibid*
[87] *Ibid*
[88] *Ibid*

mover. If it is not realized, which is the practical case, then it is not expressed that the Self is controlling its own evolution but rather there are other psychological explanations that serve that purpose. The Self is not the only activity in psyche, and there is, in Jung's lexicon, God's will, the soul, the spirit, and the irresistible urge to become what one can be. No answer need be found, but it appears that all options are possible for that which is unknown, yet fundamental to us and society. The conclusion is that Jung did not give the Self agency but only that it has that appearance when its importance is understood as one then sees that it was always there and is the source of peace.

Configurations of the Model

The various parts of the Self hint at two different configurations. The first configuration is the Self having agency or individuating energies in that it is actively seeking a result from its primordial roots to its realization. This implies that it is, by its nature, purposeful with an aim, always oriented to an outcome, in active pursuit of a goal. This "agency model" expresses the Self as an entity, a personality, with or without a physical basis or the conglomeration of mental functions that act as the director.

The second configuration is that the Self exists as a numinous aspect of our psyche because it is embedded as a patterning of wholeness that acts like a magnet in drawing us into an awareness of its existence. This "magnet model" postulates the Self as entity but with no purpose or agency. It is realized because it alerts us to its existence when there is strong affect that draws us into the unconscious, as it has a numinous, fascinating quality.

These models are subject to two further distinctions occurring in the relationship of the Self to an individual. The Self may have agency or merely a numinous, magnetic quality in order for it to *realize itself* through the agency of an individual. In this interpretation, the realization of the Self is for the incomprehensible goal of the Self *for its own purpose*; it seeks itself and we are participants in its unfolding. The parallel idea, reflected in Jung's *Answer to Job*, is that God engages man to become conscious. The other possibility is that the realization of the Self exists because the Self is actively concerned in an individual's psychological growth. In this view, the Self is not seeking its own realization, as it is not self-reflective, but rather its existence is oriented to actively create ontological development, perhaps as an evolutionary unfolding.

The taxonomy can be represented as a quaternity of four points and two pairs of opposites:

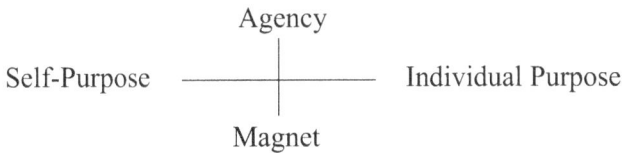

$$\text{Agency}$$

Self-Purpose ————|———— Individual Purpose

$$\text{Magnet}$$

The Self could serve as a magnet for its own realization that gives it a form of agency in the sense that it is primarily working through an individual for its own self-realization. On the other hand, it can be primarily a magnet to alert an individual that it exists, and that realization offers the possibility of understanding that there is a non-ego aspect of the psyche.

The scope of these different models and their underlying goals cannot be known because a portion of the Self will never be brought to consciousness. The Self appears to have different orientations, but neither model can therefore be determinative. In a discussion between Jung and a Japanese Zen philosopher, Jung explains that in relation to the Self, "only half is known," the conscious part, but the other half remains unknown as it embraces the vast unconscious.[89] Consciousness can be expanded by the realization of such of the Self that is revealed, but it can never be more than half of the ideal of wholeness; Jung adds, "I cannot be conscious of whether the self has attributes or not, because I am unconscious of the self."[90] The attributes of the Self's inner workings, the models, are then capable of being expressed only to a limited extent because of the different ways that psychic events appear to occur, the variations in symbols that are presented, the limitations of language to express unconscious interactions, and also the multiple motifs reflecting the Self that appear in myths, fairytales, and visions.

---

[89] Muramoto, et. al. 2002, p. 109
[90] *Ibid,* p. 113

The alternative view is that it is not either/or, but both, a partnership between the Self as agent and as magnet where it contributes to the opportunities for growth by being a creator of the conflict of opposites and seeks both its own realization and that of the individual. As a quaternity of opposites, the Self suggests that it can be safely viewed as an "organizer of the personality"[91] through presenting the principle of wholeness so that its operation includes all derivations of the taxonomy. As an emergent archetype, it can generate many forms and is able to accept multiple functions.

As the Self is preexistent and the central archetype, it stands as the organizing principle of *all* psychological development. In that sense, it must always be seen as asserting itself and making itself known in order for there to be any evolutionary progress. Neumann wrote to Jung to ask just that question: "Is not the *Self* therefore, in a certain sense, a *center in or behind the collective?*"[92] This letter, written in 1934, was never answered by Jung on this point but shows that its numinous presence as preexistent in psyche suggests it must be viewed as the primary cause. Jung in a subsequent letter to Neumann expresses the fact that Self therefore will make itself known as it "insists on becoming visible with or against the conditionality or situation, to a certain individual and fatefully different degrees."[93] Assuming this was reflective of Neumann's question, the Self becomes visible because it is the organizing principle of individual and collective life. In offering corrections to Neumann's work *New Ethic,* Jung points out, "The Self cannot be 'deployed.' It deploys itself, for it is the totality of autonomous nature ... as one cannot deploy God. One cannot orient to the Self, for one does not know it. We are oriented by it."[94] This applies to the Self as an evolutionary force, God's will, what is essential for psychological growth, so he adds, "The totality asserts itself."[95]

How it asserts itself will always remain unclear because, as a powerful magnet, its attraction is a form of agency. Warren Colman suggests a possible solution from a different point of view. He refers to interrelated

---

[91] CW 10, § 694
[92] Jung & Neumann, 2015, p. 68
[93] *Ibid,* p. 108
[94] *Ibid,* p. 367
[95] *Ibid*

correlates of the Self, "being a self," the preexistent core Self and its operation in the unconscious, and "knowing the Self," obtaining a sense of Self, an awareness of having a Self. Knowing the Self is then "more in accord with the wholeness of being" that is already there.[96] He concludes, relevant to the agency question, that the Self for this reason, is a *process* of psychosomatic development, so therefore there is no need "to posit a self that 'initiates' processes such as deintegration and reintegration; these processes *are* the self in action and activity *is* the self."[97] This is consistent with the Jung's view of the Self as an *a priori* matrix or pattern of wholeness, but it rightly and clearly suggests that the manner in which it operates on an individual in terms of psychological growth is also the Self as a process. Colman sets out a quote from Jung that the Self that embraces our whole organism is the "fertile soil from which all future life will spring."[98] This evolutionary sentiment indicates that magnetism, fascination, and agency combine to create the psychic forces of growth that not only breathes life into the embryo but also carry out a continued process of psychological development.

Colman, reinforcing the view that the Self is the process, proposes that it is active from the start of life, and because it is the totality of our being, it is also what we do, the totality of our action in the world.[99] We then live the Self, as we are the Self. He acknowledges that the ego can only know a part of the Self, but the Self can also be that unknown element that stands behind the decision to act and that should be attributed to the Self as the agent of our lives. This is a credible argument as it aligns with the fact that the Self is always there, preexistent as a core Self neurobiologically that is an infrastructure that patterns the reception of bodily and environmental stimuli but remains in the unconscious until presented as a hint and is then realized by the ego. He gives the Self a form of agency as more than a core Self by a connection to a "greater being which is in some way also the being of the self that I am."[100] This is akin to the idea of the *Atman*, which will be discussed, that we hold a part of that greater being in ourselves. There can be no objection to this

---

[96] Colman 2008, p. 352
[97] *Ibid,* p. 357
[98] CW 7, § 303
[99] Colman 2008, p. 355
[100] *Ibid,* p. 357

transcendent idea, but, again, it has the effect of not only giving the Self agency but also making it part of a cosmic plan that makes its realization for its own purpose or a wider purpose. This then casts the Self as *soul*, and Colman refers to the Self as "self or soul," which carries even more agency to the Self.[101]

It is clear that we do not know the Self until we have some realization, either initially as a hint or presentation of the Self, or in a greater form by its realization. Until then, it exists in a manner that is unconscious, so there is no way of knowing what that primal patterning is doing, other than as self-recursive infrastructure for infant growth. Creating it as perhaps the soul or a cosmic force changes its nature to more than a center and is speculative. This has the effect, unfortunately, of elevating the Self to a dimension that can never be explained clinically and that begins to lose any logical framing. In the 1935 lecture, where Jung adds that the Self is the center and also totality as that is manifested in an individual, he is expressing very clearly the limits of the Self as not that cosmic ideal. The starting point of totality that would embrace the transcendent is only a psychological fact to the extent that it is realized, such as with a numinous experience or a realization in a lesser form of an interconnection of all things. If a goal is set for the Self as a manifestation of the cosmic or a soul, the inability *that we all have* of not being able to realize the soul in that fulsome way, suggests that the Self is unattainable, and all lesser realizations are not enough.

There will always be a sense of agency for the Self because of the transcendent ideal of unity suggested by the clash of opposites, for as Jung explains, "In nature the resolution of opposites is always an energic process ... doing something that expresses both sides, just as a waterfall visibly mediates between above and below."[102] There is no justification, however, of jumping from the Self to the soul or the divine spark as conferring energy and agency. Even if it is accepted that the Self has an ideal state because it can hold the opposites, that does permit a comparison to a cosmic state. In a letter to Rev. White in 1952 when he was 77, Jung explains: "The way in which opposites are reconciled or united on God, we just don't know. Nor do we understand how they are

---

[101] *Ibid,* p. 360
[102] CW 14, § 705

united in the Self."[103] This makes it an open question and not solvable by transposing unknown energies, such as the soul or God's will to the Self.

This makes a strong case for seeing the process of the Self in concrete terms as arising from the preexistent pattern in the brain that suggests ordering. That ordering is evoked specifically when a solution to conflict draws us into the unconscious. The symbols then presented allow a chance to align with the core pattern with the conscious recognition of the central archetype. This straightforward way of explaining the Self has clinical efficacy as it makes the process legible. When aspects of the Self are then realized, the wider sense of the Self can be useful to increase its numinosity and make it an important subject of consciousness. This is at the core of what Jung is presenting, and taking it further to levels of soul or God may explain why it may lose focus and is so difficult to understand.

Clinical Vignettes of Models of the Self

Vignette 1: The Experience of Patterning

A 40-year-old man presented with a sex addiction in repeatedly visiting sex workers, as well as excessive masturbation. When his wife became aware of the issue by examining his credit card statement, he went with her to marriage counseling and undertook a one-week residential stay at an intense, addiction-based, residential therapy center. He came for analysis after that counseling and stay and thereafter for five years of twice weekly sessions.

As we entered our sixth year, he explained that he liked to come early to our sessions to go to the nearby park and walk around in an ever-decreasing circle, which he described as a spiral. He said it calmed him and gave him a chance to reflect on the session to come. I asked him to draw that pattern and he drew a spiral, not from a vertical perspective, but from a bird's eye view. As he put the drawing on his lap, he traced the spiral from the outside in. I asked him why he traced it in that direction and not from the center outward. His answer was that the feels comfortable at the center and not at the edge. "As a feeling, I feel safer, like I am when I am home." I asked him, as an experiment, to trace it

---

[103] Jung-White 2007, p. 187

from the center outward and to explain what it felt like, and he reported that he could do it on paper, but it would have made him anxious when he was at the park.

His parents had come to New York from a small village in the Gorski Kotar mountains west of Zagreb in Croatia. At the start of the analysis, he had explained that he was Croatian, but the nearby village had many Serbs. At the time, I did not accord that fact any significance as he had spoken about it, in all its aspects, as an uneventful time. The spiral suggested that he felt unsafe, so I eventually asked him about the relationship his family had with the outlying Serbs. It emerged that before leaving Croatia when he was 8 years old, he had witnessed his uncle being attacked by a neighbor with a machete who cut off one of his uncle's hands. He stated that he strongly held the image of the hand falling faster than the teacup his uncle was holding. He had not previously mentioned this horrific event, he explained, because the dispute between his family and the family of the Serbs had been going on for many generations.

He experienced the center as a point of safety and orientation. Sometimes at work, he said that he would doodle a spiral and he also mentioned that he had a picture on the wall of his study of the spiral galaxy *Messier 100*. Jung refers to the spiral as *"the symbol of indirect approach by means of circumambulation"*[104] and that the "spiral emphasizes the centre."[105] Jung also explains, consistent with these statements, that circumambulation is actually a spiral as it gradually gets closer to the center.[106]

In this case, the spiral emphasized the center as a harbor from danger, which is suggestive of an orientation to order. The production of the image did not relate to any village pathways, but he did mention that when he was a few years older, he was excited to travel to Rijeka with his father to the wealthy home of his grandfather through the *Brajdica* tunnel, which is a 360-degree spiral. He added that he did not walk in that spiral manner at other times, only when he came for his analysis, perhaps casting the therapy room as temenos.

---

[104] CW 12, § 245
[105] *Ibid*, § 246
[106] *Ibid*, § 325

Using the drawing of the spiral, we were able to go out to the terrible anxiety that ran through generations where the outside was unsafe and then back to the center. We tracked the journey out and the moment of buildup of tension and the need that emerged then for relief to get back home. Slowly a connection was made with what he had witnessed and the loss of agency he experienced connected to the loss of his uncle's hand.

The spiral served as the centering function and a means to compare states of anxiety. The center was, accordingly, numinous for him as a solid, unmovable point that brought order to unmanageable anxiety. The function of the Self as center was to reveal the source of his anxiety, and this led to a reduction of his symptoms. It acted in each session as a magnet, drawing him closer. With the loss of anxiety, masturbation decreased, as eventually did his need for visits to sex workers.

The Self manifested in his case as an innate pattern of wholeness in the form of a spiral with a center. He was not aware of this patterning; it initially meant little to him, yet he walked in a spiral to the consulting room as if he were drawn to its revelation. In this case, it was a magnet from a primal patterning, but it needed activation of the psyche, the recollection of the dreadful scene with his uncle, that would allow him to integrate the innate pattern with consciousness.

Vignette 2: No Self, Just Presence

A woman in her 60s came for analysis because she was dying from cancer. She had a lifetime of deep involvement as a Sufi, constantly attending retreats in Turkey and being regularly in contact with distinguished Sheiks. She had also studied with John G. Bennett, a disciple of Gurdjieff. She was more than happy for this story of her to be shared.

She was an extraordinary woman, of deep understanding, who had many mystical experiences and realized deeply who she was. She could be said to have had an individuated ego where she did not have to cure a conflict of opposites, but only more deeply inquire into her pending death. It was a privilege to work with her and, after a year, she went to California for what was unconventional and unsuccessful treatment. In that time, we worked online.

She expressed the inner workings of her psyche as a complete mystery with no conclusions as to its structure or its parts, and she initially gave psyche the name of God. As she became more ill, she ceased to use the term God and instead described a movement of her being toward a solid place within her to the recognition of the existence of a "presence" as she described it. As she got closer to her death, she ceased to be philosophical and spoke from the absolute reality of her being as a conduit through which that presence manifests. This was not an idea for her, but a true psychic fact. She expressed it as a presence that was a personal part of totality that was within her and that was in all things. This was her experience, and it gave her a strength and dignity that was inspiring. She explained her process of dying as a letting go into that presence and, just before she stopped treatment, dying very quickly thereafter, she explained the presence. She said that it appeared as a center point within her of the totality which constitutes the presence. The Self became that presence of totality when all other issues, hopes, and desires were stripped away so it could then be realized as both and, at the same time, as the interconnected center with totality.

I used the term "Self" when speaking about it in her last weeks, but she insisted that you cannot give it a name because it transcends concepts, as it is a *felt sense* of a completed whole that was ever there, and which would always be there. She said it is not subject to logic or discourse, nor is it subject or object. The Self was therefore, in her realization, both the underlying patterning that was the primordial presence as well as the center, but she did not give it agency. Her experience of it was as a primary miracle that was preexistent that was lost in the naming and any attribution of it as an entity was untenable. It was just there as an unnamed marvel much like the sun that can only be defined as a presence as it is beyond understanding what it is and what it may or may not do.

The late Dan Merkur explains "presence": "My term *psychic presences* is meant to convey the experience of intrapsychic preternatural entities, which present as images or phantoms and which we, in turn, reify as real."[107] Merkur quotes Grotstein that the agency of those entities appears as projections of one's conscious self, and therefore the presence does

---

[107] Merkur 2010, p. 267

not itself have agency.[108] Her experience did not create any images or theoretical ideas so there was nothing that could have agency. Moreover, in our sessions she was strongly resistant to put it into a framework for something that was perceived in a manner that made it unnecessary for it to be symbolized.

The difficulty with images and ideas is that they are translated into an intrapsychic entity that has agency. This is a necessary cognitive step resulting from their naming and objectification. This is contrasted with her experience of a presence as felt that was too vast and unknown to apply a function, so it could not be an entity. The conclusion as to the Self, based on her deep and poignant insights, is that it is the naming and conjuncture that gives the Self a function as agent *because it is an aspect of a psychological theory in which it exists.*

In *Psychological Types*, Jung explains that "the symbol always presupposes that the chosen expression is the best possible description, or formula, of the relatively unknown fact; a fact, however, which is nonetheless recognized or postulated as existing."[109] The reason that a symbol or explanation was unacceptable to her is perhaps best explained by Fordham in his reflections on images and symbols. He examines the limitations of the work of Kerenyi, who was a scholar of myths: "Religion is the subject-matter of Kerenyi's studies, but he is never inside the whole process like the mystic, who believed he was discovering how to perceive a reality of far greater significance than either external or psychic reality."[110] She was that mystic.

Vignette 3: Self as Tyrant

A 45-year-old patient wanted analysis because he was enamored with Jungian theory, a common phenomenon. He was extremely well-versed in Jung's writings and would often quote him, sometimes in German and sometimes in English to put our discussions, as he expressed it, "on track." To him, the Self was a force that had a specific function of forcing him into suffering so he could experience the opposites. He was Swiss and considered that Switzerland always stood for the Self as it was neutral

---

[108] *Ibid*, p. 268
[109] CW 7, § 814
[110] Fordham 1957, p. 44

in the war and stood as a center between tyranny and democracy. He attributed his dreams to the Self as his heritage but would often say that the Self was a hard taskmaster that was never satisfied and would not be for the rest of his life.

If an issue came up about his failed business, he attributed that to the Self. If he met a possible partner, that also was the Self at work, controlling his life. Often in his dreams, there would be an anima figure pointing out something to him, but he took that, as well, as the appearance of the Self. Yet, there were no observable symbols of the Self in his dreams, no centrality or order in the content or his contemplations, no remote connection with totality, but only the Self as a kind of little person inside his mind that was forcing its plan upon him.

The problem that this illustrates is that the concept of the Self as a function can be hijacked by complexes or be at service of a regression. The elevation of the Self to the highest function, based on it having transcendent connections, can make it the source of anxiety and suggest a psychological replacement of an Old Testament God. The other effect is that it makes all symbols and images concrete because the existence of a third party—the Self—as controller, removes responsibility for psychological growth. As a result, if he had a dream of being on the water, he literally would plan to rent a boat, and he therefore kept the intrapsychic meaning of the dream as only a poor substitute for the directed power of the Self. Because there is such importance given to the Self in Jungian thought, that was the platform upon which our work began and continued, no other explanations were able to be advanced. The Self was in the consulting room as a projected image, not as a centering or expansive alteration of consciousness but, instead, a terrorizing autocrat.

The idea of suffering as the path of individuation and his sense that it is foisted on an individual was necessary for him to explain failures. This attributes to the Self the creation of conflict so that, in the working out of problems, the uniting aspect and centering of the Self makes it more realizable. There is no way directly out of this situation caused by his vision of the Self but indirectly there was an opportunity to work through the suffering and its developmental and Shadow qualities. He was willing to take this path as it was his view that it is the suffering that bestows on the Self a function as its cause and its salvation. It then was the manipulator of that process but also the inspiration or purpose of that process that fostered his openness to be analyzed. He accepted that its realization is the chance for redemption.

The effect of his view on his process was to project a complex onto an idea, but the salvation was not realizable in that manner. The idea did not hold because he did not have anything approaching an intimation of the Self, so it was free-floating. Yet, on occasion, his dreams indicated moments of peace, a home in the middle of a storm, a place where internal figures met and shared food, an image of a neat room, a woman who was healing in his childhood. In this way, the centering function still broke through and the purpose of the Self was recast to accept its appearance in dreams that offered him hope in the suffering, not as a goal, but rather as a moment of wholeness in the suffering it had produced.

The primal patterning of the Self will always have a subtle influence as it remains in the psychoid level, even without its activation in psyche. As Jung explained, the psychoid possesses qualities of a "parapsychological" nature to create inexplicable phenomena,[111] such as the patient walking in a spiral or a centering image breaking through in a dream. The translation of the patterning of wholeness to the Self carries with it a risk and a reward.

---

[111] CW 10, § 849

Chapter 11. The Self as Divine

The idea of the Self as inclusive of totality invokes great transcendent analogies because it aligns with the sentiment of an unconscious without limits. In addition, the existence of the Self as preexistent attracts metaphysical assumptions. Totality, in particular, orients the concept of the Self to encompass the grand idea that it is the gateway to larger truths, that it will reveal a hidden secret, and is the ultimate spiritual goal.

The Self as embracing totality is, of course, a hypothesis except as Jung expresses it in his 1935 lecture, *to the extent* it is manifested in the individual. Manifestation means that an aspect of totality has become known, and its realization creates an alteration of consciousness. The alteration is necessary for manifestation because it has created a new orientation, a different vision of life, a connection with that which is life's purpose and essence. How totality is manifested must then be by way of a numinous experience in whatever form, the nature of which is to *overwhelm* the ego, rather than by a cognitive surmising or a series of hunches or intuitions. It is difficult to imagine what else beyond a mystical or religious experience would supplant the ego sufficiently to have a connection with totality.

There is perhaps no better description of this profound numinous experience that alters consciousness than by Satprem, the French writer who made his life in India:

> As if one had lived life after life for naught; forever on the sidelines; estranged from self, from others, from objects, until suddenly everything crumbles and one is on anther journey. Barely time to catch one's breath and it is time to be off, to peer out a new window. Yet none of this is strange, startling, extraordinary. Indeed it was the opposite of a hallucination; a pure little note that struck the ear with its

truth—the right note—*the* note. As if there were only one. I felt like shouting yes, yes, it is this. Absolutely this. That which I awaited for millions of years. The sweetness of total recognition.[1]

Any realization of this kind will invoke a revelation of interconnectedness, wholeness, no matter what form the content of the experience took. This can be seen in the numerous published accounts of mystics that Jung and others rely upon to express the ineffable. The smallest revelation that so changes consciousness will have the effect of providing a view of reality that goes beyond the ego and a center. It will be an engagement with the circumference at its widest dimension. As a consequence, what is realized by totality is not only the preexistent center but also the unity in which all opposites are balanced, or as Satprem calls it, the "only one." However, if that realization of the Absolute, a dimension that is beyond comprehension, is only available as Jung suggests to an individuated ego, it will be exceedingly rare. A glimpse that does not alter consciousness, in this way, is not a realization of totality by the ego.

Aspects of totality can be presented to consciousness through symbolic representation in dreams and visions. What can be observed in the 1935 Eranos statement about totality is that it is to be understood through realization of the center. This means that totality symbols are *not* the direct pathway to their manifestation but rather it is through realization of the center as embracing the ideal of unity that those symbols and visions can be understood. By symbolic representation in dreams and visions, totality symbols may lead to insight into a center as well as a gradual sense of the wholeness of an individual's psyche that portends a deeper connection. However, Jung explains, "But the man who is inwardly great will know that the long expected friend of his soul, the immortal one, has now finally come …"[2] That degree of manifestation is not available by a mere symbol of totality, such as a circle, as it does not have any effect until it causes an alteration of consciousness; finding the "long expected friend" by the inwardly great is more than an idea or a hunch but a conclusive realization by the ego. The centering function can be

---

[1] Satprem 1978, p. 20, emphasis supplied.
[2] CW 9.1, § 217

understood logically as a goal and the *idea* of totality can also be understood by the symbols, but the widest scope of the Self as totality goes beyond conjecture and some insight, so that it only exists as a spiritual or religious experience.

Personal Image of Totality

It can therefore be said, as is obvious, that totality is a mystical idea. This conclusion is inescapable and leads commentators to attempt to find a way from psychological integration to the highest realms of the Self where there is no direct path. Rosemary Gordon first refers to the Self as "an abstraction, as a metaphysical construct …"[3] but is then forced to the conclusion that we can recognize the "little self," the idea of the states of "myself" and perhaps gradual manifestation of the Self, and therefore, "the more an individual recognises the cohesion and interrelatedness of his several selves, the closer does he approach the big self."[4] If this were the case, the manifestation of the big Self requires an individual to become inwardly great, an individuated individual having a numinous experience. This is not functional for the psychoanalytic inclusion of totality, as it would just leave an absolutely abstract and confusing idea for patients and analysts. Sanford Drob suggests that the inability to reach that cosmic big Self "leaves room for a 'personal' aspect of the Absolute that is identified."[5] This fits best with the view that the dimensions of the Self as totality may not be realized, but the idea of a personal connection with totality still has a profound effect on an individual's ego. This is where the connection with the divine as the Self begins. The effects of that connection would be to a tendency to greater introversion, less alienation, stress modulation, a moral code, and an orientation to open to the center. That list does not begin to explain how a *personal* spiritual or religious orientation may have an effect on an individual and create a willingness to seek totality.

To develop a personal aspect of the totality of the Self, it requires an image of an external object to give it form and substance. The result is that the Self as including totality only becomes an object of consciousness

---

[3] Gordon 1985, p. 261
[4] *Ibid,* p. 266
[5] Drob 2017, pp. 396-7

when named as that which is *other* than the Self. The word "Self" cannot hold it, as it does not have the collective recognition of other transcendent ideations such as God, Christ, *Brahman* or similar terms that are the known placeholders for religion. For this reason, there is a tendency for the Self to find its place outside itself. How it is found or conceived, the process for its realization, the form that it may take in psychological development, depends on the individual's orientation to a chosen, named object.

The significance of a named object, such as a personal guide or a particular divinity, is that it offers a chance to maintain a focus on that object as having the same function as the Self. That object will be accompanied by an image, however blurry, as otherwise the hypothesis of the big Self is vague, a matter of faith, and the process of psychological growth shifts from seeking that goal to symptom reduction or problem solving. No individual can maintain a hypothesis about a nonexistent but virtual center or totality without a sense of proof that arises when an image is formed and comes into focus.

The possibility that the Self lies *outside* an individual and is a center embracing the collective unconscious or is a remote transcendent entity that remains in an unknown realm would not appear to advance psychological growth. As well, the internal, personal image does not create the Self or the object, as Jung accepts: "… I take my stand on Kant, which means that an assertion doesn't posit its object. So when I say 'God' I am speaking exclusively of assertions that don't posit their object."[6] The image of the object is only an assertion but, *most critically*, it still must be present in order for it to be experienced; as Jung explains, "Only psychic existence is immediately verifiable. To the extent that the world does not form a psychic image it is virtually non-existent."[7]

A personal, psychic image is essential to invoking a sense of the existence of the Self and to create it as a logical goal. To confirm a goal or the validity of a center, to relate at least in part to that center containing the totality, it also requires an image that possesses an *emotive element* or, at least, a numinous possibility. Only then can totality become embodied, brought to ground, inhabit an individual's being, and be made an object

---

[6] *Letters*, Vol. I, p. 294
[7] CW 11, § 770

of the ego. This is because the grander the personal, psychic image, the more likely that the wider dimensions of the Self can be grasped.

The need to *embody* the image arises because the *process* of the Self will inevitably create the situation that it is observed or understood as existing outside itself. This approach does not support the 1952 argument of Martin Buber that Jung was in error because he did not permit of a separate Other outside psyche.[8] Instead, it implies that the essence of the Self is preexistent, that it "exists from the very beginning,"[9] so that it must be observed in all things, in the inner psychic realm and also outside in the world of matter, for it to be fully understood. Until then, as Jung expresses, "I do not know the self. I have to discover it in my acts, where it first reappears under strange masks."[10]

The images of the Self as Other that hold this numinous potential to be embodied are of two types:

1. God Images: those which are transcendent, primordial, and embedded in the collective consciousness, such as God or Christ,

2. Empirical Assumptions: those where there is no clear image but yet they offer, upon investigation, some empirical evidence, such as a guiding spirit or an internal voice.

As to the first, God Images, Jung was clear that because of their numinosity and as the subject of autonomous subjective experience, they have substance, such as the Virgin Mary appearing in a dream: "it is equally certain that the direct perception of the archetypal world inside us is just as doubtfully correct as that of the physical world outside us."[11]

The second, Empirical Assumptions, is an idea or an unformed image, confirmed *after the fact*, that brings its own sense of internal reality and numinosity. The idea that there is a guiding spirit, the *spiritus rector,* that has directed our lives, or that there is an internal voice that speaks to us, are both versions of a Self that arises from its presence in psyche as an archetype of order.

---

[8] Buber 2017, Chapter 9
[9] CW 12, § 105n34
[10] *Letters*, Vol 2, p. 196
[11] CW 14, para. 787

The Self as God

The transposition of the Self to God occurs very naturally. When the Self is realized, the attribution of the Self as God can be made because of its ability to order an unforeseen unity arising from the great numinosity of the center. Thus, Jung explains, the Self "constitutes the most immediate experience of the Divine which it is psychologically possible to imagine."[12] This was Jung's realization and suggests that if an individual realizes the Self and, it is assumed, some aspect of totality, then it will elevate the Self beyond a center to the level of a religious experience. In many ways, the comparison with a deity is apt because even without that realization, as a metaphysical assertion, it suggests an act of creation for a new way of being, the single most significant transformation to order in the midst of chaos.

Jung's experience of the Self as having divine aspects was on such a daunting level that from that vantage point his constant reference to God, on this basis alone, is understandable. His realizations are similar to mystical experiences because a non-ego force overwhelmed his conscious mind and supplanted any doubt or confusion with a glimpse of a divine truth. These revelations altered his consciousness as it made clear the centralized, profound nature of the Self as the highest form of existence. It is not possible to think that such realizations are from merely finding a center in a dream or vision or a symbol of totality or a similar experience; it required the highest degree of receptivity for such an alteration of consciousness. The transposition to God naturally follows as that alteration completely rearranges a point of view, suddenly and indelibly.

This experience must have been the rationale behind the *Seven Sermons,* wherein he chose to adopt a particular mystical approach to creation.[13] Equating the Self with God or making that link a requirement could have derailed his psychology, which must account for his transferring the authorship in 1916 to Basilides for the *Sermons*. It is fair to say that his relationship of the Self with the idea of God became fixed thereafter and continued to emerge, as his biographers point out,[14] and his interests show. Almost 20 years after the period of his mystical experience, he makes it

---

[12] CW 11, para. 396
[13] Stein, 2015
[14] Bair 2004, p. 126-7

very clear that the Self is not God or even the idea of God, but the revelation for him exposed the highest possibility for a life. In 1936, Jung in the Zarathustra lectures explains:

> The term *self* is often mixed up with the idea of God. I would not do that. I would say that the term *self* should be reserved for that sphere which is within the reach of human experience, and we should be very careful not to use the word *God* too often. As we use it, it borders on impertinence; it is unlawful to use such a concept too often. The experience of the self is so marvelous and so complete that one is of course tempted to use the conception of God to express it. I think it is better not to, because the self has the peculiar quality of being specific yet universal. It is a restricted universality or a universal restrictedness, a paradox; so it is a relatively universal being and therefore doesn't deserve to be called 'God.' You could think of it as an intermediary, or a hierarchy of ever-widening-out figures of the self *till* one arrives at the conception of a deity. So we should reserve that term *God* for a remote deity that is supposed to be the absolute unity of all singularities.[15]

The Self is the closest comparison to his version of a God in the same sense that he chose *Abraxas* as the midpoint of the *Pleroma,* as Shamdasani points out.[16] The God is not the Christian God but one that contains all the opposites of love and hate, beauty and abomination. It was therefore "*the* God" as a configuration that can hold all opposites and is the proper form of personification. In that way, in that language, it is possible to bring the Self and that God closer together. This is echoed in so many of his other themes of the continuing incarnation of God in man, the divine within us, and the divine becoming conscious through our actions: divine self-reflection, all of which are at the heart of Jung's development of an individual and humanity.[17]

The idea, as Edinger puts it, that "the Self, is that Deity"[18] is not justified. Murray Stein suggests instead that the Self is "linked to (even fused with)

---

[15] Jung 1997, Vol II, p. 977-8, emphasis supplied.
[16] *Black Books,* Vol 1, p. 68
[17] *Letters*, Vol 2, p. 316; 322-4

the Divine" because "The Self links the ego complex to ultimate wholeness." He concludes, "Jung is *not* saying that the self is divine but rather that it is an expression of the Divine," as Divineness shapes the Self in the form of that which contains the opposites. It is *the* God that stands behind the creation of the Self, as Stein colorfully explains: "my image for this is a hen laying an egg, 'pressing it out.'"[19] There is nothing in Jung's writings, he explains, that states the Self has a divine nature. It *mirrors* the Divinity "(at least to some degree)."[20]

Stein also supports the view that the Self is better connected to *Abraxas* in the *Seven Sermons* than the God of Christianity, as *Abraxas* can hold all opposites. The Divinity that expresses the Self, is therefore "inclusive of the opposites good and evil, light and dark, male and female."[21] This makes the God-image (*Imago Dei*) as one possible representation of the Self, but it must transcend a monotheistic, particular God-image because that inevitably "tends towards one-sidedness and partiality."[22]

It is, however, natural to use the term God for what is experienced as guiding our life, that offers a chance for peace, and is the ultimate mystery. Psychologically, "the God" does not fit with the Christian God, not only for the reasons suggested by Stein but also because that God is not a mid-point in psyche. There are, however, references in Christianity that bring it closer to the Self. There is an indwelling God in the form of the Holy Spirit as Paul states in Romans (8:7-9): "but you are not in the flesh but in the spirit, if indeed the Spirit of God dwells in you." This requires one to achieve this through faith in order to receive the indwelling presence as stated in Luke (11:13). This gift arises by a rejection of the flesh so that "in me (that is, in my flesh,) dwelleth no good thing" (Romans 7:18). This does not, however, extend to create a parallel to a preexisting center in psyche that holds all opposites, light and dark, soul and body, and is a unity that does not need faith to be revealed symbolically.

---

[19] Stein 2008, p. 308
[20] *Ibid,* p. 310
[21] *Ibid,* p. 311
[22] *Ibid,* p. 313

Agency through God

There is a difference between expressing that the Self when realized as a psychological fact is equivalent to the realization of the God and that the Self has the powers of God and thus agency. Jung brought the Self and God together from his very first mention of the Self to explain the ultimate goal and continued to use it after his realizations in ways that did not emphasize the qualities of an *Abraxas*. The question therefore remains of whether he attributes the world-creating power of God to a power and agency within the Self. It is a question that needs to be answered in this context as it again is relevant to the issue of whether the Self is to be considered self-initiating for its own sake, for an individual's psychological growth, or is passive as a magnet.

It is not possible to fully transpose the power of the creator to the Self until it is realized as it then displays itself as having that dimension as creator of a new reality. Prior to that realization, the Self is better explained by the magnet model of the archetypal patterning that exists as a core Self, a primordial orientation that is preexistent. To attribute divine power to the Self before realization would imply that the Self, when eventually realized and then experienced as God, was always an aspect of God or pertaining to the power of God. This is not something Jung ever expresses, and his references appear to apply only to the full realization of the Self that is empirically the same as the presence of God.

This relationship between the idea of God and the agency of the Self is not explained with any clarity by Jung, as once the Self was realized by him, the comparisons with God flowed in his writings. However, even prior to his dream and before the *Seven Sermons,* there was an emphasis that he was describing a comparison with God empirically when the Self is realized. This can be traced back to his comments in 1912 in *Symbols of Transformation* that thereafter became an established pattern in his writings. There are also repeated hints in that period that the Self has that world-creating power, but nothing specific, however, is said by him that this leads to an agency model or confers that divinity on the Self before it is realized. He explains, for example, that Christ "as hero and god man, signifies psychologically the self as a projection of the self archetype."[23]

---

[23] *Ibid,* § 576

This makes it, he adds, "the ruler of the inner world, of the collective unconscious."[24] The reasoning in this quote and this early period is that as Christ suggests unity, it fits the role of the ruler for the collective and is therefore a representation of the Self, again *when realized*, as it then is understood as the way to that orientation and meaning.

Some greater importance for the Self as approximating the Godhead indirectly offers a suggestion of agency in *Psychologische Typen* in 1921. The Godhead, Jung states there in discussing a revelation of the mystic Meister Eckhart, has "self-generating creative instinct."[25] If the Self and the Godhead are related, which he did not do in this essay, that self-generating instinct may appear to apply to the Self, giving it divine agency. This is relevant because in a later analysis of this same point published in 1950 and concerning the Paraclete, he refers to Moses obtaining instruction from Khidr, and states, "Then follows those incomprehensible deeds which show how ego-consciousness reacts to the *superior guidance of the self* through the twists and turns of fate."[26] The mystical Khidr is a hero in the Koran consistent with Jung's continuous mention of other all-powerful figures: Hiranyagarbha, the "collective aggregate of all individual souls,"[27] the Buddha, *Purusha* (the Hindu Godhead), and the *Atman*. This self-generating power is in the Godhead or its manifestation in historical figures, and it is, by analogy, appearing to give the Self agency, as in the phrase "superior guidance of the self."

This sentiment, even though not specific in his writings, is convincing and has a tendency to elevate the Self to this highest dimension, confusing the issue of the possible agency of the Self and its true nature. As an example, Gerhard Adler, in an early work, states, "The archetype of the Deity in the human psyche Jung has expressed as the 'Self.'"[28] This appears in his Introduction to lectures given between 1936 and 1945, a period after Jung declared that the Self embraces totality. In describing wholeness, Adler calls it the "homo totus," which is an explanation, he claims, for the revelation of dreams or visions "that transcend our present

---

[24] *Ibid*
[25] CW 6, § 429
[26] CW 9.i, § 247, emphasis added.
[27] *Ibid*, § 675
[28] Adler 1948, p. 14

understanding."[29] "Homo totus" is derived from Jung's use of that term in *Psychology and Alchemy* as the "greater man within, the Anthropos, who is akin to God."[30] Adler is using that phrase as the presence of the divine in the Self that brings agency to create dreams and visions. This view is not warranted by a direct reading of Jung but is understandable as the elevation of the Self as having divine agency within an individual can be implied through a generous interpretation.

The relationship of the Self with God and the possibility of transposing agency was, it could be said, made clearer some years later in *Answer to Job* away from the Self having the power of God. In stating that the archetype of wholeness manifests spontaneously in dreams with a "tendency independent of the conscious will," Jung then adds that it does not "seem improbable that the archetype of wholeness occupies such a central position which approximates it to the *God image*."[31] Thus, he states, the archetype of wholeness "is this archetype from which we can no longer distinguish the God-image empirically."[32]

These ideas of the Self appearing *empirically* when realized as a *God-image* is not the Self having the creative power of God and does not allow that transposition of divine agency to the Self. The inclusion of the God-image, in fact, takes away the idea that the power of God is relevant and focuses instead on the idea, the image of God that arises on realization. The movement from God to God-image in relation to the Self first appears in 1948 in a revision of the earlier written *The Psychological Approach to the Trinity*,[33] then again in 1950 in Jung's revision of a 1933 Eranos lecture on the process of individuation[34] (the original Eranos lecture did not have that focus). There are other earlier references to the God-image, but these do not specifically equate the Self with the God-image appearing empirically as the same, when realized.

The proclivity to equate the Self with divine transcendent creativity does not arise with the God-image. This is made very clear in a letter in 1955 to a Pastor, where he makes the distinction between God and the God-

---

[29] *Ibid*, p. 174
[30] CW 14, § 152
[31] CW 11, § 757 emphasis added.
[32] *Ibid*
[33] *Ibid*, § 231
[34] CW 9.i, § 572

image: "You write ... that I equate God with the Self. You seem not to have noticed that I speak of the *God-image and not a God* because it is quite beyond me to say anything about God at all. ... I don't know what you must take me for if you impute such stupidities to me ..."[35] The consequence is that the Self as the center of psyche always carries with it, upon realization, such a powerful revelation that it approximates the *idea* of divinity, a God-image, and it is not possible to transpose the agency of God to the Self.

The connection between the Self and God-image is a recognition of the qualities of the Self when it is presented in a realization. Until then, the Self is undergoing a process in the unconscious. It is possible to say that this may or may not also have divine power, but that is not relevant empirically to the ego, the only test of its realization. In any event, it is not a connection between the Self and God that confers agency, and therefore there is no effective statement that the Self partakes of divine control. It, to use Jung's words in *Answer to Job,* "approximates" to the God-image. The argument for individuating energies therefore is reduced, primarily because of the evolving idea of the God-image, whose variations are explicated by Edward Edinger.[36] What is left is the *empirical* similarity of the Self with an image of God, the fascination of the non-ego and its mystery, and the ideal of transformation that it represents.

The Self having any transcendent analogues so it can be argued to have divine agency is not able to be so easily reconciled. At the time of realization, the Self is perceived as the mover to the moved, and it does suggest that it has been the guiding spirit of one's life. Edinger offers a suggestion of how to reconcile the issue by separating out the Self for an individual from the transcendent aspect of the Self as a *collective* Self: "a transpersonal center shared by a whole body of humanity."[37] That reconciliation is not, however, convincing, as it is clear that the realization of the Self *appears* as a transcendent revelation of God in the psyche of an the individual, especially if it arises as a numinous experience.

---

[35] *Letters*, Vol. 2, p. 260
[36] Edinger 1996b
[37] *Ibid*, p. xiv

The reason that the Self appears to have agency is actually because of the magnet model. The ego is drawn to the core Self because of its numinosity, and that numinosity evokes spiritual or religious sentiments. Adler's comment that the goal of the Self is to "find the way back to its own sources"[38] is a good reference to the magnetic quality of being pulled along by the primordial patterning so it is that which shines through to remind us of our essential being. The primordial pattern as preexisting, shared by the collective, a gift that can establish the microcosm, suggests it is a divine plan. However, the agency model as derived from God does not necessarily fit with clinical experience. Agency will make the Self the hero, as Jung expresses, as the jewel coveted by all and also close to a god, as he indicated with Khidr.[39] This is contrary to the manner in which the Self needs to be understood by the ego because too great an identification of that level of the Self with ego-consciousness causes inflation.[40] As well, this identification with the hero and the god would mean that the Self would be unavailable to the rest of humanity.

The idea of the Self and God, the God-image, does come together at one point because the symbols of the Self "for the central point, circle, quaternity are well-known symbols of the deity."[41] The theoretical comparison is always justifiable and may be invoked clinically as explaining the effect of realization. Jung cites the *Brahman* (*Purusha*)-*Atman* connection on the basis that this causes "The impossibility of distinguishing between 'self' and 'God.'"[42] This holds true because God is defined as a circle or roundness in many ancient traditions in addition to the profound realization it entails. The comparison of symbols of the Self to God is empirically undeniable, although this does not make the Self as God or that it has the power or agency of a God.

If God and the Self are not the same and the Self does not partake of divine power, the issue of agency remains unresolved. Although Jung suggests that they are empirically the same—"I cannot prove in practice that the self and God are identical, although in practice they appear

---

[38] Adler 1948, p. 14
[39] CW 6, § 256
[40] *Ibid,* § 254
[41] CW 9.i, § 572
[42] *Ibid*

so"[43]—the effect, on closer examination, points to another interpretation. In the letter written in 1955, he removes divine agency for the Self by speaking of individuation as a "religious process" requiring a "religious attitude" whereby the ego will submit to *God's will*.[44] In this statement about the clinical development of the Self through individuation, Jung shifts the power of creation to God's will operating *behind* the process to realize the Self. *God's will* is the supraordinate driver, what is responsible for the process, and not the Self. More specifically, he adds, "And since the self cannot be distinguished from an archetypal God-image, it would be equally true to say of any such arrangement that it conforms to natural law and it is an act of God's will."[45]

Jung uses "God's will" because he consistently asserts that all psychic processes are subject to primal, archaic laws governing the behavior of archetypes. This shifts the agency from the Self to God's will and the Self then becomes the *process* of becoming what one can be. The coupling of the Self and God-image is, however, necessary because Analytical Psychology "helps us find a way to the religious experience that makes us whole" and "teaches us an *attitude* which meets the transcendent reality halfway."[46] This does not, however, make the Self equal to God or confer on the Self that transcendent power or agency, but, in clinical practice, it creates the attitude that is fundamental to its realization. Being open to that, allowing the process of individuation to be filled with awe rather than assigning it agency, makes the Self very much a religious experience. There is every reason that it is important that it appears as divine by the experience and the symbolism, so that "Christ can be brought into relation with the concept of the 'self' as the symbolism proves."[47]

The comparison of the Self with Christ rather than God is a greater disincentive to use the agency model. Christ fails as having insufficient power to transfer those energies to the Self because of Jung's qualifying statement: "That Christ is the self of man is implicit in the gospel, but the

---

[43] *Letters*, Vol. 2, p. 285
[44] *Ibid*
[45] CW 11, § 238
[46] *Letters,* Vol. 2, p. 265
[47] *Ibid,* p. 66

conclusion Christ=self has never been explicitly drawn."[48] Christ does not confer on the Self the power of God. Instead, the Self obtains power by the process of realization according to God's will, as an innate pattern of wholeness desired when consciousness is activated by affect, and it also is a magnet that draws all to it.

There are, before leaving this topic, several statements in Jung's writings that suggest that energy exists without a comparison to God, heroes, or corresponding symbols, but are closer to the idea of God's will. In his essay on *Concerning Mandala Symbolism,* Jung appears to ascribe an energy to the Self in two other ways. The first is that he comments on the center point in the mandala, "which in itself is a source of energy."[49] In this idea, which has been already discussed but bears repeating, he states: "The energy of the central point is manifested in the almost irresistible compulsion and urge *to become what one is,* just as every organism is driven to assume the form that is characteristic of its nature, no matter what the circumstances."[50] The second is that, in commenting on two mandalas, one of which is surrounded by what he calls a "fire of desire," he states: "(this) represents … an *amor fati* that burns in the innermost self, trying to shape a patient's fate and thus help the self into reality. Like the homunculus in *Faust,* the figure shut up in the vessel wants to 'become.'"[51]

The phrase "become what one is" changes the emphasis and, in that context, is not arguing for the Self as having agency by a connection with divinity. The phrase is translated by Jung as finding the "wholeness which we have lost in the midst of our civilized, conscious existence, a wholeness which we always were without knowing it."[52] The central point, the essential part of wholeness, is manifested by becoming what one is. It is not the central point that manifests itself, but it is manifested by some other force that is not attributed to the Self. This concept of "becoming what one is" is explained in several ways that are variants of that idea. The first is that when an individual realizes the Self, they have found that the existing life-force is there, as Jung explains in relation to

---

[48] *Ibid,* p. 84
[49] CW 9.i, § 634
[50] *Ibid,*
[51] *Ibid,* § 480
[52] CW 10, § 722

a person who found in their heart the image of the sun that represents the Self.[53] The second related concept is that the source of life is not the unrealized Self but rather the continued, irrepressible longing to find one's individuality.

Amor fati, love of one's fate, a concept used by Nietzsche to indicate a refusal to regret, was a mainstay of his oeuvre as revealed in several places in his autobiography *Ecco Hommo,* "my formula for greatness is *amor fati.*" Jung incorporates this expression as the sense of living on for no purpose other than discovering one's individuality.[54] It is therefore employed by him to refer to an inner compulsion, an inner voice, that demands to live no matter what is in the way. This is the "objective activity of the psyche, which, independently of conscious volition, is trying to speak to the conscious mind through the inner voice and lead him towards wholeness."[55] This idea of an inner source, a will to life, is developed in Jung's 1932 lecture on the *Development of Personality* about that "inner voice," which Jung previously calls a "vocation:" "an irrational factor that destines a man to emancipate himself from the herd and from its well-worn path."[56] In this point of view, it is not the Self that shapes fate, but rather that irrational factor in psyche, manifested as an inner voice, the desire to become what one is, and to discover one's individuality that therefore is of *help* to the Self to manifest as the end goal of psychological becoming.

The source of energy that drives the process of seeking the Self is thus beyond explanation as God's will, the great teacher such as the Buddha,[57] the longing to become what one can be, and the collective unconscious.[58] These, Jung refers to collectively as "All the powers that strive for unity, all heathy desire for selfhood."[59] The source of energy of the Self is also the tension of opposites, the magnetic quality of order, as a reaction of psyche to affect, and to the regulating aspect of psyche in the production of symbols. Jung did not therefore give the Self energy when it remains

---

[53] CW 5, § 17
[54] *Zarathustra,* Vol. 2, p. 87
[55] CW 17, § 313
[56] CW 4, § 572
[57] CW 12, § 169
[58] *Ibid,* Prefatory Note
[59] CW 17, § 318

unrealized in the psychoid region or in the unconscious. It is thus accurate to focus the powerful, profound energy of the Self on its realization, as does Lucy Huskinson in stating that the encounter with the Self is "violent" as the ego is forever changed by the overwhelming impact.[60]

When the realization of the Self as an experience occurs, the Self begins to have an effect on the entirety of psyche, and this is where the energy for change is created by *consciousness*. There is a confrontation that faces the ego with a non-ego force: "Wholeness is thus an objective factor that confronts the subject independently of him."[61] Accordingly, it creates energy in the formation of a unity when the Self is being realized so all of the parts of psyche are resolved. "The shadow, the syzgy, and the self are psychic forces of which an adequate picture can be formed only on the basis of a fairly thorough experience,"[62] and it is then that the transformation occurs. In the *Structure and Dynamics of the Self,* the movement is based on "a process of becoming conscious" whereby the Self must be brought into "relationship with the four functions of consciousness."[63]

The Atman and Totality

To find a more direct parallel for the Self than God or the God-image, Jung turns to the *Atman* that arises in Hinduism as perhaps the most significant analogy. He was most likely first informed about the Atman because he owned a complete set of the 50-volume *Sacred Books of the East* in his library, published in English from 1895 to 1910,[64] which contained 21 volumes of translations of the Hindu Vedic system. In the Preface to Volume 1, which along with Volume 2 contains translations of the *Upanishads*, the translator states:

> One of the most important words in the ancient philosophy of the Brahmans is Atman, nom. sing. Atma. It is rendered in our dictionaries by breath, soul, the principle of life and sensation, the individual soul, the self, the abstract

---

[60] Huskinson 2002
[61] *Aion,* § 59
[62] *Ibid,* § 62
[63] *Ibid,* § 409
[64] Shamdasani 2012, p. 61

individual, self, one's self, the reflexive pronoun, the natural temperament or disposition, essence, nature, character, peculiarity, the person or the whole body, the body, the understanding, intellect, the mind, the faculty of thought and reason, the thinking faculty, the highest principle of life, Brahma, the supreme deity or soul of the universe, care, effort, pains, firmness, the sun, fire, wind, air, a son.[65]

As the *Atman* has so many aspects and functions, the translator states that because it can directly be translated as soul, mind, or spirit, he was "driven at last to adopt Self as the least liable to misunderstanding" and that in German, the *Ich* and *Non-ich* "since the time of Fichte," suggests that as a legitimate usage.[66] The reference to Fichte is that he proposes that it is necessary to clearly posit that which is non-ego so that the Self can be understood by discovering that which is not available to the ego. Fichte and other German Idealists were a great influence on Jung,[67] and this would have made the idea of the Self as *Atman* even more attractive.

It is hard to resist the conclusion that Jung would have been very satisfied to have the *Atman* expressed in this manner by the translator of the *Sacred Books of the East* as a parallel to the Self. The translator further explains the *Atman* as the "Highest Self," where the aim is to recognize one's own personal self as a mere limited reflection of the Highest Self in order to "know his self in the Highest Self, and through that knowledge to return to it, and regain identity with it."[68]

That *Atman* is explained in such a way that the translations of the *Upanishads* in Volume 1 and 2 clearly reflect the qualities of the Self that Jung had realized as that which offered the chance to hold the opposites and provide a glimpse of totality. The use of the Self as *Atman*, however, may not have necessarily been the perfect fit for two reasons. The first is that there is a tendency, as taken up by the translator of the *Sacred Books*, to give a single Sanskrit word that has multiple meanings a single form, such as *Atman,* thereby ignoring or diminishing its many other usages. As Sri Aurobindo, the spiritual teacher and scholar, explains: "The

---

[65] Müller 1895, p. xxvii
[66] *Ibid,* pp. xxviii – xxviv
[67] Bishop 2012
[68] Müller 1895, p. xxx

Sanskrit has always been a language in which one word is naturally capable of several meanings and therefore carries with it a number of varied associations. It lends itself, therefore, ... to ... a single form of words."[69] *Atman* has multiple meanings dependent on the various schools of thought of Hinduism, such as *Advaita*, *Mimamsa*, *Dvaita* or Dualism, *Nyaya* and others, some which see the *Atman* and *Brahman* as identical, as in *Advaita,* and some that marks their difference, as in *Dvaita*. Although the *Atman* is universal to all schools, it is interpreted in each in a manner that either approaches Jung's view of the Self or is very distant.

Jung's approach to the *Atman* can be gathered from the manner in which he employs the quotes of different *Upanishads* to serve as a comparison with the Self. Jung drew his idea of the *Atman* from the point of view of the classic Vedanta view of the *Upanishads*, on which this school of Hinduism is based. The *Atman* in that lineage is a drop within an individual of the ocean that is the totality where the goal is not realization of what is indwelling, but only to realize the totality it represents. He therefore had to interpolate the *Upanishads* in a particular way to make the *Atman* more personal and a subjective experience. For this, the *Sacred Books* were particularly apt. An example of helpful translation is in the *Chhandogya Upanishad,* where it is stated that the "intelligent whose body is spirit, whose form is light, whose thoughts are true, whose nature is like ether ... from whom all works, all desires, all sweet odours and tastes proceed; he who embraces all this, who never speaks and is never surprised. .... He is my self within the heart ..."[70] A further part of the same *Upanishad* appears to bring it closer to the psychological Self: "I shall obtain him (that Self)."[71] However, the reference in that *Upanishad*, as explained by the Sanskrit scholar Sri Ganganatha Jha, is to the Supreme Self as a goal,[72] and not the realization of the indwelling Self, thereby limiting the Self to the Supreme Self; it is a reference to *Brahman* and not *Atman*.

Jung also drew on the translations of the *Upanishads* by Robert Hume, a professor at Union Theological Seminary, as a comparison (c.f.) for various quotes that suggest the *Atman* as a separate personality. It is interesting that Hume's translation is only one view of the *Atman* so that

---

[69] Aurobindo 1996, p. 258
[70] Müller 1895, p. 48
[71] *Ibid*
[72] Ganganatha 1942, p. 156

commentators argue that it is an attempt to merge the varied approaches to the *Atman/Brahman* connection and is said to be "a strongly partisan interpretation of the development and meaning of the entire literature, colored in the interests of the Sankara school, and going far beyond the facts."[73] The Sankara school is *Advaita Vedanta* where the indwelling *Atman* is identical to *Brahman* and most clearly aligns with Jung's idea of the Self as the goal to be realized. In the use of Jung's own referencing of the *Chhandogya Upanishad,* in order to personalize the Self, he merges another *Upanishad* into the translation that appears to speak of an indwelling, personal *Atman*.[74] The quote is that there is the "golden person in the heart," but Jung leaves out the express phrase that follows in Sanskrit "it is Brahman."[75]

There is thus an implied tendency in Jung's analysis to separate the *Atman* from *Brahman* in order to bring it closer to the Self to make it a personal *Atman*. This must be because the translations he was using did not distinguish between the different streams and the many philosophical ideas relating to the relationship of *Atman* to *Brahman*. For instance, Jung does not draw on the *Akshar-Purushottom Darshan* school, a lineage long in existence when he was writing, which treats the *Atman,* there called the *Aksharbrahman*, as a personality having agency distinct from *Brahman,* as every aspect of it seems to approximate the Self.[76]

Jung could not use the *Brahman* as the Self because it was what he calls the "outer Atman," totality, and he explains correctly that with *Brahman* "the idea of the self is not explicitly given."[77] In accepting *Brahman* as totality, Jung creates a distinction in relation to the *Atman:*

> Brahman is the union and dissolution of opposites, and at the same time stands outside them as an irrational factor. It is therefore beyond cognition and comprehension. It is a divine entity, at once the self (though to a lesser degree than the analogous Atman concept) and a definite psychological state characterized by isolation from the flux of affects.[78]

---

[73] Hinman 1922, p.198
[74] CW 6, § 334
[75] Ganganatha 1942, p. 155
[76] Bhadreshdas 2018
[77] CW 6, para 189
[78] *Ibid*

The *Atman* in this interpretation is the manifestation of a lesser form of totality than is *Brahman*. The relationship between *Brahman* and *Atman*, phrased in this way, raises questions about the Jungian Self as *Atman* and its relationship to totality. The quote by Jung runs into the many headwinds of different philosophical and doctrinal streams of Hinduism. One view, as an example, is that *Brahman* can exist in different forms so therefore it can be the external Supreme Being but also can be indwelling in an individual that holds part of the totality. However, this may also be considered on another interpretation, contrary to the nature of *Brahman* as totality so as not able to be split into parts. It is therefore not possible that totality be reduced to a limited extent in the *Atman*, especially as the Self, by definition, must theoretically always contain all of totality.[79]

The result of the split in Jung's quote between *Brahman* and *Atman* is to make the *Atman* the principle of the *subjective* existence of totality that is accordingly always limited, and the *Brahman* is therefore experienced as a lesser psychological state as it is not subject to a subjective experience because it is an objective, incomprehensible totality. In this way, it at least makes clear that the concept of Jung's that totality subjectively exists *only to the extent that it is manifested in an individual* is found for the *Atman* as Self and as *Brahman* to that lesser extent. The Self can only be the subjective experience of what is objective, and it may contain totality as identical to *Brahman*, but it only functions subjectively and to that extent.

Even if the *Atman* and, to a lesser extent *Brahman*, is compared to a psychological state, it makes the *Atman* psychologically more important than the realization of God and adds to the idea that totality can be experienced through the subjective existence of the Self. This is not always the case in different schools of Hinduism. Unlike the psychological requirement for realization of the Self, in *Mimamsa* or Brahmanism that follows the *Brahmana* texts of the ancient Vedas, the idea of realizing the Atman is not critical to spiritual liberation as it does not result in "right action."[80] It is only Dharma, or right action, that is important for the goal of liberation (*moksha),* and therefore the *Atman* is associated more with the will as a dynamic potential in one's being, not

---

[79] Chaudhuri 1954, pp. 52-3
[80] Baju 1967, p. 187

as that which must be realized. It is closer in this usage to what might be called the watcher or pure awareness: "This realization is *not very covetable* because the pure *atman* is only existence and has neither consciousness or bliss. ... The atman is essentially an onlooker, but through identification with the ego, becomes involved in the activities of the ego."[81]

Jung explains his early usage of the *Atman* of the *Upanishads* in a Zarathustra Seminar.[82] It is through the *Upanishads* that the nature of the *Atman* is developed by him; the *Upanishads* are the final section of the Vedas, commonly dated between 700 and 300 B.C.E. In this Vedic material, Jung took the *Atman*, perhaps based on the Preface to Volume 1 of the *Sacred Books of the East,* as meaning "Self," although in other Vedic texts, it is referred to in many different ways, such as the body or the soul.[83] It appears that the *Atman* is actually used in those other texts primarily in terms of reincarnation; the difficulties and suffering of the body are overcome by the separation of the *Atman* from the body and sensations[84] so that the body is merely the vehicle for the *Atman* that will be reborn in another body. In Vedic literature, the *Atman* is repeatedly localized specifically in the heart, and, if it is to be understood at all by an individual, it is not realized by a concept of circumambulation of the center but rather by having absorbed the right teaching. Importantly, the *Atman* was reserved only for Brahmins and was not available to be understood universally.[85]

There has accordingly been criticism of Jung's use of the *Atman* as a personal Self available by subjective realization when it is, in fact, impersonal in Vedanta.[86] This criticism requires some examination as it is related to the essential link made by Jung of the *Atman* as a parallel to the Self. If the Self has any clear parallel in Jungian thought, it is the *Atman*; nothing else has that connection of the realization of an indwelling aspect of the divine leading to a complete alternation of consciousness.

---

[81] *Ibid,* p. 195-6, emphasis added
[82] Jung 1997, Vol.2, p. 555
[83] Black 2007, p. 7
[84] *Ibid,* p. 9
[85] *Ibid,* p. 27
[86] Schlamm, 2010, p. 41

If that connection is not accurate, then there are no other Western or Eastern parallels.

It appears that the first mention of a personal *Atman* by Jung is a footnote in *Symbols of Transformation*,[87] wherein Jung indicates that the *Shvetashvatara Upanishad* supports the link between a personal *Atman* and a suprapersonal *Atman*. This *Upanishad* reads, the "Divinity, who created the universe and who pervades everything, always dwells in the hearts of creatures, being finitized by emotions, intellect, will and imagination. Those who realize this become immortal."[88] The *Atman* in this form is discussed thereafter extensively in the 1921 German edition of *Psychologische Typen,* although not specifically as a personal *Atman*. However, it is made very clear thereafter that this personal *Atman* remained his view as can be seen in a 1938 lecture in Zurich that referred to it as that which belongs to each individual, similar to a soul.[89] This idea, carried over to the *Atman*, is as a personal aspect of *Brahman,* or totality, whereby *Brahman* can be realized subjectively through the *Atman* by several means, as Jung explains, including negation of phenomena "and of discriminative cognition of *Atman* as disguised from the phenomena thus negated."[90]

Atman is therefore a reasonable yet not precise fit as a parallel of the Self as it is an indwelling aspect of totality, making the Self in comparison a placeholder of totality, and that totality can be realized through the center. The lack of precision with Vedanta philosophy does not negate the comparison because it is the universal sentiment that is being explained of an indwelling aspect of totality that can be realized that is consistent with Jung's 1935 Eranos statement that totality can be understood only by the center. As *Atman,* it contains all of totality that is *within* the center. Therefore, it is possible to be able to realize an aspect of totality through the center in the same way realization of (his version) of the *Atman* will disclose *Brahman* to the extent that can be realized.

It can be said that much of Jung's approach to the idea of a personal *Atman* that is the Self can find refuge in the plain words of many

---

[87] CW 5, § 596n182
[88] Sri Ramakrishna Math 1949, p. 92
[89] Jung, 1938-9
[90] *Ibid,* p. 94-5

Upanishads, uninterpreted by different schools. Accordingly, even though the *Atman* has no process or symbolization, realizing it is liberation; the *Taittiriya Brahmana Upanishad* provides that realizing the Atman frees one from being bound by actions. Jung clarifies his own view of the connection between the Self and the *Atman* in a discussion with a Zen philosopher, where Jung explains, "This personal *atman* corresponds to the self insofar as it is at the same time the suprapersonal *atman*. In other words, 'my self' is at the same time 'the self.'"[91] This makes perfect sense in light of the manner in which he interpreted the *Shvetashvatara Upanishad,* which is the basis of enlivening personal devotion, *Bhakti,* as the *Upanishad* is concerned with reaching totality by the love of God. The concept of "my self" as "the self" is unique; the essential merging of *Atman* and *Brahman* does not arise in the *Upanishads*, but indicates his orientation that the Self we subjectively experience as a center is, in fact, at the same time, totality.

It should be noted that it is this comparison of *Atman* being the experience of *Brahman* that most explains why Jung has said that the totality is contained within the center. The best comparable idea in the *Seven Sermons* is that the totality is the transcendent *Pleroma* that contains all things, the starting point for creation. In the *Black Books,* Jung explains that "we are the Pleroma, for we are enclosed in it and part of the eternal and the endless,"[92] so each of us contains the entirety within us.

This comparison with the *Atman* is a highly metaphysical issue, and Jung, in 1958, felt compelled to justify its use in the same discussion with the Zen philosopher: "I can only acknowledge what the person says—for I do not know what the true atman really is. I only know what people say about it. I can only say of it: 'It is so' and, at the same time, 'It is not so.'" In the same discussion, he more accurately suggests, "The authentic self *corresponds* to the *atman*."[93] Although not perfectly matched, the teachings related to the *Atman* do indeed echo the Self found by Jung, as explained by this Indologist:

> The self is the most intimate part of a person, the very center of one's being, and therefore it is the smallest of the small.

---

[91] Muramoto, et al 2002, p. 113
[92] *Black Books,* Vol. 5, p. 285
[93] Muramoto, et al 2002, p. 113

Yet, as the same time, it surpasses everything. The paradox thus undercuts any exclusion of the individual from the rest of the world, for there is nothing beyond the self.[94]

The use by Jung of *Atman* as a placeholder for totality is understood by what he intended by its introduction, not its place in the Vedic system. In a February 1932 Zarathustra seminar, in analyzing the Self, Jung suggests Hindu philosophy informs him that the "innermost being of man is *cit*, which is identical to the deity."[95] In his Kundalini Lectures in October of the same year, he describes *citta*, the noun of *chit*, as "the conscious and the unconscious field."[96] This suggests indirectly that the Self as center contains psychic totality that is a reflection of utter totality: macrocosm to microcosm. In a footnote by the editor, Professor Hauer is referenced: "Citta is absolutely everything that is in our inner world ... and therefore citta is 'soul,' in the sense of being the complete inner cosmos."[97]

These two lectures serve to introduce the connection between the innermost aspect of man that *contains* the totality as *citta*, in line with the center of man that contains the totality as the Self. This is clearly what Jung had in mind when he was giving voice to the Self as a psychological inner aspect of totality, and, through finding the Self (as the center), totality may be revealed. The presence of an indwelling aspect of God is for Jung a necessary idea because of "(T)he impossibility of distinguishing empirically between 'self' and 'God.'"[98] It is this sentiment of Jung's that brings forward the concept of the *Atman*, the indwelling God in man, in which he found a connection. Psychic totality, which he often refers to as the totality of what is conscious and unconscious, is then the microcosm of the infinite that is the macrocosm, thus closing the link between the psychological Self and the *Atman*. "What is meant by the self is not only in me but in all beings, like the Atman, like Tao. It is psychic totality."[99]

The shift to the Self as the parallel to the transcendent *Atman* occurs in several ways clinically. The first is the initial experience of the Self as a

---

[94] Brereton 1990, p. 130
[95] Jung 1997, Vol. 2, p. 555
[96] Jung 1996, p. 70
[97] *Ibid*, p. 70n3
[98] CW 9.i, § 572
[99] CW 10, para. 873

sense or premonition of wholeness. It is that early connection with wholeness, although transient, that brings in the idea of God: "The concept of psychic wholeness necessarily implies an element of transcendence on account of the existence of unconscious components."[100] In terms of the *Atman,* the possible subjective experience of the indwelling divine will, perforce, invoke the ideal of an ultimate unifying totality and that is where the parallel is most useful. The second is by extrapolating from symbols of the Self a connection with divinity, at least recognized in another tradition, "for the central point, circle, and quaternity are well-known symbols for the deity."[101]

The connection with the *Atman* also suggests a particular psychological process. The *Atman* is what remains when there is a disengagement from the ego so as to sublate day-to-day experience revealing that there is a realm of autonomy lying beyond self-reflection. As Agehananda Bharati, the Western anthropologist who became an Indian monk, put it, the sublation of the ego is what is necessary and then "if only it can be peeled out from beneath the recondite, arcane, obscurantist diction in which it has been encased."[102] For the saint who has realized the Self and has "peeled out" the *Atman,* he *becomes* the Self "who observes everything with unwavering gaze because (he is) uninvolved, while the world moves around him in a continuous welter of changing phenomenon."[103]

For Jung, a direct comparison with the orthodox, impersonal concept of the realization of the *Atman* would not have answered his need for a dynamic force that can be brought into conscious awareness to become the guiding spirit. Sublation of the ego is contrary to the idea that there must be a strong, functioning ego to realize the revelations of the unconscious. It requires something else, not found in this classic idea of the *Atman,* to assert that there is an ongoing dialogue between the Self and consciousness, whereby the Self wants to make itself known. This is not an idea in Vedanta at all but exists in *Advaita Vedanta.*

---

[100] *Ibid*
[101] *Ibid*
[102] Bharati 1985, p. 227
[103] Zimmer 1952, p. 453

Advaita Vedanta

It is an issue whether *Advaita* was part of a stream of ancient Hindu thought or is more recent in origin, derived from *Sankara* in the eighth century.[104] *Advaita* is the "non-dual" philosophy, based entirely on interiority by removal of consciousness from the objective world. "The process of liberation consists in deconstruction of consciousness, that is, in a continuous removal of false identities, beginning with the idea of the identification of oneself with the suffering individual. ... Individuation is achieved here by *semantic,* rather than psychological, means."[105] The true Self that remains is the *Atman* that recognizes itself, without more, as totality.

Brahman, the supreme God, is found in the *Atman*, so *Brahman* in all its totality *is* the *Atman*, meaning it is non-dual. This causes a paradox as *Brahman* is the creator, external to the individual, yet it is also that which is the indwelling Atman. The paradox is said to be solved by the external *Atman—Brahman* being without qualities as the ultimate reality, and only with qualities as indwelling. This is a complex idea in Hindu philosophy as critics state as to *Sankara*: "if he insists on absolute unity, the ruler-ruled relationship is precluded and hence the Lord cannot be the cause at all."[106] When the Self is viewed as *Atman* by Jung, it does not have this distinction; it is not therefore an *Advaita* position.

What is most useful in understanding the Self and that which brings the *Atman* of *Advaita* closest to the Self are the teaching methods in *Advaita* for obtaining insight into the indwelling divine. *Sankara* suggests that the teacher be continuously questioned, as this indicates on the part of an individual a readiness to receive a higher form of teaching and to resolve doubts so as to let go of the ego.[107] The lineage from *Sankara* includes notable teachers, and one of the most significant is Sri Ramana Maharshi who offers a more intense method of self-enquiry. Jung was critical of Ramana and the *Advaita* consequence of abolition of the body, which Ramana described as a clod, as well as the need for discarding psyche to reach the ground of the *Atman*:

[104] Minkowski 2011
[105] *Ibid,* pp. 220-1
[106] Hirst 2005, p. 121
[107] *Ibid*, p. 71-2

> Without the Maharshi's personal ego, which, as a matter of
> brute experience, only exists in conjunction with the said
> 'clod' (=body), there would be no Shri Ramana at all. Even
> if we agreed with him that it is no longer his ego, but the
> *atman* speaking, it is still the psychic structure of conscious-
> ness in association with the body that makes speech
> communication possible. Without this admittedly very
> troublesome physical and psychic man, the self would be
> entirely without substance.[108]

In *Advaita*, the Self is best accomplished and realized, in fact, by the loss
of what marks one out as a person; it is what remains without ego
consciousness. An effective means for this process is Ramana's form of
self-enquiry, prompted by questions to be endlessly asked of oneself as
to "Who am I?" This question, using the ego, can be appropriately asked
because the thought of "I" is always paramount in the mind, making that
the prime question. Even when there is complex trauma or a greatly
diminished ego, it leads to a focus on the Self only: "to whom do these
thoughts arise?" "to whom did these events happen?" "if I am not these
thoughts then who am I?" Ramana expressed the consequence: "saying
'I am not this; no, nor am I this'—that which then remains separate and
alone by itself, that pure Awareness is what I am."[109]

This form of enquiry can be in the form of a Socratic interchange between
the questioner and the seeker that is useful for therapeutic purposes, even
though it was designed as a process of self-enquiry. It brings the focus
consistently and repeatedly back to the unreality of a cognitive answer to
events and instead to the emergence of the reality of the Self as the
essential core.

Nowhere is the function of the Self as healer better understood than in
the case of trauma. The categorization of trauma by Jung is as a
"complex"[110] and, viewed as a complex, its effect on psyche is not as to
its apparent subjective effect but rather its dynamic nature within the
layers of psyche that may result in a cumulative, or as it has been called

---

[108] CW 11, § 959
[109] Maharshi 1997, p. 40
[110] CW 8, § 204

a "cogwheeling effect"[111] with other complexes and archetypes. This activation of the psyche by the formation of a split-off trauma complex is the basis of the work of Kalsched,[112] where archetypal defenses are triggered, compounding the trauma, and Knox,[113] who carries out the analysis through an attachment perspective to interpret the cumulative experience.

The complexes are the moving parts of psyche, and it follows that a trauma complex will activate other complexes and their core archetypes and have attendant consequences for the myriad forms of dissociation. If the Self is viewed as an archetype, it too would be caught in the cycle generated by a trauma complex and the degree to which it was damaged could be argued to be a better marker than shifting subjective or emotional states. This devastation was apparent in RW, a former soldier who presented as a patient with what Wilson refers to as the "abyss experience,"[114] where extreme trauma creates utter annihilation: "a loss of a sense of continuity and a profound diminution of emotional responsiveness or psychic numbing … traumatic impact to the innermost core of psychic functioning."[115] This raises the question of what is that innermost core and how can it be approached.

RW had been a soldier in the Army of Republika Srpska (VRS) in the Bosnian-Serb conflict. He came to New York in 2010 and started analysis in 2012. RW's presenting symptoms appeared simple enough: an inability to sleep and mild instances of anxiety. He revealed, after several months, that as a soldier he had killed 27 people, only a few of whom were soldiers, by shooting and "other means" but refused to accept that this was in any way connected to his issues.

RW lived in the Tremont area of the West Bronx, one of the most dangerous areas of New York, known for the lowest level of personal income, multiple gangs, and a high concentration of homeless families. His explanation was that he is most comfortable living in a war zone. After two years of working with him in analysis, there were few changes

---

[111] Wilson 2004, p. 50
[112] Kalsched 1996
[113] Knox 2003
[114] Wilson 2004
[115] *Ibid*, p. 58

in his anxiety levels, but at least there was a sense that he was in the process as he came regularly to each session. He spent much of the time complaining about living in the Bronx, about the violence he witnessed daily, of the plight of his Dominican neighbors, and his inability to get his sink repaired. At least, through listening to the narratives he presented, some therapeutic bond appeared to be forming.

In October 2014, he was in Queens, less than a block away from the hatchet attack on four New York City police officers in Jamaica, and he heard the gunshot that killed the perpetrator. From the next session on, he did not respond to my promptings, and we would sit for long periods of time in silence. Week after week, there was no sense of him even being engaged in the analysis, as he sat there almost inert. There was no opportunity for an examination of his past or his life situation except a repeated description of his current job in a bank and the odd comment about the poor heating in his apartment, where he lived alone. No dreams were reported. I sensed a profound deadness in the room, a significant dissociation that had not been present before. The untenable idea that the core of his psyche—the Self—was destroyed had to be entertained. After a few more sessions, he terminated with an explanation that he needed some time to forget what he heard.

After four months, he contacted me for what he referred to as a "final session." He arrived in a state of deep sadness, so it was noteworthy that he had at least been engaged with his emotions. He said that he thought there was nowhere to go in our sessions as he was "broken," but he wanted to come and have a final session to say goodbye. I felt that the transference was still strong and that there was room to continue.

I suggested to him that we try an experiment for the last session where I ask him a series of questions and he would try to respond. I started off by asking him what he felt was left of him after what he had suffered, and he responded that there was not much but at least he was alive. Thus began a dialogue of me questioning him about what may lie at the source of his being: "what is alive?" and "who are you really?" I was aware that he did not have strong ego defenses and I was able to point to several false dichotomies he was trying to maintain to illustrate that the mind did not have an answer. I moved into the question of "Then, who are you?" and "Who is making up that answer?" He opened up to the fact that he had no answers, yet he was still there, and toward the end of the session he stated, "I guess something is there."

A few weeks later, he called to come back and renew his weekly commitment to analysis. In the months that followed, he appeared only slightly more functional, and no deeper therapy, aside from support, was yet indicated. However, the consistent method of direct enquiry into the Self gave me that chance to concentrate on supporting him, increasing the therapeutic alliance, and we reached a point that we both recognized where he had improved in his day-to-day functioning. He left with self-respect and an appreciation that he had changed in a manner that he could not describe.

It occurred to me that the *Advaita* method was not a "cure" because the ego remained damaged and disintegrated, and his insights into the Self, which he did have, were mostly transitory, as they were not absorbed into the field of consciousness. The result, however, was that he was more functional in that he had touched the Self and what is found of the Self can never be lost. He resumed his job from which he had taken leave, moved out of the Bronx, and met occasionally with friends. This was an improvement and, taking that as a measure, the idea of concentrating on the deepest core of the immovable and ever-present Self, where trauma has severely damaged conscious integration, has efficacy as a treatment.

It was the Self that we sought as the *Atman* that remains when the ego loses its grip and is peeled away. This is perhaps the best use of the *Atman*-Self connection, the reliance upon that indwelling aspect of totality and numinosity that can be revealed and gradually is realized as a new idea. This makes a version of the *Advaita Vedanta* method of self-enquiry a valuable tool in the ongoing search for effective ideas to work with complex trauma.

The Self, Soul, and Spirit

The relationship of the Self to the soul and the Self to the spirit is, of course, unclear, as they are all abstractions of forces within and from without that are used to explain the apparent passage of life. How the Self is characterized depends on which is the prime mover because, if the soul or spirit has that role, then the Self loses its claim to individuating energies and, to some extent, a degree of importance when it is realized.

Jung is not interested in the theoretical comparison with the Self, but only how Soul and Spirit are experienced subjectively:

> If I have called the centre the "self," I did so after mature consideration and a careful appraisal of the empirical and historical data. A materialistic interpretation could easily maintain that the "centre" is "nothing but" the point at which the psyche ceases to be knowable because it there coalesces with the body. And a spiritualistic interpretation might retort that this "self" is nothing but "spirit," which animates both soul and body and irrupts into time and space at that creative point. I purposely refrain from all such physical and metaphysical speculations and content myself with establishing the empirical facts ....[116]

Wolfgang Giegerich in his book *What Is Soul?* raises questions about the relationship between psyche, soul, and Self as used by Jung. This arises because, as he explains, Jung uses soul and psyche interchangeably, but in the English edition of the *Collected Works*, the use of soul was diminished, as it was often translated as psyche to perhaps make it more amenable to a scientific approach.[117] The interchangeability is a consequence of there being no German word for psyche as distinct from soul, so the word used for soul, *Seele*, can be translated as psyche or soul. Paul Bishop points to a specific change in Jung's language that originated in *Psychologische Typen* in 1921 from the soul (*die Seele*) to the psyche (*die Psyche*). He explains that this "represents a move *away* from an emphasis on the visual or pictorial or the imagistic ... *towards* a terminology that sounds more clinical, more technical, more scientific."[118]

Giegerich argues that soul is not the Self and soul cannot be described other than as an autonomous "nothing," as it is incomprehensible and only displays itself from time to time in various ways *where it is speaking about itself.*[119] It has its own life, an internally "logical" life as he refers to it. He quotes Jung in support,[120] substituting the word "soul" for the

---

[116] CW 12, § 327
[117] Giegerich 2012, pp. 5-7
[118] Bishop 2014, p. 142
[119] Giegerich 2012, p. 84
[120] CW 9i, § 400

English use of "psyche" to say: "In myths and fairytales, as in dreams, the soul speaks about itself ..."[121] By so defining soul and distinguishing soul from psyche, the Self appears out of place, even though it is considered by Jung as the center of psyche and responsible for psychological growth. It then can only have that place, Giegerich is forced to conclude, as a characterization of the *conjunctio* or unity caused by the fusing of the opposites in psyche.[122] It becomes, as a result, a term similar to *Abraxas* or *Mercurius*, to be used only as nomenclature for that unity, not as an active force in individuation.

To view the Self as having a greater role in psyche than merely a unity arises because growth occurs by circumambulation, so there is a center with a virtual location and purpose. If the soul is considered the prime mover, then what could remain of the purpose of circumambulation as well as the agency of the Self and the possibility that it seeks to realize itself? Giegerich, in a lengthy footnote, elucidates defects in the notion of the Self that are advanced to diminish its purpose in relation to the primacy of the soul.[123] His critique elucidates two aspects of the Self in his terms. The first is that the Self is merely a manifestation of soul because the Self would not exist without the soul. The second is that the concept of wholeness, the essence of the realization of the Self, is a uroboric feeling that is the nature of a soul display occurring within soul. Thus, the critique combines the two aspects to say that the need to realize the Self through the process of individuation is only an externality to soul and is contrary, as he asserts, to Jung's basic thesis of an objective psyche ("soul") that transforms itself.

His arguments are based on the idea that the soul exists only as total interiority and is involved in its own unfolding, unrelated to individuals. In this interpretation, there is no apparent room for the Self as revealing itself in a process of individuation. For an individual, following Giegerich's reasoning, the realization of the soul as absolutely autonomous is the only meaning that can be derived. If the Self has any function, it is accordingly only another term for the *conjunctio* that may be brought about by the soul for its own purposes.

---

[121] Giegerich 2012, p. 84
[122] *Ibid*, p. 296
[123] *Ibid*, p. 306n231

His argument is logical, not because of Jung's use of "soul" in German, but rather because it could be the soul that carries out its purpose and the Self displays a unity when realized. This does not account, however, for the presentation of the pattern of wholeness, the core Self, that operates as an emergent archetype. If it is the soul instead of the Self, it would mean it is responsible also for that patterning as prime mover. As an entity with its own logical life, it would not necessarily form symbols to reflect its biological promptings.

It does raise the strong possibility that the Self is seeking itself and, like the soul or as an aspect of soul, has its own purpose and logical life. In that case, the Self could indeed be the same as or a manifestation of whatever is considered to be the prime mover. If viewed as the Self seeking itself, this presents an important orientation and meaning. The meaning is derived for the observer witnessing its manifestations by way of wholeness and the emergence of symbols. The realization of the Self as actively seeking itself creates what Michael Sells, in speaking of the similar treatment of God in the Sufism of Ibn 'Arabi, refers to as an "identity shift" and "meaning event." In this orientation, when the divine sees its mirror reflection and realizes itself through the agency of an individual, the shift occurs for an individual that the person is no longer a separate identity but is the vehicle for the divine.[124] The meaning event is then the realization by an individual of the nature of the divine. In this sense, individuation of an individual and idea of the realization of the Self are understood as a meaning event of the revelation of the Self manifesting itself for its own sake. It is in the meaning, the orientation away from the chaos, that the Self has a role.

The Self as seeking itself can be attributed to either itself, the soul, God, or any entity because it is not a psychological process but rather a statement about the primal force of life that seeks to become conscious or desires to examine its own creation through the eyes of an individual for its own delight. It is therefore the Self's logical life as well. This still leaves the question of the relationship between the Self and the soul unclear but suggests that, even if the Self is an aspect of soul, it still has a broader role to imprint wholeness in our being and to create the longing to return to that primal source.

---

[124] Sells 1994, pp. 88-9

There is a metaphysical approach that may more closely join the Self with the concept of soul. In the *Zohar*, the central work of Kabbalah, the soul has three ascending parts that all work together. Each part is sustained by the next higher part, and the highest part is sustained by divine light. The lowest part of the soul, *nefesh,* nourishes the body, the next, *ruach,* sustains the *nefesh* and is associated with the activities of the mind and body. The *ruach,* although its function is not made clear in the *Zohar,* is the conduit for what lies above and therefore can be conceived as that which provides for contemplation of the mystery of God.[125] The highest form, *neshamah,* provides the awe and understanding of the infinite. The putative author of the Zohar, Moses de Leon, provides that the *ruach* "acts like the breeze that blows"[126] and is the intermediate spirit that connects the parts.

The word *ruach* is used continuously in the Old Testament and is called "The Holy Spirit" in the New Testament.[127] The Holy Spirit is blown into man, and the word *ruach* is therefore "wind" or "breath," which implies movement or change and thus the spirit of God that animates life, as in Genesis (Gen. 6:17, 7:15, 7:22). *Ruach* has many aspects and implies not only an animating principle but also the capacity to confer revelation. One example of the latter is Joseph given wisdom and revelations to interpret Pharaoh's dream (Gen. 41:38-39). *Ruach* in its multiplicity leads to visions (Ezek 11:24) as well as revelations and therefore can be said in this regard to have attributes of the Self; in the *Wisdom of Solomon* (1:5)*, ruach* is "holy spirit, that divine tutor."

The three parts operate at different times and suggest a unity of four: the three parts and the divine, as that can also be considered a part as it is connected to the other three. This approach of dividing the soul into parts would not be apparent from a psychological perspective because the experience of the soul does not distinguish different aspects of itself. The dual nature of the soul to nourish the body and as a connection to a higher dimension of pure soul, is briefly alluded to by Jung in a reference to that concept by Leibniz.[128] The idea of the *nefesh* to nourish the body, the idea of *neshamah,* the connection with the divine, and a need to mediate the

---

[125] Tishby 1991, Vol II, pp. 685-6
[126] *Ibid,* p. 686
[127] Wood, 1998
[128] *Letters,* Vol. 2, p. 416n2

two as *ruach,* establishes the unity of the soul. In this analogy, the Self connects to the soul that enlivens the body and is also that which connects to totality.

The Self, by its purpose as a virtual center, could be said to be the same as soul or is another name for soul. In the *Seven Sermons,* the necessity for individual life is *Creatura,* the discrimination of opposites that are in the uroboric state in the *Pleroma; Creatura* is the nature of consciousness. The opposites reside in each of us, and the process of reconciliation is the essence of psychological growth and human endeavor. If the logical life of the soul is not concerned with this, then it is an aspect of creation that is unrelated to humanity. It is thus more logical to give the Self the designation of an aspect of soul, as that is understood.

In speaking of "spirit," Jung uses the term in many contexts, but always in the same sense as an animating power of an archetype.[129] He views it as "an autonomous reality which commands a specific energy powerful enough to bend the instincts round and constrain them in spiritual form."[130] It is that energy contained within the spirit that has the power to oppose pure instinctuality, such as that instinctive force that arises from the father.[131] As the spirit has that specific, critical energy and is autonomous, it appears as the "totality of primary forms from which the archetypal images come."[132] It thus "appears as an archetype" in the collective and is expressed as a divine hero and a creator, the *Creator Spiritus.* The sense of it is that it is not at all passive but is in constant motion, represented by symbols of significance with divine power. Jung uses the term *ruach* in this way, as breath and spirit.[133]

As it is autonomous, spirit is felt as strange and existing outwardly, therefore unrelated to a soul[134] or to the Self. By granting it specific energy, represented by the hero and creator, it is that which animates life as Jung expresses, as "an inexpressible transcendental idea of all-embracing significance."[135] The essence of it encompasses that which

---

[129] Gitz-Johansen 2020, p. 667
[130] CW 5, § 338
[131] *Ibid,* § 396
[132] *Ibid,* § 641
[133] CW 7, § 217
[134] *Ibid,* § 293
[135] CW 8, § 602

appears to move life forward under the guise of many possibilities, as he explains, "When I utter the word 'spirit,' no matter how accurately I may define the meaning I intend it to convey, the aura of its many other meanings cannot be wholly excluded."[136]

If an attempt is made to suggest some logical arrangement, it is that the soul has three elements. In its primal, self-related world, it is the hand of God like the *Atman* that is indwelling in all things that appears passive but is the pattern of wholeness. It is what the editor of the *Sacred Books of the East* refers to as the Self. The Self used in this way is the breath or will of God, the *pneuma* or the spirit, which moves the soul into corporeal life, and therefore always approximates the spirit, and is also that which has the potential to unite the opposites that approximates the Self. In this way, it is also that which brings one, as *ruach,* closer to the higher, divine levels that also is the Self.

Five levels of the soul are suggested in Lurianic Kabbalah, the fourth level being the connection the soul has with other souls, and the fifth is absolute unity so that "The five levels of soul thus form a chain linking man to the Supreme Universes, and ultimately to God."[137] This concept applied to the Self makes it the total individual in which the process is enacted as well as having some grounding in every other level. This metaphysical journey is only useful to indicate the Self is not the soul or the spirit but encompasses all of them at the same time.

The Self as No-Self

It is critical to the structure and postulates of Daoist and Buddhist doctrine that there is no Self. This is necessitated because they both require discarding attachment and fixation to *any* psychic content: "the realisation of negativity is crucial to reveal ultimate Reality."[138] The goal of both can be expressed as the suppression or dissolution of the ego and its cravings, and therefore any reflection on or realization of a Self is contrary to the pure experience of being.

---

[136] *Ibid*
[137] Kramer & Sutton 1998, p. 41
[138] Abe 1975, p. 191

The essence of this deidentification with psychic content is with matters of self-reflection, the "I," the ego, individualistic awareness, sense of purpose, or any trace of subject-object. As a result, it excludes identity with the body or the concept of psychological integration along with any mental constructs that have a static end-state, such as the Jungian Self. It also denies the existence of any substantive agent or that which is preexistent and directive.

The manner in which the Jungian Self is related to the concept of no-Self can be examined on three levels. The first is whether the *processes* of reaching the goal of either are related. The second is whether Jung had any intention to include the idea of no-Self in his development of the Self. The third is whether the final state of realization of the Self and no-Self is the same.

In respect of the process, Murray Stein offers a synthesis of the stages of spiritual development in Zen Buddhism with the realization of the Self. He does this by suggesting a similarity of the stages of the Jungian individuation process with the process represented in the Zen Ox-Herding pictures.[139] The first stage of the psychoanalysis of complexes and defenses, he asserts, is similar to the initial orientation of Zen meditation practices as both yield the development of a position in psyche that is outside the ego, fundamental to the final goal. What then follows in both is a gradual series of steps that increase awareness of that quality. He quotes Jung that the psychic preparation for this development is an attempt to bring about a union of opposites and also to establish a principle "freed from the opposites," that Jung calls *Nirdvandva*.[140] Stein indicates that the Zen *Ox-Herding Pictures* reflect a process that points to the goal of individuation as "separation of from all identifications and entanglements with unconscious contents (cleansing the door of perception) and bearing witness to the archetypal powers that underlie individual and cultural psychologies."[141]

The process is similar. but the goal of realization of the Self by the ego cannot be present due to the Buddhist doctrine of "Dependent Arising," which makes the abandonment of the ego a critical aspect of each step of

---

[139] Stein 2019b
[140] CW 14, § 711
[141] Stein 2019a, p. 14

the process in Buddhist practice. The doctrine disallows recognition of the ego, as it is based on the fact that reality and its perception are continuously arising and then ceasing. This makes it apparent that it is clinging and suffering through mental processes and elements of perception that appear to create solid entities or substances, such as the Self. In that context, which is exceedingly detailed in Buddhist literature, the Self would only be another example of a phenomenon that arises and ceases under the doctrine of Dependent Arising and therefore its recognition by the ego is not to be accorded any weight.

In the practice of realization of no-Self, it is necessary to proceed with the involvement of the ego. The ego, the sense of "I," is a starting point only because the orientation to no-Self is made apparent through explanation and practice. Two teachings warn, however, that the tools of the ego: Thought, intellect, and psychic contents are contained within speech and may yield the false impression that some form of identification is acceptable, wherein the Self could shelter. In the *Chachakka Sutta*,[142] the expression of *any* aspect of self-identification, the eye, the ear, the nose, the tongue, the body, the intellect, and feeling may be linguistically acceptable, but under the condition that none of them refers to any real or psychological entities: "This is not me, this is not my self, this is not what I am" applies to all and any form of self-identification. In the *Potthapada Sutta*,[143] the Buddha explains that it is the experience of *any* aspects of self-identification that must be abandoned as they are merely temporary perceptions.

The similarity in the process then arises only because of linguistic necessity to relate to the teachings, even though the words are empty. The self as self-image and representation is still, however, present in Buddhism in order to orient to the practice. It is this self that must abandon these views of self-representation as emptiness of form by a process of disidentifying with all forms. This conundrum of speaking from a position of self-representation, yet those concepts being the barrier to be overcome, is expressed in the work of Nāgarjuna, the 3rd-century Buddhist philosopher, in his "two truths" doctrine.[144] The two truths are

---

[142] *Chachakka Sutta* 1998
[143] *Potthapada Sutta* 1998
[144] Garfield & Priest 2003

the ultimate truth of emptiness, and, as well, the *intermediate* superficial truth provided by experience. The ultimate cannot be attained without the intermediate that uses conventional representations of the manner in which the ultimate appears. There is therefore an "I" in conventional truth that describes and relates to the manner in which this ultimate truth is presented. The "I" creates assumptions and directs itself through perceptual and mental images to the essence of nonbeing, even though by Buddhist doctrine they are empty.

To fit the Jungian Self as an acceptable part of Buddhist doctrine appears to be a mistake. However, the similarity to individuation processes correctly identified by Murray Stein is that the idea of the Self, which is initially a metaphysical idea and of no intrinsic worth, is a universal model of a process and a goal, no different to Buddhist practice. Therefore, the Self, as does the no-Self, creates an abstract image during the process because of the language that is used, such as naming the Self and its functions. The Self remains metaphysical until there are symbols presented and then it is the experience, not a concept, that is translated into the Self.

This raises the question of whether Jung actually intended that the Self somehow incorporates no-Self. Some confusion arises because, at one point, he uses the term *Nirdvandva,* or a state where there are no opposites. Helen Morgan therefore asserts that *Nirdvandva* is close to *Nirvana* or nothingness—no-Self, and this inclusion was therefore an overstatement on the part of Jung because this is "much more problematic" than the link between the Self and the *Atman.*[145] This leads her to the conclusion that Jung's view of the Self may, in fact, be incomplete without the inclusion of no-Self: "we have got ourselves too shackled to this 'self' we have inherited from Jung." We must ask "What if there is no self? No God, no *atman* or *Brahman,* no 'hidden variable,' or ghost in the machine, or teleological and purposeful force or field which determines how 'things' behave?"[146]

Shoji Muramoto, in a footnote in his analysis of the conversation between Jung and Hisamatsu, a Zen practitioner and philosopher, explains that

[145] Morgan 2019, p. 24
[146] *Ibid,* p. 27, emphasis supplied.

Nirdvandva is not the same idea as *Nirvana,* which implies emptiness, but is consistent with Jung's fundamental principle of seeking a way to hold the opposites. He suggests that *Nirvana* is the denial of the opposites, so this would have been foreign to Jung. More recent publication of Jung's lectures on Yoga and Meditation, particularly in lectures given in 1938, do incidentally indicate that he was familiar with the nature of *Nirvana.*[147] In any event, Muramoto also points out that that the editor of the works of Hisamatsu suggests that the two words, Self and *Nirdvandva,* do mean the same thing, and therefore Jung could have been aware of the aspect of the Self that is nothingness.[148] The use of *Nirdvandva* is a state which is free from the opposites that is not psychologically practical: "*Nirdvandva* is a redemptive achievement not possible in ordinary human existence."[149] These are references that do not carry any relevance to individuation and are not assertions, express or implied, of the Self including no-Self.

In a separate explanation of Jung's relationship to Buddhism, Muramoto suggests several connections of which only one has any cogency. In the *Septum Sermones ad Mortuous,* the *Seven Sermons,* wherein Jung describes the *Pleroma* that holds all opposites, it is said that it includes emptiness and fullness: "I begin with nothingness. Nothingness is the same as fullness. ... Nothingness is both empty and full."[150] Muramoto concludes, "So Jung's Plermona seems to be very close to sunyata" (emptiness).[151] Basilides, the putative author of the *Seven Sermons,* was unique among the Gnostics in indicating that the *Pleroma started* from nothingness, wherein the dormant opposites are held, thus emptiness and fullness. Jung chose Basilides instead of the prevailing doctrine that creation arose from fullness.[152] Basilides creation myth, *creatio ex nihilo,* was of the origin of an original seed with a nonexistent God that came out from the emptiness.[153] This is in contrast to the creation myth of the Valentinians that it arose out of fullness, the Father, or the Monad.[154] The

---

[147] Jung 2020, p. 29
[148] Muramoto, et. al. 2002a, p. 115n7
[149] Jarrett 1986, p. 64a
[150] *Memories,* p. 379
[151] Muramoto, et. al 2002a, p. 124
[152] Stein 2015
[153] Hippolytus 1868, Book VI, p. 276
[154] *Ibid,* p. 224

great nothingness before creation therefore cannot be used as a basis for a comparison to or inclusion of no-Self in Jung's ideas of the Self.

Stanton Marlan in his work on the Alchemical *Black Sun*, suggests that the Self lacks substantiality and therefore is both complementary and antagonistic to no-Self.[155] In line with this topic, he concentrates on the no-Self derived from apophatic theology that preferences negative statements. He refers to Derrida to say that the Self therefore can be crossed out as it can never be understood and the word is always inaccurate, so it is "under erasure."[156] This makes totality something else, arising out of "larger collective forces."[157] At some level of abstraction, the Self and no-Self therefore meet, as both are unknown in content and form. This is an argument that is similar to that made by Emmanuel Levinas: "Less than identical with itself, unable to catch up with itself, unable to achieve presence and self-presence, the self cannot be considered an entity. It has dropped out of being, and out of being striving for manifestation, is disinterested."[158] This argument, however, is excluded by Jung's use of *esse in anima,* which forms a bridge between the emptiness of a concept and its psychological recognition that gives it a form.

The no-Self appears contrary to what Jung proposes because of the fundamental need for the ego to relate to the unconscious as the essential element of psychological development. Nothingness is therefore not an aspect of the Self; it does not come from nothingness, as it is preexistent and its realization does not include states of nothingness wherein the ego is not present. Jung's classic statement as to a state of nothingness characterized by complete absorption and loss of ego in the Hindu concept of "samādhi" explains his view:

> the yogis, attain perfection in samādhi, a state of ecstasy, which so far as we know is equivalent to a state of unconsciousness. It makes no difference whether they call our unconscious a 'universal consciousness'; the fact remains that in their case the unconscious has swallowed up

---

[155] Marlan 2005, p. 182
[156] *Ibid,* p. 185
[157] *Ibid,* p. 187
[158] Levinas 1991, xxxi

ego-consciousness. They do not realize that a 'universal consciousness' is a contradiction in terms, since exclusion, selection, and discrimination are the root and essence of everything that lays claim to the name 'consciousness.'[159]

The connection of the ego with the Self, necessary for its realization, disappears at the moment of samādhi and enters a state of emptiness—no-Self—with no conscious recognition. Jung was disapproving of that state for his psychology but accepted that it exists when there is a "drop in the conscious potential, the unconscious becomes the determining factor, and the ego disappears."[160] This is a state that he considers psychologically primitive, like a child, ruled by the unconscious yet is blissful because one feels "borne along by the current of life" with no need to do anything.[161] The experience is described well as where the ego "winks out, ceases to be, radically stops."[162] It is indeed a state he recognizes, although it is not the goal of individuation, as it lacks discrimination by the ego. The Self as containing all opposites would thereby, by definition, hold the nothingness of no-Self, but realization of the Self as a psychological fact does not accord with the no-Self of Buddhism.

Both the idea of the Self and the principle of no-Self are directed at the problem of the opposites. The *Tao te ching* (more recently referred to as *Daodejing*) of Lao-Tse is the guide to the Way (*Dao*). The Way is a state of being that solves the opposites by eschewing desire and is based upon "overcoming of the yearnings and cravings of the ego ... the overcoming of oneself."[163] The purpose of overcoming is to experience the unifying, preexistent *Dao* in all things, inner and outer, similar to the process of realization of the Self existing in matter that Jung explicates in *Aion*. Jung was influenced by Dao from an early time while doing research for the 1921 edition of *Psychologische Typen,* which coincided with the need to find a way to deal with the opposites. His work in this respect was refined through his preparation of a commentary on the *Secret of the Golden*

---

[159] *Aion*, § 520
[160] CW 6, § 422
[161] *Ibid*
[162] Noh 1977, p. 17
[163] Moeller 2007, p. 80

Flower.[164] The *Dao* offered a middle way between the opposites and, like the Self, was the source of ongoing creation. The *Dao* is what goes beyond a mere center point of opposites and is obtained and realized by a process; so too is the Self in its fullest expression as consisting of the opposites and their virtual unity.

The Self, if fully realized, assuming that this is possible, can evoke emptiness as one aspect of a duality. That realization would be without the ego involvement but in the context of a mystical or religious experience. This is such a rare occurrence that it is not the basis for the ontological development of the Self through individuation. The Self is, in its essence, a psychological phenomenon that presents the view of the non-ego to an ego-based consciousness in a "step by step development of the self from an unconscious state to a conscious state."[165] The relationship of the no-Self to the Self is therefore circumstantial, as the Self has a different predicate and goal.

Clinical Vignettes of the Self as Other

Vignette 1: The Self as Guru

Nicole is a 43-year-old woman from New York who became an adherent of a Tantra Yoga guru. Its tenet is that meditation exercises relating to the chakras will wake up kundalini and lead to awakening. The meditation has two specific techniques: ideation on the guru as well as mantras to be used in meditation for each chakra in order to reach Samadhi. It is important in this tradition that in reaching Samadhi it is the guru who will be found and will present himself as the highest form of *Brahman*. It accordingly maintains that there be sufficient ego at the peak moment to understand the significance of the insight. It calls for reflective self-awareness and preparation for the surrender to the guru.

Nicole had the following dream:

> I was at the edge of Rockaway Beach (in Queens, New York) and wanted to take a boat to an island I could see in the distance. It had lush vegetation, a verdant green, and it

---

[164] Coward 1996
[165] *Aion*, § 418

looked very peaceful. I easily found a rowboat as if it was waiting for me but there was no boatman in it or oars for me to row. I then saw Giri (the guru) approaching me. He was coming out of the water as if he had been submerged but his robes were dry when he approached me. He told me that I need not take the boat because there was nothing on the island.

The guru is not considered the *Atman* in Hinduism[166] but can serve the function of a symbol of the Self as well as a fitting basis for a projection of the Self. For her, it is not an intrapsychic Self but rather an external representation. As the guru was outside and served the function of directing her and indicating also a possible goal, the translation into a subjective inner Self was difficult. To say that the outside guru by its presence in the dream coming out of the unconscious is the Self made no sense to her, as he was the guiding spirit and fulfilled all of the characteristics of the Self in conveying a sense of wholeness, practices to establish a unity beyond opposites, a presence as *spiritus rector,* and ensuring the way forward along the path.

The guru's power lay in the fact that he was an archetypal form, not the same as Christ as he is not similar, as Jung calls Christ, the "typical dying and self-transforming god."[167] The archetype, however, provides for her the spirit that is missing: "we need the illumination of a holy and whole-making spirit—a spirit that can be anything rather than our reason."[168]

This dream presents the Self as an actual personality and the giver of a process with the promise of integration. In the dream, it becomes a psychological fact that assistance is needed to reach wholeness and the view she had of the Self as the island, a temenos, was an indirect route. The clinical approach was naturally to explain the guru as the Self, a numinous figure that is a symbol represented by the Self. As Jung lists the symbols of the Self as including the hero and prophet, the approach was to amplify the guru's aspects that all correspond to the Self and to leave the insights that this brought with the guru and not the psychological Self.

---

[166] Mlecko 1982
[167] CW 11, § 146
[168] *Ibid,* § 267

As the work continued, the approach echoed the idea of the *Atman* being that aspect of *Brahman* that is in each individual. This was consistent with Tantra that she practiced as the *Atman* exists there as a mid-point between the in-breath as Shakti and the out-breath as Shiva. The worship of the guru then allowed for the subjective experience of an inner aspect of that guru, as it appeared in the dream, that more easily aligns with the idea of the Self. No attempt was made to make a perfect translation, as this recognition still allowed the process of individuation to have a goal. Her psychological process and her Shadow struggles at least had the countervailing force of the idea of the Self, so that the guru served well the introduction of the ideal of a unity of the opposites.

Vignette 2: Appearance of the Dead Father

A male patient, Robert, had the following vision:

> I was at a Board meeting of my company, and I was about to speak when for a moment I saw my father, who had died the month before, sitting in one of the empty chairs. I was speechless and I realized everyone was staring at me to see why I had frozen in my seat. I heard him say, "we are being looked after" and then he faded away.

His first observation, aside from amazement and confusion, was that perhaps the dead need to communicate with us and that, if he ever needed proof of God, this was it because "this is what my father was telling me." I asked him what it meant to him that he had such a vision, and he explained that he felt as if it was probably the Holy Spirit that allowed him to have that vision and it must have always been his guide.

Robert was Catholic and had described himself as "nonpracticing, bordering on agnostic." He had come to analysis because he was overwhelmed by guilt about an affair he was maintaining, but also because he was confused about retirement, as he was 64. In the first three months of twice-a-week sessions, there was still little interest in what lies in the unconscious. Instead, each session was about work issues, family issues, and how to end his affair.

As part of most sessions, we returned to the miracle of the vision, exploring at length what the Holy Spirit was trying to do for him by bringing this message. His position was that it must have been already guiding him from his baptism, but only now he could see it. He flirted with the idea that the guiding spirit was giving him new situations to learn from his "curriculum," as he called it. The Spirit, he began to understand, was trying to work its way through him for a particular purpose: "I never realized it was there but now I can see that I have to concentrate waking up to what it is trying to teach me about how my life should go."

As an intrapsychic event, a vision, it raised the possibility that the Self had found a way to make itself known that would overcome his strong defenses. It has a sense of inevitability to it that the Self will make itself known to each individual in some manner before death or, in fact, even after. The *Bardo Thodol,* The Tibetan Book of the Dead, was accepted by Jung as a guided path into death and rebirth that made "clear to the dead man the primacy of the psyche."[169]

The discussion in the sessions started to deemphasize the vision and its numinous purpose and occurrence and concentrated on his realization of the guiding spirit. To continue with the vision or use it to explore his relationship to his father would be disorienting. Jung warned against doing so in a letter to a woman who had contact with her deceased brother:

> With regard to contact with your brother, I would add that this is likely to be possible only as long as the feeling of the presence of the dead continues. But it should not be experimented with because of the danger of a disintegration of consciousness. To be on the safe side, one must be content with spontaneous experiences. Experimenting with this contact regularly leads either to the so-called communications becoming more and more stupid or to a dangerous dissociation of consciousness.[170]

In one session, Robert referred to Paul's question in *Acts* (19:2): "Did you receive the Holy Spirit when you believed?" We discussed *John* 3:8, "The wind blows wherever it pleases. You hear its sound, but you cannot tell where it comes from or where it is going. So, it is with everyone born of the Spirit." This made a connection for him with the wind, the *pneuma,*

---

[169] *Ibid*, § 841
[170] *Letters*, Vol. 1, p. 258

a bridge to the idea of a preexistent agent of change. From there, the idea that the Spirit as a psychological phenomenon was possible.

The Holy Spirit was not perceived as constantly indwelling, but rather that it was watching and guiding, so that each decision made sense upon later consideration. It did not have the characteristics of a center and was not considered by him as a glimpse of totality but was seized upon as an orienting function that gave him comfort. The only difficulty is that he began to interpret any idea related to his day-to-day life as being a direction by the Holy Spirit so that all dreams were then assigned in a concrete way to an action. After a year, the bridge from the Holy Spirit across to the unconscious started to be found so that he could assign some of his ideas to psyche. The insistence on the Holy Spirt, however, prevented any interest in the intrapsychic principle of centering, leaving the Self as only an interpretation of the higher Spirit.

Vignette 3: Self as Nonconceptual

A woman artist who has been in analysis for very many years, concentrating primarily on her creativity, had a constant feeling that her work had an undefined, transcendent element. On one occasion, she mentioned a mobile sculpture she had created and commented that the way the four parts interacted gave her sense that there was another dimension beside the appearance of the object. She had the following dream:

> My partner and I were organizing a course to go for 10 weeks in making art. Each person was to make a little white cone out of paper and then paint it black and thereafter burn it.

I was struck by the similarity to Tibetan sand mandalas that, upon completion after several weeks, where then destroyed as reflecting impermanence. She had expressed to me that she had a noncognitive connection with her work, a tactile, embodied interaction in which she was in tune with something greater than what she had created. This constant theme of that dimension in our work was always explored by me through drawing out associations, seeking amplifications, and pointing to her embodied interaction with the concept of the Self.

The number 10 is significant as the decad; Jung quotes from *Answer to Job,* "Out of the divine number ten you will constitute unity."[171] The decad reveals the monad, that singular point that is the center and from which totality emerges as the ideal of unity. The 10 sessions are the frame for a transformation.

The assembled psyche is symbolizing a cone, a circle at its base with an extension that postulates a center at its apex as the common point. It is a geometric, three-dimensional shape where the base is connected to the apex by a straight line, its axis. In physics, it has three dimensions of space and one of time and is associated with different space-time dimensions. It is clearly a symbol of totality as it confers a transcendent quality beyond its shape.

Painting each cone black is a process of turning it from light to dark, diminishing its cognitive value as something important. There are other interpretations such as painting it black could signify its mystery so that it is not capable of being understood. In the context of the dream, it is paired with fire, destroying what was created. Fire is so laden with symbols but none of them, except that it brings light to what is occurring, are germane, as it is the consequence that is the lysis of the dream.

She already had a hunch as to totality and had captured that through her art, where it became a private revelation that she did not share with others. It was not named, made a substance, or given a particular function. It appeared that she did not need to have this translated into the narrative of the Self, and, as this dream indicates, it was an abandonment of the geometric structure and its implied center, as well as totality. It was most congruent with the Buddhist idea of no-Self, but also indicates that it was already embodied and not in need of concepts at all.

---

[171] CW 16, § 525n5

Chapter 12. The Self as Guiding Spirit

Jung refers to the Self as the "the secret *spiritus rector* of our fate."[1] In speaking of the alchemists, he also explains that the Self creates a psychological transformation, *"but only if the centre proves to be a spiritus rector of daily life."*[2] These are two slightly different ideas presented in these quotes as to the *spiritus rector,* the guiding spirit. The first is that the Self *is* the guiding spirit that determines our fate, working secretly in the unconscious, whether we realize it or not. The second reflects what Jung realized in his 1927 dream that when the Self is found as the center of psyche, it will provide orientation in daily life and allow us to control our destiny.

The first idea elevates the Self to an agent that is engineering our lives. It assumes that the Self is seeking realization and will put in place, behind the scenes, what is necessary for that to occur; it will therefore determine our fate. This is consistent with Jung's statement that "archetypal images decide the fate of man"[3] and, also, this footnote:

> 'My fate' means a daemonic will to precisely that fate—a will not necessarily coincident with my own (the ego will). When it is opposed to the ego, it is difficult not to feel a certain "power" in it, whether divine or infernal. The man who submits to his fate calls it the will of God; the man who puts up a hopeless and exhausting fight is more apt to see the devil in it.[4]

Following this approach, as the Self contains all the opposites, so it then brings about the conflict between those opposites in order for them to be

---

[1] *Aion,* § 257
[2] CW 14, § 777, emphasis supplied.
[3] CW 18, § 371
[4] CW 12, § 36n17

resolved, so this tension is deliberate and orchestrated. This means that every time a conflict arises, it is the Self that has been behind the circumstances, seeking that the opposites be resolved so that it may be realized. Even a decision to turn from the Self or abandon one's hopes suggests the intervention of the unrealized Self as guiding spirit. This is a determinist model of the unconscious psyche that is consistent with the idea of the Self as having agency.

This idea of the Self acting in the unconscious determining our fate is congruent with Jung's many statements that the unconscious indeed determines our life journey. Jung considered the psyche as objective and therefore "nothing 'arbitrary.'"[5] In explaining this in his 1924 lecture on *Analytical Psychology and Education*, he suggests that "free will" is therefore not observable and is a matter merely of a point of view;[6] it is instead the objective, autonomous psyche that molds our actions and thereby determines our fate. This is best understood that at the deepest levels of the unconscious, as Jung indicates, we have no choices to make as, for example, "there is no such thing as free will when it comes to the inferior function," that "archaic personality in ourselves" that is barely perceptible.[7] In speaking of instincts in the psychoid region, which cannot be known by consciousness, he adds that they correspond to the "will of God." They are natural forces, "absolutes which one must learn how to handle correctly."[8] God in this context, is referred to as a *daimon*, not a Christian God,

> which comes upon man from the outside, like providence or fate, though the ethical decision is left to man. He must know, however, what he is deciding about and what he is doing. Then, if he obeys he is following not just his own opinion, and if he rejects he is destroying not just his own invention.[9]

It is not a difficult proposition to advance in a clinical setting that the unconscious, in all its dimensions, dictates our fate. When we are not aware of it, we falsely believe we have free will and we do so, as Jung

---

[5] CW 17, § 68
[6] *Ibid*
[7] CW 18, § 36
[8] *Aion*, § 51
[9] *Ibid*

explains, because, "The advantage of 'free' will is indeed so obvious that civilized man is easily persuaded to leave his whole life to the guidance of consciousness, and to fight against the unconscious as something hostile, or else dismiss it as a negligible factor."[10] Neurobiological studies confirm, if that proof is necessary, that all goal setting is derived from the unconscious.[11] So much is settled in psychoanalysis.

The idea that there is a guiding spirit that works to control our fate thus arises naturally for consideration. Jung proposes, more specifically, that its origin is related to the preconscious soul of a child derived from its ancestry and the primordial archetypes that confer the best and worst qualities and is thus the "mysterious *spiritus rector* of our weightiest deeds and our individual destinies, whether we are conscious of it or not."[12]

Jung's second use of the *spiritus rector* is that when the Self is realized as a center, it then moves an individual from being buffeted by fate to align with the orienting role of the Self. There then occurs a meaning shift from being carried along by blind fate to now aligning with one's destiny as Jung explains: "If fate emerges from the word of god, then destiny is a preordained path that man can fulfill."[13] By accepting and embodying the revelation of a center of psyche, the Self as the orienting, guiding spirit, free will remains only as a moral choice to be consistent with the needs of the Self. However, this intentionality is probably not really achievable, as Jung admits:

> The question will certainly be asked whether for some people their own free will may not be the ruling principle, so that every attitude is intentionally chosen by themselves. I do not believe that anyone reaches or has ever reached this godlike state, but I know that there are many who strive after this ideal because they are possessed by the heroic idea of absolute freedom. In one way or another all men are dependent; all are in some way limited, since none are gods.[14]

---

[10] CW 18, § 1493
[11] Custers & Aarts 2010
[12] CW 17, § 97
[13] Bollas 1989
[14] CW 8, § 636

Rollo May suggests that psychological transformation through greater realization of the Self allows one to make that shift from pure fate to align more consciously with the guiding spirit: "The presence of consciousness creates the context in which the human being's response to his or her destiny occurs."[15] Destiny is thus "accomplished"[16] by conscious realization of the character of the Self that directs one to become what one can be. In this interpretation, realization of the Self offers opportunities that can be taken up by an individual to fulfill one's destiny. If that is not taken up, fate will prevail, and the opportunity provided by the Self to find orientation and meaning is lacking. As Jung suggests in a Zarathustra lecture, the very choice to explore the unconscious starts with a surrender to fate[17] as would the decision to follow the promptings of the Self. He insists therefore that "The life of an individual is his own making,"[18] meaning that the journey from fate to destiny starts as a choice and remains a choice. Seeking what is offered by the Self is a powerful *lietmotif* as a chance to rise above fate and raise one's sails to the winds of one's own destiny.

Jung's explanation for the appearance of symbols that represent the guiding spirit in dreams, visions, and fantasies is therefore that it is a representation of the Self, as it is pointing to the ultimate goal: the Self to be realized. The guiding spirit is therefore intertwined with the appearance of the Self, and its intimation can be found by a presentation or realizing it as an orienting center. The possibility that either will occur is enhanced by consciousness being attracted to the idea of a guiding spirit even more than the idea of the Self as it is more personalized and also suggests assistance in aligning with destiny. The symbol of the guiding spirit can thus appear in a concrete form in many similar forms, such as an old man[19] who knows "every road and option."[20]

According to Jung, the appearance of the guiding spirit results in the symbol leading the mind "back to the unchangeable, underlying archetypes, which are then forced into projection by this regression." This

---

[15] May 1981, p. 88

[16] CW 6, § 169

[17] *Zarathustra*, Vol.2, p. 1252

[18] *Ibid*, p. 1481

[19] CW 9i, § 406

[20] *Ibid*, § 405

occurs when the "mind of the investigator departs from exact observation of the facts before it and goes its own way."[21] He offers the prime example of Faust, who projected his unredeemed state and his struggles to "become what he really is, to fulfill the purpose for which his mother bore him ..."[22] The projection is of the opportunity to become what one can be, as the appearance of a guiding spirit symbol is likely to draw one back to the archetypal force of the Self, the central archetype, as that symbol carries the promise of aligning with one's destiny.

Nonpsychological Spirit

The guiding spirit can come to consciousness in a different way. This is by a cognitive awareness or belief that there is a force that guides us through circumstances with no necessary relationship to psyche or the Self. This second form provides a possible intimation of the Self, not a realization, but in clinical practice is as powerful as any symbol of the Self in a dream or fantasy, as it allows that guiding quality of the Self to be attached and provides the basis for the eventual realization of the Self.

This awareness or belief is probably more frequent than finding an individual who relates a guiding spirit as a symbol of the Self. This is because embracing the existence of a guiding spirit offers a very convenient and hopeful explanation for the direction and circumstances of our lives. To say that a dead uncle was behind a choice, or an inner voice spoke up, can give solace for any decision. Rather than just fate and a series of random events or seeing ourselves merely as a product of immediate and past family circumstances, there can be a sense that it has all been steered by a purposive power that is beyond our conscious existence with a goal to put us on the right course. This force cannot be attributed to our thoughts or moods with their day-to-day vicissitudes and unreliability; if it exists, it therefore must be somewhere else, and this offers a chance to see the non-ego possibilities of psyche and is a prelude to realization of the Self.

Having an orientation to a guiding spirit by belief or insight creates a dual approach to experiences: the subjective awareness of an event or series

---

[21] *Ibid*
[22] *Ibid*

of events as they have transpired and then the supply of a *subsequent* cognitive explanation of how the events occurred. The two are separated by time, the latter following the event or events either in the briefest moment or after a longer period. Evoking a guiding spirit obviously requires the recalling of the event or series of events and a desire thereafter for an explanation. The clarity of the subjective awareness as the event or events took place is not important in invoking the guiding spirit because it is the explanation that provides the linking. When that explanation is provided, it is necessarily expressed consciously as an abstract idea, such as the hand of fate, destiny, the grace of God, or an internal force responsible for life-authorship, none of which explains a process or even a relatable concept of the events at that time, but only an attribution. The explanation does not present as a narrative or a story about what is guiding, but rather is only a brief acknowledgement, such as "I have been blessed by God" or "My long-dead father showed me the right path." Yet, it is this acknowledgement, brief, abstract, and beyond thought, that is part of the human experience.

The explanation attributed to the guiding spirit does not require unraveling the reason for its origin, its location in psyche, the manner in which it carried out its purpose, or why it chose this event or series of events and was otherwise quiescent. When it occurs, the attribution of events to a guiding spirit necessarily generates a brief visual model of whatever is the subject matter, such as an angel or a deceased relative, perhaps to give the ephemeral idea some tangibility. It may evoke a feeling or emotion, but that is not necessary for its appearance, as it is more in the form of a justification for the transpiring of events. It requires no engagement with the guiding spirit, just the attribution as it has done its work and is no longer required to be present. It may provide a sense that it is still there, waiting to help again, but the suitable explanation will only arise after a series of new events have led to another attribution of its role.

The proof of the phenomenon, that it is indeed an aspect of human ontology, is revealed in myths, fairytales, prayers, rituals, symbols, and images, numerous and ancient. Angels, ghosts, a shadowy or illuminated figure, the Holy Spirit, a god, a daimon, a divine force, a deceased relative, animals, and celestial spirits are just some examples that point to something that is beyond consciousness. It arises for recognition after a change in an existing state that is accorded importance; day-to-day events alone are the not the basis for its invocation. The guiding spirit is that which has effected the change in ways that may be understood or is merely an apparent result when it is necessary to explain events or choices that have been made. The existence of the change may not immediately follow the event or series of events but can arise later, at any time, when the new state requires an explanation.

The attribution that gives rise to a guiding spirit can occur in at least three ways. The first is *spontaneously* at the appearance of what is perceived as a miracle or an unlikely event, such as a numinous, spiritual experience or, more practically, by winning Lotto or finding a life partner. The second, and more common, is an *intimation* formed after the fact that a complicated set of experiences makes perfect sense upon reflection but could not have been orchestrated consciously and requires outside help. The third is a *necessary invocation* when there is a pressing desire to find psychic equilibrium, and a guiding spirit is thus an orienting function to resolve ongoing internal conflict, such as by praising God in times of duress.

It is not necessary for psychological growth to have ever perceived a guiding spirit. The idea can be ignored by an individual with no necessary consequence to the possibility of its involvement. In daily life, the idea of a sequence of events that have led in a particular direction may or may not be the subject of reflection, even when it brings about a change. However, when there is a path to be followed, when life is seen as requiring forward movement, as in spiritual practice or psychological growth, or when a change or advancement is more noteworthy, it offers a chance to invoke a guiding spirit as an explanation.

Projecting the Spirit

Postulating the existence of the Self as *spiritus rector*—a guiding spirit— offers three possibilities: that it is either preexisting in our being, it develops within us over time, or the guidance is derived from an external source. If it is not perceived psychologically as an inner force that is preexisting or that develops, then it must appear as a magical or divine intervention.

If an inner force is suggested as the origin of the guiding principle, the psychological consequence can be that it will be projected onto an external, transcendent source, such as a God or an angel, thereby giving it a name and content. The existence of these transcendent objects makes that projection natural and convenient. There is nothing neurologically or otherwise that suggests that the guiding spirit exists, so the projection creates a numinosity, a spiritual force, increasing its acceptance. As there is no rational framework for its existence, it is always easier to accept it as being external and therefore transcendent.

The guiding spirit, when projected, may then be viewed as if one is in a personal relationship with a caring and benevolent figure or instead an impersonal hand of fate. If the consequences are negative, it is more likely to be perceived as impersonal. However, conceived, as personal or impersonal, it projects a force that is active, interfering with the existing state by creating a vector of energy in a particular direction that could be looked upon as guiding actions.

All religion, having attributed every circumstance to a transcendental figure or figures, is comfortable with the idea of a guiding spirit that can create miracles or has divine power. There is, therefore, uniformly some inclusion of a revelatory moment where a force or figure is attributed as guiding a key event: the golden light that filled the room entering the mouth of Kasyapa, who carried forward the Buddha's teaching, or the biblical magi following the star, or the visit of the Archangel Gabriel to Muhammad. In each, there is the intervention of that guiding spirit to serve as the basis for a new direction. In commenting on trinitarian thinking, Jung suggests that this is motivated by the Holy Spirit that "is never a question of mere cognition but of giving expression to imponderable psychic events."[23]

It is, in all cases of that attribution, the interference with the course of life that suggests a transcendent basis. It interrupts the ego's ideas of its power over direction and purpose, and therefore the ego cannot normalize it as an aspect of an inner, unconscious event. Jung explains in this well-known passage that for him a change in life direction is what he calls "God": "God is the name by which I designate all things that cross my willful

---

[23] CW 11, § 242

path violently and recklessly, all things that upset my subjective views, plans and intentions and change the course of my life for better or worse."[24]

When perceived as an inner force, the idea of an external guiding force can easily be discounted on the basis that in relation to the events, there were cogent, developmental ingredients that psychologically arranged each decision along the way. If it is so explained, a guiding spirit idea is less likely to arise as an explanation. So, in simple terms, a child who has been brought up with intellectual traditions and a priority placed on scholarship who in later life becomes an academic can be said to have followed a natural course without a guiding spirit. A deliberate choice would then have to be made to assign that result an underlying reason other than genetics and lineage, that would be more likely if perhaps the route appeared ever so circuitous or unlikely. On the other hand, a child who has been abused and eschews learning who then finds a book on the pavement and is inspired to seek an education and become an academic suggests there is something more at play. The concept of the guiding principle, even when it is attributed to an inner force, therefore still involves a cognitive choice of overlaying upon events a rational explanation derived from inexplicable or difficult-to-understand events that have created a change.

The consideration of a guiding spirit for a series of events is accepted in all societies as a recognized occurrence, no matter how it originates or the form it takes. A statement declaring a guiding spirit is not seen as unusual and differs from the reporting of psychic phenomena. The reasons for the difference are subtle and include a collective way to deal with the ambiguity of life, as well as a historical acceptance of that spirit through the concept of divine communication that underpins most beliefs.

Language and the Guiding Spirit

The possibility of the existence of a guiding spirit arises *at the end* of an experience or a series of experiences. This occurs, as mentioned, when it is invoked immediately after an event, is perceived later after the fact, or arises as an idea during a search for psychological equilibrium after a

---

[24] *Letters*, Vol. 1, p. 525

review of issues. In fact, by definition, it arises only by hindsight, which is the way that life is indeed understood. Jean-Paul Sartre puts it clearly:

> Nothing happens while you live. The scenery changes, people come in and go out, that's all. ... Days are tacked on to days without rhyme or reason. ... That's living. But everything changes when you tell about life; things happen one way and we tell them in the opposite sense. ... In reality it's by the end that one begins. The end is there invisible and present and that is what gives words the pomp and ceremony of the beginning. [25]

The narrative at the end must describe, should it include a guiding spirit, an intervention that was present from the beginning that continued as a thread that binds the experiences. It only takes shape and makes sense as the possibility of an invisible force that was there all the time. As it is creating an invisible thread, it points to that which is not capable of understanding and is therefore irreducible by reason.

The language used to describe the *spiritus rector* can move through different iterations because the deferred allocation of memories is recast into a new translation of what occurred. Jung uses the term *Zurück-phantasieren* (retrospective fantasizing) to indicate that reinterpretation of the past into present fantasies is what occurs, and therefore is a symbolic expression of a person's current issues. Freud, on the other hand, refers to *Nachträglichkeit*, deferred action, being the temporal deferment between the event and its interpretation in order to bring attention to those events that have been impossible to incorporate into meaning in the first place, such as trauma. Unlike Jung, Freud gives retroactive significance without alteration to a previous experience.[26]

Psychological Purpose of the Spirit

To attempt to ascribe a purpose to that which cannot be determined, described, or easily explained in psychological or practical terms confounds the problem. The guiding spirit could just as well make us a murderer as a saint, as Jung indicates: "if we normal people examine our

---

[25] Sartre 1938/2007, p. 39
[26] Explained in Stern 2017

lives, we too perceive how a mighty hand guides us without fail to our destiny, and not always is this hand a kindly one."[27] To say that the "spirit" can guide is to suggest a purpose that may either be contained within the spirit or instead comes from other influences and is mediated by spirit. Murray Stein suggests that Jung's concept of the guiding spirit, the *spiritus rector,* evolved through his need to heal the problems of Christianity, so that its purpose is derived to provide for a spirit that carries that need into the development of consciousness.[28]

The concept of "spirit" in the phrase *spiritus rector* is that as an agent of change, it implies movement in psyche, exactly the basis of the Self. It derives its explanation in that way, rather than by definition, as that which interferes in life unexpectedly. In its Christian etymological source, it is associated (Jn 19.30) with the Passion and Christ sending forth his spirit ("*emiset spiritum*") that blows out of his body. It literally means, in that paradigm, to breathe into or out of the body; it is thus equated with that which keeps us alive and has meaning as the *anima*, as in the expression for "laying down the anima" (Jn 10.18) ("*ponendi animam meam*"). As well, it is the *Spiritus Sanctus*, the Holy Ghost, that is derived from the Hebrew where it is the breath of God ("*ruah ha-godesh*"). It is thus a substance propelled by a force that has as a purpose to create a new state.

The substance called spirit is breathed out, related to the substance of God that has the particular nature of influencing events. It is said in the master work *Isidore of Seville's Etymologies*[29] that the Holy Ghost is in fact derived from the Father as well as the Son, as something breathed out of them. It is therefore always a messenger, and in the 50th Psalm, the Holy Ghost is the guiding spirit, the *spiritus principalis* and the finger of God. What is significant is that it is also called *caritas,* of loving affection, because it comes from God. This attributes to it a quality derived from its source, even though it is itself merely an agent that comes forth to make changes.

The source defines the spirit, as it has no definition of its own; the guiding spirit is thus, in psychological terms, derived from or is the Self. The source of the breath of God, any other transcendent entity, or the Self are

---

[27] CW 4, § 727
[28] Stein 1985, p. 17
[29] Isidore 2005, Vol. 1, Book VII.3-1

the fundamental bases for the attribution to a guiding spirit. If the unconscious, and in particular the Self, is postulated as being a purposive agent of change, then that attribution can be the source. This is the necessary conclusion that the guiding spirit is an agent of either a transcendent force, which cannot be understood, or an internal source, where it can be hypothesized. In the case of using the Self, it has the purpose of being an agent that guides one to the realization of the Self by means of altering consciousness.

The presence of a guiding spirit may be a more direct opportunity to realize the Self than a symbol of the Self as listed by Jung in his Definition. The appearance of a guiding spirit in a dream, vision, or fantasy is a symbol that suggests a source, a movement in consciousness, and a purpose. Most importantly, the later attribution of a series of events as being orchestrated by a guiding spirit elevates its importance because it did not require waiting for symbolization. It is a conscious formulation of the Self, which, although possibly tentative, has clinical significance as advancing realization.

A clinical example is needed to bring into focus the clinical importance of the idea of a guiding spirit. A 55-year-old patient who was a senior member of a Buddhist community provided this narrative of attribution to a guiding spirit:

> Ten years ago, I developed Crohn's disease. I had moved into the monastery in Northern Thailand, and my pain and suffering was greeted as grist for the spiritual mill. Every day when I was ill and overwhelmed, it was treated as a working out of some problem that was necessary. After two years, I had to move out and sought medical help only to be told that there was little I could do to solve this ailment. I was in Bangkok, walking down Sukhumvit Road, and I came upon a vendor who had a sign in English that he was selling medicine for bad stomachs. With the help of a young boy who could speak English and was standing next to the seller, I explained my situation. The boy took me down an alleyway (a *soi*) and to an apartment and a woman there gave me a bottle of some foul-smelling liquid and motioned to drink. I did and I never had that problem again, Crohn's was cured. It was a miracle and as I was getting on the plane to

return home, I had the sense that there was a hand on my shoulder: maybe my Abbot, but it felt like it was both in me but also outside me and that there was something guiding me to a healthy life so I could connect with the mystery.

The introduction in analysis of the idea of the Self became very natural as it was completely compatible with his idea of an internal agent that could also be external. There was no need to translate a symbol such as a circle or an animal into a representation of the Self because he had experienced the Self in action. The missing pieces of a center and totality were easily understood by later dreams and, when he spoke, he often touched his hand to his heart to indicate that there was something internal that was his truer Self.

There is no clear indication, of course, that the presence of a guiding spirit always leads to the realization of the Self. It presupposes that a connection can be made between that spirit and consciousness. This is accomplished by the fact that the ego is comfortable with a guiding spirit, as Jung explains:

> Throughout we believe ourselves to be the master of our deeds. But reviewing our lives, and chiefly taking into account our misfortunes and their consequences into consideration, we often cannot account for our doing this act and omitting that, making it appear as if our steps had been guided by a power foreign to us.[30]

In fact, it is more likely that the idea of a guiding spirit or an inner voice will be clearer than an idea of a virtual center in psyche. The distance between the appearance of a guiding spirit and the Self is not great, and the fact of that supraordinate personality and its recognition will most likely suggest a possible destiny or an orientation to transformation.

Inner Voice and the Self

Finding a source for the activation of the agency of the guiding spirit can only be explained by an attempt at some rational explanation or by a numinous religious or spiritual revelation. The difficulty of tracing the

---

[30] CW 4, § 727n17

nature of that internal source also applies to the existence of an "inner voice," an idea of a spirit or the Self that actively guides by speaking directly prior to an event or events.

We are familiar with the idea of an internal voice: the voice of God appears that way throughout the Old and New Testaments, such as Jonah being told to speak against the city of Nineveh (Jonah 3. 4-10), or the initially unrecognized voice of God spoken to Paul on the road to Damascus (Acts 9.1-6), in which case it required a specific capacity to hear it: "God does speak—now one way, now another—though no one perceives it" (Job 33.14).

There are many reported occurrences of the presence of an internal voice for Jung. He had a "waking vision" of calamity in 1913 when a voice instructs him to look clearly, as the vision is "wholly real."[31] There is a voice from the "woman within me" as the sound of the anima.[32] In referring to the "inner friend of the soul," he adds its voice is "the simplest and most natural thing imaginable."[33] This is a process he attributes to that inner companion, the Self, and "the real colloquy becomes possible only after the ego acknowledges the existence of a partner to the discussion."[34] In referring specifically to a voice in a dream, Jung provides that it adds "a clarity superior to the dreamer's actual consciousness."[35]

The inner voice has received substantial analysis and has been said, to name only a very few approaches, to be a natural consequence of reliance on external language,[36] as one level of a multilayered, wider consciousness,[37] or perhaps an aspect of a process of self-reflection. An inner voice is common as a historical explanation for good as well as evil acts either transcendent or from inner sources. Socrates described an inner voice as his daimon that warned him so as not to make mistakes; Freud referred to having heard his name "suddenly called by an unmistakable inner and beloved voice";[38] Hitler stated, "But if the voice speaks, then I

---

[31] *Memories*, p. 175
[32] *Ibid*, p. 186
[33] CW 9i, § 235, 236
[34] *Ibid*, § 237
[35] CW 11, § 70
[36] Steels 2003
[37] Morin, 2006
[38] Freud 1960, p. 261

know the time has come to act."[39] There is a very long list of those who have declared the importance of an inner voice as a private, internal authority and guide in their creativity and in making of decisions.[40] Jung, referring to an inner voice in the dream series of a patient, calls it a "spokesman of the unconscious" that has a greater intelligence than thought: "The voice gives me certain contents, exactly as if a friend were informing me of his ideas. It would be neither decent nor truthful to suggest that what he says are my own ideas."[41]

The inner voice is necessarily interpreted after it has spoken, as coming from a guiding spirit. It arises as an agent of a divine or inner force of change that is purposeful, if in fact the action taken after the voice is successful. Primarily, it can be, as the daimon deities of Greek and Hellenistic religion, mythology, and philosophy, accepted as a divine force of intervention. Yet it also could be seen as an inner being, the Self as an entirely internal crystallized entity that is speaking at the right moment. It is therefore likely that the voice, however derived, will be recognized as the guiding spirit, the *spiritus rector,* as it speaks by the imposition of an idea on an intrapsychic dilemma. The guiding spirit arises in consciousness when there is an attribution that creates it; then, and only then, it is a revelation that creates the change, as when Samuel mistook the voice of God as that of his uncle Eli (1 Samuel 3:4) until he had the revelation that God was speaking.

Jung equated the inner voice to a situation of falling back into the collective unconscious. It is the unconscious contents, he explains, that "break through into consciousness, filling it with their uncanny power of conviction."[42] It is given that conviction because it appears as a personality, an inexplicable "other," that approximates the essence of divine power so, "One can understand why that inner friend so often seems to be our enemy, and why he is so far off and his voice so low. For he who is near him 'is near to the fire.'"[43] This is caused by the unknown force that Jung calls "man's daemon, genius, guardian angel, better self, heart, inner voice, the inner and higher man, and so forth." The voice is

---

[39] Jablonsky 1994, p.259
[40] Liester 1996; Alschuler 1987
[41] CW 11, § 63
[42] CW 7, § 254
[43] CW 9.i, § 237

therefore caused by the "objective activity of the psyche" that "is trying to speak to the conscious mind through the inner voice and lead him towards wholeness."[44]

The inner voice is never presented by Jung as the Self, but rather a deeper psychic force that is advancing growth "in the most baffling way," so that it at least serves wholeness. It has the effect of taking agency from the Self, but it sounds and acts very much as the innate patterning of the Self, as centering and orienting when realized. That psychic force creates the necessary opposites for growth, and the inner voice is therefore, as Jung calls it, "Lucifer," as it creates "ultimate moral decisions without which they can never achieve full consciousness and become personalities."[45] Therefore:

> One should listen to the inner voice attentively, intelligently and critically (*Probate spiritus!*), because the voice one hears is the *influxus divinus* consisting, as the Acts of John aptly state, of "right" and "left" streams, i.e., of opposites.[46]

The Self will become the guiding spirit when it is realized, as then it is known as the source of orientation. This may change the attribution of an event or an inner voice to the Self. Until the Self is so realized, the forces that suggest attribution are diverse and there is no necessary path from their diversity to the Self. In fact, Jung does not seem to insist on that connection as he invokes all manner of influences. However, it is highly likely that the narrative necessary to understand the Self can be advanced by using an instance of the guiding spirit as also the workings of the Self.

Personification of the Guiding Spirit

In *Memories, Dreams, Reflections,* Jung speaks about his daimon that overpowered him, compelled him, and separated him from his friends.[47] The ancient name "daimon" of classical antiquity characterizes a force that compels a particular direction and cannot be resisted. Jung equates it

---

[44] CW 17, § 313
[45] *Ibid*, § 319
[46] CW 18, § 1662
[47] *Memories*, p. 356

broadly with the unconscious[48] and explains that the term is most useful when personified: "The great advantage of the concepts 'daimon' and 'God' lies in making possible a much better objectification of the *viz-a-vis,* namely, a personification of it. Their emotional quality confers life and effectuality upon them... What is merely being 'displayed' becomes 'acted.'"[49]

Unlike a direct knowing from mystical or numinous experience, for the presence of the guiding spirit to be felt as a revelation it must take a form to be the subject of the ego. Even if there is such a non-cognitive state that provides a sense of a daimon, the attribution to a guiding spirit will always require cognitive analysis after events because, as William James states, "They are illuminations, revelations, full of significance and importance ... and as a rule they carry with them a common sense of authority for after-time."[50]

The revelation of the guiding spirit and its personification requires a cognition that consists of four parts. The first is the awareness of a new orientation providing an alternative route or option for change; the second is that the alternative could not follow from logical thought but was imposed as a new idea; the third is that it is attributed to a source that is named that has imposed the new orientation; and the fourth is that it speaks with authority. In this arrangement, attribution is not the main essence of the guiding spirit, but rather it is the introduction of a new approach and the personification of that spirit.

That personification is possible because the subject chosen as the guiding spirit presents itself as "I" and requires then to be given a personality, such as daimon or the Self. That personality has the qualities that are not found in the ego and are not limited by time and space.[51] The personification arises naturally because it is not merely a mental construct but rather is consistent with that innate instinct to become more of what one can be. Jung accordingly compares the *spiritus rector* to instinct in an animal that is its ruling spirit.[52] The use of "instinct" for Jung is not

---

[48] *Ibid,* p. 336
[49] *Ibid,* p. 33
[50] James 1902, p. 380-381
[51] Liester 1996, pp. 8-13
[52] CW10, § 556

merely of an animal's prepatterned, DNA set of actions; his view is that of Aristotle in *De Anima*[53] that it is a life principle, the soul, that confers attributes. It is therefore a rational soul or the Self that is the director of life energy and is able to be personified.

Psychologically, the acceptance of a *spiritus rector* immediately provides a new point of reference for the ego without a translation of unconscious emanations, such as dreams, fantasies, and projections. There is an ontological sense that can then occur that life is not random but has a direction and a goal that can be aimed at by the realization of that spirit as the Self. For this to occur, the attribution of the guiding spirit to an external or internal source requires an object that can be named or described so as to be the subject of continued examination, experience, and ultimate acceptance. In the absence of that objectification, it may remain an elusive internal something within the vast depths of the unconscious that stays as only conjecture, even when it is sensed. It is not that the attribution to a divine force or the Self solves the question of the source or existence of the guiding spirit, but it permits it to be spoken about as a spiritual or numinous aspect of existence and translated as the Self.

For the guiding principle to be recognized, it needs to make its way from hidden, internal depths into conscious awareness or be made the subject of a spontaneous, numinous revelation. If it is perceived as developing over time, it is linear and more easily named, as it can be considered a force within the individual from the beginning, gradually breaking through the turmoil. A consideration of the personality that has been guiding over time enhances the idea of an autonomous guiding spirit that pulls the strings. It also leads to the conclusion that it has been brought into consciousness in order to show itself, and therefore it will use consciousness as needed for its purposes. In this case, it could lead to the understanding that the guiding spirit as the Self decides on the development of itself when and if it is needed. The effect of this approach is that one becomes, at most, the observer of its operation and therefore gets a sense that it is made to appear if this serves the organism.

---

[53] Aristotle 1993

The premise of the guiding spirit as the Self has several unwanted effects. The first is it cannot be realistically described, much as one cannot describe the Godhead, because its purpose and breadth are beyond comprehension. This leaves it open to being discounted and reduced to a vague idea that does not alter consciousness. The second is that giving it this form of existence means that it may be part of some larger force existing in all of us that has divine qualities, so to name it may divert the true realization of the Self as center.

The manner in which the guiding spirit is defined must therefore be that which gives it a place in human existence and accordingly, by that definition, has a purpose. To describe it as a force or the divine is nomenclature for what is unknown and is incapable of advancing its function or existence. Yet, it is there and has a purpose that may relate to its own realization where insights into that purpose give us an orientation and meaning for our own lives. The Self is the perfect vehicle for that transformation.

Integration with the Self

The opportunity to integrate a guiding spirit with the Self depends upon the impact the guiding spirit has on consciousness. If it is perceived as preexistent, that it has transcendent qualities or analogies, that it can provide an orientation, that it is striving for an ideal of unity, then it mimics the Self in those respects and may indeed be the voice of the Self.

There is a necessary distinction to be made between the apparent promptings of a guiding spirit and the audible demands of the ego. The ego, or conscious patterns of thought, informs decisions and offers a sense of meaning and direction. As well, as the ego is directed by unconscious forces, it is difficult to attribute an inner prompting or a voice to a guiding spirit rather than the more general forces of the unconscious. Any attribution to a guiding spirit then is just a metaphor to add meaning to the result of events or as a metonym where a guiding spirit is substituted directly to account for present events.

In *Formulations on the Two Principles of Mental Functioning,* Freud explains that a "state of psychical rest" is disturbed by internal demands, and when this occurs, whatever we wished for "is presented in a hallucinatory manner."[54] Only when there is disappointment that the wish is unfulfilled is there a conception of the real world; this is the reality principle and the growth of consciousness to relate to the external world. The consequence is that this can suggest the guiding spirit as a hallucination.

The discounting of a guiding spirit as arising from the ego or as a hallucination is outweighed by its importance to Christianity and Judaism. The prophets mentioned so often in the Old Testament (e.g., 2 Chr 36:15; Deuteronomy 18:14-22) were the means by which God spoke. Speaking through Jesus (Hebrews 1:2) or God undertaking to place his Holy Spirit to guide followers (Ezekial 38:26-27), makes the guiding spirit essential to belief. In one view, it is necessary to listen to the still, small inner voice to know God's purpose.[55] The guiding spirit is therefore archetypal and necessary for humanity: "Where there is no guidance, a people falls, but in an abundance of counsellors there is safety" (Proverbs 11:14; 15:22). In Judaism, the existence of a Holy Spirit is clear in the *ruach kodshechal* in Psalm 51, and the Talmud explains, "The scroll of Esther was dictated through the holy spirit" (Babylonian Talmud Megillah 7a). The guiding spirit is everywhere: "The wind blows where it will" (John 3:8).

Even though there are variations on the role of the Holy Spirit in different religions, the chance of psychological integration is most easily understood by personification of that which is thought to *already exist* by the *consensus generum*. This is in contrast to the Self that requires revelation by symbols, of which a guiding spirit may be one, and that has no prior Western antecedent. The guiding spirit is the voice of divine will, and its connection in that regard is more likely to be accepted. Jung explains that a higher authority is more easily accepted if it is of a "divine will" because otherwise:

> Civilized man has such a fear of the 'crimen laesae maiestatis humane' (a crime against the king—the ego) that whenever possible he indulges in a retrospective coloration of the facts in order to cover up the feeling of having suffered a moral defeat. He prides himself on what he

---

[54] Freud 1911, p. 219
[55] Petty 1999, p. 31

believes to be his self-control and the omnipotence of his will, and despises the man and despises the man who lets himself be outwitted by mere nature.[56]

The appearance of a guiding spirit is the single most analytical route to the Self. Aside from a numinous experience, it starts off the translation into the Self by the preexistence of a non-ego force that has a particular purpose and, most usefully, divine presentation. It parallels the Self as being significant and it appears, if it is a benevolent spirit, as seeking some orientation in the chaos that can then be understood as a possible unity. It is also translatable as a center in that it is mediating the opposites to forge a direction. The idea of a *spiritus rector* has significant clinical importance, and its presence can focus the symbols that Jung suggests of a hero or prophet and can, by its wonder, evoke the notion of it being an aspect of a transcendental force.

---

[56] *Aion*, § 48

Chapter 13. The Self as Process

Naming an object in psyche and providing that it has agency and is a goal, such as with the Self, does not explain how it operates in relation to other objects within psyche, such as the anima/animus, the Shadow, and the ego, especially the ego to which it must relate. The internal process of the Self therefore remains a mystery.

Robyn Ferrell analyzes the three metaperspectives that Freud proposes to understand the interaction of an intrapsychic object with other objects in psyche: topographical, economic, and dynamic. "Topographical" refers to the relation of the inner object to other places in psyche that are part of the same, dynamic mental apparatus:

> In the topographical figure—perhaps the most naïve way of conceiving the structure of the mind—an attempt is made to locate materially the theoretical representations in relation to each other—although not to solve the question of where they lie literally in the mind/body...[1]

The "economic" model refers to the distribution of energy in the system and therefore defines the difference, the valence, between the various objects in terms of energic contribution. The "dynamic" model describes the interrelated forces in the psyche in terms of dependencies.

The nature of the process of the Self as an entity in psyche can therefore begin to be understood in this light in relation to its function in respect of the ego, anima/animus, Shadow, and its degree of psychic energy or libido relative to these other objects. It also suggests the dependency relationship between ego and Self that cannot exist without each other. The consequence of employing these measures of energy and interrelatedness

---

[1] Ferrell 1996, p. 45

is that the Self is then understood as contributing to a combined intrapsychic effect. The understanding shifts from it merely being an entity in the mind apparatus to the effect it has on all objects in psyche and their effect on it.

The primary function of the Self as a preexisting, inner substance that seeks to balance the conflict in psyche cannot therefore be understood in isolation; it is fundamentally inserted in and part of a process whereby it interacts with other objects in the unconscious and consciousness. The interaction is complex and must respect that each object has a particular function not provided by other intrapsychic objects.

It is possible that the Self carries out the greatest role of balancing competing energies and dependencies of the other objects and is also a product of that interaction. It is, as Jung explains, that mid-point between conscious and unconscious, arising from the coincidence of opposites and when activated can alter the conscious position. In analyzing the transcendent function, the existence of a "third thing," arising from a process of the interplay of consciousness and the unconscious, a similar question is raised by a commentator of its place in psyche:

> Is it the expression of a *relationship* between consciousness
> and the unconscious when in dynamic opposition? Is it a
> *process* that ensues out of such opposition? Is it the *method*
> one uses to conduct the process? Is it the *final result,* the
> third thing that emerges?[2]

The work *Aion: Researches into the Phenomenology of the Self*[3] is dedicated to the exposition of the history and process of the Self and describes the Self in relationship to other aspects of psyche as a process and also a result. The inspiration for this work focused almost entirely on the Self arose after his second heart attack in 1946, which has been described as a significant turning point where it is suggested that "absolute knowledge in the unconscious was accessible to him."[4] He wrote to Father Victor White referring to how *Aion* came about:

---

[2] Miller 2004, p. 55, emphasis supplied.
[3] *Aion*
[4] Hannah 1976, p. 276

> I simply had to write a new essay I did not know about what. It occurred to me I could discuss some of the finer points about Animus, Shadow and last but not least the self. … Only after I had written about 25 pages in folio, it began to dawn on me, that Christ—not the man but the divine being—was to me the secret goal.[5]

Aion is one of his most difficult works, as he does not stop to explain his ideas and draws on any and all references that advance the concepts. In 1948, he gave an Eranos lecture on the nature of the anima/animus and Shadow in terms of their respective roles in straightforward terms that is reproduced in *Aion*—perhaps the same subject matter as the 25 pages he refers to in that letter. He explains in this essay, as relevant to the interrelationship of psychic objects, that the anima/animus have content that when withdrawn from projection can be integrated into consciousness.[6] In relation to the Self, he concludes that to the extent that those contents are then parts of the Self, they have a cumulative effect on consciousness that brings the ego closer to the Self.[7] This is the manner in which anima/animus and Shadow relate to the process of the Self by their integration into consciousness that allows the ego to loosen its grip to receive the Self. In expressing it in this manner, he establishes the primacy of the Self over the other psychic objects, so that anima/animus and Shadow, the significant aspects of the collective and personal unconscious, became part of the process of reconciling the opposites of which the Self is made the solution. The Self is then the central archetype and, as the ego is strengthened by bringing the anima/animus and Shadow into consciousness, it approaches the Self. This occurs because what has been made conscious provides realization of the relationship that exits between consciousness and the unconscious. This goes some way to accepting the Self as the midpoint that can hold that split, and this represents the triumph of the highest form of personality, of which Christ is an obvious representation.

The recitation of the goal of the realization of the Self in this essay establishes its significance, and thus it was impossible to ignore its

---

[5] Jung & White 2007, p. 103
[6] *Aion*, § 40
[7] *Ibid*, § 43

comparison to the greatest Western personality of Christ. The context of that Eranos lecture, which was the precursor to his analysis of the Self in *Aion* as parallel to this highest form of a personality, appeared in *Uber Das Selbst* in 1948.[8] This became Chapter IV of *Aion*, called "Self," where Jung states, as translated in the *Collected Works,* "Unity and totality stand at the highest point on the scale of objective values because their symbols can no longer be distinguished from the *imago-dei*."[9] The theme of that Eranos conference was *Der Mench: Zweite Folge*: "Man: The Second Episode." It was a conference dedicated to the postwar sentiment of the newfound, enduring strength of mankind in which an essay on the glory of the Self and comparison with Christ was congruent.

The Eranos essay invites a more fulsome analysis of Christ in the psychic field, the transcendent aspect of the Self. Jung, by first explaining in that essay that in order to assess the psychological value of the anima-animus in the psychic system, we must remember the ancient gods that represent the archetype, adding, *"Christus die uns zunächstiegende. Analogie für das Selbst und dessen Bedeutung:"*[10] "Christ is the closest to us. Analogy for the Self and its meaning." As Christ has so many theological levels, this comparison involves a journey through all of the ways that Christ and the Self are related. Thus, the ideas in *Aion* are convoluted but yield the explanation not found elsewhere of how that process of the Self that embraces the transcendent is to be understood.

This elevation of Christ as the fitting representation is the high point of the Western understanding of the Self as having a transcendent core. The chapter following in *Aion*, Chapter V, begins a deeper analysis of Christ as a symbol of the Self. Several of the chapters that then follow are about the sign of the fish, a symbol for Christ. Jung goes to great scholarly length to establish the nature of the sign of the fish in early Christianity and in Alchemy. The "Alchemical Interpretation of the Fish," Chapter XI, and the next chapter, "Gnostic Symbols of the Self," explain the process of realization of the Self *in this light*. These chapters enforce the sentiment of the power of that divine aspect of the Self as the primary essence of

---

[8] Jung 1949, pp. 285-315
[9] *Aion*, § 60
[10] *Ibid,* p. 308

psyche, so that it is interrelated to other aspects of psyche to the extent that they aid in its path to realization.

As a Dynamic Process

The underlying theme in *Aion* is that the Self is carrying out a dynamic process. The connection of the Self with God as an empirical fact draws out statements that gives the Self a sense of a never-ending activity, constantly moving within itself; this is even when a connection with God is not the apparent basis for the claim. There are many examples offered by commentators where the Self is described as a dynamic process, some of which have already been mentioned. As another example, Judith Hubback contends that the Self is dynamic, based on Fordham's process of development. As she writes, "According to him the rhythms of psyche (integration and deintegration) are the dynamic movements that lead to growth."[11] Fordham explains the Self as "a dynamic structure, having two desirable functions: it integrates and deintegrates" in order to explain how consciousness is formed in infancy.[12] The primary Self proposed by Fordham is a matrix of wholeness with potential to create states of identity for an infant through the process of deintegration and reintegration in order to *develop the ego*. The thesis of Fordham creates the Self as having a dynamic role in infant development, and this is highly consistent with the idea of a matrix, a core Self, or primal patterning, but does not suggest agency but rather a process. Fordham refers to the archetypal form of the Self being derived from the Self through its deintegration.[13] In this sense, Fordham is writing about the process of the Self formed by its emergent interactions. The latter is in line with the neurobiological explanations of Knox and Merchant, and the idea of the Self as an emergent archetype.

Sue Austin writes convincingly of the Self as unsettling when found, as it is reflective of our pockets of inner otherness. This is a reference to Jung's work on the need to find order because of the dissociability of the psyche whereby there are pockets that allow the not-I to be considered at all. The effect of the Self, viewed in this way, arises from a corresponding

---

[11] Hubback 1998, p. 279
[12] Fordham 1957, p. 97
[13] Fordham 1985, p. 45

centralizing pull to draw all to an ordered structure, which she names as "centripetal dynamics." This leads her to the conclusion that the Self as not-I emerges from the centrifugal force and is thus a "radically emergent self which seeks to engage with the presenting edges of the enigmatic, unravelling, and overwhelming unconscious communications around which it is organized, and which constantly cast it outside itself."[14]

Fordham and Austin raise the possibility that there are energies in psyche that move toward becoming all that one can be by creating the chaos of opposites and by the appearance of the not-I. Both use the notion of dynamics, but neither attributes agency to the Self but rather to the emergent process in developmental phases. This needed engagement with chaos, that process, is what in fact makes the Self appear as it is the affective response to a weaking of consciousness that then falls deeper into the unconscious. Jolande Jacobi, in this vein, summarizes the nature of the Self as a

> transconscious, central authority of psyche, which seems from the beginning to be in *a priori* possession of the goal, and with a kind of foreknowledge aims at 'the entelechy, the unity of wholeness of the human personality.' It is the organizing centre upon which all psychic phenomena depend ...[15]

This is understandable as a preexistent patterning that carries within it the goal of wholeness that has foreknowledge because of that pattern. It "aims" toward unity because that is what it is, *but* it can be said to have some form of numinosity that brings us closer to it. The internal, dynamic process is hypothetical and metaphysical that only touches the surface of the enormity of the Self. Marie Louise von Franz suggests that Jung was reticent to explain too much about the process as he knew that there were other powers behind the manifestation of the Self but "he decided not to attempt further description of them, for he thought such a description would not be understood."[16]

---

[14] *Ibid,* p. 588
[15] Jacobi 1967, pp. 30-1
[16] von Franz 1975, p. 71

Ego-Self Process

Of all psychic objects that relate to the Self, it is the ego that is most important, as the Self does not exist psychologically unless realized by the ego. The basis of the Christ analogy is derived from the manner in which the ego is overwhelmed by the transcendent power of the Self. Ego and Self are therefore in a constant developmental and psychological relationship so that one cannot exist without the other.

The "ego" is a reference to that which is constructed by consciousness over time, "a complex datum which is constituted first of all by a general awareness of your body, of your existence, and secondly by your memory data ..."[17] The ego is thus derived, and the Self, Jung suggests, "was always there."[18] The Self is "a priori existent out of which the ego evolves"[19] in the sense that the development of the ego grows from the primal patterning of the Self that is its infrastructure. The two, ego and Self, are thus not initially opposites; rather the Self until it is realized is not experienced by the ego. When it is experienced, having not been previously revealed, it will then appear as novel, a non-ego entity or a force that is alien to the ego, "absolutely other."[20] The ego and the Self finally meet upon the realization of the Self, when the ego must give way to the Self that is so overpowering there may be little choice. Therefore, Jung explains consistent with these ideas, there is always a difficult struggle with the active ego:

> For we *have* to struggle with the self. The self is not *apparently* inimical. It is *really* inimical—and it is also of course the opposite. It is not only our best friend, but also our worst enemy; because it doesn't see, it is as if not conscious of time and space conditions. We must say to the self, "Now don't be blind; for heaven's sake be reasonable. I shall do my best to find a place for you in this world, but you don't know the conditions. You don't know what military service means or tax collectors or reputations. You have no idea of life in time and space. So if you want me to

---

[17] CW 18, § 18
[18] CW 11, § 400
[19] *Ibid,* § 391
[20] CW 9.i, § 289

do something for you, if you want me to help you to
manifest, you must be reasonable and wait. You should not
storm at me. If you kill me, where are your feet?" That is
what *I* (the ego) am.[21]

The ego encounters the Self as overwhelming due to several factors, most
importantly that it is alien to the ego. It is primarily the understanding
that the Self was "always there" prior to its realization that allows it to
become a concrete object able to be realized by the ego, as it is then not
alien but an aspect of being. If the Self was instead merely an idea, then
the ego would not experience this concrete representation of the Self
through symbols. As well, the symbols arising from the core patterning,
as are the other archetypal foundations in psyche, are a mystery to the
ego but thereby have numinosity and force. The revelations of that
mystery of archetypal forces are another means that loosen the dominance
of the ego, and, as Jung put it, "create a wider personality whose center
of gravity does not necessarily coincide with the ego."[22] Although the
Self is just one factor that confronts an individual as "other," it is the Self
that provides a specific idea of possible unity that the ego craves and
thereby distinguishes itself from other forces. These characteristics of the
Self permit the ego to interact and struggle with the Self rather than
excluding it because it is so overwhelming. Wrestling with the Shadow,
being disrupted by the syzergy, does also create a relationship between
the ego and the unconscious, but they lack the same impact, as they do
not offer a solution to the conflict of those opposites as does the Self.

The connection of the ego with the Self begins when it is understood by
the ego as an internal phenomenon, the transcendent *indwelling* of a
center and a potential unity. It is the indwelling that confers on it a
transcendent quality and makes the center numinous. In order for it to
have significance as a center, it must indeed partake of that numinosity
so it is separated out from other psychic phenomena and becomes so
significant that it attracts focus; it must be touched by the magnetism.
The numinous indwelling of a center is the most important of the three
factors of realization as it is that which makes it the "other" and that gives
it meaning as an ideal in terms of the ongoing tension of opposites. It also

---

[21] *Zarathustra*, Vol. 2, p. 977-8
[22] *Aion*, § 297

is that which approximates an even wider power for that center as the proposition emerges that if it is indwelling in one person, it follows logically that it must be in all beings. This is, by necessity, a transcendent realization that draws the opposites closer to a universal unity.

The idea of realizing that indwelling occurs by revelation that we are all the same and therefore the center is collective as it must be in all things. The internal personalization or the external collectivization are both useful in refining the realization, as Jung indicates:

> It seemed to me typical that, in some cases, the new thing was found outside themselves, and in others within; or rather, that it grew into some persons from without, and into others from within. But it was never something that came exclusively either from within or from without. ... [I]n no case was it conjured into existence through purpose and conscious willing, but rather seemed to flow out of the stream of time.[23]

Jung ties the two modes of realization together so ideally the Self can be understood as both personal and collective:

> this self is not just a rather more conscious or intensified ego, as the words 'self-conscious' 'self-satisfied,' etc. might lead one to suppose. What is meant by the self is not only in me but in all beings, like the Atman, like Tao. It is psychic totality.[24]

The importance of a numinous indwelling of a center is a further step that builds the Self as an intrapsychic personification that is necessary to be recognized by the ego. It suggests to the ego that it there is a higher value to the Self and so allows it to guide moral choices. The ego does not have the same valence as the Self as a higher aspect of psyche and must, to be realized, begin to give over to the Self. In discussing a vision of a patient, Jung explains, "You see, before she can realize the nature of Tao, she must fully destroy all the ideas behind which she has been sheltered hitherto, because only one who is able to deliver himself over entirely to the river of life can experience Tao."[25]

---

[23] CW 13, § 18
[24] CW 10, § 873
[25] Jung 1997, Vol. 2, p. 695

Inflation of the Ego

As mentioned, the relationship of the ego to the Self is twofold. The first is that as the ego realizes the Self, it begins to be modified by the higher value of the Self. This is either a single instance of understanding or more likely a gradual revelation of the Self as the center of psyche. However, the process of continuous revelation of the Self, Jung explains with Christ in mind, "inevitably produces an inflation of the ego."[26] This inflation is from the expanded consciousness that arises from having some glimpse of the esoteric sentiment that results from the numinosity it contains. This warning of inflation follows from the Eranos essay of 1948, wherein Christ is considered a representation of the Self. It is the introduction of the image of God, the *imago-dei* that opens up, more than any other factor, the possibility of inflation. This is an inevitable consequence of a process whereby the supraordinate Self in its highest transcendental form is absorbed in part by the subordinate ego.

There must then be an act of cognitive discrimination that sets a boundary between the ego and the Self by maintenance of a strong ego position in order for inflation to be avoided or mediated. The possible boundary is when the ego achieves some modesty and accepts a moral defeat to be able to reclaim the unconscious from the inflated ego. If this is not established, the ego could also be assimilated by the Self, losing its integration, resulting in a primordial dream state, and this, Jung declares, would be a "psychic catastrophe."[27]

The ego-Self relationship requires a *balance* between them, some delicate position where the ego does not get lost in the Self and the Self does not inflate the ego. In the balancing of the relationship of the Self to the ego, Jung therefore suggests that each individual faces a moral issue to seek homeostasis: "for a man who is not conscientious enough has to make a moral effort in order to come up to the mark; while one who is sufficiently rooted in the world ... (must) loosen ties with the world."[28] Having set up the transcendent power of the Self in relation to the ultimate personality of Christ, the call for balance is confusing as the distance between Christ and the ego is incalculable. There is no authority in psyche for this

---

[26] *Aion*, § 44
[27] *Ibid*, § 45
[28] *Ibid*, § 48

balancing between ego and Self at that level that directs how to proceed; it cannot come from the Self but instead requires a countervailing inner authority arising from the will of God or some autonomous natural force.

It is instructive that the Self in its role as *spiritus rector*, the manifestation of the Self as a guiding spirit, is best served to create that balance through an explanation of "God's will" in a manner that retains an individual's ego so that it does not demean "the omnipotence of his will."[29] This emphasis on balancing the resistance of the ego with the power of the Self by invoking God's will as the force that motivates the Self, may be a successful strategy to reduce inflation yet maintain a strong ego. God's will is a natural, common concept that can explain the movement of the ego toward the Self and that can prevent an individual from being overwhelmed. It has effect because it removes the sense of an overpowering Self that aligns with Christ and puts the balance into a form of homeostasis advanced by the ultimate mystery of God's will. This allows the process to be amenable to greater ongoing monitoring of the feeling-value arising in the process of the realization of the Self, "how a subject is *affected* by the process."[30]

The elevation of the Self to Christ, the *imago-dei*, rather than a function of God's will or another source, appears as the most likely problem that can inflate the ego, not allowing a balance. Jung did not directly make this connection of inflation with a comparison to Christ; instead, he deals with the issue by warning against the emphasis on intellectual and metaphysical ideas such as the God-image. He admits that these images appear in dreams and can contain a "resemblance to the motifs of mythology,"[31] but they are only ideas and do not give the Self the power of God.

This balance is thus carried out best by pointing to the possibility of a unity of the two opposites of Self and the ego by invoking the higher source of God's will. The consequence is explained by Jung as: "The view that things are arranged according to God's will is one that leaves little room for causality,"[32] thus allowing the Self as represented as Christ as

---

[29] *Ibid*
[30] *Ibid*, § 65, emphasis supplied.
[31] *Ibid*, § 66
[32] CW 8, § 927

not an omnipotent force. It is useful because "Every metaphysical statement (of God's will) is, *ipso facto,* unprovable,"[33] giving the expression no set meaning.[34] In addition, in speaking of the process of individuation, Jung adds, "Psychology has no proof that this process does not unfold itself at the instigation of God's will."[35] This idea of using God's will as the reason for the numinosity of the Self is strongly prompted by the need to balance the ego with the Self to prevent overwhelming absorption in either direction. It is thus better to seek "God's will" as an explanation for the origin of the Self, or perhaps neurobiological findings, rather than comparing it to Christ.

Ego-Self Axis of Neumann

Erich Neumann raises the possibility that the ego and Self work together for the realization of the Self. Neumann's views bring the relationship of ego and Self into sharper focus and are helpful in understanding the manner in which it can be said that the ego is involved with the Self. The phrase "ego-self axis" is often used by commentators in analyzing of the Self, but it does not derive from Jung; it originates with Neumann. Neumann's explanation is, however, complex, and in order for him to postulate an axis, he had to start with the proposition that the ego and Self are opposites and then find a way that they cooperate along that axis to advance the ultimate realization of the Self.

Neumann, as a young doctor, and after completing a short Jungian training in 1933, commenced writing *The Roots of Jewish Consciousness* on the way from Berlin to Israel, after Jews were barred from practicing their professions in Germany. The immediacy of his predicament led him to provide that when ego consciousness is being transformed by the Self, the entire psyche is not also so transformed: "The dark parts, however, are merely isolated; they are not part of the transformation."[36] The consequence is that the ego's realization of the Self thus leaves out evil, and evil is projected outward: "The ego that is identified with the Self always experiences the world as negative"[37] so the polarity has not been

---

[33] CW 11, § 238
[34] CW 16, § 392
[35] CW 18, § 1555
[36] Neumann 2019, Vol. I, p. 118
[37] *Ibid*

resolved. The Self, unlike the ego, is assumed to carry the positive, and this leads him to the conclusion that the ego is always rooted in the negative, outside world to which it belongs and "In this respect it contrasts with the Self,"[38] which is only connected with the inner world. This creates the ego and Self, by this categorization, as two opposites that are differently oriented, and no link is suggested.

In a letter to Jung in 1935, in the period when Jung was making his first, comprehensive statements about the transcendent nature of the Self at Eranos, Neumann mentions that he realized that the "Self as the center of the individual process is also something general, not only suprapersonal but also structurally real."[39] There is nothing remarkable about this insight, but it led Jung to reply that if we are only an ego "we are completely bound up in people and history. That is why 'individuation' can never be realized by 'egos' and their intentions."[40] This distinction between individuation that involves circumambulation of the Self and the character of the "ego" as worldly, reflecting the disturbing times in which this was written, perhaps made clearer to Neumann that the ego and Self are unresolvable opposites.

Neumann was invited to give a lecture in 1952 at Eranos that he titled *The Psyche and the Transformation of the Reality Planes: A Metaphysical Essay,*[41] where he proposed a link between the ego and the Self, the opposites, in the form of an axis. Neumann develops the idea that both aspects, the outside world represented by the ego and the inside world that is the Self, are necessary for psychological growth. They are, as he describes them, two different *fields* of orientation, one of energetic-dynamism outward, and one that is perceived inward, leading to a "human duality of orientation (that) corresponds to a duality of reality itself."[42] These fields are constantly interacting to present reality, even though one is uncentered knowledge held by the ego and the other is the centered Self.[43] This field model of an interaction between the ego and the Self is the milieu in which realization takes place, so it is not just caused by the

---

[38] *Ibid*
[39] Jung & Neumann 2015, p. 96
[40] *Ibid*, p. 108
[41] Neumann 1989
[42] *Ibid,* p. 35
[43] *Ibid, p. 46*

numinosity of the Self gradually supplanting the primacy of the ego, as Jung proposes.

Neumann describes this process: the Self "during centroversion, directs the ego's development and individuation, and in large measure fatefully guides the unified whole of the individual's life purposes and of his or her way of coming to terms with the world."[44] This idea of *centroversion* was first suggested by Neumann in his 1949 classic work, *The Origin and History of Consciousness,* as "the innate tendency of the whole to create unity within its parts and to synthesize their differences in unified systems. The unity of the whole is maintained by compensatory processes controlled by centroversion …"[45]

The meaning that can be derived from Neumann's exposition as to the role of the Self and its relationship to the ego is that the process of centroversion involves the Self's innate tendency toward wholeness that evokes the interplay of the compensatory nature of the opposites to foster realization of the Self. The statement in the 1952 Eranos lecture about the Self directing the ego's development is not therefore explained as the Self being an entity that can direct through its power or nature, but rather that the ideal of unity as a goal and intrapsychic center is the milieu that is responsible for the process of centroversion. That centroversion, he explains, is "the primary function of the psyche, causing unconscious contents to present themselves to consciousness in the form of images."[46] The Self's role in the process of centroversion, he explains in the Eranos lecture, is as "a formally directing factor of absolute knowledge" omnipresent as a "guided order."[47]

His idea of how the Self operates in that process defines his Ego-Self axis. The ego's knowledge of the center sets up a field—a Self-field— "in which the individual moves"[48] that has then that guiding quality of order. The ego is "anonymously uncentered knowledge and does not manifest itself as centered self with centered knowledge unless certain conditions prevail." It is the *interaction* of the ego with the centered

---

[44] *Ibid.*
[45] Neumann 1954, p. 286
[46] *Ibid,* p. 295
[47] Neumann 1989, p. 47
[48] *Ibid,* p. 48

knowledge of the Self that is needed to create those conditions: "Having thus experienced the self and the original unitary world, no longer do world and psyche act as two worlds existing side by side and independently of each other, each possessing its own self-contained lawfulness." Ego and Self then form a "complementing unity."[49]

The "ego-self axis" is "the central axis which constellates the regulating phenomenon of form, and the possibility of cognition per se."[50] This axis regulates the interaction between ego and Self by the appearance of the underlying unity that leads to the possibility that it can be realized by the ego. In this movement, "We call the connection between the ego and the self an axis because the whole development and shaping of the personality circles around it."[51]

This ego-self axis operates in the unconscious but is what is required for the presentation of the Self to the conscious mind. To clarify the exposition of Neumann's view, he does not propose, as did Edward Edinger, the axis as a scale where the ego is on one end and the Self on the other and psychological development is a point on that scale, but instead it is a virtual line around which the ego and Self continuously revolve. If it is to be seen as having any characteristics of a scale, it is between knowledge of the ongoing operation of the axis and no knowledge, as Neumann explains: "But as long as the self as center remains unconscious, the ego-self axis of the personality—which might therefore be termed self-ego axis in this phrase—remains unconscious as well."[52] He points out, however, that the "effectiveness of the ego-self axis is independent of whether or not it becomes conscious, it is only when it does so become conscious that a centering of the personality which includes the conscious mind will take place."[53]

In Neumann's terms, the ego-self axis is a dynamic, evolving aspect of centroversion that moves the ego because there is an underlying, innate tendency toward the center and unity, consistent with the idea of the center in the dream. Michael Fordham considered these concepts of no

---

[49] *Ibid*, p. 55
[50] *Ibid*, p. 20
[51] *Ibid*, p. 57
[52] *Ibid*, p. 57
[53] *Ibid*. p. 57-8

practical use, "unnecessary additions,"[54] but they do serve well the explanation of the relationship between the ego and the Self as ever-changing, compensatory processes of centroversion where the Self is the matrix so that it is always ongoing in the unconscious.

Approaching an Empty Center

It is not possible that the ego's gradual absorption of the directing power of the Self will fail to give it a transcendent value. This is the natural result of the experience of the numinous Self. This will take place at some point in the process of the gradual realization of the Self, perhaps as early as its first presentation as a hunch or a sense of wholeness, but clearly later as the Self begins to be realized as an ideal of unity. It is the confrontation of the ego with the higher, non-ego aspects of the Self.

When that connection is made between the Self and transcendence, the incomprehensible nature of God offers the Self a comparison. The center, as discussed earlier in relation to the function of the center in the 1927 dream, is then an empty center as it cannot be filled by God, which is unknowable. The Self as an archetype represented symbolically as a center that is empty cannot logically then go beyond an approximation. Jung explains:

> With increasing approximation to the center there is a corresponding depotentiation of the ego in favour of the influence of an 'empty' center, which is certainly not identical with the archetype but is the thing the archetype points to. As the Chinese would say, the archetype is only the *name* of Tao, not Tao itself. Just as the Jesuits translated Tao as 'God' so we can describe the 'emptiness' of the centre as 'God'.[55]

The process of ego-Self development is effectively stalled at the point where the Self reaches transcendence. The ego's confrontation with the empty center will therefore reveal that it cannot merge with the center so viewed, and therefore it experiences an "endless approximation …"[56]

---

[54] Fordham 1981, p. 106
[55] *Letters*, Vol. 2, p. 258
[56] *Ibid*, p. 259

Jung's solution is difficult to understand: The ego must "acknowledge many gods before it attains the centre where no god helps it any longer against another God."[57] This subtle sentence implies that transcendence will bring up many God-images, but they will not, by their ideation, inhabit the center, but if that center is found, it surpasses the images and finds the complete unity, which is the actual divinity. The issue then is how to move beyond the God-image that naturally arises from intimations of the Self.

In a letter Jung writes in November 1959, he explains that images are a result *"of something"* and the God-image is "the expression of an underlying *experience* of something which I cannot fully attain to by intellectual means."[58] When the center is empty, it is then filled by or projected onto a God-image because "'God' therefore is *in the first place* a mental image equipped with instinctual 'numinosity,' i.e., an emotional value bestowing the characteristic autonomy of the affect on the image."[59] This is the mechanism that results in transcendence for the Self drawing one closer by its power and affect but that must give way to the actual realization of the divine. The full realization of the Self reveals the interconnectedness of spirit and matter, of inside and outside, of all things and is therefore, theoretically, the all-oneness.

As Christ is the greatest Western god-image that can represent the Self, Jung then provides: *"Christ exemplifies the archetype of the self."*[60] Christ is important, as it is the Western God-image, and that gives the Self the highest emotional value, drawing the ego closer to the Self. From this value flows other symbols that are derivative: the heavenly kingdom, or Adam before the Fall. As mentioned, Christ is not the perfect God-image, as it lacks wholeness because it excludes the evil, dark side. It can only be restored to wholeness artificially by the doctrine of *privatio boni,* that evil is only the absence of God, which Jung discusses at length in *Aion.*[61] The Self consists of good and evil in equal measure and therefore "can

---

[57] *Ibid*
[58] *Letters,* Vol. 2, p. 522, emphasis supplied.
[59] *Ibid*
[60] *Aion,* § 70, emphasis supplied.
[61] *Ibid,* chap V

only be described in antimonial terms,"[62] but the Christ image only serves one pole of the opposites.

As Christ is not a perfect representation of the goal, its role in the process of the Self is not sufficient to move to a higher revelation. "In the Christian concept ... the archetype is hopelessly split into two irreconcilable halves."[63] In an interesting footnote, Jung explains that, in the present time, it is indeed inadequate, but it was not for the pre-psychology age where Christ *was* wholeness and did not merely symbolize it.[64] Thus, Christ is devoid of an antimonial nature but can still be realized as pointing to the higher reaches of the Self, an aspect of totality, as "the idea of totality is, at any given time, as total as one is oneself."[65]

This missing relationship of Christ to evil, when analyzed in present times, may not still suggest the idea of totality. This may be occur when all sides of Christ are viewed as the four points of intersecting opposites as a quaternion, as Jung suggests in this illustration and comment:

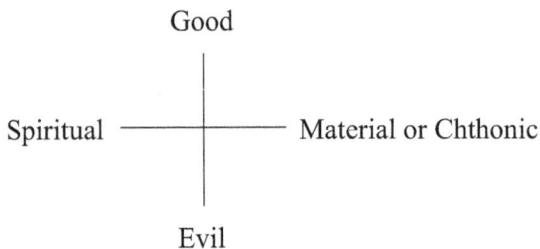

Good

Spiritual ———————— Material or Chthonic

Evil

Figure 5: The Christ Quaternion[66]

The resultant quaternion of opposites is united on the psychological plane by the fact that the self is not deemed exclusively "good" and "spiritual"; consequently its shadow turns out to be much less black. A further result is that the

---

[62] *Ibid*, § 115
[63] *Ibid*, § 76
[64] *Ibid*, § 115n75
[65] *Ibid*
[66] *Ibid*, p. 63. Republished with permission of Princeton University Press from C.G. Jung, *Collected Works*, Vol. 9ii, p. 63; permission conveyed through Copyright Clearance Center.

opposites of "good" and "spiritual" need no longer be separated from the whole.[67]

This quaternion represents light and dark and another set of opposites, spiritual and material, that are further aspects of Christ; material being the antithesis of spirituality. This is the double set of opposites that are a composite that is a greater sign of the ideal of unity of the psychological Self, even if not an exact match to Christ, because it is closer to the process of individuation that proceeds on their potential unity.

This exegesis, somewhat convoluted in the complicated ideas in *Aion*, is necessary to indicate the process by which the Self embraces transcendence. It is not then a goal of rising to the level of Christ and thereby reaching totality, but rather a symbol that creates a movement under tension between the poles of opposites within wholeness so that it advances forward but never reaches a final goal. Christ then serves, in its antimonial nature, as an example of the never-ending tension between primal opposites and therefore truly "exemplifies the Self." The God-image may lead to an empty center, but instead, the ideal of a unity of opposites advances the Self toward its proper realization. This logic indicates that the God-image is not the goal but a way station in the process of the Self.

His examination of Christ as representing the Self in this Chapter of *Aion* is significant for establishing three concepts. The first is that the Self can be ideally represented by a quaternion structure of four points that are two pairs of opposites that explains how the Self progresses in its process from the tension of opposites. The second is to allow the God-image of Christ to remain a prime symbol of the Self as a contemporary, psychological postulate. As a psychological postulate, it is an image of a quaternion and therefore a balanced wholeness. The third is an introduction to Jesus as the principle of "sonship" at the end of the essay on Christ as the spiritual inner man, the Anthropos.

The idea of sonship, the relationship of God to man through the son that leads to the Anthropos, is explained by Basilides, the Gnostic whose name was attributed by Jung to his *Seven Sermons*. His explanation is that there are three parts to sonship. The first son is that which remained with the

---

[67] *Ibid*, § 116

Father; the second was lower; and the third was impure.[68] This in turn is seen by Jung as spirit, soul, and body. The significance of the Self as an aspect of sonship and the significance of the Anthropos arises by the presence of the third sonship that is, although impure, the "divine seed," even though unconscious and formless in man, so that he can be considered the "spiritual inner man."[69] This is then the *indwelling* of God in the son and gives rise to the Self as a parallel with Christ as dormant in the unconscious, *within an individual,* seeking its higher form. This is the Anthropos, the indwelling divine in man. This correspondingly implies movement within the Self, which lies dormant in an individual that must then be realized. It follows logically from the association of the Self with the god-image of Christ, both from a psychological perspective containing wholeness and from the notion of "sonship," that the seed of wholeness makes an individual the Anthropos where realization is *in potentia.*

These complicated parallels and relationships are inevitable when the transcendent quality of the Self appears from early recognition of its numinosity to a greater appreciation of its place in psyche; the Self is a cornucopia of transcendent ideas. Most importantly, it shapes the Self as a higher, esoteric goal and indicates we each have the indwelling potential for wholeness, although it can never be perfected. An archetype is not perfected as its realization is a *suspension* between conflicting opposites and can only lead to "an approximate state of wholeness."[70] Psychologically, Jung points out, the individual can never reach the perfect man who is crucified because it is in the realm of being archetypal and not an actual event, so it is only an imperfect image.

This is a critical point made in *Aion* in relation to the Self, explaining that understanding of the Self as the psychologizing of wholeness through symbols is only the revelation of the imperfect archetype of wholeness. It is not seeking a perfect enlightenment or complete wholeness but that the ideal of a unity becomes the foreground and the chaos remains in the background. In addition, these symbols and the process of the Self are always contained within a paradox of opposites and unity, as the "union

[68] *Ibid,* § 118
[69] *Ibid*
[70] *Ibid,* § 123

of opposites can be thought of only as their annihilation."[71] Consequently, the Self always operates within an inherent state of conflict that creates the need for redemption through individuation, even in the situation where it has a transcendent dimension. This may appear as a technical, metaphysical explanation of the Self, but *Aion* defines the *process* of the Self as the ongoing psychological work of reconciling the paradox of opposites. The transcendent symbol of Christ merely echoes that process by postulating that an inner unity is inherent because of sonship, an indwelling, to create God in man. That indwelling, the ideal of unity, must be realized for that unity to occur. It is true that it complicates the idea of the Self, but it also takes away an emphasis of the nature of the Self, *per se,* and shifts it to the Self as a process.

Jung forecasts this difficulty arising from the paradox of the Self in his letter to Father White, wherein he was delving deeper and deeper in *Aion* into the historical development of the Christ figure by examining the fish symbol, so often a Christ allegory. He was obviously looking for that greater connection of the Self with Christ to find that unity, but it was not to be found in that manner but rather in its antimonial nature. In *Aion,* this symbol of the fish is explored extensively,[72] more so than any other symbolic representation. The analysis illustrates that, at its core, the transcendent nature of the Self projected as the fish is intrinsically paradoxical as consisting of opposites as well as suggesting a unity: "The ambivalent attitude towards the fish is an indication of its double nature."[73] This promotes the idea of opposites, repeated consistently even in the transcendent symbols of Christ, as the grundnorm, the actual foundation of the Self. It does not contain the concordance he found with the *Atman,* but it is the manner in which Western ideas, his audience, can struggle to approximate the Self *as a process.*

Transitions in the Process

Chapter XIII, *Gnostic Symbols of the Self,* is not only directly concerned with the Self but also provides powerful symbols and imagery that Jung uses to explain the process of the Self. It is here, in describing the doctrine

---

[71] *Ibid*
[72] *Ibid,* Chapters VI, VIII, IX, XI
[73] *Ibid,* § 187

of the Gnostic sect of the Nassenes, that Jung sets out the relevant metaphors and symbols, and offers a profound revelation about how the Self develops over time within an individual. This revelation, as already mentioned, is the basis of viewing the Self as a magnet that keeps the process in movement. He invokes the comparison of the Self to the *aqua doctrinae*, the living water, which in its symbolic form makes it a magnet as it "perfects every nature in its individuality and thus makes man whole too."[74] The magnetic attraction creates a process whereby it is "the magnet that draws to itself those part or substance in man that are of divine origin ..."[75] The magnetic action is the creator of a process that carries out the attraction and consists of three properties: a passive substance like the *aqua doctrinae,* an autonomous being that represents "the dark and unfathomable,"[76] and the *Logos*, a philosophical idea.

For the Gnostics, these were aspects of an "incarnate" God that has numinosity and, psychologically, "revolutionizes the ego-oriented psyche by setting up, in contradistinction to the ego, another goal or centre which is characterized by all manner of names and symbols: fish, serpent, center of the sea-hawk, point, monad, cross, paradise, and so on."[77] This symbolization begins to create the higher, more conscious man, "that indescribable whole, the antithesis of the subjective ego-psyche, is what I have called the self, and this corresponds exactly to the idea of the Anthropos."[78] The *Anthropos* as the dormant God within that can be awakened becomes the realized *Anthropos*, the Perfect Man, which represents the process of the Self from dormant to realized. It is the magnetic pull of these symbols that draws one to the transcendent aspect of the Self.

Chapter XIV, *The Structure and Dynamics of the Self,* draws on these Gnostic symbols to explain the process and progress of the Self. For a more complete analysis of the detailed symbolism and the formula for the process of the Self in this chapter, I direct the reader to my previous work on the Self: *Becoming Whole: Jung's Equation for Realizing God.*[79]

---

[74] *Ibid,* § 289
[75] *Ibid,* § 291
[76] *Ibid,* § 293
[77] *Ibid,* § 296
[78] *Ibid*
[79] Stein 2012

At the start of his analysis of the process of the Self, Jung reminds us that it is a *complexio oppositorum* that holds all the opposites. He then adds, "It is quite possible that the seeming paradox is nothing but a reflection of the enantiodromian changes of the conscious attitude which can have a favourable or an unfavourable effect on the whole."[80] Enantiodromia is the term used for a movement of one thing to its opposite, where their opposite nature suggests movement between them. He is presenting that the process may not only be moved by the tension of opposites, but also by the general movement in psyche from one pole to the other. This occurs because consciousness and the unconscious are inherently opposites; in fact, consciousness is considered masculine and the unconscious feminine,[81] so psychic totality is inherently unstable. As it has the quality of a deliberate process, the Self presents as a daimon, an active figure that is necessary to provide that stability not found and thus, as Jung puts it, "can appear in all shapes from the highest to the lowest."

To describe the process of the Self, Jung uses the quaternity, a geometrical symbol that is a totality symbol and holds all elements of the opposites and their reconciliation:

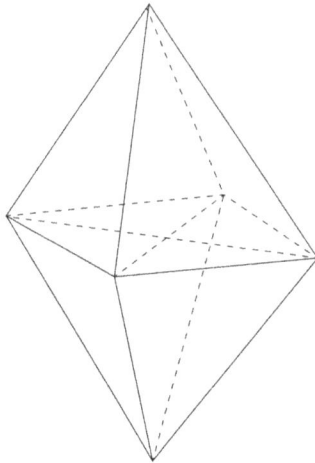

Figure 6: Quaternity Symbol[82]

---

[80] *Aion,* § 355
[81] *Ibid,* § 426
[82] *Ibid,* p. 227, Redrawn.

It illustrates the double set of opposites joined at the midlevel, a theoretical center created by the opposites, and a higher and lower aspect. As an example, in what he calls the *Anthropos* quaternion, it is represented by the biblical characters Moses and Jethro as opposites, and the reconciliation of those opposites leads from the lower man, called the Lower Adam, to the Anthropos, the Higher Adam.

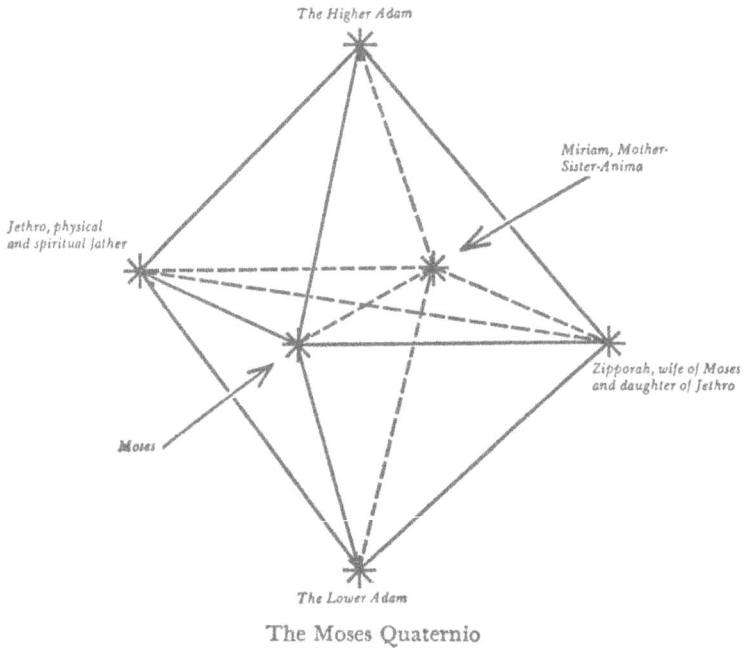

The Moses Quaternio

Figure 7: Moses Quaternio[83]

Based on this complex movement in psyche, Jung proposes a formula, appearing as a geometrical structure that indicates the process of the Self from a lower form with the *Anthropos* dormant in an individual to one where the Anthropos is the highest form. That structure is:

---

[83] *Ibid*, p. 259. Republished with permission of Princeton University Press from C.G. Jung, *Collected Works*, Vol. 9ii, p. 259; permission conveyed through Copyright Clearance Center.

$$
\begin{array}{ccc}
\quad b_3 & & \quad d \\[2pt]
\diagup\ \diagdown & & \diagup\ \diagdown \\[2pt]
c_8 \qquad a_3 = A = a & & c \\[2pt]
\diagdown\ \diagup & & \diagdown\ \diagup \\[2pt]
d_3 & & b \\
\| & & \| \\
D & & B \\
\| & & \| \\
d_2 & & b_1 \\[2pt]
\diagup\ \diagdown & & \diagup\ \diagdown \\[2pt]
a_2 \qquad c_2 = C = c_1 & & a_1 \\[2pt]
\diagdown\ \diagup & & \diagdown\ \diagup \\[2pt]
b_2 & & d_1
\end{array}
$$

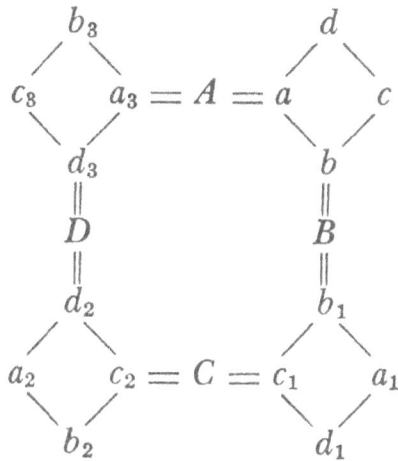

Figure 8: The Self Equation[84]

The equation obviously appears as a puzzle but illustrates the path and process of the Self. It provides a profound statement that goes beyond the mere idea that the Self is realized by it being recognized by the ego through symbols or that it is embodied when comprehended fully. He states, "The process depicted by our formula changes the original unconscious totality into a conscious one."[85] The "A" at the top of the formula is initially the unconscious man, as in the *Anthropos* Quaternion, and by traversing from A to B to C to D, and then back again to A, the process of the Self is complete and results in the completely conscious *Anthropos*.

The process is a circular pattern and thus, incidentally, it is itself a symbol of the Self and circumambulation. "The formula presents the symbol of self, for the self is not just a static quantity or constant form but is also a dynamic process."[86] From the unconscious *Anthropos*, the incarnate Self that lies in each individual must first deal with the Shadow, which is B. On each corner is what he calls a "tetrameria," which works counterclockwise to indicate an intrapsychic process that must take place to achieve progress. The first passage of the Self is to the Shadow because

[84] *Ibid,* § 410. Republished with permission of Princeton University Press from C.G. Jung, *Collected Works*, Vol. 9ii, p. 410; permission conveyed through Copyright Clearance Center.
[85] *Ibid*
[86] *Ibid,* § 411

it is here that the opposites are most at play. This is the challenge reflected for each patient in the consulting room dealing with complexes that are derived from a failure of the constellation of the archetype.

By the constant enantriodroma of conscious and unconscious positions, there is some resolution of the issues buried within the Shadow, and a hint is presented of a possible unity. That possible unity is C, Paradise, which is the first revelation of the Self that arises from the deeper processes that have been engaged in psyche. Jung describes that this gives rise to the first intimation of the *Lapis*, the alchemical stone, the stone that is not a stone because it contains the spirit, the uniting of spirit with matter. It is a symbol of the ideal unity, and that is what arises in C, the presentation or sense of wholeness.

The passage to D is unique and is the single-most important step in the process of realization of the Self. It is the extraordinary insight that the Self does not just exist in each individual but also exists in matter. In this way, spirit and matter, the ultimate set of opposites, are joined, suggesting the highest form of the existence of a complete unity. It would mean that an individual is aware of the possibility that the Self in them is also in all others, as well as matter; it is in a tree, a stone, a chair, and at that point, it really becomes totality. Then and only then the interconnectedness of all things allows the Self to be realized as a greater form of totality because it is in all things and therefore is all things.

The ultimate state of union of spirit and matter, the Self in all things, is in the *rotundum* that cannot be reached as it is a perfect state of roundness and thus absolute wholeness. Therefore, the realization of the Self, at most, stops at D and the perfect man—the return to "A", the realized Anthropos, is not created. "The *rotundum* is a highly abstract, transcendent idea, which by reason of its roundness and wholeness refers to the original man, the Anthropos."[87]

The Highest Stage of the Process

The idea that the *rotundum* cannot be reached so that the true realization is the *Lapis,* the symbol of the apperception of the Self in all things, changes the nature of what it means to realize the Self. It also means that

---

[87] *Ibid,* § 389

the Self is not to be considered personal but rather universal so that it exists in all things: in me, in others, in matter. It is an aspect of totality in the sense that the Self embraces all that is conscious and all that is unconscious, but also, in this realization, it is because it is universal in all things. This manifestation of the Self as existing in all things, involuted in matter, is the final stage of the process, as Jung did not extend it further to a complete wholeness where there was no ego, no Self, no thing.

At this highest level, totality is understood to the extent it is manifested in an individual by the fact that it is also a uniting symbol as mediator in the tension of opposites, as well as a unitary dimension (*unus mundus*) in which they are all completely reconciled. That *mundus* is the undivided world before it was even divided into heaven and earth that Jung calls, "the original, non-differentiated unity of the world or of Being."[88] To realize totality as the *unus mundus* would be equivalent to reaching the *rotundum*, perfect roundness, or being as one without any differentiation. To even understand that there is a *unus mundus* and that there exists this end state of realization of the Self is perhaps the zenith of realization for an individual. This requires a mystical or numinous experience because there can be no mental formulation of a world without opposites, where spirit and matter are commingled. This was, however, Jung's insight as he expresses obliquely, "For the spirit alone penetrates all things, even the most solid bodies."[89] This is the realization of Jung of the *Brahman* through the *Atman* that involves a complete absorption in the divine, the significance of which is established as ego returns. This is then the culmination of Jung's desire to seek out the goal that Christ suggests that began his purpose in writing *Aion* and which exists as a possibility, the rarest of possibilities, because of his expansion of the Self into a process directed by the personal *Atman,* a living entity in psyche that suggests and fosters wholeness.

The appearance of symbols that indicate a center or totality are therefore only a starting point for the *process* of the realization of the Self that arises in the unconscious when the tension of opposites creates affect that activates psyche to project the Self. According to the formula, this will arise not only by symbolization of the Self but also by the wider

---

[88] CW 14, § 660
[89] *Ibid*, § 9

confrontation with the Shadow, because it is then that there is affect when attraction and repulsion of the opposites become patent. Until that time, or in the absence of the confrontation, the Self as magnet may make itself known by symbols or by a presentation, but, as it needs energy to activate the psyche, it requires that conflict for a center to be found in which there is some stasis. In this manner, seeing the Self as agent, as Mercurius, gives force to the proposition that psychic peace must be found: "The idea of Mercurius as a peacemaker, the mediator between warring elements and producer of unity …"[90]

The formula reveals that the struggle leads to Paradise, which is related to the alchemical idea of the *albedo,* that "regained state of innocence,"[91] a newfound place of simplicity. *Albedo* in alchemy is indeed the product of the transformation of unconsciousness into "illumination."[92] This is the initial realization of the Self that appears as a product of the struggle with the Shadow, a sense of wholeness and peace, and creates at once or gradually an alteration of consciousness.

The *Lapis*, the realization of the Self in matter, is the highest, practical form of realization that requires more than the acceptance of the metaphysical idea of the *unus mundus.* This level starts with the appearance of symbols confirming the Self as the center of psyche and, if possible, providing elements of totality. This is the pre-state of the Self for the appearance of the *Lapis.* For this later stage of realizing the *Lapis*, it will require a realization of the universality of the Self in all things in such a manner that it is a *permanent* alteration in consciousness rather than a transient insight that is forgotten eventually. Such a revelation would require a breakthrough into consciousness of the archetypal power of the *unus mundus* to so overwhelm a doubting consciousness that it must be realized. This is not the full realization of the Self, as that is not possible, but is one that leads to the appearance of the *Lapis*, which has cracks and is incomplete.

If the proposition is that the Self seeks its own realization through its agency, then the possibility is that the movement is unerringly toward this goal. As Jung points out in reviewing the mystical insights of those "who

---

[90] *Ibid,* § 10
[91] *Aion* § 373
[92] CW 13, § 82

write hundreds of treatises about something that did not exist and was therefore completely unknowable,"[93] this desire always brews in the unconscious of all individuals to be revealed to the extent of an individual's receptivity, when necessary. The longing is there, great in some, in the same way that vegetation is variegated, some of it weeds, some Banyan trees. There does not appear to be any door to knock upon to reveal that realization of the *unus mundus* as, with all numinous experience, it comes unbidden, in its own time or not at all. The hint of it will occur in dreams where it is modulated and hidden, or in fantasies, where it can be contemplated, but there is no definable path to the end state.

The formula recognizes the longing, is based on its existence, and asserts that the Self is only known as center or totality after the long voyage of struggling with the opposites and then only to the extent that it is manifested in an individual. Furthermore, it suggests that there is a reflective, continuous movement, a never-ending process in a circular way from unconsciousness to consciousness, so that the Self is always evolving, even when it appears to have stagnated. Attributing movement to the Self is the explanation of the entire process that provides a holding container without which the soundings of the Self may appear to be confusing and hard to integrate. However, that insight requires an individual's profound, unerring commitment to the process, which very well may be at the discretion of the Self.

Mystical Experience and the Process

The idea of the Self as expressed by Jung is not shared in contemporary psychology to the same extent and form. As a center or an idealized unity, the Self is clearly a sound conceptual ideal, but when it extends to a psychic force that has agency that enters into an intimate relationship with *Brahman* or the *unus mundus*, it becomes unique. The existence of the Self is therefore, for those who have not had its realization, only a *deduction* derived from Jung's revelations and from the *consensus generum* reflected in the idea of the *Atman* and appearing through a long history of its symbolic presentation in dreams and visions.

---

[93] CW 13, § 52

The idea behind what Jung calls a numinous experience, of which mystical and religious experience are forms, is that there is a possibility of a direct knowing, of full realization, of that which reveals a fundamental truth and has the effect of altering consciousness. The nature and scope of that experience is set out in my book *Working with Mystical Experiences in Psychoanalysis: Opening to the Numinous*.[94] The essence of a mystical experience is most useful in clarifying the nature of the Self as totality that may be included in the realization of the Self and the effect that it has on the entirety of the process.

There is the possibility that the existence of the Self as a mid-point and as embracing totality can certainly be the subject of a mystical experience. This is primarily because the Self is an archetype of wholeness and orientation that can break through by accumulated libido and foster that experience. However, the limited range of symbols that amount to realization of the Self as center and totality will not be the form in which the realization necessarily takes place. These symbols are usually presented in a gradual process of struggling with the unconscious and developing affect sufficient to activate psyche. A numinous experience does not need symbols but rather involves a direct knowing of a truth, which encompasses underlying wholeness. This will create a more fulsome understanding of and identification with the divine ground so that the insight, as Jung attributes to the mystic Meister Eckhardt, is entirely an "inner possession," with no need for explanation.[95]

A numinous experience of the Self does not depend on the process Jung set out in *Aion* of working through Shadow material, having clarity and peace caused by that process, and then beginning to see that the Self is in others and in matter. Instead, it is a jump to the last phase, the complete merging, a glimpse or a grasping of the *Rotundum*, where the realization is that the Self, in whatever form it manifests, is present in all things and is totality.

To understand how the Self is revealed in a numinous experience, it is necessary to understand what is that truth, the unity that holds the opposites in the form of the Self. In a 1936 Eranos lecture, Boris

---

[94] Stein 2019a
[95] CW 6, § 416

Petrovitch Vysheslawzeff, a professor of moral theology in Paris, explains the different forms of unity that arise with opposites. This is a seminal lecture where he brings these forms into comparison with the *Atman* that Jung uses to represent the Self.[96] The first form of opposites is "indifferent" because it is rigid and unchanging as the *necessary* parts of the construction of an interrelated whole and thus indelibly joined, such as now and then, cause and effect, with no need for resolution. The second is an either-or opposition, love and hate, good and evil that can never be reconciled, as they have an inextricable repugnance. The third is the harmony of opposites wherein there is a complementary relationship that is capable of being united. He states in relation to the third form: "Jung's greatest philosophical and psychological achievement is to have discovered in the mind a series of harmonious polarity and in particular the polarity of conscious and unconscious."[97]

It is therefore not all opposites that can be reconciled psychologically; it is only those where there is a complementary relationship. Vysheslawzeff suggests that the Absolute, the Godhead, does not rely on that complementary relationship to come into existence, so it otherwise remains *unable to be reached* and is then the "mysterious limitlessness which is revealed to intuition."[98] This suggests, most significantly, that realization of the Absolute is at an entirely different level from the potential for unity or seeing that potential in matter. In psychoanalysis, it is the working out of the relationship between unconscious material and consciousness that yields a sense of wholeness. Mystical experiences, on the other hand, are not concerned with complementary opposition, as was Jung, but suggest a harmony of either-or opposition because they establish a new, higher realm or truth where the opposites are subsumed in a larger matrix. Mystical experiences are those of finding absorption in *Brahman* or entering the Kingdom of God. This is why, as Vysheslawzeff points out, that Hinduism does "not believe in harmony, because it represents a passing state."[99] The only true harmony is not the passing state but the final unity, the complete *conjunctio*, the *heiros gamos*, the *Rotundum*, and the perfected *Anthropos*, none of which can be reached by or is relevant

---

[96] Vysheslawzeff 1969, pp. 11-13
[97] *Ibid*, p. 14
[98] Zenkovsky 1953, p. 815
[99] Vysheslawzeff 1969, p. 17

to the Self. This takes a numinous experience out of the process of the Self. The statement in the 1935 Eranos lecture by Jung that totality is to be *understood* through realization of the center can only mean that the numinosity of the center when realized, thereby only suggesting the *Lapis*, can be an *approximation* of a mystical insight.

The Self as the coincidence of opposites exists then on two levels. The first is that it develops from the complementary relationship (centroversion) between conscious and unconscious. Because of the psychological struggle that ensues, and as more unconscious material is integrated into consciousness, the sense of wholeness occurs. Symbols in this development would necessarily echo the emerging sense of wholeness, such as a circle or a center point. A mystical or numinous experience, if it occurred, would have the effect of establishing a truth that necessarily absorbs the opposites and symbols, if they arise at all, and are more likely to be those of a transcendental unity of all-oneness. This is a state of the interconnectedness of all things and the direct revelation of the divine as witness to its own creation or intertwined with that merging. This is beyond the Lapis that hints at a unity that is perfect wholeness as compensatory opposites are irrelevant.

The emergence of symbols, it is noted in relation to numinous experiences, is still possible because they may not be at the level of an absorption into all-oneness and can be something less, such as a feeling of harmony looking at stars, or a momentary sense of peace that comes unbidden. In those cases, it is an experience hinting at totality and the resolution of either-or opposites, even if it is only fleeting. The mystical experience has, as its main characteristics, that it arrives unbidden, is overwhelming, and, most importantly, it alters consciousness. In all cases, it is the breaking through of unconscious contents containing the primordial archetype of totality and can lead to further insights or deeper realization of the Self until it is at the level of a *permanent* alteration by a complete unitive experience that, most likely, does not exist in a Western setting.

It is interesting that the numinous experience of all-oneness may not evoke any characteristics of the Self, as Jung cast totality in a different form as the entirety of conscious and unconscious, the "psychic totality." In this form, the Self does indeed open the possibility of a wider Self "the *self*, his wholeness ...is both God and animal—not merely the empirical man, but the totality of his being, which is rooted in his animal being and reaches out beyond the merely human towards the divine."[100] However, this is not the Self most likely realized in a numinous experience. The numinous or mystical experience does not reveal the Self but rather *what stands behind the Self*. The idea of what stands behind is particularly clear in the comparison with the *Atman*, where it is the divine *Brahman* that is being manifested. It is this higher truth that is the basis for an experience that has the effect of altering consciousness; it is what remains when there are no opposites so therefore there can be no definition of the "Self" in the state of ultimate transcendence.

Totality as used in relation to the Self is then the sum of all psychic contents and that which contains the *possibility* of the ideal of unity of either-or opposites. The sense of wholeness, the symbols of that wholeness, the breaking through of numinosity, are all consistent with totality as both psychic integration and a hint at the ideal of a *conjunctio*. The actual realization of totality, if it occurred as a mystical experience, would not in any event leave the ego in place, so it cannot be part of the process of the Self. As Vysheslawzeff understood: "When the 'self' transcends all opposites and rises above them, it transcends also the opposition of conscious and unconscious."[101]

---

[100] CW 5, § 460
[101] Vysheslawzeff 1969, p. 21

Chapter 14. The Self and the World

The process of individuation is solitary and requires a commitment and orientation that is not common: It is said to be the work of a lifetime. In all such journeys, there is a move away from the *participation mystique* of the collective to an individual's search for his or her destiny. Such an introverted movement is necessary for, as Murray Stein explains, "A process of individuation requires questioning one's own most cherished cultural certainties and dearly held convictions. It means letting go of earlier identifications ..."[1] However, the countervailing idea, as John Beebe points out, is that the highest form of character that can be changed by individuation is *integrity*, and "this cannot find a place without relationship—which means relationship to others, to self, to culture."[2]

At least four questions arise from the conflict between individuation as an internal process and the life of the collective. These questions need to be addressed, as it is no longer possible to hide from the mounting problems of the conditions of urban life and the threat of a climate disaster, as just two examples. This leads to a consideration of whether the realization of the Self is any longer possible in the increasing stress of urban living, how the progress for realization of the Self relates to the well-being of the community, how can we account for the higher goal of the Self in relation to environmental issues, and what role does the Self have in the face of so much destruction? This is not an attempt to enter into a polemical stance for psychoanalysis but is entirely a theoretical analysis from the point of view of the Self.

The relationship of the individual to the community, culture, and the world is not expressed by Jung in the context of individuation as being required for realization of the Self. It is then a situation where the external

---

[1] Stein 2019c, p. 275
[2] Beebe 1992, pp. 123-4

world serves an individual's needs for realization, not the other way around: "Individuation does not shut one out form the world, but gathers the world to oneself."[3] Eric Neumann wrote to Jung in 1934 suggesting that the individual "inasmuch as he individuates, stands in the close relationship, namely, a compensatory relationship to the community."[4] He suggests, in relation to the collective, "I must confess that the fact that the prophet or the individuated person have a compensatory function in relation to the people or the respective community makes it more probable to me that the general center of the happening and the Self stand in closer connection."[5] Accordingly, he intimates that the random happening of events is compensated by those who are individuated; it is a compensatory not a cooperative relationship.

This idea that those who have reached the full realization of the Self somehow balance the collective is a difficult proposition. It is the sentiment that those who individuate may create an opportunity for others by being a catalyst for realizing the Self. Even this relationship is not apparent in Jung's ontological position of *esse in anima* or the development of a solipsistic, experiential reality, so that what an individual experiences in relation to the community are, according to Jung, "… in its most simple form, an exceedingly complicated structure of mental images. Thus there is in a certain sense, nothing that is directly experienced except the mind itself." The external world only *appears* to manifest for the individual, and the world is produced *ex animo* "between yourself and your surroundings." This leads to some connection because "the self appears in deeds and deeds always mean relationship."[6] The most that is provided by Jung is that realization of the Self relieves unconscious tensions, thereby making a person a better citizen, indirectly improving social conditions:

> But individuation means precisely the better and more
> complete fulfilment of the collective qualities of the human
> being, since adequate consideration of the peculiarity of the

---

[3] CW 8, § 433
[4] Jung & Neumann, 2015, p. 43
[5] *Ibid,* p. 44
[6] *Zarathustra*, Vol. 2, p. 795

individual is more conducive to a better social performance than when the peculiarity is neglected or suppressed.[7]

The idea that the Self as an archetype is *emergent* because the primal patterning is informed by the environment that includes social interaction is the postmodern, post-Jungian approach, which differs from Jung's realization. It is derived from the idea that the patterning of wholeness is not just a genetic coding in the brainstem but is a catalyst for developmental processes that follow. Accordingly, as Jean Knox put it in her pioneering writing, archetypes "are emergent structures resulting from a development interaction between genes and environment that is unique for each person."[8] This statement does not, however, establish a relationship for a developed adult that has specificity in relation to society.

What is clear is that the environment can have a brutal, negative effect on the realization of the Self, and when added to the normal psychological barriers, the connection with the Self may not emerge. The day-to-day barriers to realization of the Self are legion. Psyche can be activated by these events, but symbols may not be presented in dreams or visions, or they are lost on presentation as unimportant, or they do not have sufficient impact to alter consciousness. That slippery pathway between a symbol and its realization does not make the Self in *most* modern circumstances more than an unimaginable or abstract goal. There are many factors that analysis cannot conquer, such as the pandemic, war, oppressive regimes, and economic hardships. These are all seen as transient phenomena in which analysis can hang on and perhaps even provide opportunities for affective consciousness to seek a center. However, there is another factor of the difficult possibility of realizing the Self in the contemporary day-to-day urban living that appears to be relentless. This means that the impact of the collective on the development of the emergent Self and the possibility of realization may face the *most significant barrier* and diminish the impact of the Self in the modern world.

---

[7] CW 7, § 267
[8] Knox 2004, p. 4

Urban Life and the Self

The impact of contemporary urban life on the Self has not been included in the considerations of the emergent archetype. It is, however, the milieu in which the majority of the world lives. Underlying, ceaseless, and cumulative urban problems have been accepted as a recognized form of trauma—"urban trauma"—in studies starting in the 1980s as an "ongoing, recurrent disease."[9] In the last few decades, urban trauma as a concept has been extended to the displacement of urban populations by the undermining effects of globalization and neoliberalism, such as can be witnessed in the current destruction of houses each day in the city "beautification" process of New Delhi, never-ending gentrification of working class areas as in Atlanta, Baltimore, or La Barceloneta in Barcelona, as well as housing becoming severely unaffordable as in Hong Kong and San Francisco. There are many other forms of displacement, such as abandonment of urban areas that are unlivable because of gun violence and rising crime, the continued impact of war in urban centers, and the frightening beginning of the movement of climate change refugees. All of this—these insoluble, ongoing stresses of urban living and displacement—has been called "attritional lethality" or "chronic" urban trauma, a process that "occurs gradually and out of sight ... a violence of delayed destruction that is dispersed across time and space, an attritional violence that is typically not viewed as violence at all."[10] The impact of this form of collective trauma on the emergent Self is profound, and the realization of the Self, if that has occurred, has not had an impact and perhaps cannot have an impact on that which has become an underlying effect of urban living.

This continuous, underlying urban trauma is not always a result of major upheavals but is more aptly called "slow violence," described as not consisting of "one-off spectacular events but as continual, incremental discriminatory dispossessions of community and places."[11] Its current effects are visible for all to see, even if it has become so commonplace that it is now taken for granted. If examples are necessary, it is there in the postapocalyptic landscape of homelessness in Seattle, the intractable

---

[9] Sims, et al, 1988
[10] Nixon 2011, p. 2
[11] Pain 2019, p. 387

slums of Cañada Real Galiana near Madrid, the ruins of the destruction of the Heygate Estate in South London, or the scarring and racial tensions in the enclave of Cliché Sous Bois in the suburbs of Paris. Urban trauma does not apply only to these hardships and dispossessions where they are, as the examples listed, so obvious, but also to all of the relentless intrusions from the urban environment that enter deep into psyche: "traumatogenic effects of oppression that are not necessarily overtly violent or threatening to body well-being … but do violence to the soul or spirit."[12] To this could be added that they do violence to the Self.

The notions of recurrent urban trauma were certainly not in the purview of Jung. He offered no applicable commentary on slow urban trauma brought about by the non-war displacement of inhabitants, or non-war terror, or the effects of noise and local violence, as these were not problems of his time. The urban stress at that time was in fact relatively benign; since Jung's passing in 1961, there has been an increase of approximately 3.3 billion more people concentrated in cities, now constituting approximately 55 percent of the world's population that will grow to almost 70 percent by 2030.

The reality of unavoidable and repeated trauma resulting from urban living was contrary to his view of the city as it appeared in his dream and the numerous references where he equated it with wholeness, such as:

> The city represents a totality, closed in upon itself, a power which cannot be destroyed, which has existed for centuries and will exist for many centuries more. Therefore, the city symbolizes the totality of man, an attitude of wholeness which cannot be dissolved.[13]

He equated the central place of the Self with a city,[14] probably derived from the idea of the four-square Heavenly City,[15] or the notion of the city as the center of the earth,[16] as well as its nurturing, maternal setting,[17] identifying the Self with the feminine.[18] There is only a hint that

---

[12] Brown 1995, p. 107
[13] Jung 1935 § 268
[14] *Aion*, § 353
[15] CW 11 § 123
[16] CW 12, § 63
[17] CW 9i, § 156; CW 5, § 313

he understood the lack of individuality in cities: "individuals in big cities are wiped out, becoming just particles of a herd."[19]

Urban problems have rapidly increased in Europe due to the refugee influx, lack of affordable housing because of greater wealth disparity, increased crime rates related often to the introduction of Oxycodone, heat island effects and climate catastrophes of rapid global warming, and the active, recurrent risk of urban terrorism. These complex urban problems have obvious consequences with psychological implications: the indignity of racism, poverty, homelessness, family dysfunction, absent fathers, crime; a loss of a connection with peace and nature; and the resultant states of loneliness, alienation, depression, and despair. The greater the rate of population increase, the corresponding exacerbation of the psychological problems of depression, suicide, opioid addiction, alcoholism, and psychosis. Governments have merely flayed about, and the problems have not responded to tentative solutions.

The idea of slow, daily violence caused by the danger and vicissitudes of urban life is perhaps closer, if an analogy is needed in Jung's writings, to the treatment of Job: one indignity after another: "He laments that the calamities which struck him came so quickly one after another that he did not even have time to 'catch his breath' between each occurrence."[20] The acts against Job were all distinct but had a cumulative effect. In *Answer to Job*, Jung makes reference only to the clear deeds of divine oppression that, although incessant, could form distinct acts and objects:

> Just as there is a link between the wound and the weapon, so the affect corresponds to the violence of the deed that caused it. ... Although, by giving way to the affect, one imitates all the bad qualities of the outrageous act that provoked it and thus makes oneself guilty of the same fault ... the violence is meant to penetrate right to one's core, and the individual to succumb to its action.[21]

---

[18] CW 5 § 306
[19] *Zarathustra*, Vol. 1, p. 660
[20] Schwab 2005, p. 117
[21] CW 11, § 561-2

How can the Self be realized when there is such insidious stress? The problem that has lessened the recognition of urban stressors as a form of trauma having an effect on individuation is the absence of a clearly defined act. In the case of slow violence, the lack of a direct object leads to unrelated and vague intrusions being understood as a consequence of urban living by the population at large, even though they are indeed significantly disruptive. The problems are then perceived as a matter of urban governance. Psychologically, the events such as incessant, intermittent noise, impossible traffic, being a witness to violence or homelessness, hearing about a local or distant terrorist act, to name only a few, do not create a consistent, concrete object with which the ego can relate. Trauma is traditionally classed as an interaction between an abuser and an abused, yet with this form of urban trauma, there is a long trail of abusers, none of which have a distinct identity or, if they do, are absorbed into new abusers; it is rather a collective, systematic imposition on a diffuse population in an amorphous manner.

The lack of attention to complex urban trauma in Jungian theory is a function of the emphasis placed on the subjective effect of an event and not its objective character; the cause of the trauma is largely treated as irrelevant. The linking of intrapsychic fluctuations through shifts in society is evidenced by Jung in *Civilization in Transition,* but in all cases it is the personalization of the external events, as he put it, in the "individual test-tube."[22] This individual, subjective emphasis as the means to evaluate external effects does not consider the nature of the external event or the shifting societal structures. This is driven home in the early writings of Jung in his distinction in terms of the degree of impact of external events on hysteria and dementia praecox: "Hysteria is a caricature of the normal, and therefore shows distinct reactions to the stimuli of the environment. In dementia praecox, on the other hand, there is always defective reaction to external stimuli."[23] The degree to which urban trauma is treated as a subjective event in psyche rather than a specific, external form of trauma, will, in this view, make its nature and effect unclear.

---

[22] CW 10, § 450
[23] CW 2, § 1068

It should be mentioned that Otto Gross indicates that changes in the societal structures should be considered as part of the psychological milieu that must be considered and changed: "Thus he saw the necessity of linking internal, intrapsychic, change with external social and political change …"[24] In that model, the effect of urban trauma as a distinct form could be examined as representing a shift in society around which an understanding of its complexities and a treatment could be formed. There has been, however, little attempt to bring together the effect of the rapidly changing urban environment into psychoanalysis probably because from the test-tube view, we are bound by the emphasis of Renos Papadopoulos that "the majority of individuals do not require professional attention because a great deal of their healthy functioning remains intact and unaffected by the devastation …"[25]

The realization of the Self is a very delicate proposition. It implies that the symbols of the Self will be recognized and can be translated into the appearance of a center in psyche. It is called the "work of a lifetime" because it is not merely an insight into a particular complex but rather it is the induction of psyche into a new orientation. This clearly requires a strong and aware ego and, although that may be available to some, it certainly, in this modern world of urban trauma, is not available to many. This makes much of the process of the Self available to be realized in interludes from the chaos and suggests that the community in general cannot achieve realization of the Self. Those who might in the early to mid-20th century have had the privilege and aptitude to realize the Self would not have that capacity in modern urban areas that will shortly make up 70 percent of the world's population.

The Self and Community[26]

With the assumption that an individual can progress in an environment that permits the process of the Self, is there a duty to assist or aid in the development of social cohesion in the community? Do we need each other to realize the Self? The French philosopher Gilbert Simondon

---

[24] Heuer, 2001 p. 663
[25] Papadopoulos 2007, p. 308
[26] This section contains revised material from my paper to be presented at the Eranos Conference 2022 on "Jung's Red Book for our Time: Searching for the Soul under Postmodern Conditions."

suggests that there is always a *reciprocal* relationship in individuation; the latter term he uses in a similar manner to Jung: "Both individuations, the psychic and collective, are reciprocal to one another; they allow for the definition of a category of the transindividual, which can be used to explain the systemic unity of the interior (psychic) individuation and the exterior (collective) individuation."[27] A way to understand this viewpoint is that the individual by his or her presence is beneficial to the community, and the community is helpful for that individual to become individuated.

This idea of reciprocity is apparent in the *Window on Eternity* image in *The Red Book* that appears as a statement on the relationship of individual realization of the Self to the community. This image is Figure 2 and is discussed earlier in this work in relation to Jung's dream of the center in 1927 in which he realized the Self as a luminescent tree on an island. In that dream, there were other identical centers for others to realize the Self but with smaller replicas of the island.

The glowing center is explained first in the legend to the reproduction of the image in the German Edition of the *Secret of the Golden Flower* in 1929 as a "luminous flower in the centre, with stars rotating about it. Around the flower, wall with eight gates. The whole conceived of as a transparent window."[28] The image is a mandala, so that it suggests wholeness. The center in the Image is a very large rose of ruby-colored glass. It is an overpowering image of wholeness that is protected from destruction by the wall that keeps the psychic energy within that is necessary for individuation.

Around the center are small, jewellike centers that are for the collective. This directly establishes a reciprocal arrangement. Accordingly, Jung's realization of the center obtains significance as the center of a larger structure that is the environment of the collective, and the collective, in turn, is offered a numinous goal that is unmistakable. If the structure of the collective was degraded or the center was not present, the Image would lose its significance: Each is sustained by the interdependency.

The large center is suitable because, for an individual in the collective to realize the Self, it is necessary that there be affect-laden, clear symbols

---

[27] Simondon 2009, p. 8
[28] Willhelm 1961, p. 136, Fig 2

capable of holding their significance. For the less realized person, the idea of the self as center is then not abstract, as it is contained within the notion and sense of all roads leading to the center, providing an orientation and accepting the existence of a point from which all else radiates.

Simondon goes further and emphasizes that the individual who seeks individuation is in a "veritable theatre of individuation" that includes the collective[29] and that is necessary because the individual cannot solve problems alone and needs the collective: "The collective unit provides the resolution of the individual problematic, which means the basis of the collective reality already forms a part of the individual...."[30]

The collective is important for the realization of the Self if it creates a temenos for each individual, a pathway to a different level of realization, and by offering the suggestion that it is a collective, interdependent journey. "The implication is that it is only within the unity of the collective—as a milieu in which perception and emotion can be unified— that a subject can bring together these two sides of its psychic activity and to some degree coincide with itself."[31]

In dystopian times, the idea of a supporting community to provide a safe temenos for realization of the Self seems fanciful. In such times, it is said, "individual judgement grows increasingly uncertain of itself and that responsibility is collectivized as much as possible. ... In this way, the individual becomes more and more a function of society, which in turn usurps the function of the real life carrier ..."[32] In those times, a mana-personality is indeed the only individual that can fully realize the Self, represented by the massive center that is instructive for the community. Nevertheless, it is clear that the individual is the center of social history and without the process of individuation in the context of a supportive community, it is difficult to stand against the collective shadow. The lack of that support indicates that the possibility of realizing the Self is therefore diminished and suggests that it needs a supportive community, a concept that may need to be contemplated by psychoanalysis.

---

[29] Simondon 1964/1992, p. 298
[30] *Ibid*, p. 307
[31] Combes 2013, p. 33
[32] CW 10, § 504

The World Self and the Natural Environment

The issue to be addressed is whether the Self has a relationship to the natural environment. The Self as experienced in psyche by way of symbols in dreams and visions does not suggest any particular connection to the natural environment. The symbols that arise that may be representative of the Self may include images from the natural environment, such as a tree as Jung had in his dream, animals, or pristine settings. Any of those, by their significance in the context of the dream or vision, could be said to be intimations of a center point, wholeness, or a hint as to aspects of totality. However, all of these are in service of internal revelations, and there is no direct connection with the actual object or situation in the natural environment.

In the equation Jung uses for explaining the process of the Self in *Aion,* the underlying theme is that the spirit has become abstracted and introverted, removed from the operation of the material world and the resolution of that split creates the near-perfected Self. This split between spirt and matter and its relationship to the Self is best understood through the equation in *Aion,* as well as the dream of the physicist Wolfgang Pauli of the World Clock. The vision of Pauli was of a composite set of circles that made it a three-dimensional structure. It was a vision of totality that embraced the circle, a surrounding square, a triangle, and the cycles of time. According to Jung, it was an embodiment of space-time.[33] The significance of this vision has been acknowledged scientifically as the possible link between physical and psychic processes.[34] It amounted for Pauli to a conversion, a numinous experience,[35] and as a statement of the close link between the structure of psyche that includes the Self and the natural world.

The spirit/matter split appears most obvious in the historic Christian depreciation of the body. A good starting point for that analysis is Augustine and his orientation to an individual as a spiritual being that is understood by *inwardness*, so that the needs of the body distract from that goal. This makes the materiality of the body of less consequence: It is only spirit that is relevant and the idea of an internalized spiritual vocation

[33] CW 12, § 312
[34] Sherbon 2012
[35] CW 11, § 110

"produced changes in the apprehension of the body from the twelfth century onwards."[36] As Jung reports, this led to the sublimation of sex[37] and a movement away from nature[38] that inevitably suggests the orientation that God is pure spirit.[39] The result was a "despiritualization of nature,"[40] a turning away from the essence of the natural world.

Both spirit and matter were postulated by Jung as able to have some connection through synchronicity because there is a factor that exists "which mediates between the apparent incommensurability of body and psyche, giving matter a 'psychic' faculty and the psyche a kind of 'materiality.'"[41] Yet, they remain opposites, and as the Self consists of and is a coincidence of opposites, the resolution of that incommensurability would be an essential aspect of only the last stage of the realization of the Self.

In the equation in *Aion,* the movement to D, the *Lapis Philosophorum,* is the realization of the Self in matter, the last possible stage. It is the coming together in alchemy of "body, soul, and spirit,"[42] or the realization that they are integrated. This is the ultimate, practical realization recognized in alchemy as the *deus terrenus,* the light above all lights.[43] The link between the *Lapis* and the *Anthropos,* the individual in which the Self or God is indwelling, suggests totality. It is for the individual to make that link between the indwelling Self and matter. What is to be experienced, according to the ancient alchemist Hermes Trismegistus is the "Gold in a mean ... the very Soul."[44]

The Self is experienced by its realization, gained by the resolution of spirit and matter, the primordial opposites. Matter, the external world, is then joined with spirit. At that stage, the Self is connected with the material world of the environment as both are united in the *unus mundus.* This is not an everyday occurrence, so for all others the opposites remain split,

---

[36] Louth 1997, p. 120
[37] CW 3, § 279
[38] CW 5, § 339
[39] *Ibid,* § 99
[40] CW 9ii, § 370
[41] CW 10, § 780
[42] CW 9i, § 177
[43] *Ibid,* § 289
[44] Salmon 1692, p. 244

and the spirit does not reach out for unity with the external world. This rare joining requires that an individual has understood that the wholeness within is an aspect of existence that is in all things, my body, your body, the natural world, and even in inert material. It is not explained in the equation as a mystical or numinous experience where one is absorbed in the divine, although it could arise in that way, but rather that the conscious mind is aware that the Self is in all things.

In practical terms, the realization of the Self in all things would necessitate an engagement with the natural world as having equal valence and mutual concern. The natural world is therefore necessary for the *Lapis*, the stone, to receive the projection of the Self, for without that the essence of the Self would not become a psychological fact. The realization of the Self is what offers the possibility of a reconciliation of opposites of spirit and matter in an absorption where there is an all-oneness because "opposites are not to be united rationally."[45] For Jung, the split between spirit and matter is the ultimate split: "Matter is the counterpole to God."[46] This means that as the Self is gradually realized by symbols and an emerging sense of wholeness, something is created, and although the split is not reconciled, there is still a "positive act of creation which assimilates the opposites as necessary elements of coordination ..."[47]

It is not necessary to consider that the Self is in nature and that the Self is also the spirit within an individual in order for the opposites of spirit and matter to be reconciled. This is because the Self is a mediator between the opposites, "a mediating and unifying force located in between the phenomenal and noumenal realms, yet containing both."[48] It contains spirit as well as matter and is the place where the two are united. This is a realization that concentrates on the nature of the Self and not the observation of the material world having a spirit. This is a subtle difference that suggests that the critical understanding is that the Self is primarily the midpoint or center between opposites and, for that reason, reconciles the opposites within itself.

---

[45] CW 6, § 169
[46] *Black Books*, Vol 5, p. 269
[47] CW 6, § 541
[48] *Letters*, Vol 2, p. 258

The result is that the Self is in the natural world as well as in us because it holds both as it does all opposites, and this suggests that it is everywhere at once. As the world is a set of opposites, the Self is the world Self, the *anima mundi*, the "world mother" that is omnipresent.[49] Viewed in this way, it coincides with the Holy Ghost and *Mercurius* as the guiding spirit responsible for "all the phenomena of life and the psyche."[50] Jung treats it as spirit in that it is an animating principle,[51] a divine spirit.[52]

The Self is the World Self as, Jung expresses, as it "coincides with that of the collective unconscious whose centre is the self."[53] This makes the *Lapis* a joining that has some imperfections "a bit of the world soul."[54] The *anima mundi,* Jung explains, "paints a picture of the self, the indescribable totality of man."[55] Jung proposes that the *anima mundi* is also like the *Atman* of the Upanishads,[56] thereby bringing it closer to his idea of the Self.

When viewed as the world soul, the Self is in nature as well as containing nature within it as the mediator of opposites; it is in all things, totality as an animating principle. Its place as the world soul makes it the soul of all things as it is what creates phenomena, which makes the concepts of *Atman, Brahman*, and Christ completely apt as its dimension and nature. From this position, no harm can be done to nature that is not harm to oneself.

This would, it follows, call for environmental action if realized. It would require an individual to understand that the indwelling divine is also in the air, in the effects of climate, in the plight of the homeless. This is the case for those who have realized the Self to that great extent. However, for those who seek the Self, even though the ideas may still be a hypothesis, there seems a duty to integrate with the environment, be mindful of how it is imperiled, and to fight for it with as much longing as one has for the ultimate unity and peace of the Self.

---

[49] CW 5, § 550
[50] CW 8, § 393
[51] *Ibid*, § 219
[52] CW 11, § 160
[53] *Ibid*, § 265
[54] CW 13, § 102
[55] *Ibid*, § 172
[56] CW 9i, § 554

The Self and Destruction

If the Self is given agency and is responsible for psychological growth, the question must be asked of why there is so much destruction, violence, trauma, disadvantage, discrimination, poverty, hunger, inequality, and evil. Is it merely that the Self holds good and evil so that it directs both according to its whim? It is not a comforting argument that the Self contains light and darkness because if that is fully accepted, it would require great moral confusion as to whether to introduce the Self to patients. It is also not enough to answer that the Self is at work as a guiding spirit for each individual in the face of genocide. It then requires resorting to the justification that there are higher forces involved that we cannot understand and it is all as it should be. This is not merely a philosophical question because by postulating a Self as *spiritus rector*, some answer must be found for the majority of humanity that is not undergoing psychoanalysis and where the possibility of realizing the Self is an illusion.

The problem is created by attributing agency to the Self so that it is *responsible* for outcomes. As shown, Jung was never specific about the Self having agency but rather states that when it is realized, it becomes the guiding spirit. Until then, even when it is realized as a hunch or presentation, it will begin to reorient consciousness and thereby, in that partial realization, direct the manner in which an individual develops. Putting the darkness in the world at the feet of the Self should not exist as an idea when it can be viewed otherwise as a magnet that attracts and fascinates by its mere existence.

There is no doubt, as neurobiology confirms, that the Self as a core centering pattern exists in the brain structure and is the infrastructure for, or at least contributes to the interaction of a neonate with the environment. As a core pattern, an archetype, it will appear in dreams and have an unconscious role in a movement toward centering in each of our lives. When there is a time of chaos, when the internal conflict is significant and the ego structure is less coherent, it makes sense that the patterning will emerge more easily. It is natural that psyche will be activated and seek relief and homeostasis. This occurs because the patterning has the force of an archetype and, being outside consciousness, has a numinosity or higher value. As a magnet, the understanding can occur that there is indeed an internal process that is innate, and thus consciousness can expand to accept the other in psyche. When this occurs, it is possible that the center can be seen as a predominant characteristic of all life and as a universal principle that brings one closer to the image of a God.

There is no secret to the Self. It is not a mysterious substance that is alien and can never be understood and that controls us as a puppet master. It is there to be found just as talents are uncovered or the connection of an individual with a higher power can be discovered. It is not responsible for anything other than the revelation of itself that occurs because it is a primal patterning and creates a numinous fascination when it rises to the surface. The Self is therefore not responsible for destruction and, for most lives, will go unnoticed but still be played out each day in the desire to correct oneself or become more centered and have a moment of peace.

As containing all opposites, the Self contains good and evil in equal measures. The possibility that it has agency and will exert its evil forces for some reason is incongruent with the pace of psychological growth and its principles. The fact that it is aligned by Jung with the transcendental is the only means by which it has agency. This means that when it seeks that higher range of divinity, it then may need to refine the individual through a test of fire. These are God's ways. The best explanation is Jung's underlying theme that God needs man to become conscious, to complain about injustice, and to question God's will. The critical comment of Maimonides is for those who know God and psychologically realize the Self, "If a man knows this, every misfortune will be born lightly by him."[57]

---

[57] Maimonides 1963, Guide III: 23, p. 497

Chapter 15. Clinical Notes on the Self

The Self is always a concept. It is understood as such and is a reflection of a sense of being centered or a feeling of momentary wholeness or balance. The Self as a representative term for wholeness will thereby produce symbols from the unconscious for many dreams that point to the innate patterning in the brain and psyche. It must be accepted clinically that the Self as Jung found in his extraordinary dream in 1927 and then in 1935 wherein the center also held all of totality, created for him indelible psychological facts as the concept was proved. When a patient has a dream of equal exactitude, it is most likely not to fit in the matrix of insights already held by such a mana-personality as Jung to be thereby rendered a realization. Jung's realization was part of a very long process of incubation and experimentation, drawing daily mandalas in a privileged setting, looking for something that gave him meaning. In the dream, he found the Self but the "other Swiss" did not, even though they climbed up to the plateau, nor did those in the marketplace from which they had climbed higher.

The complex framework of the Self in Jungian thought is similar to the insights of other great beings whereby the rest of us must try to give them meaning even though we are not sure of exactly what is meant. When Jung quotes, for instance, *tat tvam asi* (that thou art) as a "complete identity of inside and out,"[1] to take one of several thousands of examples, we then have to breathe into it our own understanding. That understanding is on a massive sliding scale from Jung (or those greater who realized *tat twam asi)* to the rest of us in descending order. This means that every interpretation of the Self in a clinical setting will never be accurate to its full extent but will only be an approximation according to our own insight, scholarship, embodiment, and complexes.

---

[1] CW 6, § 189

It is therefore incumbent upon the analyst, it appears, to primarily provide a matrix so as to create a personality for the Self. Unless the symbols and their meaning arise as a numinous experience, which is possible but rare, there is no context for the Self in analysis, and there are no modern equivalents that carry the certitude that here lies something of value. It would be reasonable to assert that without a context being provided, the Self has limited clinical significance, even though theoretically it is what is driving the entire process.

Translating the Self

Analytical psychologists must vocalize the nature of the Self because it is the foundational tool of their chosen profession. As well, if explained properly, it will alert the patient to the possibility that it offers. A translation of what is experienced as a symbol of the Self in relation to the matrix of Jung's insights is therefore needed. Translation is required because for many symbols of the Self, they may point to wholeness, such as a circle, but they are not as explicit as an ideogram that undoubtedly conveys what it means, such as a sign in a restaurant of a cigarette with a red line through it. Such an ideogram is explicit because it partakes of a shared understanding, which is not the case for the symbols of the Self. Consequently, a dream with a symbol of a circle in a square as representing totality may be an intimation of the Self, but it is not apparent to the dreamer and requires translation.

Symbols of a center, a hero, a guide, a circle, to name a few, can be interpreted as pointing to a center, but it does not have to be explained as the Self initially as an abstract concept but rather as our desire for a center and an innate, neurobiologically proven, core patterning. It does not seem possible to present the entirety of the concept of the Self at an early stage of analysis, even if that was attempted. Instead, those aspects of the Self that are revealed can be left to an explanation of a centering process, centroversion, and the desire of an individual for wholeness. It then must be left up to the magnetism of the Self to produce more as consciousness is pulled closer to wholeness and its implications. Accordingly, the translation of symbols of wholeness to the Jungian Self is a gradual process, with each instance of its appearance revealing, as appropriate, an explanation of the concept of the Self to provide that matrix for understanding.

Stating the Goal

There are two contrary lines of approach that are revealed in the Self that have been discussed at length. The first is the agency view, whereby the Self is seeking to realize itself and is autonomous, objective, and creates and destroys for its needs. Meaning, in this viewpoint, lies for the individual in the awareness of the Self's journey. The alternative, the magnet view, is that the individual is drawn into a lifetime of reflection so that the Self can be realized through the agency of the individual.

The first approach has many Jungian adherents on the thesis that the divine is seeking itself to observe its creation and man is merely the conduit through which it acts. In this case, the role of mankind is either to seek individuation or not obscure that observation or to become conscious through that process, so the Self can develop to a state where it is capable of carrying out its goal. The need for an individual to be conscious of that possibility perhaps first appears in the *Scrutinies* section of *The Red Book:* "the Gods need a human mediator and rescuer. With this man paves the way to crossing over and to divinity."[2]

If this agency approach is taken, then the analytical framing is that all that occurs in psychoanalysis is that the Self brings one closer to its realization that then explains the difficulties that rise when seeking its emergence. This matrix, ignoring the metaphysical arguments, suggests an active Self always working hard to advance itself. Symbols in a dreams and visions can then confirm this role, and the goal of the Self can become the accepted goal of the individual. However, symbols in dreams, visions, or those evident in projections, do not necessarily reveal the Self in this light. As well, the process needed for the symbol to represent the Self, the attribution of the symbol to a centering function, the extrapolation to the metaphysical idea, do not guarantee a lasting or significant realization.

The agency view, however, at least confers a meaning and purpose, if it is accepted, that may have a salutary effect. If it is understood that the Self is seeking its realization through symbols or appears as a guiding spirit, it creates the possibility of a new foundation for consciousness. It takes the burden off random events and orients an individual to the transcendent qualities of psyche. It is not possible to discount this idea as

---

[2] *Red Book,* p. 358

being unsustainable or speculative as it is no less plausible than the magnet view. This is, in fact, congruent with Jung's approach to the Self when bringing it into psychological usage, assigning to it the ultimate goal, and comparing it to the *Atman* where it is an aspect of the divine within an individual.

Location and Personification

The goal is not merely to understand the Self but to embody it so that it can be given a location. Until that time, it is an idea that may have transient effects on psychological circumstances. The Self is susceptible to embodiment if it has such a location, although Jung consistently refers to it as a "virtual" center. The presence in a location in the body, such as the middle of the chest or the pit of the stomach, tends to be a reference point for what is otherwise abstract. This is not suggested by Jung, but it makes the Self a physical point of reflection.

The *Atman* is specifically located in the heart in all schools of Hinduism, so that it is given a place that aids in its personification. In addition, it also offers a transcendent possibility, a hint of something beyond our understanding that it is working toward a higher goal. It must be understood that the realization of the Self is not a linear process and requires a constant confrontation with the ego in all its respects, offering the chance to relocate it each time it is appropriate. This makes it the substance that confronts problems and that points to a goal. It is interesting that in the final pages of *Mysterium*, Jung's last and most mystical work, he reminds us:

> The self, in its efforts at self-realization, reaches out beyond the ego-personality on all sides, because of its all-encompassing nature it is brighter and darker than the ego, and accordingly confronts it with problems which it would like to avoid. Either one's moral courage fails, or one's insight, or both, until in the end fate decides.[3]

A personification, at least, creates an entity that "in its efforts at self-realization" can stand as the Self in a location. A clinical example may be useful. A patient who is going through a difficult divorce and has had

---

[3] CW 14, § 778

repeated symbols in his dreams of a wise old man telling him to listen to what the old man is saying, began to localize that figure. Jung suggests that the old man, whom he states is an archetype that first appears as the father, is a personification of meaning and spirit.[4] This old man appeared initially in a dream as two old men walking together at a social engagement and again as being in the middle room of a house where parts of himself (who announced themselves as such) were gathered. This led to the possibility of speaking about the center and the Self and its possible agency role. Thereafter, he associated it as living in his heart, and would often touch his chest thereafter as an awareness of the old man in him.

Personification is at the heart of the synthetic method, first evident in Jung's 1912 *Wandlungen und Symbols der Libido*. Personification of the Self is particularly important because when the Self has a location, it can be brought back to awareness and made the subject of repetition, adding to the narrative and the induction of psyche into the power of the Self.

Clinical Conclusion

The Self has at least six aspects that must be recognized in the therapeutic process for it to alter consciousness. The first is the underlying chaos of opposites. As the Self has the most significance as uniting opposites, there is no understanding of the Self possible if that interaction is not grasped. The second is the idea of finding a center, centroversion and its commonplace notion of being centered. The third is the role of the center as mediating opposites and the concept of the primal patterning, a core Self, that seeks homeostasis. The fourth is establishing the numinosity of a center as why it is emerging into consciousness. The fifth is the power of that center, its guiding hand, its desire to work with the individual for it to be realized. The final aspect is that it is the prize to be won and that all psychological work is aimed at the goal in order to keep the Self embedded in the individual's psychological work.

Manifestation of totality is the outlier aspect of the Self, and although that gives it its power and transcendence, it is something that must develop organically from dreams, visions and a sense of wholeness, but is not able to be easily translated. A dream with totality symbols may in

---

[4] CW 5, § 515

fact alert the patient to the idea of the expansive nature of the Self, but that is not indelible, as it depends on the individual's receptivity, which cannot be predicted. Speaking of totality in the absence of its realization will demean in many instances the discovery of the center as it makes it more of a metaphysical idea that is not grounded in personal revelation.

The Self is the marvelous aspect of ourselves that pushes for wholeness in the rush of day-to-day. How it does so, as agent or magnet, is not relevant except by the use of agency as a technique to raise the significance of the Self as a guiding spirit. The Self is the core of all psychoanalytic work, and the more that attention is drawn to it, the more that it will settle on the patient, as if by a fine mist, until it permeates the conscious mind. It is truly a gift of Jung's to move from mere psychological solutions to a sense of wholeness that creates a presence in the world.

Abbreviations

Aion:

>Jung, C.G. (1951). *Aion: Researches into the Phenomenology of the Self.* 2ed. The Collected Works of C.G. Jung, Vol 9, Part II. R.F.C. Hull, Trans. Bollingen Series XX. Princeton: Princeton University Press.

Black Books:

>Jung, C.G. (2020). *The Black Books 1913-1932: Notebooks of Transformation.* S. Shamdasani, Ed. M. Liebscher, J. Peck, & S. Shamdasani, Trans. New York: W.W. Norton.

CW:

>C.G. Jung. *Collected Works of C.G. Jung.* R.F.C. Hull. 2ed. Bollingen Series XX. Princeton: Princeton University Press. 19 Volumes + Index + Vol. A and B.

Letters:

>Jung, C.G. (1973). *C.G. Jung Letters.* G. Adler & A. Jaffe, Eds. Princeton: Princeton University Press. 2 Volumes.

Memories:

>Jung. C.G. (1989). *Memories, Dreams, Reflections.* A. Jaffe, Ed. R. & C. Winston, Trans. New York: Vintage Books.

Red Book:

>Jung, C.G. (2009). *The Red Book: Liber Novus.* S. Shamdasani, Ed. M. Kyburz, J. Peck, S. Shamdasani, Trans. New York: W.W. Norton.

Zarathustra:

>Jung, C.G. (1989). *Nietzsche's Zarathustra: Notes of the Seminar given in 1934-1939.* J.L. Jarrett, Ed. Princeton: Princeton University Press.

References

Abe, M. (1975). Non-being and Mu the metaphysical nature of negativity in the East and West. *Religious Studies, 1975*, 181-192.

Addison, A. (2018). *Jung's Psychoid Concept Contextualized*. London: Routledge.

Adler, G. (1948). *Studies in Analytical Psychology*. New York: W.W. Norton.

Adler, G. (1979). *Dynamics of the Self*. 1948. London: Coventure.

Alcaro, A., Carta, S., & Panksepp, J. (2017). The affective core of the self: A neuro-archetypical perspective on the foundations of human (and animal) subjectivity. *Frontiers in Psychology, 8(1)*, 1-13.

Aleghieri, Dante, & Longfellow, H.W. (2017). *Paradiso*. Mineola, NY: Dove Publications.

Allport, G.W. (1955). *Becoming*. New Haven: Yale University Press.

Alschuler, A.S. (1987). Recognizing inner teachers: Inner voices through-out history. *Gnosis, 5,* 8-12.

Altmanspacher, H. (2014). Psychophysical correlations, synchronicity and meaning. *Journal of Analytical Psychology, 59(2)*, 181-188.

Altmanspacher, H. (2018). Dual-aspect monism according to the Pauli-Jung conjecture. *Review Simbio-Logias, 10(14)*, 60-78.

Ameriks, K. (1997). Kant and the self: A retrospective. In D.E. Klemm & G. Zoller, Eds. *Figuring the Self: Subject, Absolute and Others in Classical German Philosophy*. London: Routledge.

Anderson, J. (2012). An investigation of *Moksha* in the Advaita Vedanta of Shankara and Gaudapada. *Asian Philosophy, 22(3)*, 275-287.

Arendt, H. (1978). *The Life of the Mind*. Vol. 1. New York: Harcourt, Brace, Jovanovich.

Aristotle. (1930) *Physics*. R.P. Hardie & R. K. Gaye, Trans. Oxford: Oxford University Press.

Ashbery, J. (1988). The Skaters. In *Rivers and Mountains*. New York: Ecco Press.

Astor, J. (1995). *Michael Fordham: Innovations in Analytical Psychology*. London: Routledge.

Aurobindo, Sri. (1996). *The Upanishads*. Twin Lakes, WI: Lotus Light.

Aurobindo, Sri. (2005). *The Life Divine II*. The Complete Works of Sri Aurobindo, Vol 22. Sri Aurobindo Ashram Press: Pondicherry, India.

Austin, S. (2009). Jung's dissociable psyche and the ec-static self. *Journal of Analytical Psychology, 54(5)*, 581-599.

Bachelard, G. (1960). *The Poetics of Reverie: Childhood, Language, and the Cosmos*. D. Russell, Trans. Boston: Beacon Press.

Bachelard, G. (1964). *The Poetics of Space*. M. Jolas, Trans. London: Orion Press.

Bair, D. (2004). *Jung: A Biography*. London: Little Brown.

Baju, P.T. (1967). Religion and spiritual values in Indian thought. In C. Moore, Ed. *The Indian Mind: Essentials of Indian Philosophy and Culture*. (pp.183-215). Honolulu: University of Hawaii Press.

Barthes. R. (1982). *Empire of Signs*. R. Howard, Trans. New York: Farrar, Straus and Giroux.

Baumann, C. (1946). Presentation of "An alchemical text interpreted as if it were a dream" by C. G. Jung. Presented to The Analytical Psychology London Club on October 18, 1946, unpublished.

Beebe, J. (1996). *Integrity in Depth*. College Station, TX: Texas A&M University Press.

Bennet, E.A. (1985). *Meetings with Jung: Conversations Recorded during the Years 1946-1961*. Zurich: Daimon Verlag

Bhadreshdas, Sadhu. (2018). *Akshar-Purushottam Darshan – An Introduction*. Ahmedabad, India: BAPS.

Bharati, A. (1980). *The Ochre Robe: An Autobiography*. (2nd ed.) Santa Barbara, CA: Ross-Erickson.

Bharati, A. (1985). The self in Hindu thought and action. In A. J. Marsella, G. De Vos, & F.L.K. Hsu, Eds. *Culture and Self: Asian and Western Perspectives* (pp. 185–230). New York: Tavistock.

Bishop, P. (1995). *The Dionysian Self*. Berlin: Walter de Gruyter.

Bishop, P. (1996). The use of Kant in Jung's early psychological works. *Journal of European Studies, 26(2),* 107-140.

Bishop, P. (1999). The birth of analytical psychology from the spirit of Weimar Classicism. *European Studies, 29(4),* 417-441.

Bishop, P. (2008). *Analytical Psychology and German Classical Aesthetics: Goethe, Schiller and Jung. Volume 1: The Development of the Personality.* London: Routledge.

Bishop, P. (2009). *Analytical Psychology and German Classical Aesthetics: Goethe, Schiller, and Jung. Vol. 2: Constellation of the Self.* London: Routledge.

Bishop, P. (2012). Jung's *Red Book* and its relation to aspects of German Idealism. *Journal of Analytical Psychology, 57(3),* 335-363.

Bishop, P. (2014). *Carl Jung.* London: Reaktion Books.

Black, B. (2007). *The Character of the Self in Ancient India: Priests, Kings and Women in the Early Upanisads.* Albany: SUNY Press.

Bob, P., & Laker, M. (2016). Traumatic stress, neural self and the spiritual mind. *Consciousness and Cognition, 46,* 7-14.

Bogart, G. (2009). *Dreamwork and Self-Healing: Unfolding the Symbols of the Unconscious.* London: Karnac Books.

Bollas, C. (1989). *Forces of Destiny: Psychoanalysis and Human Destiny.* Northvale, NJ: Jason Aronson.

Bonhoeffer, D. (2009). *Berlin: 1932-1933.* Dietrich Bonhoeffer Works, Vol. 12, C. Nicolaisen & E-A Scharffenorth, Eds. Minneapolis: Fortress Press.

Borghesani V., & Piazza M. (2017). The neuro-cognitive representations of symbols: the case of concrete words. *Neuropsychologia, 105,* 4-17.

Bourdieu, P. (1991). Censorship and the imposition of form. In J. Thompson, Ed. *Language and Symbolic Power.* (pp. 142-143). Cambridge, MA: Harvard University Press,

Bradbrook, M.C., & Lloyd Thomas, M.G. (1939). Marvell and the concept of metamorphosis. *The Criterion, 18,* 236-254.

Bradley, R. (2012). *The Idea of Order: The Circular Archetype in Prehistoric Europe.* Oxford: Oxford University Press.

Bredin, H. (1984) Metonymy. *Poetics Today, 5(1):* 45-58.

Brereton, J. (1990). The Upanishads. In *Approaches to the Asian Classics,* W.T de Bary & I. Bloom, pp. 115-135. New York: Columbia UP.

Brooke, R. (2009). The self, the psyche and the world: a phenomenological interpretation. *Journal of Analytical Psychology, 54(5),* 601-618.

Brooks, R.M. (2019). A critique of C.G. Jung's theoretical basis for selfhood: Theory vexed by an incorporeal ontology. In J. Mills, Ed. *Jung and Philosophy.* London: Routledge.

Brown, L.S. (1995). Not outside the range: One feminist perspective on psychic trauma. In C. Caruth, Ed. *Trauma: Explorations in Memory.* (pp. 100–112) Baltimore: Johns Hopkins University Press.

Buber, M. (2016). *Eclipse of God: Studies in Religion and Philosophy.* Princeton: Princeton University Press.

Cambray, J. (2005). The place of the 17th century in Jung's encounter with China. *Journal of Analytical Psychology, 50(2),* 195-207.

Cauvin, J. (2000). *The Birth of the Gods and the Origins of Agriculture.* Cambridge:
Cambridge University Press.

Chachakka Sutta (1998). Translated from the Pali by Thanissaro Bhikkhu. *Access to insight.* http://www.accesstoinsight.org/tipitaka/mn/mn. 148.than.html

Chaudhuri, H. (1954). The concept of Brahman in Hindu philosophy. *Philosophy East and West, 4(1),* 47-66.

Chittick, W.C. (1979). The Perfect Man as the prototype of the Self in the Sufism of Jāmī. *Studia Islamica, 49,* 135-157.

Cicero, M.T. (2014). *De finibus, bonorum et malorum = On ends.* Cambridge: Harvard University Press.

Cleary, T. (1991). *The Secret of the Golden Flower: The Classic Chinese Book of Life.* T. Cleary, Trans. San Francisco: Harper Collins.

Colman, W. (2006). The self. In: R.K. Papadopoulos, Ed. *The Handbook of Jungian Psychology: Theory, Practice and Applications.* (Chapter 7). East Sussex: Routledge.

Colman, W. (2008). On being, knowing and having a self. *Journal of Analytical Psychology, 53(3),* 351-366.

Combes, M. (2013). *Gilbert Simondon and the Philosophy of the Transindividual.* T. LaMare, Trans. Cambridge: MIT Press.

Corbin, H. (2014). *Jung, Buddhism and the Incarnation of Sophia: Unpublished Writings from a Philosopher of the Soul.* J. Cain, Trans. Rochester, VT: Inner Traditions.

Coward, H. (1966). Taoism and Jung: synchronicity and the self. *Philosophy East and West, 46(4), 477-495*

Cummins, R. (1975). Functional analysis. *The Journal of Philosophy, 72(20),* 741-765.

Custers, R., & Aarts, H. (2010). The unconscious will: How the pursuit of goals operates outside of conscious awareness. *Science, 329,* 47-50.

Damasio, A. (2010). *Self Comes to Mind. Constructing the Conscious Brain.*
New York: Pantheon, Hardcover.

Deleuze, G. (1993). *The Fold: Leibniz and the Baroque.* T. Conley, Ed. Minneapolis: University of Minnesota Press.

Dennett, D. (1991). *Consciousness Explained.* Boston: Little, Brown.

Derrida, J. (1970). Structure, sign, and play in the discourse of the human sciences. R. Macksey & E. Donato, Trans. In D. H. Richter, Ed. *The Critical Tradition: Classic Texts and Contemporary Trends.* New York: St. Martin's Press.

Derrida, J., Bennington, G., & Bowlby, R. (1989). Of Spirit. *Critical Inquiry, 15(2),* 457-474.

de Voogd, Stephanie. (1991). Fantasy versus fiction: Jung's Kantianism appraised. In R. K. Papadopoulos & G.S. Saayman, Eds. *Jung in Modern Perspective: The Master and his Legacy.* (pp. 204-228). Bridport, UK: Prism Press.

Dourley, J. (2006). Jung and the recall of the gods. *Journal of Jungian Theory and Practice, 8(1),* 43-53.

Dourley, J. (2015). Conspiracies of Immanence: Paul; Tillich, Pierre Teilhard de Chardin and C.G. Jung. *Journal of Analytical Psychology, 60(1),* 75-93.

Drob, S. (2017). *Archetype of the Absolute: The Unity of Opposites in Mysticism, Philosophy, and Psychology.* Santa Barbara, CA: Fielding University Press.

Dyczkowski, M.S.G. (1989). *The Canon of the Śaivāgama and the Kubjikā Tantras of the Western Kaula Tradition*, Delhi: Motilal Banarsidass.

Edinger, E.F. (1960). The Ego-Self paradox. *Journal of Analytical Psychology, 5(1)*, 3-18.

Edinger, E.F. (1996a). *The Aion Lectures: Exploring the Self in C.G. Jung's Aion.* Toronto: Inner City Books.

Edinger, E.F. (1996b). *The New God-Image: A Study of Jung's Key Letters Concerning the Evolution of the New God Image.* Willmett, IL: Chiron.

Eisen, R. (2004). *The Book of Job in Medieval Jewish Philosophy.* Oxford: Oxford University Press.

Eliade, M. (1959). *Cosmos and History: The Myth of the Eternal Return.* W.R. Trask, Trans. New York: Harper & Brothers.

Ewing, K. P. (1987). Clinical psychoanalysis as an ethnographic tool. *Ethos, 15,* 16-39.

Ewing, K. P. (1990). The illusion of wholeness: Culture, self, and the experience of inconsistency. *Ethos, 18(3),* 251-278.

Fairburn, W.R.D. (1944). Endopsychic structure considered in terms of object-relationships. *The International Journal of Psychoanalysis, 25,* 70-92.

Fawcett, E.D. (1909) *The Individual and Reality: An Essay Touching the First Principles of Metaphysics.* London, Longmans, Green, and Company.

Ferrell, R. (1996). *Passion in Theory: Conceptions of Freud and Lacan.* London: Routledge.

Fichte, J.G., P. Heath, & J. Lachs (2003). *Science of Knowledge: With the First and Second Introductions.* Cambridge: Cambridge University Press.

Fordham, M. (1957). *New Developments in Analytical Psychology.* London: Routledge.

Fordham, M. (1960). The relevance of analytical theory to alchemy, mysticism, and theology. Journal *of Analytical Psychology, 5(2), 113-128.*

Fordham, M. (1963). The empirical foundation and theories of the Self in Jung's works. *Journal of Analytical Psychology, 8(1),* 1-24.

Fordham, M. (1981). Neumann and childhood. *Journal of Analytical Psychology, 26(2),* 99-122.

Fordham, M. (1985). *Explorations into the Self.* London: Academic Press.

Foundation of the Works of C.G. Jung, Ed. (2019). *The Art of C.G. Jung.* New York: W.H. Norton.

Freeman, K.S. (1997). *Blakes Nostos: Fragmentation and Nondualism in the Four Zoas.* Albany, New York: State University of New York Press.

Freud, S. (1893-1895). Psychotherapy of hysteria. In J. Strachey, Ed. and Trans., *The Standard Edition of the Complete Psychological Works of Sigmund Freud* (Vol. 2). London: Hogarth Press.

Freud, S. (1895). Project for a scientific psychology. In J. Strachey, Ed. and Trans., *The Standard Edition of the Complete Psychological Works of Sigmund Freud* (Vol. 15). London: Hogarth Press.

Freud, S. (1901). The psychopathology of everyday life. In J. Strachey, Ed. and Trans., *The Standard Edition of the Complete Psychological Works of Sigmund Freud* (Vol. 6). London: Hogarth Press.

Freud, S. (1911). Formulations on the two principles of mental functioning. In J. Strachey, Ed. and Trans., *The Standard Edition of the Complete Psychological Works of Sigmund Freud* (Vol. 12). London: Hogarth Press.

Freud, S. (1915-1916). Introductory lectures on psycho-analysis. In J. Strachey, Ed. and Trans., *The Standard Edition of the Complete Psychological Works of Sigmund Freud* (Vol. 15). London: Hogarth Press.

Freud, S. (1920). Beyond the pleasure principle. In J. Strachey, Ed. and Trans., *The Standard Edition of the Complete Psychological Works of Sigmund Freud* (Vol. 18). London: Hogarth Press.

Freud, S. (1930). Civilization and its discontents. In J. Strachey, Ed. and Trans., *The Standard Edition of the Complete Psychological Works of Sigmund Freud* (Vol. 21). London: Hogarth Press.

Ganganatha, J.H.K. (1942). *The Chandogya Upanishad.* Poona, India: Poona Oriental Book Agency.

Garfield, J.L., & Priest, G. (2003). Nāgārjuna and the limits of thought. *Philosophy East & West Volume, 53(1),* 1–21.

Giegerich, W. (2001). *The Soul's Logical Life.* Frankfurt: Peter Lang.

Giegerich, W. (2005). *The Neurosis of Psychology: Primary Papers towards a Critical Psychology.* Vol. 1. New Orleans: Spring Journal Books.

Giegerich, W. (2012). *What is Soul?* New Orleans: Spring Journal Books.

Giller, P. (2000). *Reading the Zohar: A sacred text of Kabbalah.* (Chapter 4). Oxford, Oxford University Press.

Gitz-Johansen, T. (2020). Jung and the spirit: a review of Jung's discussion of the phenomenon of spirit. *Journal of Analytical Psychology, 65(4),* 653-671.

Goethe, J. W. von. (1986). *Goethe's 'Maximen und Reflexionen.'* R.H. Stevenson, Ed. and Trans. Glasgow: Scottish Papers in Germanic Studies.

Gordon, R. (1985). Big self and little self: Some reflections. *Journal of Analytical Psychology, 30(3),* 261-271.

Grotstein, J.S. (1998). The numinous and immanent nature of the psychoanalytic subject. *Journal of Analytical Psychology, 43(1),* 41-68.

Halevi J. R. (2001) The Kuzari. In *Prophecy.* Amsterdam Studies in Jewish Thought, vol 8. Dordrecht: Springer.

Hall, J.A. (1960). Enantiodromia and the unification of opposites: Spontaneous dream images. In Carson, J. Ed. *The Arms of the Windmill: Essays in Analytical Psychology in Honour of Werner H. Engel.* (pp. 59-67). Baltimore: John D. Lucas Printing Company.

Hannah, B. (1976). *Jung, His Life and Work.* New York: G. Putnam's Sons.

Hannah, B., & von Franz, M-L. (2004). *Lectures on Jung's Aion.* Wilmette, IL: Chiron Publications.

Harding, E. (1973). *Psychic Energy: Its Source and its Transformation.* Princeton: Princeton University Press.

Harms, D. (2011). The geometry of C.G. Jung's *Systema Munditotius* mandala. *Jung Journal, 5(3),* 145-159.

Hartmann, H. (1964). The development of the ego concept in Freud's work. In *Essays on Ego Psychology: Selected Papers in Psychoanalytic Theory.* (pp. 268-296). New York: International Universities Press.

Hauer, J.W. (1934). *Symbole und Erfahrung des Selbstes in der indoarabischen Mystik.* Eranos-Jarbuch. Zurich: Rhein-Verlag.

Hegel, G.W.F. (1977). *Hegel's Phenomenology of Spirit.* A.V. Miller, Trans. Oxford: Oxford University Press.

Heisig, J.W. (1979). *Imago-Dei: A Study of C.G. Jung's Psychology of Religion.* Lewisburg, W Virginia: Bucknell University Press.

Heuer, G. (2001). Jung's twin brother. Otto Gross and Carl Gustav Jung. *Journal of Analytical Psychology, 46(4),* 655-688.

Hillman, J. (1983). *Inter Views: Of Psychology, Biography, Love, Soul, Dreams, Work, Imagination, and the State of the Culture by James Hillman with Laura Pozo.* Woodstock, Conn.: Spring Publications.

Hippolytus. (1868). *The Refutation of All Heresies.* J. H. MacMahon, Trans. Edinburgh: T. & T. Clark.

Hinman, E.L. (1922). Review of the thirteen principal Upanishads. *The Philosophical Review, 32(2),* 197-199.

Hirst, J.G.S. (2005). *Samkara's Advaita Vedanta: A Way of Teaching.* London: RoutledgeCurzon.

Hobson, A. (2014). Consciousness, dreams, and inference: The Cartesian theatre revisited. *Journal of Consciousness Studies, 21 (1-2),* 6-32.

Horgenson, G. (2004). What are symbols of? Situated action, mythological bootstrapping and the emergence of the Self. *Journal of Analytical Psychology, 49(1),* 67-81.

Horgenson, G. (2020). The geometry of wholeness. In R. Main, C. McMillan, & D. Henderson, Eds. *Jung, Deleuze, and the Problematic Whole.* (pp. 125-141). London: Routledge.

Hubback, M.A. (1998). The dynamic self. *Journal of Analytical Psychology, 43(2),* 277-285.

Human, R. E. (1934). *The Thirteen Principal Upanishads.* (2 ed). London and New York: Oxford UP.

Huskinson, L. (2002). The self as violent other: The problem of defining the self. *Journal of Analytical Psychology, 47(3),* 437-458.

Huxley, A. (1956). *Adonis and the Alphabet.* London: Chatto and Windus.

Ibn 'Arabi. (2016). *Kernel of the Kernel.* Cheltenham: Beshara Publications.

Isadore. (2005). *Isidore of Seville's Etymologies.* P. Throop, Ed. Charlotte, Vermont: MedievalMS.

Jablonsky, D. (1994). *Churchill and Hitler: Essays on the Political-Military Direction of Total War.* London: Routledge.

Jacobi, J. (1967). *The Way of Individuation.* R.F.C. Hill, Trans. New York: Harcourt, Brace, Jovanovich.

Jacoby, M. (2017). *Individuation and Narcissism: The Psychology of Self in Jung and Kohut.* London: Routledge.

James, W. (1890/2007). *The Principles of Psychology: Volume 1.* New York: Cosimo Inc.

James, W. (1902). *The Varieties of Religious Experience.* New York: Longmans Greek & Co.

Jarrett, J.L. (1981). Schopenhauer and Jung. *Spring: A Journal of Archetype and Culture,* 193-204.

Jarrett, J.L. (1986). Eros in the creation of consciousness: Nietzsche and Jung on the clash of opposites, *Psychological Perspectives, 20(1),* 62-71.

Jorg, J. (2012). C.G. Jung in the 1930s. *Jung Journal, 6(4),* 54-73).

Jung, C.G. (1921). *Psychologische Typen.* Zurich: Rascher & Cie.

Jung, C.G. (1934). *Uber Die Archetypen DES Kollektiven Unbewussten,* Eranos-Jarbuch. Zurich: Rhein-Verlag.

Jung, C.G. (1935). Traumsymbole Des Individuationsprozesses. Eranos-Jahrbuch. Zurich: Rhein-Verlag.

Jung, C. G. (1938-9). *Modern Psychology, 3: Notes on Lectures Given at the Eidgenossische Technische Hochschule.* B. Hannah, Ed. Privately published manuscript, Zurich, 1959.

Jung, C.G. (1939). *The Integration of Personality.* S. Dell, Trans. New York: Farrar & Rinehart, Inc.

Jung, C.G. (1942). Psychology Today. H. Nagel Trans. *Spring,* 1-12.

Jung, C.G. (1942a). *Der Geist Mercurius.* Eranos-Jahrbuch. Zurich: Rhein-Verlag.

Jung, C.G. (1948). *Uber Das Selbst.* Eranos-Jahrbuch. Zurich: Rhein-Verlag.

Jung, C.G. (1983). *The Zofingia Lectures.* Princeton: Princeton University Press.

Jung, C.G. (1984). *Dream Analysis: Notes on the Seminar Given in 1928-1930 by C.G. Jung.* W. McGuire, Ed. Princeton: Princeton University Press.

Jung. C.G. (1996). *The Psychology of Kundalini Yoga: Notes of a Seminar Given in 1932 by C.G. Jung.* S. Shamdasani, Ed. London: Routledge.

Jung, C.G. (1997). *Visions: Notes of the Seminar Given in 1930-1934.* C. Douglas, Ed. Princeton: Princeton University Press.

Jung, C.G. (2008). *Children's Dreams: Notes from the Seminar Given in 1936-1940.* L. Jung, & M. Meyer-Grass, Eds. E. Falzeder & T. Woolfson, Trans. Princeton: Princeton University Press.

Jung, C.G. (2014a). *Analytical Psychology: Notes of the Seminar given in 1925 by C.G. Jung.* W. McGuire, Ed. London: Taylor & Francis.

Jung, C.G. (2014b). *Dream Interpretation Ancient & Modern: Notes from the Seminar Given in 1936-1941.* J. Peck, L. Jung, M. & Meyer-Grass, Eds. E. Falzeder & T. Woolfson, Trans. Princeton: Princeton University Press.

Jung, C.G. (2019). *Dream Symbols of the Individuation Process: Notes of C.G. Jung's Seminars on Wolfgang Pauli's Dreams.* S. Gieser, Ed. Princeton: Princeton University Press.

Jung, C.G. (2020). *Psychology of Meditation and Yoga.* Princeton: Princeton University Press.

Jung, C.G., Jung, E., Wolf, T. (1982). *C.G. Jung, Emma Jung and Tony Wolf: A Collection of Remembrances.* F. Jensen & S. Mullen, Eds. San Francisco: The Analytical Psychology Club of San Francisco.

Jung, C.G. & Neumann, E. (2015). *Analytical Psychology in Exile: The Correspondence of C.G. Jung & Eric Neumann.* M. Liebscher, Ed. Princeton: Princeton University Press.

Jung C.G, & White, V. (2007). *The Jung-White Letters.* A.C. Lammers & A. Cunningham, Eds. London: Routledge.

Kalsched, D. (1996). *The Inner World of Trauma. Archetypal Defences of the Personal Spirit.* London & New York: Routledge.

Kalsched, D. (2013). *Trauma and the Soul: A Psycho-spiritual Approach to Human Development and Its Interruption.* New York: Routledge.

Kant, E. (1798/1974). *Anthropology from a Pragmatic Point of View,* M. Gregor, Trans. The Hague: Martinus Nijhoff.

Kant, E. (1965). *Critique of Pure Reason. 2nd Edition.* N.K. Smith, Trans. New York: St. Martins.

Klemm, D.E. (1997). Schleiermacher on the self: Immediate self-consciousness as feeling and as thinking. In D.E. Klemm & G. Zoller, Eds. *Figuring the Self: Subject, Absolute and Others in Classical German Philosophy.* (pp. 169-190). London: Routledge.

Knox, J. (2003). Trauma and defences: their roots in relationship: An overview. *Journal of Analytical Psychology, 48(2),* 207-233.

Knox, J. (2004). From archetypes to reflective function. *Journal of Analytical Psychology, 49(1),* 1–19.

Knox, J. (2010). Response to Erik Goodwyn's "Approaching archetypes: reconsidering innateness." *Journal of Analytical Psychology, 55(4),* 522–33.

Kohut, H. & Wolf, E.S. (1978). The disorders of the self and their treatment: An outline. *International Journal of Psychoanalysis, 59,* 413-.

Kramer, C., & Sutton, A. (1998). *Anatomy of the Soul: Rabbi Nachman of Breslov.* Monsey, NY: Breslov Research Institute.

Lacan, J. (2006) The instance of the letter in the unconscious or reason since Freud. In *Ecrits.* B. Fink, Trans. (paras. 494-528). New York: Norton.

Levinas, E. (1991). *Otherwise than Being or Beyond Essence.* L. Lingis, Trans. Berlin: Springer.

Liester, M.B. (1996). Inner voices: Distinguishing transcendent and pathological characteristics. *The Journal of Transpersonal Psychology, 28(1),* 1-30.

Lodge, D. (1993). *The Modes of Modern Writing: Metaphor, Metonymy, and the Typology of Modern Literature,* London: Edward Arnold.

Lorenzen, D.N. (1972). *The Kāpālikas and Kālāmukhas: Two Lost Śaivite Sects,* Berkeley and Los Angeles, CA: University of California Press.

Louth, A. (1997). The body in Western Catholic Christianity. In S. Coakley, Ed. *Religion and the Body.* (Chapter 7). Cambridge: Cambridge University Press.

Lowenthal, D. (1961). Geography, experience, and imagination: Towards a geographical epistemology. *Annals of the Association of American Geographers, 51(3),* 241-260.

Loy, D. (1988). The path of no-path: Sankara and Dogen on the paradox of practice. *Philosophy East and West, 38*, 127–146.

Main, R., McMillan, C., & Henderson, D. (2019). Introduction. In C. McMillan, R. Main, D. Henderson, Eds. *Holism: Possibilities and Problems.* (pp. 1-14). London: Routledge.

Maimonides, M. (1963). *The Guide For the Perplexed.* S. Pines, Trans. Chicago: University of Chicago Press.

Maharshi, R. (1997). *The Collected Works of Ramana Maharshi.* A. Osborne, Ed. New York: Samuel Weiser.

Mather, M. (2014). *The Alchemical Mercurius: Esoteric Symbol of Jung's Life and Work.* London: Routledge.

Matt, D.C. (2006). *The Zohar: Pritzker Edition.* Stanford, CA: Stanford University Press. Vol. XI.

May, R. (1981). *Freedom and Destiny.* New York: Norton.

Merchant, J. (2006). The developmental/emergent model of archetype, its implications and its application to shamanism. *Journal of Analytical Psychology, 51(1), 1,* 127-146.

Merchant, J. (2012). *Shamans and Analysts: New Insights into the Wounded Healer.* London: Routledge.

Merchant, J. (2016). The image schema and innate archetypes: theoretical and clinical implications. *Journal of Analytical Psychology, 61(1),* 63-78.

Merchant, J. (2019). The controversy around the concept of archetypes and the place of an emergent/ developmental model. *Journal of Analytical Psychology, 64(5),* 701-719.

Merkur, D. (2010). *Explorations of the Psychoanalytic Mystics.* Amsterdam: Rodopi.

Metzinger, T. (2003). *Being No One: The Self-Model Theory of Subjectivity.* Cambridge, MA: MIT Press.

Minkowski, C. (2011). Advaita Vedanta in early modern history. *South Asian History and Culture, 2(2),* 205-231.

Mitchell, W.T. (1983). Metamorphoses of the vortex: Hogarth, Turner and Blake. In R. Wendorf, Ed. *Articulate Images.* (pp. 125-168). Minneapolis: University of Minnesota Press.

Mlecko, J.D. (1982). The guru in Hindu tradition. *Numen, 29(1),* 33-61.

Moeller, H-G. (2007). *Daodejing: The New, Highly Readable Translation of the Life- changing Ancient Scripture Formerly Known as the Tao Te Ching.* H-G Moeller, Trans. Chicago: Open Court.

Miller, J.C. (2004). *The Transcendent Function: Jung's Model of Psychological Growth through Dialogue with the Unconscious.* Albany, NY: SUNY Press.

Morgan, H. (2019). Response to 'Psychological individuation and spiritual enlightenment: some comparisons and points of contact' by Murray Stein. *Journal of Analytical Psychology, 64(1),* 23-27.

Morin, A. (2006). Levels of consciousness and self-awareness: A comparison and integration of various neurocognitive views. *Consciousness and Cognition, 15,* 358-371

Müller, F.M. (1895). The Upanishads. In *Sacred Books of the East,* Volume 1. F.M Müller, Trans. London: Curzon Press.

Muramoto, S., Young-Eisendrath, & Middeldorf, J. (2002). *The Jung-Hisamatsu Conversation. In* P. Young-Eisendrath & S. Muramoto, Eds. *Awakening and Insight: Zen Buddhism and Psychotherapy.* (pp. 105-118). London: Routledge

Neumann, E. (1954). *The Origins and History of Consciousness.* R.F.C. Hull, Trans. Princeton: Princeton University Press.

Neumann, E. (1989). The psyche and the transformation of the reality planes: A metaphysical Essay. In *The Essays or Eric Neumann. Volume 3, The Place of Creation.* H. Nagel, E. Rolfe, J. van Heurck & K. Winston, Trans. Princeton: Princeton University Press.

Neumann, E. (2019). *The Roots of Jewish Consciousness: Volume One: Revelation and Apocalypse.* A.C. Lammers, Ed. London: Routledge.

Nietzsche, F. (1961). *Thus Spake Zarathustra.* R. J. Hollingdale, Trans. Harmondsworth, England: Penguin.

Nisargadatta, Sri Maharaj. (1973). *I Am That: Talks with Sri Nisargadatta Maharaj.* Bombay: Chetana Press.

Nisargadatta, Sri Maharaj. (1993). *Experience of Nothingness: Sri Nisargadatta Maharaj's Talks on Realizing the Infinite.* R. Powell, Ed. San Diego: Blue Dove Press.

Nixon, R. (2011) *Slow Violence and the Environmentalism of the Poor*. Cambridge, MA: Harvard University Press.

Noh, J.J. (1977). *Do You See What I See?* Wheaton, IL: Quest.

Ostrowski-Sachs, M. (1971). *From Conversations with C. G. Jung*. Zurich: Juris Druck & Verlag.

Pain, R. (2019). Chronic urban trauma: The slow violence of housing dispossession. *Urban Studies, 56(2),* 385-400.

Palmer R.R. (2014). *A Political History of Europe and America, 1760-1800*. Princeton: Princeton University Press.

Panksepp, J. (1998). The periconscious substrates of consciousness: Affective states and the evolutionary origins of the self. *Journal of Consciousness Studies, 5*(5-6), 566–582.

Papadopoulos, R.K., (1984). Jung and the concept of the other. In Papadopoulos, R.K, Saayman, G.S., Eds. *Jung in Modern Perspective*. (pp. 54-88). Wildwood House, Hounslow, England

Papadopoulos, R.K. (2007). Refugees, trauma and Adversity-Activated Development. *European Journal of Psychotherapy and Counselling, 9(3),* 301-312.

Paracelsus. (1952). *Selected Writings*. J. Jacobi. Ed. New York: Pantheon.

Peer, M., Salomon, R., Goldberg, I., Blanke, O., & Arzy, S. (2015). *Proceedings of the National Academy of Sciences, 112 (35),* 11072-11077.

Perera, R. (2019). Cartesian creatures: Watching ourselves watching the world. *Journal of Consciousness Studies, 26 (3-4),* 131-154.

Perls, F.S. & Stevens, J.O. (1982) *Gestalt Therapy Verbatim*. Toronto: Bantam Books.

Petty, J. C. (1999). *Step by Step: Divine Guidance for Ordinary Christians*. Phillipsburg, NJ: P&R Publishing.

Plotinus. (1992). *The Enneads*. S. MacKenna, Trans. Burdett, NY: Larson Publications.

Potthapada Sutta (1998). *Potthapada Sutta: About Potthapada*. Translated from the Pali by Thanissaro Bhikkhu. Access to Insight. http://www.buddhasutra.com/files/potthapada_sutta1.htm

Poulet, G. (1966). *The Metamorphosis of the Circle*. C. Dawson & E. Colman, Trans. Baltimore: John Hopkins University Press.

Progoff, I. (1959). *Depth Psychology and Modern Man*. New York: Julian Press.

Pulver, M. (1960). The experience of Light in the Gospel of St. John, in the 'Corpus hermeticum,' in Gnosticism, and in the Eastern Church. In J. Campbell, Ed. *Spiritual Disciplines: Papers from the Eranos Yearbooks*. Princeton: Princeton University Press.

Pykett, J. (2018). Geography and neuroscience: Critical engagements with geography's 'neural turn.' *Transactions of the Institute of British Geographers, 43(2)*, 154-169.

Quispel, G. (1948/1969). Gnostic man: The doctrine of Basilides. In J. Campbell, Ed, *The Mystic Vision: Papers from the Eranos Conference*. London: Routledge & Kegan Paul.

Saks, E.R. (2007). *The Center Cannot Hold: My Journey through Madness*. New York: Hachette.

Salman, S. (2013). *Dreams of Totality: Where We Are When There's Nothing at the Center*. New Orleans: Spring Journal Books.

Salmon, W. (1692). *Medicina Practica or Practical Physick*. Book 2: *Hermes Trismegistus: Tactus Aureus*. London: T. Hawkins.

Sandner, D.F., & Beebe, J. (1992). Psychopathology and analysis. In R. Papadopolos, Ed. *Carl Gustav Jung, Clinical Assessments*. London: Routledge.

Sartre, J-P. (1938/2007). *Nausea*. L. Alexander, Trans. New York, New Directions.

Satprem. (1978). *By the Body of the Earth or The Sannyasin Unending History*. M. Fitzpatrick, Ed. New York: Harper & Row.

Schlamm, L. (2010). Revisiting Jung's dialogue with yoga: Observations from transpersonal psychology. *International Journal of Jungian Studies, 2(1)*, 32-44.

Schopenhauer, A. (1958). *The World as Will and Representation*. Vol 2. E.F.J. Payne, Trans. New York: Dover Publications

Sells, M. (1994). *Mystical Language of Unsaying*. Chicago: Chicago University Press.

Serrano, M. (1966). *C.G. Jung and Hermann Hesse: A Record of Two Friendships*. F. McShane, Trans. Einsiedeln: Daiman Verlag.

Shamdasani, S., Ed. (2009). *The Red Book, Liber Novus: A Reader's Edition*. M. Kyburz, J. Peck, & S. Shamdasani, Trans. New York: W.W. Norton.

Shamdasani, S. (2012). *C.G. Jung: A Biography of Books.* New York: W.W. Norton.

Sherbon, M.A. (2012). Wolfgang Pauli and the fine-structure constant. *Journal of Science, 2(3),* 148-154.

Schwab, R. (2005). *Rav Schwab on IYOV: The Teachings of Rabbi Shimon Schwab on the Book of Job.* Brooklyn: Mesorah Publications.

Simondon, G. (1964/1992). The genesis of the individual 1964. In *Incorporations.* J. Crary & S. Kwinter, Eds. New York: Zone.

Simondon, G. (2009). "The position of the problem of ontogenesis." G. Flanders, Trans. *Parrhesia, 7,* 1-16.

Sims, D.W., Bivins, B.A., Obeid, F.N., Horst, H.M, Sorensen, V.J., & Fath, J.J. (1988). Urban trauma: A chronic recurrent disease. *Journal of Trauma, 29(7),* 940-947.

Sorge, G.V.R. (2020). The construct of the 'mana personality' in Jung's works: a historic-hermeneutic perspective. Part 1. *Journal of Analytical Psychology, 65(2),* 366-388.

Spivack, C. (1969). The Elizabethan Theatre: Circle and Center. *The Centennial Review, 13(4)*-443.

Sri Ramakrishna Math. (1949). *Svetasvataropanisad.* Mylapore, Madras: Sri Ramakrishna Math.

Steels, L. (2003). Language re-entrance and the 'inner voice' In *Machine Consciousness. Journal of Consciousness Studies Supplement. 10,* 173-185.

Stein, L. (2012). *Becoming Whole: Jung's Equation for Realizing God.* New York: Helios Press.

Stein, L. (2015). Jung and Divine Self-Revelation. *Jung Journal, 9(1),* 18-30.

Stein. L. (2019a). *Working with Mystical Experiences in Psychoanalysis: Opening to the Numinous.* London: Routledge.

Stein, M. (2008). 'Divinity expresses the self …' An investigation. *Journal of Analytical Psychology, 53, 305-327.*

Stein, M. (2019b). Psychological individuation and spiritual enlightenment: Some comparisons and points of contact. *Journal of Analytical Psychology, 64(1),* 6-22.

Stein, M. (2019c). *Individuation.* Vol. 1 of the Collected Writings of Murray Stein. Asheville, NC: Chiron.

Stein, M., Brutsche, P., & Fisher, T. (2012*)*. C.G. Jung in the historical context of the 1930s. *Jung Journal, 6(4)*, 7-11.

Stern, D.B. (2017). Unformulated experience, dissociation, and *Nachträglichkeit*. *Journal of Analytical Psychology, 62(4)*, 501-525.

Snorri Sturluson. (2005). *Snorri Sturluson: The Prose Edda, Norse Mythology*. J.L. Byok, trans. London: Penguin.

Tishby, I. (1991). *The Wisdom of the Zohar: An Anthology of Texts*. D. Goldstein, Ed. Portland, OR: Littman Library.

Trinka, W. (2001). Dreams, psychic mobility and inner beings. *Free Associations, 8(4)*, 562-575.

Ulman, R.B., & Brothers, D. (1988). *The Shattered Self: A Psychoanalytic Study of Trauma*. Hillsdale, NJ: The Analytic Press.

Urban, E. (2005). Fordham, Jung and the self: a re-examination of Fordham's contribution to Jung's conceptualization of the self. *Journal of Analytical Psychology, 50(5)*, 571-594.

von Franz, M-L. (1975). *C.G. Jung: His Myth in Our Time*. W.H. Kennedy, Trans. New York: G.P. Putnam's Sons.

von Franz, M-L. (1992). *Psyche and Matter*. Boston: Shambhala.

von Franz, M-L. (1995). *Projection and Recollection in Jungian Psychology: Reflections of the Soul*. Chicago: Open Court.

von Franz, M-L. (1996). *The Interpretation of Fairy Tales*. Revised Edition. Boston: Shambhala.

von Franz, M-L. (2000). *Aurora Consurgens: A Document Attributed to Thomas Aquinas on the Problem of Opposites in Alchemy*. R.F.C. Hull & A.S.B. Glover, Trans. Toronto: Inner City Books.

Vandekerchkhove, M., Bulnes, L.C., & Panksepp, J. (2014). "The emergence of primary anoetic consciousness in episodic memory." *Frontiers in Behavioural Neuroscience, 7(210)*, 1-8.

Von Hoffman, A. (2008). The lost history of urban renewal. *Journal of Urbanism: International Research on Placemaking and Urban Sustainability, 1,3*, 281-301.

Vysheslawzeff, B.P. (1969). Two Ways of Redemption: Redemption as a Solution of the Tragic Contradiction (1936). In J. Campbell, Ed. *The Mystic Vision: Papers from the Eranos Yearbooks*. London: Routledge & Kegan Paul.

Weger, U., & Herbig, K. (2019). The Self as activity. *Review of General Psychology, 23(1),* 251-261.

Wilhelm, R. (1962). *The Secret of the Golden Flower: A Chinese Book of Lif*e. New York: Harvest.

Wilson, J. P. (2004) The abyss experience and the trauma complex: A Jungian perspective of posttraumatic stress disorder and dissociation, *Journal of Trauma & Dissociation, 5(3)*, 43-68,

Wood, L.J. (1998). *The Holy Spirit in the Old Testament.* Eugene, OR.: Wipf and Stock.

Yeats, W.B. (1989). *The Collected Poems of W.B. Yeats.* R.J. Finneran, Ed. London: Palgrave Macmillan.

Young-Eisendrath, P. (1997). The self in analysis. *Journal of Analytical Psychology, 42(1),* 157-166.

Zabriskie, B. (2001). Jung and Pauli. In C.A. Meier, Ed. *Atom and Archetype: The Pauli/Jung Letters 1932-1958.* Princeton: Princeton University Press.

Zinkin, L. (2008a). Your self: Did you find it or did you make it? *Journal of Analytical Psychology, 53(3),* 389-406.

Zinkin, L., et, al. (2008b). Discussion of Zinkin's paper "Your Self: did you find it or did you make it?" *Journal of Analytical Psychology, 53(3),* 407-420.

Zimmer, H. (1952*). Philosophies of India*. J. Campbell, Ed. Princeton: Princeton University Press.

Zenkovesky, V.V. (1953). *A History of Russian Philosophy. Volume 2.* London: Routledge.

Index

www.ingramcontent.com/pod-product-compliance
Lightning Source LLC
Chambersburg PA
CBHW020331270326
41926CB00007B/132